Theatre Censorship
in Contemporary
Europe

Exeter Performance Studies

Series Editors:
Helen Brooks, Reader in Theatre and Cultural History, University of Kent
Jane Milling, Professor in Drama at the University of Exeter
Duška Radosavljević, Reader in Contemporary Theatre and Performance, Royal Central School of Speech and Drama, University of London

Founding Editors
Graham Ley, Peter Thomson, and Steve Nicholson

Exeter Performance Studies explores performance in relation to historical context. The series is a home for a wide variety of work engaging with processes of making and doing, as well as materiality, policy and cultural practice. It publishes the best new scholarship, presenting established authors alongside pioneering work from new scholars, including titles which provide access to previously unavailable material and engage in processes of decolonisation and methodological innovation.

Selected previous titles:

The Censorship of British Drama 1900–1968,
by Steve Nicholson

London's Grand Guignol and the Theatre of Horror,
by Richard J. Hand and Michael Wilson

From Mimesis To Interculturalism: Readings of Theatrical Theory Before and After 'Modernism', by Graham Ley

Critical Essays on British South Asian Theatre,
by Graham Ley and Sarah Dadswell

Theatres of the Troubles: Theatre, Resistance and Liberation in Ireland,
by Bill McDonnell

Forms of Conflict: Contemporary Wars on the British Stage,
by Sara Soncini

John McGrath: Plays For England,
Introduced by Nadine Holdsworth

Theatre Censorship in Contemporary Europe

Silence and Protest

edited by
Anne Etienne and Chris Megson

UNIVERSITY
of
EXETER
PRESS

First published in 2024 by
University of Exeter Press
Reed Hall, Streatham Drive
Exeter EX4 4QR
UK

www.exeterpress.co.uk

Copyright © 2024 Anne Etienne, Chris Megson and the contributors

Paperback edition published 2026

The right of Anne Etienne, Chris Megson and the contributors to be identified as authors of this work has been asserted by them in accordance with the Copyright, Designs and Patents Act 1988.

Exeter Performance Studies
ISSN 3049-7302 Print
ISSN 3049-7310 Online

A CIP record for this book is available from the British Library.

https://doi.org/10.47788/TJBJ7381

ISBN 978-1-80413-051-3 Hardback
ISBN 978-1-80413-224-1 Paperback
ISBN 978-1-80413-052-0 ePub
ISBN 978-1-80413-053-7 PDF

Cover image: *The Curse*, directed by Oliver Frljić, at Teatr Powszechny in Warsaw, 2017; photograph courtesy of Magda Hueckel and Teatr Powszechny.

Every effort has been made to trace copyright holders and obtain permission to reproduce the material included in this book. Please get in touch with any enquiries or information relating to an image or the rights holder.

EU Authorised Representative: Easy Access System Europe – Mustamae tee 50, 10621 Tallinn, Estonia, gpsr.requests@easproject.com

Typeset in Sabon LT Std by S4Carlisle Publishing Services, Chennai, India

Contents

Contributors   vii
Acknowledgements   xii
Note on translation and referencing   xiii

Introduction: Censorship in Times of Convulsive Change   1
    Anne Etienne and Chris Megson

PART 1: FORMS AND SOURCES OF CENSORSHIP   23

    Intervention 1. Capturing Space: Crashing Down the Gates
    of the Maltese Utopia   25
    Vicki Ann Cremona and Marco Galea

1 Voices from Semi-Peripheries: Pressure, Self-Censorship,
    and Micropolitics of Resistance in the Western Balkans   34
    Milena Dragićević Šešić and Aleksandra Jovićević

2 The Emperor's New Clothes: Ideology and Censorship in
    Contemporary Russian Theatre   52
    Alex Trustrum-Thomas

3 Risings and Cancellings: Implicit Censorship on a Free Irish Stage   70
    Anne Etienne and Lisa Fitzpatrick

PART 2: GHOSTS OF THE PAST   91

    Intervention 2. Censorship in Hungary: Comedy, Silence,
    and Subversion   93
    Andrea Tompa

4 Nothing New on the Eastern Front: Censorship in
    Contemporary Slovenia   103
    Denis Poniž

5 *Un-Divine Comedy. Remains* and Self-Censorship
    as Work-in-Progress in Poland   119
    Agnieszka Jakimiak

6 Opera Censorship in Europe: Production, Circulation,
    and Reception in a Transnational Market   137
    Andrew Holden

    Intervention 3. The Tenacity of Tradition: Performativity in the
    Dutch Black Pete Controversy   156
    Lonneke van Heugten

Part 3: Staging Taboos — 167

Intervention 4. Racialized Censorship in the Age of Culture Wars — 169
Roaa Ali

7   Images of Protest: Religion, Theatre, and Censorship — 178
Chris Megson

8   Religion and Politics: Silencing Greek Theatre in the Twenty-First Century — 195
Olga Kolokytha, Yulia Belinskaya, and Matina Magkou

9   Booing and Banning: Freedom and Prohibition in Spain's 'National Fiesta' — 211
Duncan Wheeler

Intervention 5. Play on the Periphery: Irrational Queerness as Resistance to Censorship in Gestalta's Shibari Performance Art — 228
Hannah Probst

Index — 239

Contributors

Roaa Ali is Lecturer in Cultural Sociology at Birmingham City University, and Honorary Research Fellow at the University of Manchester. She is an interdisciplinary educator and researcher focusing on race, inequality, and diversity in the Creative and Cultural Industries (CCIs); Arab American theatre; and identity and the politics of cultural production. Her most recent publications include an article titled 'The Trouble with Diversity: The Cultural Sector and Ethnic Inequality' (*Cultural Sociology*) and a monograph for Routledge titled *Contemporary Arab American Drama: Cultural Politics of Ethnicity, Otherness and Visibility* (2023).

Yulia Belinskaya, MA is a prae-doc researcher at the Department of Communication, University of Vienna. Her work addresses the hybrid public sphere and dissident media. This involves research on digital media activity, social movements and communities, street art, pornography, and obscenity, but also restrictive media policies and governance of communicative spaces.

Vicki Ann Cremona is Chair of the School of Performing Arts at the University of Malta, and Professor within the Theatre Studies Department. She is particularly interested in the connections between theatre and power. She has published mainly about carnival, Maltese theatre, commedia dell'arte, Tunisian theatre, and theatre laboratories. She has also co-authored, co-edited, and translated various books. Her latest book publication is *Carnival and Power: Play and Politics in a Crown Colony* (2018), and she is one of the editors of *Theatre Scandals: Social Dynamics of Turbulent Theatrical Events* (2020).

Milena Dragićević Šešić, former President of the University of Arts, Belgrade, is founder of the UNESCO Chair in Interculturalism, Art Management and Mediation, and Professor Emerita of Cultural Policy and Management, Cultural Studies, Media and Memory Studies. She has published twenty monographs and edited books, and 250 essays. She is a UNESCO, EU, and Council of Europe policy expert. Her international research projects include Horizon 2020, COST Actions, Erasmus +, and Creative Europe. She was Commandeur dans l'Ordre des Palmes Académiques (French Ministry of Education) in 2002; ENCATC Fellowship Laureate in 2019; and University of Arts Laureate in 2004 and 2019.

Anne Etienne is Senior Lecturer in Modern & Contemporary Drama in the Department of English, University College Cork. Her research focuses on theatre censorship, Arnold Wesker, and contemporary Irish theatre.

Her publications include *Theatre Censorship: from Walpole to Wilson* (2007), and the co-edited volumes *Populating the Stage: Contemporary Irish Theatre* (2017), *Arnold Wesker: Fragments and Visions* (2021), *Adult Themes: British Cinema and the X Certificate in the Long 1960s* (2023), and the *Palgrave Handbook of Theatre Censorship* (2024). She is co-editor of the series 'Palgrave Studies in Cultural Censorship'.

Lisa Fitzpatrick is Senior Lecturer in Drama at the University of Ulster in Derry. She is the author of *Rape on the Contemporary Stage* (2018); recent publications include *The Theatre of Deirdre Kinahan* (with Maria Kurdi, 2022) and *Plays by Women in Ireland 1926–1933: Feminist Theatres of Freedom and Resistance* (with Shonagh Hill, 2022). Her current work on gender-based violence in conflict and post-conflict societies includes a collaboration with Kabosh Theatre Company, Belfast. She is co-convenor of the Feminist Working Group at the International Federation for Theatre Research, and associate editor of *Theatre Research International*.

Marco Galea teaches Theatre Studies at the University of Malta. His main area of specialization is theatre in Malta in the nineteenth and twentieth centuries, and he is particularly interested in issues of language, identity, and representation. He has published articles and book chapters in this area and has edited a number of books. In recent years he has been coordinating, on behalf of the School of Performing Arts at the University of Malta, efforts to create a digital archive for the performing arts in Malta.

Andrew Holden completed his PhD at Oxford Brookes University with a thesis entitled *Opera Avanti a Dio!: Opera and Religion in Liberal Italy*. Publications include a book chapter, 'From Heaven and Hell to the Grail Hall via Sant'Andrea della Valle: Religious Identity and the Internationalisation of Operatic Styles in Liberal Italy', in Axel Korner and Paulo Kühl (eds), *Italian Opera in Global and Transnational Perspective: Reimagining Italianità in the Long Nineteenth Century* (2022). His book on the abolition of theatre censorship in the UK is titled *Makers and Manners: Politics and Morality in Post-War Britain* (2005).

Agnieszka Jakimiak is a PhD student at Royal Holloway, University of London. She works as a theatre director (*nosexnosolo*, 2019; *Eats the Soul*, 2017), an essayist, and a playwright. She has been working as a dramaturg with Polish and international theatre directors, such as Oliver Frljić (*The Curse*, 2017), Anja Suša (*The Republic*, 2019), and Weronika Szczawińska. She researches traces of censorship and self-censorship within performing arts. Her current work combines self-referential analysis and institutional critique, and remains focused on interrogating forms of distribution of power and challenging hegemonic practices in theatre.

Aleksandra Jovićević is Professor of Performance Studies at the Department of History, Anthropology, Religion, and Arts Performance (Storia, Antropologia, Religioni, Arte, Spettacolo; SARAS) at La Sapienza University of Rome, Italy, where she teaches performance studies and theatre theories. She is also a director of the master's programme in Video Editing and Digital Storytelling for Live Performance at the same university and a visiting professor at the UNESCO Chair for Cultural Policy at the University of Belgrade. Her most recent publication is *Orson Welles and Theatre: Shakespeare and Beyond* (*Orson Welles e il teatro: Shakespeare e oltre*, 2022).

Olga Kolokytha is the academic director of the MAs in Music Management and in Music for Applied Media at the University for Continuing Education Krems. She was the lead researcher for the University of Vienna in the Horizon 2020 project CICERONE on cultural and creative industries in Europe. She is on the editorial board of the journal *City, Culture and Society* and is an elected member of the board of the Research Network Sociology of the Arts of the European Sociological Association. Her research interests include cultural policy and management, sociology of culture, and culture in conditions of crises.

Matina Magkou is a postdoc researcher at the SIC.Lab Méditerranée of the University Côte d'Azur in France and holds a PhD in Leisure, Communication and Culture from the University of Deusto in Spain. Her current research focuses on intermediary cultural spaces, digital transformation processes, and commons and the city. Her research interests include cultural policy and cultural relations. She has worked for festivals and theatre productions, and continues collaborating as a cultural manager and consultant to cultural networks and organizations evaluating projects, facilitating learning processes, and managing complex projects.

Chris Megson is Reader in Drama and Theatre at Royal Holloway College, University of London. His research focuses on post-war and contemporary British playwriting, and documentary and verbatim theatre. His publications include *Get Real: Documentary Theatre Past and Present* (co-edited with Alison Forsyth, 2009), *Decades of Modern British Playwriting: The 1970s* (2012), and numerous chapters for edited collections including *Performing the Secular: Religion, Representation and Politics* (2017) and *Arnold Wesker: Fragments and Visions* (2021). He is a series editor of 'Playwriting and the Contemporary: Critical Collaborations' (Liverpool University Press), and Methuen Drama Student Editions.

Denis Poniž is Emeritus Professor of European and Slovenian Drama at the University of Ljubljana, Slovenia, and a visiting professor at several European universities. His research is concerned with Slovene poetry and drama, and the semiotics and anthropology of theatre. In 2008–12 he led the research project 'Censorship and Self-Censorship in Slovene Drama and Theatre 1945–1990'. When the project was stopped without explanation, he continued to research the censorship of contemporary European and American playwrights. He has published twenty-five books and over 600 articles and book chapters. He is also a poet and playwright, and a literary translator from both Serbian and Croatian.

Hannah Probst will receive their postgraduate qualification in Transcultural Theatre Studies from the Universität Leipzig (Germany), where she is a research assistant at the Centre of Competence for Theatre. Their work focuses on the intersections between theatre, sexuality, and social control, as well as performance and the politics of remembering and forgetting. She holds a BA in Drama and Law, Societies and Justice from the University of Washington (Seattle, Duwamish/Coast Salish lands).

Andrea Tompa is a writer and an associate professor in the Hungarian Theatre Department at Babeş-Bolyai University in Cluj, Romania. She holds her PhD in Russian Literature. She has worked as a theatre critic for two decades and was the editor-in-chief of theatre magazine *Színház* until 2019. Her major field of research is contemporary Hungarian theatre and twentieth-century Hungarian theatre history in Romania. She is also a novelist: her first novel, *The Hangman's House*, was published by Seagull Books in English; her novel *Omerta* was published by Suhrkamp Verlag in Germany. She lives in Budapest.

Alex Trustrum-Thomas is a postdoctoral visiting scholar at the University of Warsaw (Poland) and the V.N. Karazin Kharkiv National University (Ukraine), funded by the Leverhulme Trust. His publications include 'From Stalinist Socialist Realism to Putinist Capitalist Realism: Tracing Cultural Ideology in Contemporary Russia', in J.A.E. Curtis (ed.), *New Drama in Russian: Performance, Politics and Protest in Russia, Ukraine and Belarus* (Bloomsbury Academic, 2020). He holds a DPhil from the University of Oxford.

Lonneke van Heugten is a writer, dramaturg and poet-performer who conceptualizes and curates cultural events. Her PhD at the Amsterdam School for Cultural Analysis (ASCA) grapples with the cosmopolitics and limits of imagining community in European cultural policy and theatre practices. She was awarded the Dutch National Theatre Institute Award for her MA thesis in International Performance Research (University of Warwick and University of Amsterdam): *Theatre as a Vortex of Behaviour in Dutch Multicultural Society* (Tectum Verlag, 2013). She also acts as a coach and occasionally teaches, notably at the Department of Theatre Studies at the University of Amsterdam.

Duncan Wheeler holds the Chair of Spanish Studies at the University of Leeds. A published translator, he was inducted into the Spanish Academy of Stage Arts in 2016 in recognition of his teaching and research of theatre. He is the Hispanic Studies Editor of the journal *Modern Language Review*. His latest book is titled *Following Franco: Spanish Politics and Culture in Transition* (2020). In addition to his academic publications, he regularly writes for the media in Spain, the UK and the USA (*The Economist, Guardian, Newsweek, El País, Times Literary Supplement*, etc.).

Acknowledgements

First and foremost, we would like to extend warmest thanks to the contributors to this volume: their expertise, patience, and enthusiasm throughout this project has been much appreciated. We are grateful to the team at University of Exeter Press, and particularly to Anna Henderson, Commissioning Editor, Nigel Massen, Publisher, and David Hawkins, Production Editor, for steering us through the commissioning, editorial, and publication process so supportively and efficiently.

We would like to thank the following for their assistance in the preparation of this volume: Szymon Adamczak, Richard Ashby, Emma Cox, Maria Delgado, Zsofi Domsa, Graça dos Santos, Helen Freshwater, Geoff Gould, Adrian Heathfield, Joe Kelleher, Radka Kunderová, Bryce Lease, Sara Magness, Aneta Mancewicz, Steve Nicholson, Sophie Nield, Dan Rebellato, Eleanor Roberts, Aniko Szucs, Elaine Turner, and the research group LIBEX. We are very grateful to Magda Hueckel for use of her photograph for our cover image. Finally, we express gratitude to our anonymous peer reviewers for their constructive suggestions and encouraging remarks.

This book is dedicated, with thanks and appreciation, to Professor Thomas Pughe, and to the late Professor David Bradby and Professor Anthony Hozier.

Note on translation and referencing

Regarding the translation and formatting of the titles of foreign works, including the titles of published and unpublished plays, we have presented the title in its original language and style followed by the English translation in brackets; thereafter—for ease of reference—we refer to the title in its English translation. When referring to the titles of plays published in English, or titles with an accepted English translation, we have presented the title translation in italics in headline style—for example, *Nie-Boska komedia. Szczątki* (*Un-Divine Comedy. Remains*); for unpublished English titles, we have not used italics and have presented the title, translated by our contributors, in sentence style—for example, *Politika kao sudbina* (Politics as a fate).

Introduction
Censorship in Times of Convulsive Change

ANNE ETIENNE AND CHRIS MEGSON

To celebrate the 400th anniversary of Molière's birth in 2022, Ivo van Hove directed the original, banned text of *Tartuffe, ou l'hypocrite* at the Comédie-Française for the first time since it was performed for Louis XIV in 1664. The three-act comedy about religious hypocrisy much amused the king, but he forbade its public presentation to avoid antagonizing the clergy. Molière rewrote the play into a version in five acts, *Le Tartuffe, ou l'imposteur*—the alternative wording avoided the emphasis on false piety— which was eventually performed in 1669. In March 2023, an adaptation of Molière's play by Frank McGuinness opened at the Abbey Theatre in Dublin: the eponymous Tartuffe, a character who claims morality but acts otherwise, has an intriguing contemporary appeal. As the Abbey's poster for *Tartuffe* announces: 'The only crime lies in being found out'. Such a declaration on hidden duplicity is pertinent to the focus of this book: unlike Tartuffe, an effective censor tends to leave no trace of their actions and conceals their core motivations.[1]

While totalitarian regimes kept strict control of artistic expression until the 1990s, Western democracies left behind, in a more or less distant past, systems of officially institutionalized, or direct, censorship. A wide range of censorial practices have been mobilized, historically, to silence playwrights, invigilate dramatic texts (preventive, a priori, pre-production censorship) and control theatrical performances (punitive, a posteriori, post-production censorship), as long as their operation was neither suspected nor challenged. In all cases, censorship was maintained until its exercise elicited protests, thereby revealing it to be, variously, an embarrassment (England), a waste of money (France), or an affront to the principle of freedom of speech (Scandinavia). Helen Freshwater's conclusion that 'censorship remains a live issue', and that the abolition of official systems of censorship cannot be relied upon as evidence of 'progress towards increasing tolerance', provides an apt springboard for the multiple reflections on contemporary censorship gathered in this book (2009: 167).

Theatre Censorship in Contemporary Europe: Silence and Protest investigates contemporary practices of theatre censorship in Europe (east to west and, to a lesser extent, north to south), taking 1989 as a starting point to reassess how the seismic transformations in Europe in the decades following the fall of the Berlin Wall, and particular national politics, have affected artistic creation and free expression. Shedding light on national and cross-national case studies, the contributors explore the limits and resistance of artistic expression to map censorship in its mechanisms and effects today. Our primary aim is to identify the sources of censorship following the abandonment of institutionalized and state-regulated systems. In particular, we wish to attend to the following questions: What are the contexts (political, societal, legal, cultural) of theatre censorship in Europe post-1989? Given the abolition of state-sanctioned and institutional forms of censorship, in what ways and to what extent does censorship manifest and proliferate in contemporary European theatre cultures? How does censorship respond (or not) to governmental, cultural, economic, societal, moral, and religious circumstances and injunctions? And how have theatre-makers courted or countered controversy in this period? Cumulatively, the chapters track how new mechanisms of censorship operate to control artists or performances, and detail how theatre practitioners respond to constraints placed upon their work across territories. Our contributors also analyse how political, religious, and moral taboos impact on theatre and performance, and differ across Europe. We invite readers to consider not only the varied mechanisms of censorship including in its more covert manifestations, but also what is censored, when, and why, particularly in relation to the sensitive issues of religion, race, sexuality, and nationalism. By focusing on the work of key playwrights and directors, as well as significant production case studies, and reflecting on the consequences of censorious manifestations on artistic policies and cultural activity, the volume offers fresh perspectives on the practice and impact of censorship in Europe.

Contexts and definitions of censorship

Since centralized systems of censorship were discarded across Europe at different moments of the twentieth century (1906 in France, 1954 in Denmark, 1968 in England, 1974 in Portugal, to the ideological revolutions in Eastern Europe triggered by the fall of the Berlin Wall in 1989), various forms of pressure on artists and suppression of material have emerged and developed to replace them. Censorship has shed its visible, historical, state-controlled, physical identity to transform into a series of polymorphous phenomena that largely escape detection—and often controversy—because they elude definition.

Previous studies have established conceptual perspectives on the hidden mechanisms of censorship that have developed since state-sponsored censorship systems were abolished. In her introduction to *Global Insights on Theatre Censorship*, Catherine O'Leary identifies myriad types of restriction that may be construed as censorship:

> Censorship can include deletions, rewritings and insertions within a text; the proscription of actions, inflections or visual components in performance; the prohibition of individual works; the withdrawal or cancellation of works; the blacklisting, imprisonment or exile of an author; and, in extreme cases, even the killing of authors whose works are deemed a threat to the established order […;] the humiliation, harassment and exclusion of authors; the imposition of fines and travel restrictions; loss of employment; and public campaigns against writers […;] restrictions on the length of performance runs and types of venue. […] Threats, fines, restrictions on paper supplies and imprisonment may all be applied, and prizes and subsidies used to reward or exclude. (2016: 5, 6)

O'Leary highlights the difficulty in reaching a consensus on the definition of censorship, both pragmatically and conceptually—a difficulty that is intensified in the contemporary period by the official absence of legislatively embedded censorship apparatus, and the proliferation of agents and modes of repression and punishment. Traditional censorship always takes an institutional form: it is established by legal texts and regulated by the state via more or less independent bodies/institutions. In some cases, writers claimed that they were not aware of the precise criteria of the censor—either because there were, indeed, very few fixed criteria for the censors themselves, or to highlight how censorship affected writers even before they put words to the page. Its purpose is the suppression or prohibition of any parts of printed or performed texts that are considered obscene, politically unacceptable, or blasphemous.

Reflecting on the omnipresence of censorship across time, Michael Thompson notes the way in which censorial practices are responsive to context: 'censorship apparatuses and practices reflect the specific characteristics of the political and cultural systems in which they are deployed at particular times, and reveal interesting things about those systems and circumstances' (2016: 265). Our approach stems from this notion of a site- and time-specificity in the creation and reception of censorship. One of our key preoccupations is to identify how strategies, agents, and effects of censorship have mutated in contemporary Europe and manifested—as the subtitle of this book indicates—between the poles of silence and protest. We intend the word 'silence' to refer variously to the subjugation of playwrights when their works are censored in whole or part; the silence of theatregoers when censorship has been effective in removing potentially sensitive material without their knowledge; the silence in situations where censorship is so indirect it is not even suspected; and the silence when authoritarian censorship muzzles everyone. Meanwhile, the word 'protest' refers to forms of opposition from theatre artists and their allies when their work is censored (in democracies); complaints from political, religious, and other groups who attempt to block access to a performance, occupy the auditorium, and/or even climb on stage; and protests by audience members during performance on the grounds, for instance, of outrage and offence. Protests can target the artist, the theatre, or the censorial practices, but protest can also be seen as a form of censorship: the noise of protests and counterprotests creates echo chambers that divert from identifying censorship, prompting the fundamental question—who is the censor? Indeed, Lara Shalson contends that censorship is to be found in the intersection between forms of performance and protest when street protests (sometimes referred to as 'mob censorship') criticize the artist's work and seek to restrict access to the production; as she points out, with reference to the examples of Gurpreet Kaur Bhatti's *Behzti* (2004) and Brett Bailey's *Exhibit B* (2010) in the British context, this can result in institutions deciding to cancel a production (2021: 29–38).

Freedom of thought, freedom of speech, and freedom of expression are supposed to have been acquired, but are they—as Nicole Moore argues—'utopic principle[s], forever unfulfilled', or rather in unresolved and dangerous tension with the right to offend (2015: 1)? Freedom of expression includes the right to offend and the right to protest in a dynamic that solicits dialogue. Censorship occurs when access to the stage is denied and performances are cancelled, when protest leads to silence and intimidation rather than dialogue, and when freedom of expression is mobilized as an incitement to hatred and crime. As such, the attempt to elucidate what censorship is by locating its opposite is problematic: freedom of expression is not an antonym for censorship.

Matthew Bunn observes that 'using the word "censorship" to describe impersonal, diffuse forms of thought-regulation leads to a problematic erosion of specificity for censorship as an analytical category' (2015: 40). When indirect, implicit, structural censorship is at play, the word is rarely pronounced. The censoring act not only remains unclaimed, but it is effaced and disguised, conjured away like a sleight of hand. In 2020, an eponymous text about the notion of a liquid city by Regina Guimarães was quietly and surreptitiously removed from the programme of *Turismo*, directed by Tiago Correia, at the Teatro Municipal do Porto in Portugal: Guimarães's text had failed to advocate the philosophy of a town councillor (and former Councillor for Culture), Paulo Cunha e Silva, and was effectively silenced ('Dramaturga' 2020). The result of such actions is that consensus prevails: funding bodies—either public or private—must not be upset, and nor should programmers be thwarted. For Laurent Cauwet (2017), censorship today originates in the 'domestication de l'art' (subjugation of art), a control that appears innocent by diverting—in its double meaning of taking detours and providing entertainment. Censorship is difficult to identify when it has been revamped and transformed into communication, when the term is brandished for its shock effect, or again when its opacity prompts metacensorial responses. For instance, in 2017, the Royal Court Theatre in London cancelled the revival of Andrea Dunbar's play *Rita, Sue and Bob Too* (1982) in response to allegations against the co-founder of the Out of Joint theatre company, Max Stafford-Clark, and concerns about the play's representation of abuses of power against women; the production was reinstated in the programme when the Royal Court's decision was condemned as an act of censorship (Press Association 2017).

In the twenty-first century, protests have amplified and multiplied, drawing attention to public outrage at the unjust treatment of artists and the political suppression of their work. Vocal opposition to the arrest and trial of Russian director Kirill Serebrennikov in 2017–18 alerted the international community to his plight and the limits of artistic freedom of expression in Russia (as discussed by Alex Trustrum-Thomas in Chapter 2). Described by Harriet Sherwood and Andrew Roth as 'the only theatre company in Europe to be prohibited on political grounds' (2021), Belarus Free Theatre is perhaps the most notorious example of a company subjected to unrelenting state persecution: in October 2021, in fear of torture and imprisonment, several company members left Belarus after Alexander Lukashenko's regime tightened its grip on the country following disputed election results in 2020 (Rees 2022). The remarkable perseverance of company members has helped draw international attention to the worsening political situation in Belarus. In Hungary, increasing state interference in theatrical affairs can be traced back to Viktor Orbán's election to the premiership in 2010: the nomination of actor-director György Dörner to lead the state-subsidized New Theatre in 2012—supported by the extreme right-wing, antisemitic party Jobbik—prompted artists to voice their opposition in Hungary and beyond ('Open, Liberal Theatre' 2012). Protests in 2019 against proposed government legislation to limit artistic independence by rendering theatre funding a political operation via state-appointed directors were part of a wider opposition to Orbán's new legislation (as Andrea Tompa explores in her contribution to this volume). In 2016, protests at the Abbey Theatre in Dublin against a male-dominated programme commemorating the centenary of the Easter Rising revealed a form of censorship by omission through the historically embedded marginalization of women (discussed by Anne Etienne and Lisa Fitzpatrick in Chapter 3). In 2023, the French Observatory for Creative Freedom measured an 'unprecedented number of cancelled events in all fields of art and culture' ('Déprogrammer' 2023), not only proving the quantitative presence of censorship, but also raising questions about the rights and responsibilities of artistic programmers. Among those events, Aeschylus's *The Suppliants* was cancelled at the Sorbonne in March 2019, when students protested against the use of blackface on the publicity poster, and of black and white masks in the planned performance. While the university expressed its support for the play's director in the name of artistic freedom—a point made by Ariane Mnouchkine when she justified her choices in the making of *Kanata* in 2018—accusations of racism were declaimed as the students physically blocked access to both performers and spectators ('Pièce de théâtre' 2019). Laurène Marx's *Pour un temps sois peu* (For a time being, 2021), an autobiographical play on gender, normativity, and trauma, elicited protests from trans groups when it played in Toulouse in November 2022 because the role was performed by a cisgendered actress. Though the complaint enabled a round-table discussion in Toulouse, the Théâtre 13 in Paris, taking a conservative approach, opted to cancel the January run altogether. In February 2023, the University of Groningen in the Netherlands cancelled the student production of Samuel Beckett's *Waiting for Godot* (1953) because its director refused to enforce gender parity on stage—Beckett (and his estate) being famously inflexible on that issue.

The case of Brett Bailey's *Exhibit B* is interesting for two reasons. When it was due to open in London in 2014, it was doubly censored by a boycotting campaign and protesters blocking the doors of the venue, and by the Barbican which yielded to pressure and cancelled the piece (Farrington 2019). Bailey's installation had toured Europe since 2010 before the first protests emerged in Berlin, in October 2012, organized by Bühnenwatch ('stage watch'), a coalition of activists and theatre-makers initially founded in opposition to blackfacing and its roots in German colonial history.[2] France's colonial past in Korea and Algeria had motivated the censorship of playwright Michel Vinaver's *Les Coréens* (1956), *Les Huissiers* (1957), and *Iphigénie Hôtel* (1959), under the cover of the state of emergency enforced during the Algerian War of Independence (1954–62). The performance of his bilingual play *11 septembre 2001/11th September 2001* (2002), about the attacks on the Twin Towers in New York, was also cancelled in Los Angeles in 2005 three weeks before the opening (Sermon 2007). Though indirect—the French Embassy in Washington informed Vinaver and director Robert Cantarella that they would no longer receive the agreed $5,000 for the production, insisted on its logo being removed from the play's programme, and excised an advert for the play intended to be printed in its monthly newsletter—this new instance of censorship appears as a political manoeuvre in appeasing American sensibilities in the post-9/11 context of the 'War on Terror'. As Frédéric Hervé notes, dramatists have often delocalized the action of their plays to avoid censorship (2016: 125). These varied examples reignite conversations about diversity, 'political correctness', 'cancel culture', and the painful, intractable, and omnipresent legacies of colonialism. They also recall the two poles that have historically defined the domain of any censorship system: the invisibility of its exercise, and complaints (from artists and audiences alike) against its decisions.

The disparate case studies outlined above also indicate contemporary tendencies in terms of the evolution of taboos and forms of censorship. They compel scholars and audiences to consider debates on censorship that are now inflamed by global culture wars, exacerbated by the proliferation of (social) media that capitalize constantly upon ideas of freedom of expression and the right to offend. Such questions linger in the absence of a centralized, official censor whose duties were to avoid a breach of the peace by removing any content of a religious, political, or sexual nature that may trigger unrest, complaints, protests, or parliamentary inquiries. For the Observatoire de la liberté de création—a focus group of some fifteen organizations created by the French Ligue des droits de l'homme—'culture should not be a place of power, but of questions, dialogue and sharing' ('Déprogrammer' 2023): this statement underscores freedom of artistic expression without denying that such expression has legal limits. If a judge has the power to determine whether a production is offensive and to enforce adequate punitive measures, does this mean that any other method of preventing a production can be defined as censorship? As Janelle Reinelt invites her readers to look beyond censorship as a 'common-sense catchword' (2007: 3), we would venture a definition of censorship that is both elaborated and challenged in the ensuing chapters: censorship is any attempt to modify the integrity of the artistic work and its reception.

The research context

As more archives have opened, seminal studies on theatre censorship have been published, most of them scrutinizing national territories. The endurance of theatre censorship in twentieth-century Britain has been elucidated by Steve Nicholson's magisterial four-volume *The Censorship of British Drama 1900–1968* (2003–15), and in his thematically focused *British Theatre and the Red Peril: The Portrayal of Communism 1917–1945* (1999). Placing theatre censorship and its abolition in a parliamentary political context, *Theatre Censorship: From Walpole to Wilson* (2007), edited by David Thomas, David Carlton, and Anne Etienne, offers the first survey of direct and indirect forms of censorship in Britain after 1968 based on practitioners' testimonies. Helen Freshwater's *Theatre Censorship in Britain: Silencing, Censure and Suppression* (2009) similarly covers a wide chronological territory, extending her thematic analysis beyond the Lord Chamberlain's collection to the infamous prosecution of Howard Brenton's *The Romans in Britain* in 1981 and the protest against *Behzti* in 2004. Graça dos Santos has devoted multiple studies to Portuguese theatre during the dictatorship of António de Oliveira Salazar, who established a surveillance system which, under the name 'Estado Novo' (New State), administered until 1974 censoring practices that reviewed the texts both to be performed and in performance, thereby centralizing resources to prevent and punish (2002 and 2006). Laura Bradley's seminal study of theatre in East Germany, *Cooperation & Conflict: GDR Theatre Censorship, 1961–1989* (2010), highlights the complexity of official and indirect forms of censorship as well as self-censorship against such key historical events as the construction of the Berlin Wall and the Prague Spring.

Other important studies have examined the censorship question through an international lens—sharing some similarities with this volume in respect of their transnational or temporal scope—and have significantly expanded our knowledge of censorship formation and practices. Catherine O'Leary, Diego Santos Sánchez, and Michael Thompson's *Global Insights on Theatre Censorship* (2016) adopts a wide chronological approach which invites dialectical comparisons between explicit and implicit censorship. However, with rare exceptions, their purview is limited to specific linguistic territories (English, Spanish, Portuguese) and eschews a contemporary timeline.[3] Caridad Svich's edited collection, *Out of Silence: Censorship in Theatre & Performance* (2012), highlights exclusively contemporaneous cases of censorship without the constraint of a specific geographical agenda, preferring to interrogate—to illuminating effect—how censorship (whether official or self-imposed) affects the artists' creative process.

Global studies have extended the scope of scholarly enquiry on censorship not only through time, but also in their investigation of differing cultural modes and genres. Exceptional among a field led by scholars, the novelist J.M. Coetzee's *Giving Offense* (1996) gathers his personal reflections on censors and the effects of their gagging efforts, focusing on the censored authors' responses. Robert C. Post's edited collection, *Censorship and Silencing: Practices of Cultural Regulation* (1998), structures its investigation of censorship in relation to three models of state power—'repressive', 'tutelary', and 'egalitarian'—and covers a historical spectrum from the early modern period to the present. Meanwhile, in *Censorship and the Limits of the Literary: A Global View*, Nicole Moore envisages literature and censorship not as opposites, but as engaged in an agonistic relationship (2015: 2). Her edited volume identifies five new critical directions in the study of censorship that have emerged in Western democracies or the ex-Soviet bloc to illustrate the multiplicity not only of phenomena across the world, but also of censorship theories and terminologies. In 2020, the French journal *Communications* dedicated an issue—edited by Catherine Brun and Philippe Roussin—to the notion and global manifestations of 'post-censorship', querying how cultural productions or controversial images and words are captured and neutralized. They demonstrate that, as Roland Barthes suggests, censorship models in democracies do not prohibit as much or as effectively as they filter consensual opinions (2020: 13–14). Laurent Martin's *Les Censures dans le monde: XIX–XXI siècle* (*Censorships in the World: Nineteenth to Twenty-First Centuries*, 2016) covers an impressive range of countries and periods. The tripartite structure of the collection affirms the necessity of a historical approach: the first section is devoted to state- and church-regulated censorship in the nineteenth and early twentieth centuries; the following two sections observe how, in the twentieth and twenty-first centuries, censorship has functioned in democracies, and in totalitarian regimes.

Recent publications have also illuminated how the abolition of the old regime of the censor has complicated our understanding and observation of censorship. Beate Müller identifies three reasons for the renewed research in censorship debates from the 1980s to 1990s, the first two being motivated by the historical context: in the USA, the Republican agenda of Presidents Ronald Reagan and George H.W. Bush was accompanied by 'attempts to curb some civil and aesthetic liberties' (2004: 3); in Europe, the fall of the Berlin Wall in 1989 and the demise of the Soviet bloc in 1991 resulted in the opening of state archives, which included censorship records. But as official systems of direct censorship gave way to new or mutated forms of censorship, the functions and nature of censorship in contemporary culture required reconceptualizing (2004: 4). Müller, Freshwater (2009), and O'Leary (2016) have explained comprehensively how Michel Foucault's writings on discipline and the repressive hypothesis, Pierre Bourdieu's consideration of strategies of euphemization and the formation of self-censorship, and Judith Butler's articulation of an implicit and productive censorship have challenged and modified our understanding of censorship as a fixed phenomenon engineered by an identifiable exterior source. Thus, as Matthew Bunn explains, 'New Censorship Theory' has 'recast censorship from a negative, repressive force, concerned only with prohibiting, silencing, and erasing, to a productive force that creates new forms of discourse, new forms of communication, and new genres' (2015: 26).

The contemporary era is rarely examined in censorship studies, even though the past few decades have witnessed an increase in the limits placed upon free expression and heated debates abound about the issue. Analyses are more often to be found in press articles written in immediate response to controversial cases. Academic publications on censorship tend to explore the past rather than the present and be focused on national discourses. Clearly, language barriers further impact on the international range of outputs on offer for a topic that defies geographical boundaries. This volume builds on previous work by establishing European parameters for the study of contemporary forms of theatre censorship, but no publication to date has attempted the geographical range or temporal scope.

Insofar as the chapters contained in this collection interrogate forms of censorship, we have attempted to standardize the terms used: 'direct' to refer to overt intervention by political representatives; 'indirect' (or 'implicit') to encompass financial mechanisms as well as the conscious or unconscious phenomena of omission and marginalization. To these must be added threats towards the playwright and other practitioners involved in a production—including threats of prosecution—as well as self-censorship. However, what became evident in our dialogue with contributors was that such standardization may sometimes inhibit the articulation of how censorship functions on more than one level and through a constellation of pressures, and how it is experienced by artists and researched in a given national context. For instance, self-censorship is sometimes understood as a form of indirect censorship experienced by artists. Our approach thus embraces Freshwater's 'inclusive definition that responds to the diverse experiences of censorship' (2004: 225) in her exploration of the 'new censorship' debates, so that we have privileged an observation of various practices of censorship and their effects on performance and (trans) national theatrical ecosystems. This emphasis is prompted by our primary research questions, which are concerned with the evolution of censorship practices in a focused timeline (from 1989 to the present) and within a contested geographical territory, which is also a symbolic community: Europe.

Structure and methodology

In their responses to the volume's historical approach, our contributors discern new or barely revamped modalities of censorship that require critical scrutiny and attention. At a time when the concept of Europe is being interrogated and challenged locally and globally, several chapters in the volume reflect on how national systems of censorship have disappeared or rather reinvented themselves; they also question the nature and contemporary identities of censorial practice to invite new definitions of the tension between the stage, repression, and power. The early ideas for this book took shape in the aftermath of the Abbey Theatre controversy of 2016, mentioned earlier, while the date of its submission for publication coincided with new censorship legislation in Russia elicited by Vladimir Putin's full-scale invasion of Ukraine in 2022.[4] By focusing on Europe within a defined yet still open time period (the 'contemporary'), when the nation states of Europe falter under the pressures of extreme populism, nationalism, financial 'austerity', migration crises, the climate emergency, and the horrifying military conflagration in Ukraine, the chapters in this collection examine the processes and consequences of theatre censorship in unstable sociopolitical environments, and the role of theatre in subverting, resisting, and challenging oppression.

The selected chronology of the book hinges on a political event which ostensibly marked the end of a polarized ideological divide between East and West: the fall of the Berlin Wall in 1989 represents for the editors' generation a momentous change in global perspectives, comparable to the 1960s revolutions for the previous generation. However, since then the European Union has witnessed both ongoing political shifts and evolving censorship practices that do not always follow the East/West partition but also encompass political, moral, and religious issues prevalent equally in the north, south, and centre of Europe. While we aim to engage with a spatial coverage which encompasses East/West as well as North/South coordinates, we do not claim to be exhaustive, nor could we accommodate all European national territories within one volume. The privileging of the East–West axis stems from a number of reasons. The volume chronologically hinges on an event which primarily focuses on the East/West ideological debate. Following this, the geographical configuration complicated the historical approach (Portugal, for instance, is both South and West, but yet was also representative—under Salazar's dictatorship—of the kind of strict pre-production censorship model that would be usual behind the Iron Curtain). The inclusion of Russia was motivated, at first, by the escalating censorship under Putin, and subsequently by the Russian full-scale invasion of Ukraine. In addition, rare cases of theatre censorship have taken place in Scandinavia since the national official systems were abolished.[5] Prominent studies on national territories have already been published (for example, dos Santos 2002, Nicholson 2003–15, Bradley 2010) and some of these have tackled the beginning of our chronological scope (for instance, Popescu on Romanian theatre [2000, 2004] and Santos Sánchez's 2018 collection on Lusophone theatre). Where a monograph has been devoted to the contemporary period—such as Popescu—we have privileged other national contexts. In this volume, we have expanded not only the chronological scope but also the field of enquiry to embrace alternative types of performance—including chapters on bullfighting (by Duncan Wheeler) and shibari (Hannah Probst)—in order to investigate the notion of the audience as censors. So as to observe how censorship intervenes in the tension between silence and protest, contributors also explore protest as performance (Vicki Ann Cremona and Marco Galea, and Lonneke van Heugten) and how taboos emerge transnationally, requiring opera productions to invigilate and modify canonical librettos (Andrew Holden).

To enable contrasts and echoes across the work, the book is structured in three parts, which correspond to the research priorities of the volume. Part 1 ('Forms and Sources of Censorship') examines contemporary censorship strategies and their impact on theatre-making processes today. Part 2 ('Ghosts of the Past') explores the tension between past and present, in terms of censorship methods and the legacy of history. Part 3 ('Staging Taboos') foregrounds a range of sensitive topics and performances that may be deemed unspeakable and/or unwatchable. Our contributors explore the ongoing practices of censorship in Western democracies and post-communist societies as well as a range of performances that have sparked controversy because they tackle the continuing historical legacy of unpleasant pasts (for example, systemic racism). Theoretical considerations developed in previous studies (Freshwater 2004, Bunn 2015, O'Leary et al. 2016) have informed our understanding of censorship but our approach is phenomenological and historical. For this reason, we have placed Part 2, 'Ghosts of the Past', at the centre of the volume to emphasize the core importance of the memory of censorship, as the other parts examine contemporary forms and contemporary taboos in an implicit comparison with a past that lingers. If censorship has morphed into new forms, how have these been influenced and shaped by previous national formats? If the traditional repression of religion, politics, and sexuality on stage has changed, what are the contemporary taboos? In observing contemporary, fragile democracies, how does history haunt artists in the West, in the ex-Soviet bloc, and in the former Yugoslavia? More importantly, is the abolition of the centralized censorship systems of the past a positive development for theatre artists? For the author Anna Lengyel, historical forms of censorship at least prompted creative responses:

> The Berlin Wall has perhaps been the fourth wall in Hungarian theatre. The change of the system had a complicated impact. Freedom meant intellectual and artistic freedom, but it also meant that hidden political truths and reading between the lines became redundant. Therefore what was certainly the most cathartic element of good theatre before the change suddenly lost all meaning. In a way it was the strongest theatres that found themselves in the deepest void. (2009)

To engage with these questions, we have included a combination of longer and shorter pieces. The five shorter ones, titled 'Interventions', function as dialogic bridges between the three parts of the volume. While the chapters tend to be more expansive in scope, the interventions examine single case studies and/or particular fields of investigation. These pieces open the discourse to urgent questions about censorship in relation to notions of performativity, protest, political power, the public sphere, and freedom of speech—thereby expanding the volume's exploration of theatre censorship to related concepts, and opening future avenues for research. They sometimes connect to peripheral topics: either mutations of censorship around rather than of theatre, or new questions about a specific aspect of performance in the context of protest, or the seeming acceptability of—for example—blackface performance. Several of the interventions relate to identity politics, the issue of political correctness, and culture wars—pressing concerns that are linked, amongst other things, to language use and which have a direct bearing on the work of theatre practitioners, especially playwrights. Some of our contributors are—or have been—actively engaged in the artistic and cultural spheres, and their proximity to theatre practice bears upon their scholarly work in this volume—work that gives international readers direct access to a wealth of new research.

Contents

Part 1 of the volume, 'Forms and Sources of Censorship', opens with an intervention by Vicki Ann Cremona and Marco Galea titled 'Capturing Space: Crashing Down the Gates of the Maltese Utopia', which examines the concept of theatricality within the framework of a specific protest movement. On 16 October 2017, Malta was shaken by a car bomb explosion that killed a leading journalist, Daphne Caruana Galizia. Through her blog, Galizia had started to reveal corruption and political intrigue that was hotly denied by the suspected perpetrators. Her assassination sparked two contrasting attitudes: one which tried to play down the murder and another that insisted on bringing her death and her revelations to the fore. This resulted in the growth of civil society groups—many of them led by women—who adopted methods deemed unconventional to a Maltese public: to protest in the street, in court, and in the media demanding truth and justice. Cremona and Galea argue that theatricality creates the necessary space to voice dissent in the face of censorship that prevents protesters from using institutional channels of communication in order to express controversial or contrary views to those put forward by the political order, especially when the latter is the gatekeeper to these channels.

In Chapter 1, 'Voices from Semi-Peripheries: Pressure, Self-Censorship, and Micropolitics of Resistance in the Western Balkans', Milena Dragićević Šešić and Aleksandra Jovićević investigate different mechanisms of censorship in the performing arts since 1989, focusing on the Balkan countries. The abolition of official censoring bodies has made way for new strategies and subtle forms of economic and social suppression of topics that are seen to endanger traditional, national values. The consequences of the new forms of control are all the more damaging and difficult to estimate since there are no official records. Rather, contemporary cultural management has developed a sophisticated mechanism of impacting artistic decisions, while the political sphere uses populist forms of political communication to incite right-wing groups to generate fear and threaten the critical artist. In the Western Balkans, issues that may provoke malaise in public opinion (such as the critique of nationalism, religion, or politics, and challenges to heteronormativity) do not raise controversy because their presentation on 'official' stages signals that they do not challenge dominant values. However, when crossed with themes related to cultures of memory (shame, guilt), and when performances question the accepted narrative of history, they may cause a reaction, ranging from vocal opposition to direct censorship. Dragićević Šešić and Jovićević explore various direct forms of censorship and examine the micropolitics of resistance of civil society actors, with reference to examples of courage shown by numerous independent artists, artistic collectives, theatre groups, and even some public institutions.

In Chapter 2, 'The Emperor's New Clothes: Ideology and Censorship in Contemporary Russian Theatre', Alex Trustrum-Thomas illuminates intensifying censorial practices in Vladimir Putin's Russia. Considering developments since 2012, this is one of the first studies to address the issue of intensifying censorship in Russian theatre in an emboldened conservative-authoritarian political climate. In 2013, the then new Russian Minister for Culture, Vladimir Medinskii, dismissively compared contemporary Russian art to the emperor's new clothes. This turned out to be the firing gun for a state-directed assault on so-called alien ideas in Russian culture more broadly. This has restricted the possibilities for free expression, as censorship in its numerous guises has forced institutional theatres into conformity and silence—a situation that has worsened since the Russian invasion of Ukraine in 2022. Through analysis of legislation documents, official statements, interviews with theatre-makers, policy in practice, and key events as they unfolded, Trustrum-Thomas maps out the forms and mechanisms of censorship in contemporary Russian theatre against a background of a shifting political landscape and a society in transition.

In Chapter 3, 'Risings and Cancelling: Implicit Censorship on a Free Irish Stage', Anne Etienne and Lisa Fitzpatrick focus on the cultural selection processes at play on the contemporary Irish stage by examining what is absent (artists who have been historically relegated to the margins) or disappearing (artists who have been pushed aside by economic forces). This censorship is not centralized or formalized, but operates opaquely, implicitly, to maintain a status quo that is arguably reflective of social assumptions about gender, language diversity, and regionalism in the arts sector, as their case studies demonstrate. For Clare McIntyre, 'If women's theatre is supposed to be dead at the moment, it's because of who is doing the judging; that is, who is running the theatres. It's directors who determine what is seen and on what stages' (1999: 56). Taking its cue from the 1916 Easter Rising, the #WakingTheFeminists movement protested against the under-representation of women in the Abbey Theatre's 2016 centenary programme. This campaign acted as a positive incentive to review the canon as well as gender parity in terms of employment and was encouraged by the Arts Council. However, Etienne and Fitzpatrick also consider how successive Arts Council policies shape the Irish theatre ecosystem so that subsidies function as an indirect form of censorship. In 2022, the Arts Council of Northern Ireland denied the theatre company Aisling Ghéar its annual funding; in Cork, Corcadorca closed its doors, unable to continue with a diminished budget. The authors argue that this is the insidious and 'implicit' effect of the drip-feeding policies that have had a deleterious impact on small Irish theatre companies.

Part 2 of the volume, 'Ghosts of the Past', begins with an intervention from Andrea Tompa: 'Censorship in Hungary: Comedy, Silence, and Subversion'. Neither direct censorship nor violent interference in culture—that is, the closing of institutions, physical threats to cultural figures, the aggressive interruptions of performances by police, or the banning of shows—is characteristic of contemporary Hungary; rather, censorship practices are masked as legal and manifest in the form of budget cuts, restructuring, and reorganizations. Tompa contends that Hungary has always had a tradition of 'sloppiness': a chaotic, flexible, and complex modus operandi of censorship. Since the elections of 2010, however, state interference in the arts sector has grown exponentially. In her analysis, Tompa reflects on practices of censorship in Hungary since 2010—including through indirect governmental intervention—and responses to these practices.

In Chapter 4, 'Nothing New on the Eastern Front: Censorship in Contemporary Slovenia', Denis Poniž analyses the case of Slovenia. To orientate the reader, he briefly examines censorship in the former Yugoslavia from 1945 to 1991, but his analysis focuses on the later period (1991 onwards), specifically in the newly formed state of Slovenia. While the communist regime that controlled the former Yugoslavia officially denied having any kind of artistic censorship, theatrical endeavours were controlled in other informal and covert ways, which were twice as effective. Soon after 1991, it was obvious that the new, democratic state was not immune to the attempts of informal censorship; however, censorship was now carried out not by the government and party administration, but by unofficial groups within individual political parties and by groups that controlled capital and financial flows. The ideological motivation for such decisions is concealed under the guise of operating in a free market with a supply and demand model. Throughout his discussion, Poniž analyses several examples of such 'new' censorship and argues that its basic principles are identical to those of the ideological censorship in a one-party system.

Chapter 5, written by Agnieszka Jakimiak, is titled '*Un-Divine Comedy. Remains* and Self-Censorship as Work-In-Progress in Poland'. Jakimiak was a member of the dramaturgical team working on Oliver Frljić's production of *Un-Divine Comedy. Remains* in Kraków in 2013. This production was censored by the management of the National Old Theatre in the aftermath of a leak to the press concerning the potential controversies that the performance might cause. The decision to suspend the production was justified by the theatre as a response to harsh attacks from the press. Meanwhile, theatre critics and theoreticians approached the case from the perspective of questioning the aesthetics of the potential performance or its ideological premise (*Un-Divine Comedy. Remains* was to tackle the issue of Polish antisemitism). The notion of self-censorship is conventionally applied to a singular decision made by a person responsible for making a certain (artistic) utterance. However, in the light of institutional critique, the subject which applies self-censorship may be understood as a collective institutional body. Jakimiak investigates the potential of analysing self-censorship as an 'inside job' deployed by institutions to prevent the outside from interfering with their structure, but also as a tool that potentially replaces an institutional crisis with an 'artificial' one. Jakimiak examines the source and the consequences of the act of self-censorship undertaken by the management of the National Old Theatre in the light of current national politics of memory, and attempts to establish what this act means for politically engaged theatre institutions in Poland.

In Chapter 6, 'Opera Censorship in Europe—Production, Circulation, and Reception in a Transnational Market', Andrew Holden focuses primarily on three national contexts which exhibit different cultural and market conditions for opera—the UK, Germany, and Italy. In exploring censorship and contemporary opera, Holden expands the critical terrain of the volume while raising issues that pertain to censorship and the performing arts more widely. He highlights some of the distinctive features of opera which impact on processes of censorship—particularly the relationship between music, text, and staging; the continuing dominance of the Western operatic canon; and perceptions of its relevance and accessibility as an art form—to reveal the importance of seeing opera censorship in a transnational context, as well as the impact of digital reception and criticism, and audience and public activism. Holden assesses how activism, from the progressive to the populist, is impacting on opera production in different manifestations of the current culture wars. Some of the productions examined by Holden have generated considerable media publicity—Damiano Michieletto's *Guillaume Tell* at Covent Garden (2015) was altered following an audience backlash against choreography which simulated a gang rape, and then toured to Palermo. In Germany, Hans Neuenfels's production of *Idomeneo* (2006) was temporarily withdrawn in Berlin because of security concerns arising from its depiction of a decapitated Prophet Muhammad. Many European opera companies supply hired productions for non-European markets like the Royal Opera House, Oman: Holden assesses the role of European theatres in censoring their own productions for hire and the implication for the work of individual artists with reference to two productions hired by Oman, *Maria Stuarda* (Welsh National Opera, 2013) and *Aida* (Teatro Regio di Torino, 2017).

Part 2 of the volume concludes with an intervention from Lonneke van Heugten, titled 'The Tenacity of Tradition: Performativity in the Dutch Black Pete Controversy'. The critique of blackface in the Dutch Saint Nicholas celebration appeared in the media as early as the 1920s. Since the 1960s, activist groups have organized protests and, in recent years, the United Nations and the Children's Ombudsman have condemned the figure of Black Pete ('Zwarte Piet') as racist. Nevertheless, Black Pete still features in a televised parade, elementary schools, shopping malls, and diverse cultural products. Comments such as 'he is just a fictional character' often surface in public debate, implying that critics misunderstand the tradition's conventions. The disavowal of the power dynamics in such responses allows for a volatile role reversal of who is censoring whom. Van Heugten exposes the affective dimensions and tenacity of a European tradition that carries over unwanted pasts, while opening up the prospect of a future-orientated cultural politics.

Following on from van Heugten's analysis of race in the context of Black Pete, the final part of the volume, 'Staging Taboos', opens with an intervention from Roaa Ali titled 'Racialized Censorship in the Age of Culture Wars'. In the UK, culture wars have increasingly become a frequent infiltrator of political and media discourse. The more contested term of 'cancel culture', which purportedly refers to the cancelling, or silencing, of those who have a prominent public profile in response to comments or cultural texts deemed discriminatory, is having a potent impact on the concepts of creativity, freedom of speech, and social justice: the term 'culture wars' has been effectively appropriated and weaponized by the right to create draconian political and cultural measures that aim to curtail racialized and marginalized voices. In recent years, two theatrical examples from the UK stand out as a worrying development regarding censorship in the arts: the National Youth Theatre's cancellation of the play *Homegrown* (2015), by Omar El-Khairy and Nadia Latif, and the obfuscation of the production of Lung Theatre's *Trojan Horse* (2018), which both touch on racialized religious minorities and their freedom of expression. The censorship in these is a product of direct state interference in the case of *Homegrown*, and the indirect instrumentalization of the state's policing of the arts in the case of *Trojan Horse*—both relating to the controversial Prevent Strategy in the UK. Ali thus investigates censorship and the weaponizing of cancel culture as ways of silencing racialized voices, connected to an agenda that maintains white privilege, if not supremacy, and that is invested in policing, and at times criminalizing, racialized sections of society.

In Chapter 7, 'Images of Protest: Religion, Theatre, and Censorship', Chris Megson identifies religion as both an embattled site of contestation in contemporary European theatre and a lens through which debates on freedom of expression have been brought into sharp focus. In the first part of the chapter, attending primarily to the British context since 2000, Megson discusses examples of individual and institutional self-censorship motivated by 'sensitivities' about Islam and the representation of Muslim lives on stage; he also explores several productions that were the target of protests, led primarily by evangelical Christian groups, on the grounds of their perceived blasphemy. In the second part of the chapter, Megson examines some of the scholarly reappraisals of theatre censorship in the early 2000s, which reflect on high-profile case studies such as the cancellation of *Behzti* at the Birmingham Rep in 2004. A shared preoccupation of this scholarship is the advocacy for greater dialogue between practitioners, scholars, and audiences on problematic issues of stage representation, especially in contexts where performances on religious themes might, or are likely to, cause offence. The final part of the chapter considers a case study—the Italian theatre director Romeo Castellucci's production of *Sul concetto di volto nel figlio di Dio* (*On the Concept of the Face, Regarding the Son of God*) from 2010. In this piece, a large-scale, close-up fragment of a Renaissance painting of Christ is desecrated and then resurrected on stage. This aspect of the production triggered fierce protests from religious groups, particularly when it was performed in Paris. Megson shows how these protests, and Castellucci's response, reflect two distinct and possibly irreconcilable perspectives on theatre's 'attentiveness' to religious iconography on stage.

In Chapter 8, 'Religion and Politics: Silencing Greek Theatre in the Twenty-First Century', Olga Kolokytha, Yulia Belinskaya, and Matina

Magkou argue that, although the system of censorship committees was abolished in Greece in 1986, there have been prominent incidents of artistic censorship since then. They discuss three cases of censorship in Greek theatre: Terrence McNally's *Corpus Christi* (2012), Pigi Dimitrakopoulou's *The Nash Equilibrium* (2016), and Fernando Pessoa's *The Hour of the Devil* (2017), which were censored for religious and ethical/political reasons. All productions were cancelled following strong public protests. In the case of *The Nash Equilibrium* in particular, artists, culture professionals, and the board of the National Theatre protested against censorship and the decision of the theatre's artistic director to cancel the run. The case studies are framed by a reflection on freedom of expression in the sociopolitical context of Greece after 1986. The authors identify the different contexts and causes of censorship and discuss how audiences, culture professionals, and cultural organizations participate in and/or react to different censorship practices in contemporary Greece.

The final chapter, Chapter 9 by Duncan Wheeler, is titled 'Booing and Banning: Freedom and Prohibition in Spain's "National Fiesta"'. In his analysis, Wheeler critically interrogates the discourse of anti-censorship as central to the identity politics of the bullfighting lobby. During the Francoist dictatorship (1939–75), it was often said that bullrings were the most democratic spaces in Spain as the audience had the right to challenge authority, and presidents (who rank the matador's performance) were frequently booed. Since the Catalan ban in 2011, defences of bullfighting have increasingly been framed in relation to freedom, and attending a bullring equated to exercising a democratic right. This libertarian logic finds its correlative within the ring where ticket holders are free to boo, in a manner that would be deemed unacceptable in most theatrical spaces, if they believe that any of the players (bullfighter, breeder, president) has delivered an under-par performance. Wheeler thus explores the bullfight as a fascinating locus for debates on politics, public performance, and censorship in contemporary Spain.

The volume ends with an intervention from Hannah Probst: 'Play on the Periphery: Irrational Queerness as Resistance to Censorship in Gestalta's Shibari Performance Art'. Probst is interested in how the work of the performance artist Gestalta explores relational queer subjectivity and how shibari intersects with questions of censorship not only because of its focus on the body and sexualized stigmatization, but also through a socioaesthetic dimension that creates a community of observers and observed. For instance, what embodiments of queerness do shibari performances interrogate, or affirm, and how do these embodiments resist the censure of queerness imposed by increasingly dominant assimilated queer subject positions? The performance examined challenges dominant notions of queerness, thereby resisting the informal censorship performed by assimilationist queer social movements.

The chapters in this volume identify some of the manifestations of censorship in contemporary European theatre and performance—direct or indirect interference; protests and threats; imprisonment; and self-censorship. We are mindful that many, if not most, cases of effective censorial silencing are left unreported and are therefore unknown to us. Despite this, our contributors investigate the ways that practitioners and theatre organizations apprehend, experience, and respond to (overt or covert) censorial practices. There is, perhaps inevitably, a notable emphasis on the influence of the past on the present—on the complex legacies of European history in shaping current systems of censorial prohibition in specific social, political, cultural, and national settings. In the present era of incendiary culture wars, cancel culture, and global movements determined to challenge and dismantle forms of systemic inequality, the chapters in this collection also evidence the considerable pressures and 'sensitivities' involved in staging works that foreground race, religion, and queerness. Above all, our contributors—situated in their various countries and contexts—attest to the extraordinary perseverance, resilience, and pugnacity of theatre-makers across the continent in times of convulsive change.

Notes

1. It should be noted, however, that Alex Trustrum-Thomas's chapter in this volume gives a clear example of when theatre censorship, in the Russian context, was intended to be visible as a way of warning other artists.
2. Katrin Sieg (2015) analyses the first public outcries in Germany against blackface in 2012.
3. O'Leary and Lázaro's collection (2011) embraces a wider European scope in their study of the censorship and reception of English literature.
4. For example, in Norway in 2014, following a press campaign led by Bishop Halvor Nordhaug, the production of *In God's Name*—a play about freedom of creed which was part of the official culture programme for schools—was cancelled in eighteen out of twenty-eight schools.
5. Yana Meerzon and Mikhail Kaluzhsky's *Performing Censorship: The Russian Case* (2025) provides a timely, and alarming analysis of the consequences of censorship on Russian theatre, tracing its evolution under Putin's totalitarian dictatorship back to Tsarist and Soviet practices. Focusing on the twenty-first century and the period since the invasion of Ukraine, the volume examines how state censorship is not only reshaping but often purging theatre to respond to Putin's national and cultural agenda, as the punitive policies and regulatory mechanisms that restrict productions force artists to self-censor (195).

References

Bradley, Laura. 2010. *Cooperation and Conflict: GDR Theatre Censorship 1961–1989* (Oxford: Oxford University Press)

Brun, Catherine, and Philippe Roussin (eds). 2020. *Communications: Post-Censure(s)*, 106. https://doi.org/10.3917/commu.106.0013

Bunn, Matthew. 2015. 'Reimagining Repression: New Censorship Theory and After', *History and Theory*, 54.1: 25–44. https://doi.org/10.1111/hith.10739

Cauwet, Laurent. 2017. *La Domestication de l'art: politique et mécénat* (Paris: La Fabrique)

Coetzee, J.M. 1996. *Giving Offense: Essays on Censorship* (Chicago and London: University of Chicago Press). https://doi.org/10.7208/chicago/9780226111773.001.0001

'Déprogrammer une oeuvre est un renoncement, pas un acte de courage'. 2023. *Libération*, 7 January

dos Santos, Graça. 2002. *Le Spectacle dénaturé: le théâtre portugais sous le règne de Salazar (1933–1968)* (Paris: CNRS Editions). https://doi.org/10.4000/books.editionscnrs.38952

―――― 2006. 'La scène sous surveillance', *Ethnologie française*, 36.1: 11–17

'Dramaturga Regina Guimarães acusa de censura direcão do Teatro Municipal do Porto'. 2020. *Observador*, 3 February

Farrington, Julia. 2019. 'Brett Bailey/Exhibit B', *Index on Censorship*, 15 May

Freshwater, Helen. 2004. 'Towards a Redefinition of Censorship', in *Censorship and Cultural Regulation in the Modern Age*, ed. by Beate Müller, Critical Studies: Volume 22 (Leiden: Brill), pp. 225–45. https://doi.org/10.1163/9789401200950_010

―――― 2009. *Theatre Censorship in Britain: Silencing, Censure and Suppression* (Basingstoke: Palgrave Macmillan)

Hervé, Frédéric. 2016. 'Stratégies censoriales et professionnelles dans le cadre du contrôle des films en France (1945–1975)', in *Les Censures dans le monde XIXe–XXIe siècle*, ed. by Laurent Martin (Presses Universitaires de Rennes), pp. 121–34. https://doi.org/10.4000/books.pur.45014

Lengyel, Anna. 2009. 'Where History Has Been Written: The Budapest Katona József Theatre', 10 June <https://www.artidea.org/blog/2009/06/502> [accessed 19 February 2023]

McIntyre, Clare. 1999. 'Plays by Women', in *State of Play, Issue 1: Playwrights on Playwriting*, ed. by David Edgar (London: Faber and Faber)

Martin, Laurent (ed.). 2016. *Les Censures dans le monde XIXe–XXIe siècle* (Presses Universitaires de Rennes). https://doi.org/10.4000/books.pur.44936

Meerzon, Yana, and Mikhail Kaluzhsky. 2025. *Performing Censorship: The Russian Case* (Palgrave Macmillan).

Moore, Nicole (ed.). 2015. *Censorship and the Limits of the Literary: A Global View* (London: Bloomsbury)

Müller, Beate (ed.). 2004. *Censorship and Cultural Regulation in the Modern Age* (Amsterdam and New York: Rodopi). https://doi.org/10.1163/9789401200950

Nicholson, Steve. 1999. *British Theatre and the Red Peril: The Portrayal of Communism 1917–1945* (Exeter: University of Exeter Press)

―――― 2003. *The Censorship of British Drama 1900–1968, Volume 1: 1900–1932* (Exeter: University of Exeter Press)

―――― 2005. *The Censorship of British Drama 1900–1968, Volume 2: 1933–1952* (Exeter: University of Exeter Press)

―――― 2011. *The Censorship of British Drama 1900–1968, Volume 3: The Fifties* (Exeter: University of Exeter Press)

―――― 2015. *The Censorship of British Drama 1900–1968, Volume 4: The Sixties* (Exeter: University of Exeter Press)

O'Leary, Catherine. 2016. 'Introduction: Censorship and Creative Freedom', in *Global Insights on Theatre Censorship*, ed. by Catherine O'Leary, Diego Santos Sánchez, and Michael Thompson (New York and London: Routledge), pp. 1–23

O'Leary, Catherine, and Alberto Lázaro (eds). 2011. *Censorship Across Borders: The Reception of English Literature in Twentieth-Century Europe* (Newcastle: Cambridge Scholars)

O'Leary, Catherine, Diego Santos Sánchez, and Michael Thompson (eds). 2016. *Global Insights on Theatre Censorship* (New York and London: Routledge). https://doi.org/10.4324/9781315714417

'Open, Liberal Theatre under Fire in Hungary'. 2012. *Guardian*, 26 January

'Pièce de théâtre annulée à la Sorbonne après des accusations de Blackface'. 2019. *Radiofrance*, 26 March

Popescu, Marian. 2000. *The Stage and the Carnival: Romanian Theater after Censorship* (Bucharest: Paralela 45)

—— 2004. *Scenele teatrului românesc 1945–2004: de la cenzură la libertate* (Bucharest: Unitext)

Post, Robert C. (ed.). 1998. *Censorship and Silencing: Practices of Cultural Regulation* (California: Getty Research Institute)

Press Association. 2017. 'Royal Court Reverses Decision to Cancel *Rita, Sue and Bob Too*', *Guardian*, 15 December

Rees, Jasper. 2022. '"I was not ready to be killed": The Secret Theatre Forced into Exile by the KGB', *Independent*, 11 March

Reinelt, Janelle. 2007. 'The Limits of Censorship', *Theatre Research International*, 32.1 (March): 3–15. https://doi.org/10.1017/S0307883306002471

Santos Sánchez, Diego (ed.). 2018. *Theatre and Dictatorship in the Luso-Hispanic World*. (Abingdon and New York: Routledge). https://doi.org/10.4324/9781315405100

Sermon, Julie. 2007. '*11 septembre 2001*, de Michel Vinaver. Irreprésentable?', *La Voix du regard*, 20: 35–46. https://doi.org/10.4000/agon.1750

Shalson, Lara. 2021 (2017). *theatre & protest* (London: Bloomsbury Methuen Drama)

Sherwood, Harriet, and Andrew Roth. 2021. '"We are in limbo": Banned Belarus Theatre Troupe Forced into Exile', *Guardian*, 6 December

Sieg, Katrin. 2015. 'Race, Guilt, and *Innocence*: Facing Blackfacing in Contemporary German Theater', *German Studies Review*, 38.1 (February): 117–34. https://doi.org/10.1353/gsr.2015.0007

Svich, Caridad (ed.). 2012. *Out of Silence: Censorship in Theatre & Performance* (Roskilde: EyeCorner Press)

Thomas, David, David Carlton, and Anne Etienne. 2007. *Theatre Censorship: From Walpole to Wilson* (Oxford: Oxford University Press) https://doi.org/10.1093/acprof:oso/9780199260287.001.0001

Thompson, Michael. 2016. 'Conclusion: The Power of Theatre', in *Global Insights on Theatre Censorship*, ed. by Catherine O'Leary, Diego Santos Sánchez, and Michael Thompson (New York and London: Routledge), pp. 259–67

Part 1

Forms and Sources of Censorship

Intervention 1
Capturing Space: Crashing Down the Gates of the Maltese Utopia

VICKI ANN CREMONA AND MARCO GALEA

> In strong democracies such as Malta's, there is absolutely no doubt that everyone has the right to protest and manifest their opinions. Likewise, everyone has the right to walk around and enjoy the capital city and elsewhere safely with their families and kids.
> [Spokeswoman for Michael Farrugia, Minister of Home Affairs, Malta] (Farrugia 2019)

When walking down a street, absorbed in our everyday activities, we do not necessarily attribute any specific meaning to our being in space. It is when we walk down the same street with intention, such as that of protesting, that the space we are in acquires symbolic value. The space of protest is a captured space; ordinary activity is disrupted, and the extraordinary takes over in order to stage action that is intended to express dissent in a forceful manner. Protest is a form of freedom of speech; it allows ordinary citizens, whose voices 'have little chance to be heard' because they 'lack access to great newspapers or television broadcasts', to render their opinions visible (Dworkin 1994: 13). All action becomes deliberately performative—it is done with the intent of forcing all those who witness it to acknowledge the disruption and, more importantly, its purpose. The theatrical capture of public space establishes a particular relationship between participants and observers that changes the perception and meaning of what occurs within it. Participants become actors and the objects they carry become symbols: their placards become text, protest T-shirts become costumes, umbrellas and walking sticks become props. However, the nature of the protesters' action and the connections established with sympathizers watching on the periphery of the protest are different to those occurring in a theatre, where the extraordinary is anticipated. The spatial articulation of dissent is based on a horizontal relationship among participants; it is not simply linked to the idea of 'being in common' in a space, but of 'transforming separation into community', where the members identify with the cause and with each other, creating a sense of adherence and belonging (Rancière 2016). This type of relationship may be contrasted with the imposition of a vertical power structure that reappropriates the public space, in the same way it reappropriates public discourse through the reinforcement of its normal regulation and its structures of control. Power wielded by the authorities to repress or impede public protest is a form of censorship. The struggle for appropriation of public space in Malta by protesters and authorities demonstrates, on the one hand, the protesters' will to stage public performances in order to keep alive public awareness of the assassination of a journalist, Daphne Caruana Galizia, and to remind the authorities of their duty to deliver justice. On the other hand, it highlights the contrasting effort by state agencies to inhibit public demonstrations in order for the event and its causes to fade from public memory.[1]

On 16 October 2017, Daphne Caruana Galizia was killed in a terrifyingly spectacular way—a bomb, placed under her car seat, was detonated minutes after she left her home, digging a crater in the road, burning the car, and strewing her body parts across a nearby field (Garside 2019). Daphne, as everybody knew her, had become a household name through her blog: *Running Commentary*. Her articles focused mainly on denouncing corruption, mostly attributable to the collusion between big business and politicians. Not only did she comment on what was happening in Malta on a daily, and even hourly, basis, but often she revealed news about the scandalous, underhanded dealings of prominent members of government, civil servants and people in their close circles, as well as those of certain members of the Opposition. Her blog compensated for the failure of the local media establishment to investigate shady deals, given that most media outlets were obliged to exercise self-censorship. In Malta, the two main political parties—Labour and Nationalist—own television and radio stations, as well as news portals, and the state media are controlled by whichever party is in power. This means that hot issues, especially those involving corruption, are only presented in censored form or are completely omitted from the news. Independent newspapers, which depend on big business for investment and advertising revenue, are often obliged to water down their criticism of dubious political decisions, especially when collusion with big business is suspected.

Although in most democratic regimes, censorship, political or otherwise, has been officially removed, there are various ways of silencing those who expose corrupt power. Libel suits, and their extreme form, Strategic Lawsuits Against Public Participation, better known as SLAPP suits, sometimes serve as a legal form of coercing someone into silence. Personal harassment and violence are used to silence critics; assassination has proved to be 'the most effective way of censoring someone whose views one does not wish to be heard' (Petley 2009: 8). Daphne was on the receiving end of all these kinds of attack: her financial assets were frozen, her dogs killed, and her front door burned down. When all this failed to silence her, she was murdered.

Since Daphne ran her own blog, she could write freely about the scandals she revealed. Due to this, she became certainly the most widely read journalist in Malta. She was trusted by many sources because they were sure that she would not give in to pressure to reveal them. Daphne's influence on Maltese society was particularly poignant in the last years of her life, when sources trusted her with information they would have never revealed to any of the local press. This matter became an issue even after her death, when her family refused to hand over her computer to the Malta Police for fear of her sources becoming known. The computer was eventually entrusted to the German police, as they were seen as a safer option (Balzan 2021).

Daphne's notoriety also made her the most hated journalist in Malta. Her style and middle-class prejudices made her an easy target for attack, especially by those who had an interest in damaging her image in order to deviate from the truth. Her digressions into gossip, usually targeting persons she showed up as corrupt or inept, did not help. She was seen as a powerful political adversary by the Labour Party in power and was, in fact, labelled a 'witch' on Labour media. There were satirical programmes featuring her as one, whipping up deep sentiments of hate towards her in people who had never read her blog (Cremona 2018). The former leader of the Opposition actually referred to her as a 'biċċa blogger' (an insulting term roughly equivalent to 'an insignificant blogger') (Pace 2017). Although Daphne's blogs attracted a wide readership and denounced government corruption, they did nothing to stem the popularity of the politicians she attacked. Despite her revelations about the persons involved in the Panama Papers, the 'witch' label helped to persuade their supporters to disbelieve her and continue to vote for politicians heavily involved in corrupt practices.[2] In contrast, the powerful image of the wreckage of the popular journalist's car and the graphic narrative of one of her sons rushing out of the house to witness his mother's dismembered body roused unprecedented sentiments of anger that produced a collective voice of protest and dissent. It has become increasingly obvious that Daphne was assassinated at a time when she was isolated from all centres of power. Whoever planned her murder banked on the fact that any political outcry could be easily contained; the protest movement it roused was totally unexpected by her adversaries. A public judicial inquiry has concluded that 'The State failed to recognise the real risks to the journalist's life [...] and failed to take the reasonable steps to avoid these risks' (Camilleri and Schembri Orland 2021).

The assassination of Daphne Caruana Galizia, a supreme act of censorship, had the adverse effect of bringing public debate about the causes she was fighting for into the spotlight. There were three main types of reaction: the taking up of her investigative work by independent journalists, the artistic expression of anger and engagement with the traumatic event and the climate that led to it, and the formation of protest groups whose work attracted a wide following in the absence of credible political leadership.[3] This intervention will discuss censorship and public reaction in relation to the theatricality of public protest and political theatre production.

The protest movement that arose immediately following Daphne's death was, initially at least, mainly led by women in a country where politics is generally dominated by men. Two main protest groups that were constituted in the aftermath of the murder were an informal gathering of women known as 'Occupy Justice', and a more formal non-governmental organization called 'Repubblika' which, for the first two years of its existence, was presided over by women. The protesters made the appropriation of public space one of their hallmarks. Protest marches were organized in the main street of the capital city, Valletta; tents were erected in protest in front of the prime minister's office; traffic was halted by students occupying a main thoroughfare near the university; large posters and streamers were placed in strategic places without permission; the main monuments representing important Maltese figures were made to carry T-shirts featuring Daphne's face and the last words she wrote on her blog: 'There are crooks everywhere you look now, the situation is desperate' (Caruana Galizia 2017). Daphne's face was stencilled or painted on several buildings and quotes from her writings were painted on walls. This raises the question: to what extent is the unauthorized use of public space considered justifiable by protesters, when it is intended as an open affront to a democratically elected government, but also as a strong expression of resistance to a corrupt power?

We have selected two examples to examine this issue. The first revolves around the appropriation of a monument commemorating the victims of war, known as the Great Siege Monument, which features three bronze figures symbolizing faith, fortitude, and civilization. The monument was selected because it is situated in the main street of Valletta, in a strategic position opposite the national law courts. It was transformed into a memorial for Daphne, with her photo positioned at its base and messages, slogans, candles, and flowers placed along its perimeter. The monument became a source of embarrassment to the authorities, and was hotly contested by supporters of the party in government, who had portrayed the journalist as a public enemy. Following Rancière, it could be claimed that dissensus was transmitted through the very aesthetic of the memorial, which embodies not so much the commemoration of Daphne's death, but rather 'the constantly renewed suffering of men and women, their re-created protestations, their constantly resumed struggle' (Rancière 2010: 170). Ad hoc street protests have included singers and poets, and projected videos, which at times have featured art and poetry dedicated to the journalist. Monthly remembrance vigils continue to be staged there, challenging the authorities to deliver justice. After some months, the government decided to recapture the space by clearing the memorial every night. The protesters invariably replaced Daphne's photograph, flowers, and candles every day, in what became a choreography of appropriation and counter-appropriation. At one point, the government's solution was to declare that the monument needed restoration and board it up, thereby negating access to the site. The protesters reacted by using the hoarding as a huge canvas to affix slogans, taunts, poems, drawings, and photographs, which made the site even more visible. These were also regularly removed, until the protest movement reappropriated the space by pulling down the hoarding and turning the monument into a memorial once more. Almost at the same time, the daily removal of the makeshift memorial was contended in court by activist and blogger Manuel Delia; he won the case against the minister Owen Bonnici on 30 January 2020. Bonnici had to reconsign all the candles that had been removed daily from September 2018 to January 2020.

The public protest, which grew steadily from the first demonstrations in 2017, culminated in November and December 2019, when protests were held almost daily. They centred mainly around the building of the new Parliament that had been relocated at the entrance to Valletta: this, ironically, had proved so expensive that there was not enough money left over to rebuild the theatre next door, which had been destroyed in the Second World War. The Parliament building, designed by world-renowned architect Renzo Piano, was conceived in such a way as 'to flatten hierarchies between the people and their representatives' by keeping much of the ground floor open, or completely visible through glass, in order to 'demonstrate the transparency of the parliamentary system' (Bevan 2015). It was also meant to allow people to walk through the footprint of the building. The decision to appropriate the most prominent open public space in the capital city for Parliament was seen by many, however, as the self-attribution of the political class as primary actors in Maltese society. During the protests, the architectural intent to free spatial constrictions by connecting the 'outside' space occupied by ordinary citizens to the 'inside' space of their representatives was betrayed by the physical establishment of boundaries intended to gag dissenting voices and sever all possible physical contact by pre-empting the penetration of the inside by the outside.[4] By taking over the space in front of Parliament, the protesters were reclaiming the original philosophy behind the building's design. Their repeated occupation of the space marked the 'institution of a part of those who have no part', in that they shifted political action from its designated formal space into the public space, transforming the status of the seat of power into one of spectatorship (Rancière 1999: 11).

The protesters' action, prolonged over several days, robbed the politicians of their agency: once performers of political life, they were forced into the position of helpless spectators of what was happening around them. The repeated spectacle of peaceful protest, characterized by masses of protesters clamouring for political resignations in front of the highest seats of power, Parliament and the Prime Minister's Office, became a more effective tool for change than any participation in political dialogue. Public voices that had been censored in state and party media made themselves heard in the streets. The disruption they caused was such that they could no longer be ignored by the local media, especially since this type of censorship was being circumvented also thanks to the involvement of foreign media organizations, who sent their reporters to film and report on the protests. The Maltese case proved once again that in an increasingly connected world, international journalism plays a key role in countering censorship by bringing to the fore events or issues that local authorities try to ignore or sideline. Spectacular theatricality, however, is needed to attract and maintain this type of international attention.

Through their actions, the protesters censored the politicians by preventing them from carrying out their work. A specific example is provided by the incidents on 2 December 2019, when Anġlu Farrugia, the Speaker of the House of Representatives, refused members of protest organizations access to the Strangers' Gallery, the designated area for the public to observe parliamentary proceedings. His decision highlighted the will to shut out those who had 'no part' in the proceedings. One Member of Parliament justified this decision by stating that it was inconceivable to 'allow people inside the Strangers' Gallery to distract us while we are trying to do our job' ('We Are Not Scared' 2019). Once again, the protests disrupted parliamentary activity as public attention shifted to the spectacle unfolding in front of the building, where protesters created a human barricade that impeded politicians from leaving Parliament or its immediate precincts. Their acts of defiance provided spectacle. Parliament had been effectively upstaged by the protesters.

Censorship, as we have seen, is exercised when state efforts are focused on suppressing the voices of those who reveal public scandal, in order to safeguard important political players or financial interests, trying meanwhile to paint a picture of political serenity and social cohesion. In these cases, public debate is maintained by independent thinkers and movements. Theatre provides another type of political engagement: by creating a direct and immediate channel of communication with an audience in the here-and-now, it impacts audience members through their different levels of sensibility, communicating awareness of different perspectives through its art. Following Daphne's death, state and party media tried to suppress her voice and her revelations by expecting the country to move on and avoid debate about the current state of affairs. Consequently, the task of critically examining Maltese society and its political culture fell to the arts, which became a major channel in cultivating the much-needed critical discourse that only a few independent journalists and public speakers were undertaking.

When theatre censorship was abolished in Malta in 2012, it was not followed by a rush of performances on political issues. However, a few significant plays were written and staged, mainly by female playwrights, directors, and casts—notably *Tebut isfar* (Yellow coffin) by Clare

Azzopardi, which was staged in October 2018 at the Valletta Campus Theatre, and *Repubblika Immakulata* (Immaculate republic) by Simone Spiteri, presented at Spazju Kreattiv, Valletta, in March–April 2019. The dramatists tackled subjects which caused controversy among the Maltese public but were deliberately underplayed by the official media channels. Whereas Azzopardi denounced business interests that are destroying communities along with the landscape they inhabit, Spiteri claimed that these business interests are holding the country in their grasp by financing the whole political system. The seriousness of the issues the writers raised became blatantly obvious when business magnate Yorgen Fenech, accused of masterminding Daphne's murder, was also outed as having had shady dealings with politicians from both sides of Parliament. Another theatrical intervention in the debate was Herman Grech's *They Blew Her Up*, a docudrama staged at Spazju Kreattiv in March 2021, exploring Daphne's personality, her opinions, the reasons for her murder, and the subsequent investigations, which are narrated through different perspectives for and against the journalist.[5] This type of debate was almost absent from public life.

All these plays had short runs in the sheltered space of small theatres, and so the political debate staged was only witnessed by a few hundred spectators. The lack of cultural visibility of theatre is also a form of censorship: official statistics show clearly that the cultural environment in Malta does not nourish an interest in the general public towards theatre (Cremona and Galea 2020: 197). This indifference highlights the importance of theatre critics who bring to public attention the issues that are displayed and debated through artistic means, and of the broadcasting media which should relay the messages to which artists give voice to the general public and attract their attention and interest. While theatres are allowed to function freely, their work is sidelined from the public eye, and their contribution to the public debate is not as powerful as it could be. Theatre hardly features in mainstream news portals, and certainly never for its political content. Newspapers and news portals have diminished the role of theatre critics, relegating them as undiscriminating rapporteurs of cultural events that seem to have no relationship to the real world.

The assassination of Daphne roused rallying sentiments that political persuasion had failed to mobilize. Public protest, articulated both in the streets and in the theatre, and publicized through national and international independent media, has proved an effective way of fighting censorship. The capturing of space normally shared by a wide section of the population permitted no indifference to what was being staged, thereby obliging one and all to take up a position in relation to what was happening. The appropriation of public space captured public attention; its theatricality sustained it. The theatre provided a badly needed space for eloquent discussion and reflection. Yet in the Maltese context, this type of discussion could not sufficiently breach the theatre walls. In contrast, the theatrical framing of the more spontaneous expressions of anger within contested public space provided a more direct means of confronting censorship. However, the prevalence of this type of confrontation comes at a price: the complexity of the message is lost to the power of the slogan.

Notes

1. For a detailed analysis of the theatricality of the Malta protests and its significance with regard to the relationship between power and resistance, see Cremona (2022). The present intervention focuses specifically on how public space is appropriated to stage the performance of protest.
2. The Panama Papers consisted of 11.5 million documents leaked from Panamanian offshore law firm and corporate service provider Mossack Fonseca, which were analysed by the International Consortium of Investigative Journalists. They showed numerous illegal financial transactions resulting from political corruption, tax evasion, money laundering, violation of trade sanctions, and breaking exchange laws. The scandal involved world leaders, politicians, public officials, businessmen, and celebrities from over 200 countries. Daphne Caruana Galizia revealed three accounts with links to Maltese politics: one held by Keith Schembri, Prime Minister Joseph Muscat's chief of staff, another by cabinet minister Konrad Mizzi, and a third, named Egrant Inc., whose owner is unknown but which was, for a time, attributed to the prime minister's wife, Michelle Muscat. The companies were financed through another account, 17 Black, registered in Dubai, which was in turn receiving funds from the private Maltese electricity company, Electrogas. 17 Black was owned by tycoon Yorgen Fenech, who has been charged with masterminding the journalist's assassination.
3. An online newspaper, *Shift News* (theshiftnews.com), and a blog, *Truth Be Told* (manueldelia.com), appeared after the journalist's death with the intent of exposing and denouncing political and financial scandals. Journalists from the *Times of Malta* joined an international consortium dealing with the Panama Papers, and a global consortium called The Daphne Project was formed to continue pursuing her investigations (https://forbiddenstories.org/case/the-daphne-project/).
4. In 2021, when public protests were prohibited during the Covid-19 pandemic, a state agency placed large planters at the site used by protesters, making it difficult for people to converge in great numbers. However, even this space was reclaimed through the placement of placards displaying anti-government slogans. This act was denounced as vandalism and reported to the police ('Planters Outside Parliament' 2021).
5. This play, supported by the Association of European Journalists, was also staged in various European cities after its Maltese premiere.

References

Balzan, Jurgen. 2021. 'Maltese Police Do Not Have Daphne Caruana Galizia Laptop', *Newsbook*, 16 June

Bevan, Roy. 2015. 'Parliament Building in Valletta, Malta by Renzo Piano Building Workshop', *The Architectural Review*, 30 September

Camilleri, Neil, and Kevin Schembri Orland. 2021. 'Full Report: Public Inquiry Holds The State Responsible for Daphne Caruana Galizia's Murder', *Malta Independent*, 29 July

Caruana Galizia, Daphne. 2017. 'That Crook Schembri Was in Court Today, Pleading That He Is Not a Crook', *Running Commentary: Daphne Caruana Galizia's Notebook*, 16 October

Cremona, Vicki Ann. 2018. 'Of Bitches and Witches', *Times of Malta*, 26 April

—— 2022. 'Empowering Civil Society: The Theatricality of Protest in Malta', *New Theatre Quarterly*, 38.2: 125–38. https://doi.org/10.1017/S0266464X22000033

Cremona, Vicki Ann, and Marco Galea. 2020. 'The Amateur Theatre in Malta', *Amfiteater*, 8.1: 197–208

Dworkin, Ronald. 1994. 'A New Map of Censorship', *Index on Censorship*, 23.1-2: 9–15

Farrugia, Claire. 2019. 'Is Malta Embracing Activism?', *Times of Malta*, 15 December

Garside, Julie. 2019. 'A Bomb Silenced Daphne Caruana Galizia. But Her Investigation Lives On', *Guardian*, 17 April

Pace, Yannick. 2017. 'Caruana Galizia's Sister to Delia: "You denigrated Daphne in her lifetime. Do not exploit her in death"', *MaltaToday*, 26 October

Petley, Julian. 2009. *Censorship: A Beginner's Guide* (Oxford: Oneworld Publications)

'Planters Outside Parliament Provide Space for Occupy Justice Protest'. 2021. *Times of Malta*, 16 June

Rancière, Jacques. 1999. *Disagreement: Politics and Philosophy*, trans. by Julie Rose (Minneapolis: University of Minnesota Press)

—— 2010. *Dissensus: On Politics and Aesthetics*, trans. and ed. by Steven Corcoran (London: Continuum Books)

—— 2016. 'Occupation', *Political Concepts: A Critical Lexicon*, 3 <http://www.politicalconcepts.org/occupation-jacques-ranciere/> [accessed 24 November 2021]

'We Are Not Scared of the Protesters Locking Us in Parliament—Silvio Parnis'. 2019. *Malta Independent*, 3 December

1
Voices from Semi-Peripheries: Pressure, Self-Censorship, and Micropolitics of Resistance in the Western Balkans

MILENA DRAGIĆEVIĆ ŠEŠIĆ AND ALEKSANDRA JOVIĆEVIĆ

This chapter investigates different mechanisms of censorship in the performing arts which have developed since 1989 in the countries of the former Yugoslavia and the wider region of Central Europe. It aims to show how and why performances were censored. Our research addresses several questions: Who has the power to ban certain productions; and how do power shifts within different political, social, and cultural environments provoke different types and methods of censorship? How do artists, theatre managers, critics, and spectators react in situations of censorship? Finally, what are the consequences of the four forms of censorship that we have identified: direct/explicit censorship (preventive and repressive), indirect/implicit censorship, street-censorship, and self-censorship? (For perspectives on forms of censorship, see Keane 1991: 39, Thomas et al. 2007: 225–53, Freshwater 2009, Farrington 2013, Arts Professional 2019).[1]

Our analysis concentrates on countries of the former Yugoslavia impacted by war and the dissolution of the country during the period of transition from socialism to capitalism. However, as the cultural context cannot be separated from the wider European political context (for example, the growth of illiberalism and the spread of populism) and cultural sphere (festivals, touring, and guest director projects), the wider region of Central and Eastern Europe will be referenced, particularly Southeast Europe and the Western Balkans. Furthermore, due to the military, political, and ideological conflicts of the 1990s, an important characteristic of former Yugoslav cultural space must be noted: namely, a division of public and counterpublic cultural spheres. A cultural counterpublic realm tends to be found in authoritarian, populist, illiberal societies: the term refers to all cultural agents of civil society that create their own 'ecosystem' of institutions and media activities (Dragićević Šešić 2016: 151–53).

Historical context

After the Second World War and during the Cold War, in European countries that belonged to the Soviet bloc, state-organized censorship was implemented in different forms. In Yugoslavia, however, due to its position as a federal, non-aligned country outside of the Soviet bloc (Perović 2007) that wanted to display to the world 'socialism with a human face', censorship was not institutionalized but transferred to self-governing cultural institutions (see Trencsényi et al. 2018). Since power shifted back and forth between the Communist Party's conservative and liberal factions, with frequent changes in the political climate, what was tolerated at one moment became intolerable the next. Furthermore, the federal structure of the country, and the increasing rivalry between the party elites and their bureaucratic bodies in the six federal republics, led to varying standards: a publication banned in one republic could be published in another, a banned production could be transferred to one of the other republics and could even win a prize at a festival there. The cause célèbre of Yugoslav theatre dissidence is Croat playwright Ivo Brešan (1936–2017) whose four early plays faced problems with theatre censorship inside and outside of Croatia, because they offered a gloomy view of post-war conditions and indicted the narrow-mindedness and oppression of communist ideology. As in many similar cases, these plays were never officially banned: if they were attacked publicly, it was under the guise of aesthetic norms, and they were then quietly removed from the repertories, or cancelled in the midst of rehearsals.

Moreover, informal political censorship had a greater power in restricting the intellectual and artistic freedom of Yugoslav theatre artists. According to some recent research on dissident theatre, based on oral interviews with writers, actors, and directors (Jovićević 2007, 2008), more than seventy theatre productions were censored in Yugoslavia between 1945 and 1991, but only two were banned officially by court orders (Klaić and Pejović 1996). Productions were often censored before the premiere, or cancelled in the middle of rehearsals (an intervention that could be executed silently and invisibly to the public by the so-called artistic committees that were mostly composed of party members in every Yugoslav theatre), and almost no official documents or material traces survive of these cases. In short, as recollected by people in the oral interviews mentioned above, nothing tangible remains: only hints, rumours, and indirect evidence. Most Yugoslav theatre professionals accepted invisible censorship as a fact of life, even if it made theatre look 'tame and conformist, an ally of the state machine' (Klaić 1986: 7). There was no hardcore dissidence, no real underground theatre, except for a few distinct critical voices of considerable reach (see Jovićević 2007: 203–09, 2008: 237–49; Dragićević Šešić 2016: 151–53).

In the 1980s, during the chaotic period that preceded the dissolution of the country, as well as wars and economic transition, several control bodies (such as the artistic committees or, in some cases, the committees for taxation of cultural industry products) were replaced by subtle strategies of economic and social oppression, as well as by forms of self-censorship, which were more diversified than in the socialist era. Following the death of President Tito in 1980, it seemed that political theatre started to flourish in Yugoslavia and censorship eased. However, this was a false impression and censorship remained strong during this period. First, *Bijela knjiga* (The white book) was published in 1984, subtitled 'On certain ideological and political tendencies in artistic creation, literary, theatre and film criticism, as well as on public statements of a certain number of cultural workers in which politically unacceptable messages are contained'. This volume—produced by the President of the Central Committee of the Communist Party of Croatia (CK SKH), Stipe Šuvar, and his collaborators—shows how artistic freedom was constantly controlled, manipulated, and castigated. For instance, a range of literary and theatre works dealing with the 1948 break with Soviet politics and its consequences were extensively discussed and analysed. Second, a large number of people were sentenced, on average, to several years' imprisonment for committing 'verbal' political offences: that is, for expressing critical opinions (either in public or private) about the Yugoslav regime. This *verbalni delikt* (verbal offence) was unique in the large scale of legal measures used against anyone who tried to express their disagreement with the regime. Other more subtle but no less efficient methods of oppression were used: dismissal from work, campaigns of abuse in the press without opportunity for right of reply, censorship of all forms of public activity, social isolation through threats, and blackmail of friends and acquaintances.

Since the 1990s, the official culture in most Southeast and Central European countries is not so strictly controlled but rather shaped by ruling partocracies that regard parties' interests as public interests. This is especially the case with populist right-wing parties that promote culture as an instrument of national identity-building, or with neoliberal parties that promote culture as an economic value (thus prioritizing 'popular' performances). The Church (or organizations close to the Church) also exercises significant influence, often under the guise of moral leadership, and frequently interferes with different requests for censorship of theatre productions or exhibitions. Most of this political and religious pressure results in some form of indirect censorship (including pressure on theatre managers and artists by right-wing groups) that damages the public realm (mostly via institutional self-censorship, which pushes artists to resign or even into self-imposed exile).[2] It sometimes also encroaches on the counter public realm through 'financial censorship', the lack of an audience, and the withdrawal of private support for independent projects (Cvetičanin 2017).

Recent empirical research in the new postsocialist democracies, and also in some 'old' EU countries, shows a discrepancy between policy statements and the reality of different forms of censorship in the performing arts (see Orel 2015, Karaulić 2016, Ljumović 2019, Tanurovska-Kjulavkovski and Vaseva 2021). Censorship practices today range from direct verbal and physical threats, cancellations, protests, legal actions, governmental interference in artistic institutions, and even exile and imprisonment, to the subtle pressures of the market, targeted budget cuts, and self-censorship. Prominent cases include the arrest of Kirill Serebrennikov in Moscow and the regular death threats received by Oliver Frljić, who is *persona non grata* in all former Yugoslav republics and whose productions are frequently banned.

Definitions of censorship

Because national contexts and their dominant ideologies vary, and empirical research in this domain offers different approaches and taxonomies, we have opted for an incomplete taxonomy that considers the most representative examples of censorship in the contemporary Western Balkans:

a) Direct censorship: effected by governments, regional and local authorities, and also public theatre managers in fear of criticism or political reprisal;
b) Indirect censorship: mostly economic, it is implemented by public authorities and the private sector through subsidies, sponsorship, and advertising;
c) Street-censorship: public protest reinforced by tabloid media campaigns that intimidate critical artists; death threats and threats of violence from pressure groups (as experienced by the Serbian branch of Women in Black);[3]
d) Self-censorship: whether motivated by the fear of losing one's employment, financial support, or public status, or of direct repressive measures, it is exercised by theatre managers, artistic directors, playwrights, and actors.

Sometimes direct censorship is mistaken for institutional self-censorship, but often the borders are blurred in these cases. Direct censorship concerns only those actions that are carried out to prevent invited practitioners from creating a show or performing in a host venue. It is implemented by theatre managers or directors of cultural centres, and occurs when the manager of a cultural institution thinks that it is their duty to defend the values of the political party that appointed them, or when they react to local authorities' directives giving a clear indication that a certain playwright or actor is not welcome in 'their' city. Although they are not publicly acknowledged, blacklists do exist, and blacklisted artists are effectively silenced.

For example, Slobodan Milatović, a Montenegrin theatre director, was subjected to two instances of censorship. His production of *Politika kao sudbina* (Politics as a fate, 1984), which he scripted and directed at Belgrade's Student Cultural Centre, occupied a political 'grey zone' (Šiklova 1990). During rehearsals, the building was deliberately set on fire three times; on the third occasion, the artistic collective was determined to proceed with the premiere. However, police officers entered the premises and, under the pretext that a bomb had been planted, evacuated the building. Subsequently, the performance was not scheduled, which seemed to be the objective of the authorities.

Later, in 1996, Milatović's work was censored by the mayor of Podgorica (the capital of Montenegro), in what amounted to an evident abuse of power. The play *Što je čoek do li biciklista?* (What is a man but a bicycle rider?) is a political satire based on Zoran Kopitović's popular text *Muzej biciklističkog ustanka u Crnoj Gori* (The museum of bicycle upheaval in Montenegro). Co-produced by two provincial and subsidized theatres, the Nikšić Theatre and the Zahumlje Theatre, the play was given only one performance at the Festival of Experimental Scenes in Podgorica, at which point the mayor declared it could not be shown again due to its political subversion. In both cases, the public authorities tried to avoid direct confrontation by communicating with theatre managers only, without explicit negative public statements about those productions (Ljumović 2019: 214–15).

The most prevalent type of censorship is indirect censorship: often invisible to the wider public, it is exercised and justified by managerial claims of inadequate resources (human, financial, technical, and/or spatial) and, sometimes, by arguments related to repertoire or programme themes. Several significant examples emerged after the political changes in Serbia in 2012 that brought a nationalist populist party to power: local governments began accusing cultural organizations of anti-patriotism and, in 2014, withdrew their financial support. The Fortress Theatre Festival (an NGO led by writer and theatre director Vida Ognjenović) was supported by local authorities for several years. Local power changed, and new authorities decided to create a festival—naming it 'Theatre in the Fortress'—as a public (city) organization. Facing accusations from a few independent media platforms that they had recuperated the Fortress Theatre Festival, city authorities of Smederevo responded that the festival could proceed, though without municipal financial support. Since the festival was unsustainable without public funding, it moved to another region (Vojvodina), and relaunched in the village of Čortanovci. The censorious decisions of theatre managers tend to result from threats to and public defamation of performing artists and authors, especially when they are issued by political or Church authorities, or media close to the regime. Because the reason for censorship cannot be acknowledged without controversy, theatre practitioners are informed that a cultural venue 'unfortunately' will not be able to host their performance, even when this involves the cancellation of corporate sponsorship.

Bitef Theatre (born out of Belgrade's International Theatre Festival) is almost unique in that it regularly hosts alternative and independent productions, and engages radical artists who deal with current political and social issues: examples include *Ako dugo gledaš u ponor* (If you stare long enough into Ambis, 2021) by Zlatko Paković, *Udarna vest* (Breaking news, 2021) by Milena Bogavac and Marko Grubić, *Jami District* (2017) by Kokan Mladenović and Milena Bogavac, and *Trilogia Pass-port* (2012) by András Urbán. Other public venues are more cautious when approached by writers from the independent cultural scene and indirect censorship (always justified with other reasons) is common practice.

Thus, some performances that belong to the micropolitics of resistance, such as Zlatko Paković's *Srebrenica: Kad mi ubijeni ustanemo* (Srebrenica: When we dead awaken, 2020), were staged only in alternative, independent spaces such as the Centre for Cultural Decontamination in Belgrade where many artistic events have been if not prohibited, then attacked by mainstream politicians. As one of the rare institutions in the region offering a space for experimental and politically critical artists, the centre has also been closed down several times in its history.

The fact that most independent theatre companies are not subsidized by national or local governments is not a reflection on quality or taste, but evidence of indirect financial censorship. In the period from 2015, NGOs such as the Centre for Cultural Decontamination—whose theatre productions include *Encyclopaedia of the Living* by Jeton Neziraj and Zlatko Paković (2015); *Predator* by Vladimir Arsenijević and Srđa Anđelić (2017), and *Authentic Interpretations: '68*, directed by newly appointed director Ana Miljanić (2019)—DAH Theatre, which is internationally renowned for its pacifist and intercultural projects, Reflektor and Mim theatres, and many other alternative companies and actors, have received no public subsidies and survive only due to international financing. In consequence, independent companies and practitioners are derided as foreign gold-diggers and mercenaries by government-sponsored media, right-wing journalists, and organizations that advocate different forms of street-censorship.

Campaigns spearheaded by the tabloid media lead directly to street-censorship, but also to withdrawals of sponsorship or media promotion, contributing to the further silencing of theatre companies that cannot count on public or corporate support. Street-censorship actions are especially frequent when it comes to intercultural projects such as the 'Mirëdita, dobar dan!' festival (which means 'Good afternoon' in both the Albanian and Serbian languages), or the 'Days of Sarajevo' festival in Belgrade: though often seemingly protected by the police force, they are always attacked by right-wing and nationalist groups. This illustrates the inability of theatre boards and managers to find an adequate response to right-wing street-pressures. Such incidents confirm 'the symbolic violence and cultural impact of this new form of radical civil action that is rarely the subject of cultural policy study' (Vickery 2021: 8).

The interruption of a performance of *Saint Sava* in May 1990 at the Yugoslav Drama Theatre in Belgrade is the best-known case of street-censorship in the former Yugoslavia.[4] Key to understanding the context of this act—the capacity of a small group of nationalist protesters to cancel a run—is the fact that it took place when Slobodan Milošević was the most powerful politician in Serbia. Milošević imposed himself as the guardian of Yugoslav unity, while his security services and police tolerated, protected, and even incorporated right-wing Serbian nationalist groups in their activities.

Saint Sava was based on the text of Serbian author Siniša Kovačević, premiered in Zenica (in Bosnia and Herzegovina), and directed by Macedonian director Vladimir Milčin, with the main role played by Žarko Laušević, a Belgrade actor of Montenegrin origin (this was perhaps the last 'Yugoslav' theatre production). An organized group of Serbian nationalists led by a priest, Žarko Gavrilović, and Vojislav Šešelj, the leader of Serbian radicals, condemned the performance (Šešelj later played a substantial role in war crimes for which he was sentenced by the Appeals Chamber of the International Residual Mechanism for Criminal Tribunals in The Hague). The protesters criticized the production for its perceived denigration of one of the greatest Serbian myths—the myth of Saint Sava (Sveti Sava was represented as a young man with sexual desires), and decried a 'vulgar performance that destroys the image of Saint Sava as a humble and pious person' ('Prekid' 2018).

The street protesters entered the theatre, disrupted the show, and physically attacked spectators who defended the actors' right to perform: the actors tried to calm the situation by inviting the protesters to wait until the end of the performance, but the rioters refused. The production was halted and has never been restaged in Serbia (there was no such resistance in Bosnia, where the show premiered). Twenty-five years later, in 2015, Tanja Miletić Oručević presented *Sveto S ili Kako je 'arhivirana' predstava Sveti Sava* (Saint S or how the Saint Sava performance was 'archived') at the Bosnian National Theatre in Zenica: it was not programmed in Belgrade due to the 'politics of oblivion'—the deafening silence attached to self-censoring actions in public theatres (see Dragićević Šešić and Stefanović 2017).

Perhaps the most widespread form of censorship, self-censorship encompasses the pressures that prevent artists from creating freely works that may touch upon political or religious topics. Self-censorship often escapes analytical scrutiny because it relates to individual artistic processes and decisions that are themselves invisible. First-hand evidence in the form of self-reflections and media interviews with practitioners on this issue are rare, as artists understandably shy from acknowledging they compromised out of fear; nonetheless, we have noticed that, in times of political crisis and wars, most theatre repertoires are based on classical escapist texts and comedies (Jovićević 2002, Medenica 2002). Self-censorship forces an artist to pay lip service, to act as a *ketman*—a person of captive mind to use the term employed by Czeslaw Miłosz (1990)—not openly allying with power, but setting the stage for the mutual exchange of benefit. Self-censorship brings temporary benefits and the whole system of production relies on this aspect.

Disclosures of self-censorship most often come from theatre and festival managers in relation to their programming decisions: their dilemma is whether to keep their personal and artistic integrity by inviting blacklisted artists, thereby eventually endangering their own position or that of their institution, or to make a compromise (by inviting another artist instead) that would strengthen the relations between an institution, authorities, and sponsors. Institutional self-censorship usually happens when independent theatre companies, with radical subversive political performances, are not allowed to perform in public theatres in provincial venues: refusal is justified with arguments about 'rented' or 'already occupied' theatre halls. For example, *Patriotic Hypermarket* (2011), a play by Jeton Neziraj and Milena Bogavac, based on the testimonies of both Albanian and Serbian war victims, premiered at the Bitef Theatre in Belgrade, but was not staged around Serbia and Kosovo. Written by Doruntina Basha, *Prst* (Finger, 2013) depicts the lives of a mother and her daughter-in-law whose son/husband is 'missing': it was performed at the Bitef Theatre, but no other venues wanted to host it because Basha is a Kosovo Albanian writer. These examples show that Srebrenica remains taboo, which impacts on the regional touring of controversial productions. Such performances often treat themes related to cultures of memory and question the understanding of history and current geopolitics; in so doing, they often provoke negative public reactions that intimidate theatre managers.

Performing arts in the new democracies

After the bloody Yugoslav Wars (1991–95; 1998–99) and the dissolution into seven republics, cultural productions in the Balkans faced numerous new taboos linked to religion, nation, sexuality, gender, immigration, and historical interpretation. The issues and performances that provoke a sense of malaise and discomfort in the mainstream public discourse of Central European and Balkan countries are different from elsewhere in Europe. They mostly relate to the critique of national and patriarchal values (for example, the satirical or critical use of national symbols), dominant religion, or official state politics, and, to a far lesser extent, to representations of sexuality (only when linked to non-heterosexuality). Right-wing intellectuals and media accused playwrights of anti-patriotism, of being favourable to globalization and cosmopolitanism, sometimes of treason (Lompar 2011, Avramović 2013): this pressure, further intensified by citizens' groups, impacted on their artistic freedom and diminished the space for the representation of cultural counterpublics and the work of practitioners who are seen as 'critical opposition'—such as directors Oliver Frljić, Kokan Mladenović, Zlatko Paković, and András Urbán, dramatists Jeton Neziraj and Milena Bogavac, and companies such as DAH Theatre. Some of them left their native countries, while others work only in provincial theatres or on independent stages with low or no budget, or are forced to establish their own organizations in order to access funding opportunities abroad.

More sophisticated cultural policies have been developed over the years to threaten theatres with the withdrawal of financial support, possible public defamation through commercial and government-sponsored media (an increasingly frequent instrument of intimidation), or, more perniciously, by inhibiting creative freedom with consequences that are harder to calculate (i.e. self-censorship). All of this has produced different forms of censorship disguised, for example, as the responsibility of a theatre managing director not to endanger the existence of an institution. Barbara Orel presents the example of self-censorship (of host venues) and indirect censorship (of theatre-makers) in relation to two productions: Janez Janša's *Slovensko narodno gledališče* (*Slovene National Theatre*, at the Stara elektrarna, Ljubljana, in 2007), and Oliver Frljić's *25.671* (at the Prešernovo gledališče, Kranj, in 2013), which won awards at the National Festival Borštnikovo srečanje (see Orel 2015). Both companies wanted to tour Slovenia and approached theatre and cultural venues around the country. In these examples, the venues engaged in self-censorship due to the fear of negative publicity but the performances were subjected to indirect censorship, as each venue found a different reason that prevented them from hosting the performance. The consequences of this are damaging for artists and cultural institutions, with the latter finding different excuses, mostly aesthetic or technical, to avoid engaging radical artists in their programmes.

There are public stages (national and city theatres) that do not raise critical concerns or challenge official statements and values. But there are also the stages of counterpublics—the independent cultural scene, whose aim is to provoke and critique majority opinions and official statements. During brief and occasional periods of bold governance in public cultural institutions, critical artists might sometimes be invited to develop projects. These periods usually end up with their removal—for instance, Željko Hubač as dramaturg at the National Theatre in Belgrade between 2014 and 2018, or Kokan Mladenović as Atelier 212's director from 2009 to 2012—and the appointment of replacements who create 'neutral' repertories (which are popular and politically acceptable) that will not endanger their positions.

The culture of memory within the theatre repertory generates both controversy and a justification for censorship. In the Western Balkans, the transitional period began with the search for new national identities and the rejection of Yugoslavia and Yugoslavian identity as the 'repression tool of Titoism' and the former socialist state. Numerous symbols of Yugoslavia ended up in the communal garbage (portraits of Tito that existed in every school and office, Yugoslav and party flags, various badges and communist memorabilia) and, as such, became the material for some radical artistic interventions and installations.[5] Nationhood was a theme for exploration on national stages. Theatre repertoires became important tools in the construction of national identity and, when using glorious historical moments (such as the Serbian resurrection against the Turks in 1804, or victories in the Second World War) as national mythology, were received with acclaim (for example, productions of plays related to the role of the Serbian army in the First World War [*Battle of Kolubara*, 1983; *Valjevo Hospital*, 1990]; performances featuring heroes and heroines of Montenegrin history at the National Theatre of Montenegro [*Princess Ksenija from Montenegro*, 1995]; heroes of Bosnian medieval history in Bosnian theatres; operas of Croat composers in Croatian national operas, and so forth). But, if national legends and myths were elaborated without apology, this could also provoke strong negative emotional reactions, as was the case with the performance of *Saint Sava* at the Yugoslav Drama Theatre in Belgrade.

It is enough to look at the Yugoslav Drama Theatre's memoryscapes: how this most important Yugoslav and then Serbian theatre suppresses the memory of all events that are harmful to its reputation by applying structural amnesia as the tactic of forgetting (Dragićević Šešić and Stefanović 2017: 629). Throughout the 1980s and 1990s, this theatre succeeded in balancing its approach to the needs of different audiences. On the one hand, it consolidated its cosmopolitan and Yugoslav orientation with the anti-war stance—as evidenced, for example, by the production of *Troilus and Cressida* directed by Dejan Mijač in 1994; on the other, it opened up a space for so-called taboo topics in national history—for instance, *Prince Paul* in 1991, directed by Dimitrije Jovanović, enhanced Serbian nationalist sentiments (Radulović 2018). Other subsidized theatres embraced the classical repertory in order to avoid any kind of political commentary on ongoing Yugoslav wars that could cause controversy and divide an audience.

The performance of memory has been part of a national reconstruction process but also a source of conflict, especially when these performances deal with recent memories—for instance, at Atelier 212 under the leadership of Kokan Mladenović. Although Mladenović had the political support of the City Mayor and the City Council for Culture, his bold repertory decisions were unacceptable to many actors of the ensemble. The decision to stage *Zoran Đinđić* (directed by Oliver Frljić, 2012) provoked criticism from all nationally orientated parties and the actors realized that they would be severely attacked: as a result, seventeen actors in the company refused to take a role in this performance, and were replaced by guest-actors.

Micropolitics of resistance

In her research on how politics operates within art productions in the former Yugoslavia, theatre manager Ana Letunić concluded, based on Chantal Mouffe's premises, that 'politics operates both inside and outside of the artistic work [...] resulting in the concepts of curatorial and artistic agency that aim at a production of culture as dissent', and at the creation of different public spheres, among them, the articulation of a cultural counterpublic realm as a necessity to avoid any kind of censorship or pressure (Letunić 2019: 347). The counterpublic realm manifests through the micropolitics of resistance that are practised by numerous independent artists, artistic collectives, curators, and cultural workers—such as the directors Kokan Mladenović, Zlatko Paković, Jeton Neziraj, and the late Igor Vuk Torbica, and organizations such as Heartefact Fund, DAH Theatre, Zorica Jevremović's Pocket Theatre, Centre E8, and Reflektor Theatre. Their activities were and are supported by independent venues such as the Centre for Cultural Decontamination, Rex (the cultural centre of the B92) in Belgrade, Metelkova and Bunker in Ljubljana, Točka and Lokomotiva in Skopje, and Lauba in Zagreb. All these activities, co-productions, residencies, tours, and festivals produce a cultural counterpublic sphere and represent a micropolitics of resistance that enhances the quality of artistic and cultural life, as well as the self-esteem of many artists, cultural professionals, and audiences. From time to time, they have been connected to isolated islands of freedom in the public sector: the programming actions of Željko Hubač at the National Theatre in Belgrade; Dubravka Vrgoč's and Ivica Buljan's leadership of the Croatian National Theatre (HNK) in Zagreb; Oliver Frljić's leadership of the Croatian National Theatre (HNK) in Rijeka; the Festival Without Translation organized by the Užice City Theatre since 1996; or the more recent Bitef Theatre collaborations with NGOs and civil society movements.

There are many strategies and tactics within the counterpublic, which are deployed to oppose the official culture and its values: initially, there is a need to build platforms and structures where independent artists can gather and create freely in a self-organized manner. Furthermore, it is necessary to show solidarity and care for other actors in the field; and, finally, there should be resistance to being co-opted and recuperated by the system. In some cases, it is difficult for artists who belong to cultural counterpublics to participate in cultural manifestations that are politically governed and used for the promotion of official culture. It was especially difficult when independent festivals and institutions, or organizations that were supposed to be independent, became hijacked, reclaimed by politicians and the authorities.

One recent example is the Festival at the Crossroads in Niš in 2019. After hearing that the festival had accepted the patronage of the Serbian president Aleksandar Vučić, the director Kokan Mladenović withdrew his production of Goran Petrović's *Sitničarnica 'kod srećne ruke'* (*Smalltalk Place at 'Lucky Shot'*). Nebojša Bradić (Belgrade), Darko Lukić (Zagreb), and Aleksandar Milosavljević (Novi Sad), who were the selectors of the festival, and Dejan Petković (Niš), withdrew from the festival's board, while theatre directors Igor Vuk Torbica and Kokan Mladenović refused further collaboration with the National Theatre in Niš, which organizes this event. This example shows how the realms of official public and counterpublic might sometimes overlap (for example, in the creation of the concept and programme of a festival). The festival's name—Festival at the Crossroads—designates its mission to connect regional theatres and contribute to a more cosmopolitan theatrical vision, so connection with the current political regime was not foreseen. The director of the National Theatre in Niš, Spasoje Ž. Milovanović, tried to present himself as open and free by inviting prominent members of counterpublics, but then, by accepting patronage from the President of the Republic of Serbia, he endangered the mission of the festival and allowed political authorities to misuse the work of artists for their representational purposes.

Persona non grata—Oliver Frljić

Croat director Oliver Frljić often confronts his audience with hidden and disturbing taboos.[6] Through his radical productions, Frljić constantly provokes post-Cold War societies, including the former Yugoslavian republics, Poland, and Germany, with all that is difficult to understand and what is suppressed and falsified in their recent past.

Despite his controversial reputation, only one of Frljić's productions has been openly banned: *Nie-Boska komedia. Szczątki* (*Un-Divine Comedy. Remains*), which was to be performed at the National Stary Theatre in Kraków in November 2013 (see Chapter 5 of this volume). Frljić's appointment as director of the Croatian National Theatre in Rijeka triggered a large-scale public debate in 2014 until he finally left in 2016 due to a number of unresolved issues with city authorities. He and his collaborators approached the venue as a 'found object', treating it as an alternative theatre space rather than as a national theatre. They not only made audacious changes to the repertory—for example, presenting a trilogy on Croatian fascism (*The Bacchae*, *Aleksandra Zec*, and *Croatian Theatre*)—but they also tried to communicate with citizens who never go to the theatre by putting various slogans and banners outside of the building.

On the first day of his appointment, Frljić and his theatre collaborators installed an enormous billboard on the theatre's façade stating 'Theatre for the People'; for the following season, they replaced this text with a quote from the Croatian constitution, 'Freedom of Thought and Freedom of Speech'. On Croatian Independence Day (25 June 2014), they hung an LGBT flag with a banner stating 'Happy Independence Day'. Then, on 5 August 2015, they organized a performance/event to commemorate the twentieth anniversary of Operation Storm (in 1995), when part of Croatia was liberated from Serbian occupation but also when the Croatian army forced more than 200,000 people of Serbian ethnicity from their homes. On this very significant day, nobody mentioned the victims of this operation. Therefore, Frljić invited five women of different nationalities onto the stage to tell their stories of how they were raped. The first problem for the authorities was that their stories did not confirm official national narratives about the war; the other problem was that all of the speakers were women.

By means of billboards and performances inside and outside the theatre, Frljić opened a dialogue not only with the city of Rijeka but with the whole of Croatian society, turning the theatre from a *site*-specific into a *community*-specific theatre. Frljić's projects go far beyond the emancipation of the audience in that he aims to deconstruct social values, beliefs, and traditions: 'What I was trying to do was the performative deconstruction of that institution and its structure; […] all norms, all fundamentals were being questioned' (Frljić 2017). Whenever a protest against him occurs, he calls it a 'positive misunderstanding'. For him, theatre work is not about a good or a bad performance, but about the question of how to extend the tools of performativity of the medium itself: the theatre is not just what we see on stage but also the perception created before and after the show.

One of Frljić's strategies entails the permanent questioning and interrogation of existing power structures within the theatre. In February 2017, Frljić presented *Klatwa* (*The Curse*) at Teatr Powszechny in Warsaw, a new version of a play written by Stanisław Wyspiański in 1899. Frljić's interpretation of the play was critical of the Catholic Church and included a scene in which an actor performs oral sex on a statue of Pope John Paul II. This provoked public outrage, was condemned by the Church, the media, and different conservative and clerical groups, and led to street protests. In addition, threats of violence were made against the actors and the director, and this also affected Frljić's leadership of the Malta Festival in Poznań in 2017.[7]

Other instances of Frljić's work have generated similar controversy. At the opening of his production of Nikola Tumbas's *Kukavičluk* (*Cowardice*, 2010), a theatre manager, Ljubica Ristovski, received a threatening letter from the president of the Saint Sava Youth demanding that Frljić be expelled from the city of Subotica, and that the performance be amended: the sequence in which the names of Srebrenica victims are pronounced should be expunged, and 'if you do not implement those demands, we will physically interrupt the show and remove the actors from the stage' (Ristovski 2022). Ristovski persisted, reinforced the theatre security, mobilized everyone in the theatre, and the performance took place. However, the production was performed only twenty times because the Subotica audience was intimidated, and did not want to be seen attending the performance. In addition, the show did not tour and has not received festival invitations, as it tackled Srebrenica's genocide, one of the most important taboos in Serbia.

In 2012, in Belgrade's theatre Atelier 212, Frljić's production of Zoran Đinđić—about the assassination of the Serbian prime minister in 2003—infuriated the audience, especially a scene in which an actress vomits on the Serbian flag. The performance provoked public outrage (in the press, on social media, and in academic spheres), but the show remained in the repertory until the end of the theatre season. Eventually caving under pressure, the director of Atelier 212 resigned in 2012. In 2014, in Rijeka (Croatia), Frljić devised *Aleksandra Zec*, which addresses the brutal murder of a Serbian family at the beginning of the war in Croatia in 1991.

Frljić also engendered much controversy with the production *Our Violence, Your Violence* (2016), using as its premise Peter Weiss's seminal essayistic novel *The Aesthetics of Resistance* (1975). Pondering the role of art in today's society, he worked on religious stereotypes and on European Islamophobia. Especially inflammatory for the audience was the re-enactment of Carolee Schneemann's famous performance *Interior Scroll* (1975) by an actress wearing a hijab. Of all Frljić's productions, this one was the most contentious because its focus was on different violences in the name of different religions. Every time outraged citizens attempted to censure the show from outside the theatre, it seemed that the cultural counterpublics prevented the production from being banned: in November 2016, during a theatre festival in Sarajevo, the audience gathered in front of the theatre demanding the right to see the show, even if it was officially cancelled; in May 2017, during a theatre festival in Split, the audience started chanting a popular children's song to silence the protesters who had entered the theatre and tried to interrupt the performance.

The production of *Balkan macht frei* at Munich's Residenztheater originally set out to tell the story of the refugees from the Balkans, but it later developed into a kind of autobiographical narrative of an imaginary Balkan theatre director engaged to work in a German theatre. As with most of Frljić's productions, such as *Damned Be the Traitor of His Homeland* (2010) and *Gorki: Alternative für Deutschland* (2018), *Balkan macht frei* began with a direct accusation of the audience for their comfortable position and indifference in the face of the suffering of refugees, who had just begun their mass exodus to Europe. In an extended monologue, the director's alter ego, Franz, attacks the audience for enjoying the spectacle of refugees, a speech that prompted several people to walk out of the performance on the opening night. Franz is then subjected to 'torture', a scene of 'real water boarding' which provoked several spectators to protest loudly, while some even climbed onto the stage and attempted to stop it (Balme 2015). After the premiere, many reviews focused on the dilemma presented by this scene: is it ethical to perform torture on stage, or even to watch it, and is this actually theatre or just an act of brutal performance? Some critics declared the production to be a piece of non-theatre because the hyperrealistic scene surpassed the restrictions of theatrical representation and had crossed an ethical line, which required active resistance by the audience (ibid.). However, Frljić's approach was prompted by an adjacent consideration: 'When I want to create a conflict with the audience, my dream is to have antagonism between every audience member. The goal is to divide them as much as possible and thus to reaffirm their uniqueness. The task is not to unite them, not to find a common denominator or a common system of values that we share' (Frljić 2017).

It is interesting to note that Frljić is unconcerned with what can be defined as a success. On the contrary, most of his productions give the impression of being unfinished, a kind of misperformance, a sort of bad amateur theatre, strongly influenced by performance art. The connoisseurs of performance art can recognize many citations from the works of, indicatively, Joseph Beuys, Carolee Schneemann, Marina Abramović, Vito Acconci, and Paul McCarthy. The audience has a similar reaction to his productions as it had to these performances—they are disgusted, they protest or leave the theatre, but they are never indifferent.

Always an object of political and social control, theatre in the Western Balkans has in recent years been subjected to different forms of moral and religious coercion. If, during socialist times, the staging process was surveyed from page to stage for its political potential and/or social threat (by self-governing artistic committees), this system of censorship has now been replaced by an unstructured one, in which pro-regime tabloid media and 'moral' right-wing groups veto productions at the moment of their opening. Our examination of censorship has revealed diverse kinds of pressure, ranging from direct and indirect (financial and administrative) censorship, through self-censorship already built into social structures and discursive practices, up to physical violence that prevent performances from happening.

What are the consequences of these forms of censorship within the theatre ecosystems in the Western Balkans? On the one hand, it is the silence of those who are leading public institutions and prefer to avoid making controversial decisions; on the other hand, cultural counterpublics are reinforced through the development of a community of care and solidarity that reaches beyond national borders. All public performances are potentially political acts echoing variations of representative democracy, which, according to Jacques Rancière, generate and reformulate public life, even if these changes are very slow or marginal. Performances produce an organized public that is an abstraction. Because the public can be mobilized occasionally in moments of crisis, modern democracies continuously count on this effect (see Rancière 2004, 2006). The aspiration of contemporary artists like Frljić or Jeton Neziraj is to make their art useful. That is a standpoint that requires new theoretical reflection. The central goal of such reflection is to analyse with precision the meaning and political function of art within society. However, as we have seen, censorship in the so-called new democracies, precisely in transitional democratic societies, is a very volatile phenomenon. Its negative aspects can affect the process of building a public, and without a democratic public, as Jürgen Habermas puts it, there is no chance of building an 'effectual' democracy (Habermas 1991). Therefore, censorship in whatever form it may appear, even in the most subtle way, refined or interiorized, is always a threat to the openness of society, to art in general, and to the freedom of human thought.

Notes

1   Street-censorship is a form of public protest that aims to inhibit artists and suppress artworks. It is mostly organized by right-wing movements that use narratives of public moral outrage (on the 'promotion' of gay culture, the right to abortion, or the defence of religious beliefs), and threats to national pride and security, as pretexts for action. Street-censorship occurs in authoritarian countries when the police allows pressure groups to intimidate and threaten, and to fulfil actions that they agree upon but are not able to implement themselves because of the right to free expression.
2   For example, in 2013, Oliver Frljić cancelled his contracted collaboration (*Aleksandra Zec* and *Crime and Punishment*) with the Gavella Theatre in Zagreb when the theatre manager, pressured by clerical groups, withdrew the poster for the production of *Fine mrtve djevojke* (*Fine Dead Girls*), written by Mate Matišić and directed by Dalibor Matanić, which showed two nuns kissing.
3   The Serbian branch of Women in Black grieve and memorialize the victims of Srebrenica's genocide through the performances they present in collaboration with the independent DAH theatre company every 11 July. In symbolic installations/living memorials, they attempt to construct a monument to the victims. Though silent and non-violent, their performative protests have a strong impact on passers-by, who are rarely indifferent: they feel either anguished, ashamed, irritated, or mildly bemused, and may insult the performers or even try to attack them physically. See Jovićević (2018: 297–315).
4   In Macedonia in 1989, for similar reasons, several historical societies tried to prevent the performance of *Spiro Crne* by Blagoja Risteski and director Vladimir Milčin at the Prilep National Theatre, 'Vojdan Černodrinski'. These societies, in reaction to the performance, staged a trial of the play debating Milčin's and Risteski's artistic interpretation of history. However, this artistic tandem continued to develop different theatre projects trying to demystify official history narratives. See Stojanoska (2020: 49–61).
5   For instance, Branimir Karanović's *photo installation* (2002), Ivan Grubanov's *United Dead Nations* (2015), Mrdjan Bajić's *Yugomuseum* (1998–2007), Zoran Naskovski's delegated performance *Apollo 9* (1999), and theatre performances such as Oliver Frljić's *Proklet bio izdajica svoje domovine* (*Damned Be the Traitor of His Homeland*) at the Mladinsko Theatre in Ljubljana in 2011.
6   For further information about Oliver Frljić, please see Jovićević 2018a.
7   In 2016, the Malta Foundation and the Ministry of Culture and National Heritage entered into a three-year contract for the organization of the Malta

Festival Poznań, which obliged the Ministry to pay annual subsidies. However, the Ministry refused to pay the PLN 300,000 subsidy when Olivier Frljić was appointed as one of the festival's curators in 2017.

References

ArtsProfessional. 2019. <https://www.artsprofessional.co.uk/news/research-investigate-censorship-arts> [accessed 16 December 2021]

Avramović, Zoran. 2013. *Rodoljubci i rodomrsci: savremeni srpski patriotizam i nacionalno dezintegrativna misao i praksa* (Beograd: Službeni glasnik)

Balme, Christopher. 2015. 'In Extremis: Theatre Criticism, Ethics and the Public Sphere', *Critical Stages*, 12

Cvetičanin, Predrag. 2017. *Between Politics and Capital: Unwanted Culture in South-East Europe* (Niš: Centre for Empirical Cultural Studies of South-East Europe)

Dragićević Šešić, Milena. 2016. 'Dissidents', in *Culture and Human Rights: The Wroclaw Commentaries*, ed. by Andreas Wiesand, Kalliopi Chainoglou, and Anna Sledzinska-Simon (Berlin: De Gruyter), pp. 151–53

Dragićević Šešić, Milena, and Milena Stefanović. 2017. 'Organizational Trauma— Types of Organizational Forgetting in the Case of Belgrade Theatres', *Issues in Ethnology and Anthropology*, 2: 621–40

Farrington, Julia. 2013. 'Taking the Offensive', Conference report, *Index on Censorship*

Freshwater, Helen. 2009. *Theatre Censorship in Britain: Silencing, Censure and Suppression* (London and New York: Palgrave Macmillan)

Frljić, Oliver, in conversation with Marta Keil and Agata Adamiecka-Sitek. 2017. 'Whose National Theatre Is It?', *Polish Theatre Journal Online*, 1–2

Habermas, Jürgen. 1991 (1962). *The Structure of Transformation of the Public Sphere* (Cambridge, MA: The MIT Press)

Jovićević, Aleksandra. 2002. 'Trenutak srećnog samozaborava', *Teatron*, 27.118: 42–49

―――― 2007. 'Ingenious Dramatic Strategies Reach Across the Yugoslav Theatre Space', in *Towards a History of the Literary Cultures in East-Central Europe: Theoretical Reflections*, ed. by Marcel Cornis-Pope and John Neubauer (Cambridge: Cambridge University Press), pp. 257–65

―――― 2008. 'Censorship and Ingenious Dramatic Strategies in Yugoslav Theatre (1945–1991)', *Primerjalna knjizevnost*, 31: 237–49

―――― 2018a. 'More Than Activism, Less Than Art: The Heritage of Bertolt Brecht and Theodor Adorno in Contemporary Theatre', *Forum Modernes Theater*, 1+2: 37–46.

―――― 2018b. 'Postmodern Antigones: Women in Black and the Performance of Involuntary Memory', in *Theatre and Cultural Performances in the Context of Yugoslav Wars*, ed. by Jana Dolečki, Senad Halilbašić, and Stefan Hulfeld (London: Palgrave Macmillan), pp. 297–315

Karaulić, Jovana. 2016. 'The Challenges of the Participatory Theatre', *Ars Academica*, 4: 149–64

Keane, John. 1991. *The Media and Democracy* (London: Polity)

Klaić, Dragan. 1986. 'Obsessed with Politics: Currents in Yugoslav Drama', *Scena: Theatre Arts*, 9: 7–19

Klaić, Dragan, and Katarina Pejović (eds). 1996. *The Dissident Muse: Critical Theatre in Eastern and Central Europe, 1945–1989* (Amsterdam: Theater Institute)

Letunić, Ana. 2019. 'Instrumental Value of Culture and Curatorial Response from European Independent Performing Arts Field', in *Forschungsfeld Kulturpolitik— eine Kartierung von Theorie und Praxis: Festschrift für Wolfgang Schneider*, ed. by D. Gad, K.M. Schröck, and A. Weigl (Hildesheim: Georg Olms Verlag), pp. 341–49

Ljumović, Janko. 2019. 'Slobodan Milatović (1952–2019): superstar crnogorske pozorišne alternative', *Matica*, 80: 205–20

Lompar, Milo. 2011. *Duh samoporicanja: prilog kritici srpske kulturne politike* (Novi Sad: Orpheus)

Medenica, Ivan. 2002. 'Srpske i druge drame: pozorište u Srbiji 1990–2000', *Teatron*, 27.119–20: 7–18

Miłosz, Czeslaw. 1990. *The Captive Mind* (New York: Vintage)

Orel, Barbara. 2015. 'O (ne)moći umetniške geste upora', *Dialogi*, 51.1-2: 172–79

Perović, Jeronim. 2007. 'The Tito–Stalin Split: A Reassessment in Light of New Evidence', *Journal of Cold War Studies*, 9.2 (Spring): 32–63. https://doi.org/10.1162/jcws.2007.9.2.32

'Prekid predstave "Sveti Sava" & komentari'. 2018. *XXZregionalniportal*, 21 April <https://www.xxzmagazin.com/prekid-predstave-sveti-sava-komentari> [accessed 10 December 2021]

Radulović, Ksenija. 2018. 'War Discourse on Institutional Stages: Serbian Theatre 1991–1995', in *Theatre in the Context of the Yugoslav Wars*, ed. by Jana Dolečki, Senad Halilbašić, and Stefan Hulfeld (Palgrave Macmillan), pp. 107–22

Rancière, Jacques. 2004. *The Politics of Aesthetics: The Distribution of the Sensible*, trans. by Gabriel Rockhill (London and New York: Continuum)

—— 2006. *Hatred of Democracy*, trans. by Steve Corcoran (New York: Verso)

Ristovski, Ljubica. 2022. Unpublished interview with authors, 20 January

Šiklova, Jirina. 1990. 'The Grey Zone and the Future of Dissent in Czechoslovakia', *Social Research*, 57.2 (Summer): 347–63

Stojanoska, Ana. 2020. 'Wie Rock'n'Roll scheiterte: Dramatext und politisches Theater—die mazedonische Situation', in *Macht der Kultur: Politik und Theater—Erinnerungen an die Gegenwart*, ed. by J. Ljumović (Cetinje: Fakultat der Dramakunste; Podgorica: Konrad Adenauer Stichtung), pp. 49–61

Tanurovska-Kjulavkovski, Biljana, and Ivana Vaseva. 2021. 'Why Are We the Way We Are? The Critical Body as Subversive Cultural Performance in 1990s Macedonia', in *REALIZE! RESIST! REACT! Performance and Politics in the 1990s in the Post-Yugoslav Context*, ed. by Bojana Piškur et al. (Ljubljana: Moderna Galerija), pp. 151–91

Thomas, David, David Carlton, and Anne Etienne. 2007. *Theatre Censorship: From Walpole to Wilson* (Oxford: Oxford University Press)

Trencsényi, Balázs et al. 2018. *A History of Modern Political Thought in East Central Europe: Volume II: Negotiating Modernity in the Short Twentieth Century and Beyond, Part I: 1918–1968* (Oxford: Oxford University Press)

Vickery, Jonathan. 2021. 'The Status of Artist, Cultural Rights, and 2005 Convention: A Tribute to Professor Milena Dragićević Šešic', *The Journal of Law, Social Justice and Global Development*, 25: 131–45. https://doi.org/10.31273/LGD.2019.2506

2

The Emperor's New Clothes: Ideology and Censorship in Contemporary Russian Theatre

ALEX TRUSTRUM-THOMAS

The Serebrennikov case

In 2012, the *enfant terrible* of contemporary Russian theatre, Kirill Serebrennikov, was made artistic director of a fusty old Soviet-era theatre called the N.V. Gogol Moscow Drama Theatre, located in a former railway depot outside of Moscow's hallowed 'Garden Ring'—the ring road that delineates the city centre from the peripheries.[1] All of Moscow's most historic and renowned theatres are located within the Garden Ring, so that the building's location on the geographical margins of Moscow's theatre landscape reflected both its own status and that of its incoming artistic director, as marginal outsiders. Nonetheless, the appointment of Serebrennikov in the first place would in hindsight turn out to be the high-water mark of what one critic called a 'golden age' in Russian theatre (Freedman 2010: 389).

This was the time of the so-called Medvedev Thaw: the four-year interlude between the first and second periods of Vladimir Putin's presidency (2000–08; 2012–) when, observing the constitutional limit of two terms in office, Putin allowed his right-hand man, Dmitrii Medvedev, to occupy the presidency while he replaced Medvedev as prime minister. During this four-year period, the political buzzwords were 'modernization' and 'progress', whilst contemporary art was embraced as an integral part of Russia's future prosperity. The fashionable Serebrennikov could be seen hobnobbing with the senior government ideologist Vladislav Surkov, even attending round tables with President Medvedev himself. The sincerity of this progressive cultural policy at the highest level of politics was demonstrated in the most material way—with genuine financial support on a large scale. The results were visible almost immediately—there were substantial increases year-on-year across a range of indicators, including the number

Alex Trustrum-Thomas, "The Emperor's New Clothes: Ideology and Censorship in Contemporary Russian Theatre" in: *Theatre Censorship in Contemporary Europe: Silence and Protest*. University of Exeter Press (2024). © Alex Trustrum-Thomas. DOI: 10.47788/KHBJ9609 of premieres, the number of spectators, the number of theatres operating, and the overall takings at box offices (Parkhomovskaia 2017: 19). Serebrennikov and his new theatre—which he gave the snappier name 'Gogol Centre'—were major beneficiaries of the Medvedev cultural investment programme. Thanks to the progressive technocratic leadership of Sergei Kapkov (the head of Moscow's Department of Culture from 2011 to 2015), Serebrennikov was given the financial backing to renovate and modernize the theatre, which soon became one of the most fashionable places to be seen on an evening out in the Russian capital.[2]

Preceding Serebrennikov's appointment by three months was the return of Putin to the presidency, with Medvedev once again taking up the post of prime minister vacated by Putin. This switching back and forth between the two highest positions of power in the country, which were supposed to be democratically elected—a procedure which Putin and Medvedev brazenly admitted they had agreed in advance—was met with huge public disapproval, mass street protests (albeit largely limited to Moscow), and claims of widespread vote rigging. For the theatre world, however, Putin's return was not initially significant. Major projects such as 'Platforma'—an experimental, interdisciplinary platform for the contemporary performing arts, run by Serebrennikov's Seventh Studio in a converted warehouse in east Moscow—had been allocated funding in 2011 on a three-year cycle. When that came to an end in 2014, the direction of travel in Putin's third presidential term was becoming clear. Three now-infamous laws had been passed in quick succession that captured the spirit of the new age, informally known as the 'gay propaganda law', the 'law on swearing', and the 'law protecting the feelings of religious believers'.[3]

The 'gay propaganda' law forbade the so-called propaganda of 'non-traditional sexual relations' being promoted to minors, defined as those under eighteen. This law still technically allowed depictions of homosexuality behind closed doors to those of legal age—for example, in a theatre performance clearly labelled and enforced as eighteen plus. However, it banished such depictions from the public sphere, and had the effect of legitimizing homophobia and encouraging extrajudicial persecution of queer individuals, including through physical violence. The 'law on swearing' sought to regulate language usage in many spheres of life—in print, on screen, on stage, and in public. Initially the law was most strictly enforced on screens, where films and TV programmes would not be given licences if they contained swear words. For a long time, it seemed as if a blind eye was being turned to the theatre as performers continued to use 'non-normative' language on stage without serious repercussions. Around the turn of the decade, however, that began to change, as theatres found themselves attracting unwelcome attention if they allowed language on stage that was seen to contravene the law. The third law, allegedly brought in to 'protect the feelings of religious believers', represented an extraordinary volte-face for a ruling elite who had all spent the formative years of their lives in the Soviet Union, as members of the Komsomol, the KGB, and the Communist Party. This was hardly a late blooming of religious piety in the lives of these former apparatchiki, however. It was rather an attack on the liberal intelligentsia, who had become increasingly critical of the blend of Russian ethnonationalism and the social conservatism of the Russian Orthodox Church, which were being employed in tandem by the government as a way of shoring up its faltering support base after the unconvincing 2011–12 election cycle. The turning point came in 2014 with the annexation of Crimea from Ukraine, which was overwhelmingly popular amongst Russians—Putin's popularity ratings went from a low ebb to an all-time high almost overnight. The subsequent war with Ukraine in the Donbas region and the corresponding information war with the West only served to reinforce the conservative-nationalist turn in government policy. Thus, when the funding for projects such as 'Platforma' came to an end, the political landscape had shifted significantly.

When Putin appointed Vladimir Medinskii as Minister of Culture in his new government, alarm bells started to ring in the arts world. Medinskii had no background in the arts, but he held a doctorate in history and, like Putin, he had a passion for the Second World War.[4] This concern was reinforced by Medinskii's public statements, such as in 2013, when he spoke out regarding funding for contemporary art:

> I popped into the Manezh [exhibition centre], where the Moscow Biennale was still on. I was walking around and thinking to myself, 'Why does no one cry out "The emperor has no clothes!"?' Why should we, under the guise of contemporary art, have to look at something abstract-cubic, something gnarled, in the form of a pile of bricks? And paid for by state money! To say nothing of the fact that it is incomprehensible to the vast majority of people in Russia. (Iablokov 2013)

The work in question was by a well-known invited artist from China, Yin Xiuzhen, whose installation at the Moscow Biennale reflected on the erasure of cultural memory as a result of the rapid expansion and reconstruction of urban landscapes in Chinese cities (Diakonov 2013). With echoes of the denunciation of 'formalism' in the Soviet Union in the 1930s, this was an emerging turn in cultural policy—away from the modernizing and the contemporary, towards a conservative, populist agenda, underpinned by a classical realist aesthetic. This was confirmed a year later when an official document titled 'Fundamentals of State Cultural Policy' was drawn up and given the presidential seal of approval. Amongst other things, this document asserted that cultural policy was an 'inseparable part of national security', and that culture has a 'social mission' as an 'instrument to transmit the code of moral, ethical, and aesthetic values comprising the core of national uniqueness to the next generations' (Decree 808 2014). I have elsewhere considered this document, along with many of the other legislative changes that occurred over the course of Putin's third term (2012–18), and come to the conclusion that the new cultural policy introduced in 2014 represented a return to many of the tenets of Soviet-era socialist realism—the state artistic policy from 1934 until 1991, where culture was treated as an instrument in the creation and moulding of the ideal Soviet citizen, and for this reason was heavily regulated through censorship (Trustrum-Thomas 2020).

As J.A.E. Curtis has pointed out, we should not necessarily be surprised that Putin and the ruling elite were drawn to reinstating aspects of Soviet cultural policy—after all, Putin was a KGB agent and Communist Party member for most of his adult life until the dissolution of the Soviet Union in 1991, and the majority of the ruling elite are of a similar age and background:

> The notion of a dirigiste state dictating the content and methods of artistic projects is one with which they [the arbiters of cultural policy] feel entirely comfortable, and if the politics of communism are no longer relevant, then the political goals of an authoritarian ruling class are still well served by these new, tight controls over cultural practices. (Curtis 2020: 10)

Furthermore, when considering the issue of censorship, it is also worth bearing in mind the definition of culture set out in this 2014 document (which laid down guidelines for all subsequent cultural policy-making): '"Culture" is the sum total of formal and informal institutions, phenomena, and factors influencing the preservation, production, transmission and distribution of spiritual values (ethical, aesthetic, intellectual, civic, and so on)' (Decree 808 2014). With this formulation of what constitutes culture at the highest level of policy-making, it is easier to understand why the government set out to instrumentalize the cultural sphere in support of its conservative-nationalist turn. If 'culture' influences and produces 'spiritual values', then a military-patriotic agenda in the arts would, in theory, rally the population behind the government in its foreign wars and in its conflict with the West—perhaps thereby distracting from intractable domestic problems such as economic stagnation, unpopular pension reforms, falling real-term incomes, and a severely weakened currency as a result of international sanctions and capital flight. Against this background, the dynamic, experimental theatre produced by the likes of Serebrennikov's Seventh Studio stood out: like the Manezh exhibition, it too seemed 'abstract-cubic', 'gnarled', and 'incomprehensible to the vast majority of people in Russia' (Iablokov 2013).

For most of Putin's third term, Serebrennikov's theatre, the Gogol Centre, was flourishing. Serebrennikov's directorial work both on stage and on screen was recognized at home and internationally. However, the net was tightening. In 2016, the presidential spokesperson Dmitrii Peskov countered accusations from the theatre world that the government was intensifying censorship by stating, 'If the state gives money to a production, it has the right to determine the themes' ('Peskov' 2016). This was in line with Medinskii's view that the Ministry of Culture should be more selective with its allocation of funding and should assert more control over what was produced. As described here and elsewhere, the problem that independent-minded theatres have in Russia is that they are almost wholly reliant on the state for their existence (Trustrum-Thomas 2020: 61). Over 70% of theatre budgets on average comes from the state, and in some cases a remarkable 90% of the cost of a ticket is comprised of state funds (Sergeev et al. 2017). Without an established tradition of philanthropy, private investment, or corporate sponsorship in the arts (until thirty years ago, these things were impossible and the state paid for everything), it is extremely difficult for theatres to escape the stranglehold of financial censorship, whereby the government can exert pressure to conform at any moment by pulling the purse strings.

Serebrennikov was a well-known face at opposition protests and had publicly spoken out against the unofficial war with Ukraine, which was claiming the lives of thousands of people on both sides, all the while unacknowledged by the Kremlin. He was becoming increasingly critical of the authorities in public interviews, stating for example in 2015 that 'everything has become rotten, stale, eaten away by corruption, monstrous lies, stealing, and cynicism' and that the Ministry of Culture was 'hostile' to his work (Belov and Super 2015). A scandal that erupted in 2013 around Serebrennikov's pre-production of a state-funded biographical film about the composer Pyotr Tchaikovsky had resulted in him scrapping the project altogether and pledging to finance the film with money from abroad instead ('Rezhisser' 2013). This was allegedly due to the controversial issue of the composer's homosexuality—a part of Tchaikovsky's biography that the Russian state refuses to acknowledge. Four years later, in July 2017, Serebrennikov's ballet *Nureyev*—about the life of Soviet ballet dancer Rudolf Nureyev who famously sought asylum in the West in 1961 (partly on account of his homosexuality)— was due to premiere at the Bolshoi Theatre, but three days beforehand it was unexpectedly postponed until the following spring. The artistic director of the Bolshoi insisted that the show was postponed because it was not ready, but numerous media reports emerged claiming that Medinskii was behind the decision ('Otmena' 2017). There was allegedly concern that the production could draw negative attention to the theatre in the light of the so-called gay propaganda law. The problems around *Nureyev*, however, were overshadowed one month later when, whilst on location in St Petersburg filming a biopic about legendary late-Soviet rock star Viktor Tsoi, Serebrennikov was arrested and driven overnight back to Moscow in a police van.

What followed has been well documented in media reports around the world (see Yaffa 2020). Serebrennikov was charged with fraud and embezzlement, and subjected to a farcical three-year court case. He spent over a year and a half under house arrest, during which time he managed to complete and release the film about Tsoi, called *Leto* (*Summer*), premiered his adaptation of Pushkin's *Malen'kie tragedii* (*Little Tragedies*) at the Gogol Centre, and continued to rehearse new stage works, all remotely via video link. During the same period, Putin was reinaugurated for another six-year term in office (his fourth term overall), and *Nureyev* eventually premiered at the Bolshoi in December 2017, with Serebrennikov notably absent. The premiere was well attended by many of the ruling elite from government and business, whilst ordinary theatregoers queued from three o'clock in the morning to get a ticket on the day of their release for one of only two scheduled performances. There was a sixteen-minute standing ovation at the end of the show when the actors returned to the stage for the curtain call, many of whom were sporting T-shirts bearing Serebrennikov's image and the words 'Free the Director' ('Bravo' 2017). This seemingly paradoxical moment exemplifies what the journalist Peter Pomerantsev describes in his book about post-Soviet Russia titled *Nothing Is True and Everything is Possible* (2015)—essentially the extreme moral relativism of the Russian ruling elite and political class, in which the very people who pass repressive laws and persecute artists in the daytime can attend controversial openings and applaud those same artists in the evening.

Serebrennikov was released from house arrest in the spring of 2019, just a few days before the awards ceremony for that year's Golden Mask Festival (Russia's most prestigious theatre awards). Appearing in public for the first time since his arrest, he was rapturously received as he collected two awards in person—for 'Best Director' in the drama category for *Little Tragedies*, and 'Best Ballet' for *Nureyev*. The jubilation did not last long, however, as Serebrennikov's court case was still ongoing, and the theatre world was shaken by a new scandal a few months later, when a young actor, Pavel Ustinov, was arbitrarily arrested near the scene of an unsanctioned protest for free elections in Moscow's Pushkin Square. Ustinov was not participating in the protest and yet was subsequently sentenced to three and a half years in prison on the flimsiest of grounds. His alleged crime was violence towards a Russian Guard officer, who, as video footage of the event shows, lost his footing and slipped over whilst violently wrestling Ustinov to the ground as he stood on the street using his mobile phone.[5] After a public campaign on the young actor's behalf by the Moscow theatre establishment, Ustinov's sentence was eventually reduced on appeal to one year suspended, meaning that he did not go to prison. Whilst this was celebrated as a victory of sorts for civic activism, many others were not as lucky in having such public support, and the liberally inclined theatre world had been given a stark reminder of the dangers of involvement in opposition politics.

Serebrennikov's trial concluded in June 2020, when the director was sentenced alongside two of his colleagues from Seventh Studio—the former general director of the company, Iurii Itin, and the former general producer, Aleksei Malobrodskii. They were collectively found guilty of embezzling 129 million roubles (*c*.£1.29 million) from 'Platforma', out of a total of 200 million roubles (*c*.£2 million) allocated to the project. Serebrennikov was given a suspended sentence of three years' imprisonment and a fine of 800,000 roubles (*c*.£8,000).[6] On top of this, he and the others were ordered to pay back the 'stolen' state money in full, and their assets were confiscated as capital until they did so. Serebrennikov stated at the time that he would never be able to pay off this sum of money.[7] Despite their utter rejection of the accusations, the outcome of the case was seen as a victory by the director's supporters, because Serebrennikov would not be going to prison. The sad irony was that, in the distorted world of the Russian judicial system, the verdict was akin to an admission of his innocence—the sentence would have been much too light if the accused had been genuinely guilty of the charges (Korniia 2020).

To illustrate the nature of the court case itself, one moment speaks volumes—the debate around the immersive performance of Shakespeare's *A Midsummer Night's Dream*, produced by Seventh Studio and directed by Serebrennikov. It premiered in 2012 as a part of the 'Platforma' project financed under former President Medvedev, was performed fifteen times, and then transferred to the Gogol Centre, where it continued to be performed in the repertory for several years. Nevertheless, the state prosecution claimed that the production of *A Midsummer Night's Dream* had never taken place and had in fact been simulated in order to embezzle money from the state. This was despite the evidence brought forward by the defence, which included posters, flyers, tickets sold, numerous reviews published by professional theatre critics, nominations for national theatre prizes, and a deluge of eyewitness statements by spectators who had attended one of the many performances of the show. The sheer absurdity of this instance in the court proceedings was the point at which it became difficult to see the case against Serebrennikov as anything other than a show trial. Any illusions that this could be a genuine case disappeared, and all that was left was the question of who had ordered the attack on Serebrennikov, and why.

The nature of a show trial is to make an example of someone, as a message to others. The message here seemed to be clear enough, and it was being sent to all the other independent-minded artistic directors of theatres in Russia, and to the cultural sphere more generally: fall in line, be silent on political matters, do not criticize the authorities, be grateful for whatever money the state gives you, or risk the same fate, because the state prosecutors and the courts are so closely entwined with the government that anything can be 'proven' against you. Russia's judicial system is rated as one of the worst in the world, according to the World Justice Project.

In 2020, it was placed at 94 out of 128 countries, with guilty verdicts handed down in well over 99% of cases on average in recent years (World Justice Project 2020). As a mechanism of censorship—and for encouraging self-censorship—the threat of a criminal investigation and court trial is one of the most powerful that the authorities have at their disposal for putting pressure on theatre-makers in contemporary Russia, as it was in Soviet times. Self-censorship has been acknowledged as a major problem facing theatre in Russia by several leading directors, including Konstantin Bogomolov (Shestakova 2012), Maksim Didenko (Shpileva 2016), and Mark Zakharov (Solomonov 2014). In Didenko's view, 'Today there are many mechanisms in our country that create an atmosphere in which people start to censor themselves. [...] The main instrument in the creation of self-censorship is fear' (Shpileva 2016).

Following Serebrennikov's 'guilty' verdict, it became known a few months later, in November 2020, that the Moscow Department of Culture—the legal owner of the Gogol Centre—was not planning to renew its existing contract with the director, which ran until the following February. Serebrennikov reflected on his dismissal on his Instagram account at the time: 'Everything in this world, having started, comes to an end. But something new starts in its place. [...] Theatre and freedom are broader, more important, and therefore more alive than any state bureaucrat' (Serebrennikov 2021). He was succeeded in his post by Aleksei Agranovich, a fifty-year-old stage and film actor who had carved out a niche for himself directing awards ceremonies for film festivals. Agranovich was an inside choice, to the extent that he knew the Gogol Centre well from playing roles in two of Serebrennikov's more recent works—*Obyknovennaia istoriia* (*A Common Story*) (adapted from the novel by Goncharov, premiered in 2015), and the aforementioned award-winning *Little Tragedies* (premiered in 2017). As one commentator noted at the time regarding the choice of Agranovich, 'he will keep the same repertory, the same company, and will give the same opportunities to stage works to those who formerly did so, including the theatre's former artistic director' (Tokareva 2021). Sure enough, when the schedule for the new 2021–22 season at the Gogol Centre was announced later that summer, first up on the bill was none other than a new Serebrennikov work—an adaptation of Giovanni Boccaccio's *The Decameron*, evidently chosen for its pertinence in the context of the ongoing global coronavirus pandemic.

The choice of Agranovich—who was not outspoken and was no less capable than Serebrennikov of getting in with the right people in the right places to secure funding for artistic projects—appeared to have been a lifeline for the Gogol Centre in the form conceived by its founder. However, in a culture where being artistic director of a state theatre is often a lifetime appointment, the symbolic gesture of removing Serebrennikov from his position was the conclusion of the criminal case against him and, as has been speculated, was perhaps the motive from the start. His popularity and celebrity status as a national cultural treasure meant that his name had to be sufficiently tarnished before he could be unseated. There were no such difficulties when, little over a year later, the Moscow Department of Culture decided to dispense with Agranovich's services as well, after he signed an open letter in opposition to Russia's full-scale invasion of Ukraine, launched on 24 February 2022. At the conclusion of the 2021–22 theatrical season, Serebrennikov publicly declared that his project to transform the N.V. Gogol Moscow Drama Theatre into a modern, dynamic, artistically exciting space was dead. The theatre was subsequently returned to its original name by the new management—Anton Iakovlev and Aleksandr Bocharnikov, two little-known figures who had no connection to Serebrennikov or his circle, and who most importantly had never spoken out against the war ('Za odin' 2022). From this we are reminded that for as long as the state holds all the levers of power over theatrical production—from financing and the appointment of senior positions, to legislation dictating what can and cannot be said and shown on stage—no theatre-maker or company is free to practise their profession without fear of reprisals for stepping out of line.

The emperor's new clothes

As in English, the idiom 'the emperor has no clothes' entered into the Russian language from the popular children's story 'The Emperor's New Clothes' by Hans Christian Andersen, first published in Danish in 1837. Andersen's story is a parable about the trappings of power and keeping up appearances. In the rigid social hierarchy of the feudal world and with potentially violent retribution for speaking out of turn, it is only the naïve child who is able to speak the truth and point out that the emperor is in fact wearing no clothes, thus breaking the taboo. The emperor has been humiliated and he knows it, but he is too proud or scared to admit it, and the procession continues regardless. Such are the trappings of power. When, therefore, the then new Russian Minister of Culture, Medinskii, likened contemporary art to the emperor's state of undress, it was intended as a similar act of unveiling. It was as if to say that everyone involved in the exhibition—from the organizers, to the art establishment, to the crowd of people assembled to consider the artistic merit of a pile of bricks—were all blind to the truth: that there is no merit here, that a pile of bricks is a pile of bricks, and that it is a waste of time, space, and state money.

Medinskii-as-unveiler proposes to dispel (or at least defund) the illusion that upholds contemporary art as an institution, in favour of his preferred artistic style—realism (figurative painting and sculpture, Stanislavskian acting, Chekhovian drama, and so on). This was reinforced by Medinskii's professed appreciation for socialist realist art, on the grounds that 'at least [Soviet artists] knew how to paint' (Diakonov 2013). One of the many problems with Medinskii's view was that it made a claim to knowledge of universal artistic Truth and denied the epochal particularity of human cultural history. In his view of art, one artistic style can be truthful, and another can be false whilst wrongfully claiming to be truthful (the naked emperor), and he believes he knows which is which. This short-sightedness would not matter had he not been the Minister of Culture for a vast multi-ethnic, multiconfessional country containing many distinct cultures, identities, and histories.[8] For the Ministry of Culture to make funding decisions and institutional appointments guided by such a narrow perception of artistic validity has an impact across the social spectrum, as much on peripheral ethnic or social minorities as on the accursed liberal cultural elite in the capital.

What undermines Medinskii's attempt at unveiling is the fact that any claim regarding the emperor's state of undress works both ways. After all, contemporary art emerged in the twentieth century as a reaction to—and unveiling of—the questionable truth premises underlying realism, in particular figurative painting. The Minister of Culture needed only to be reminded of his compatriot Kazimir Malevich's 1915 work *Chernyi kvadrat* (*Black Square*), a ground-breaking masterpiece of world art hanging within strolling distance of his office, in the New Tretiakov Gallery. He should also have recalled what had happened in the past when the state in Russia took upon itself the job of determining and regulating cultural production: it was precisely for his assaults on realism on the stage that the greatest theatre director of the Soviet avant-garde, Vsevolod Meyerhold, was arrested, tortured, and shot in 1940, with the execution order being signed by Stalin himself. Although the Putin regime was less bloodthirsty before the war than its infamous predecessor, it was a sign of the changing times when Meyerhold's name appeared on more than one occasion in the media in connection with Serebrennikov's persecution, with some commentators drawing comparisons between the fate of the two men (see Latynina 2017).

The idiom regarding the emperor's new clothes is a popular one in Russia, particularly in the cultural sphere, where it is a not uncommon attack levelled by different sides at one other. Its usage is more recently associated with the jailed politician and opposition leader Aleksei Navalny, who has employed it in reference to Putin. Navalny's opening statement, for example, in his speech in court on 29 April 2021, where he was being sentenced on trumped-up charges of slander, was: 'I want to say, my dear judge, that your emperor has no clothes' (Navalny 2021). He repeated the phrase a further five times in his speech. For Navalny, Putin is the ultimate symbol of the naked emperor, exposed and unveiled countless times by him and his team of corruption investigators, yet carrying on regardless. However, just as Medinskii's condemnation of contemporary art is unlikely to have made anyone in the art world seriously reconsider their opinion of it, Navalny's declarations that Putin is the naked emperor did not bring about a great moment of revelation in the minds of the Russian public. The problem, according to philosopher Slavoj Žižek, is that nobody seems to care any more if the emperor is naked or not. For Žižek, Andersen's story does not work in our day because 'it seems that appearances no longer have to be protected' (2012: 92).

Modelling censorship

Looking beyond the Serebrennikov case, there appeared to be a certain model taking shape for controlling, regulating, and censoring theatre in Russia at the turn of the decade. This was illustrated in the case of the Sovremennik Theatre—a large, state-funded theatre founded during the Soviet 'thaw' era (1956–64), and occupying a historic building in central Moscow. On 19 July 2021, a play called *Pervyi khleb* (*First Bread*) premiered at the Sovremennik.⁹ It was written in Russian by a young ethnic Tatar dramatist, Rinat Tashimov, and directed by a Polish director working in Russia, Beniamin Koc (both men were in their early thirties at the time).¹⁰ Set in a remote Tatar village in the depths of Western Siberia, the play addresses the desire of a young man to go to war—and possible death—as an escape from the reality of life in his village with his family, and all the social obligations that accompany it. It paints a bleak picture of life in a small provincial Russian village, which offers no prospect of a future to the young man besides premature death in combat—particularly prescient in the context of the mobilization of fighting-age men in Russia the following year. Three days after the premiere, on 22 July, news broke in the media that a formal complaint had been lodged against the production to the public prosecutor's office by an organization called Officers of Russia. The latter claimed to have received numerous complaints from Russian military veterans regarding the 'extreme use of non-normative lexicon [i.e. profanities]' and the 'open propaganda of same-sex love' in the play. The organization also declared that one of the monologues, performed by the decorated Soviet and Russian actor Lia Akhedzhakova, contained 'appalling unethicalness, rudeness, and offence' to veterans and their families ('Na teatr' 2021). They demanded that the play be altered before its next stage performance, which was due to take place the following day.

Given the play's subject matter and its anti-war message, it was not surprising that the play was targeted, and that the complaint came from Officers of Russia—an organization that represents military veterans but has expanded in recent years to include a quasi-legal paramilitary unit of 'young volunteers' (at least some of whom in fact receive payment), well known for its aggressively patriotic pro-Kremlin views. Akhedzhakova, speaking on the independent Russian TV channel Rain, commented on the situation, stating that the denunciation could only have come from within the theatre world, because there had only been one performance of the show, and there had not been any veterans in the audience (or at least not in the quantity that the Officers of Russia were claiming). As such, the complaint had clearly come from someone who was displeased with the theatre, or more likely with its new artistic director, Viktor Ryzhakov. Best known for directing plays by the celebrated contemporary Russian dramatist Ivan Vyrypaev, Ryzhakov took over at the Sovremennik at the start of 2020, having for seven years been artistic director of the Meyerhold Centre, which under his watch became, like the Gogol Centre, well known for its creative freedom, experimentation, and progressive views.[11] Ryzhakov was one of three artistic directors who were removed from their posts by the Moscow Department of Culture for signing an open letter in opposition to Russia's invasion of Ukraine in 2022.[12]

Between the premiere and the second showing of *First Bread* on 23 July, in the light of the criticism and unwanted attention, the Sovremennik altered Akhedzhakova's monologue, removing the profanities from it. On the day of the second performance, the notorious pro-Kremlin ultranationalist group SERB publicly threatened to disrupt the show. Its activists caused a nuisance outside the theatre, including by placing funeral wreaths with the words 'We are burying the Sovremennik' at the theatre's doors (Molchanov 2021). SERB has a history of targeting theatre performances that it deems to be undesirable. In 2019, it successfully disrupted a performance at Moscow's legendary documentary theatre, Teatr.doc. In that incident, SERB activists broke into the theatre during a performance of *Voina blizko* (*War is Close*), created and directed by one of the theatre's founders, the late Elena Gremina (1956–2018). They threw a cup containing faeces into the backstage area, which led to the evacuation of the premises. On another occasion one month previously, in an attempt to demonstrate that the theatre was breaking the law on the prohibition of gay propaganda to minors, SERB had created fake eighteen-plus ID for a seventeen-year-old teenager and planted him in the audience of a performance of *Vyiti iz shkafa* (*Coming Out of the Closet*) by Anastasiia Patlai, a documentary play containing the coming-out stories of gay Russians. Around twelve men then disrupted the performance and would not allow the actors to continue until the imminent arrival of the police caused them to disperse. Such actions rarely resulted in punishment or criminal investigation, and indeed it was widely considered that SERB was financed and coordinated by the security services and the Kremlin. One former member of the group claimed in 2019 that it had received funding directly from the interior ministry for its activities ('"Meduza"' 2019). Probably because of another denunciation, later that year it was announced that Teatr.doc was being investigated by the authorities for possible propaganda of drugs, terrorism, and homosexuality (of which it was cleared in January 2020). Well known for its critical views towards the authorities and for staging uncompromising documentary plays on important social issues, Teatr.doc was a repeated target of attacks after Putin's return to the presidency in 2012 and the conservative-authoritarian turn in Russian politics that ensued.

Although the Sovremennik denied the accusations of censorship levelled at the theatre after altering the performance of *First Bread* in response to the complaints, essentially the enforcers had got their way. First, this proved the power of these groups over the cultural sphere and their ability to influence what can be said and shown. Second, it justified their continued funding by the state and by unofficial state actors, thus making such attacks more likely in the future. If Ryzhakov had been seen as a liberal choice upon his appointment at the Sovremennik (which is, after all, not a fringe theatre like the Meyerhold Centre and the former Gogol Centre, but a well-known state theatre in the centre of the capital), then the scandal around *First Bread* appeared to have served a useful function in clipping his wings early on in his ultimately short-lived tenure. If there had been any lingering doubt about the purpose of state-funded 'social organizations' such as Officers of Russia, it was finally swept away by the Sovremennik case.[13] It was a clear demonstration of how closely entwined these nominally independent organizations are with state structures, and how they can be mobilized as instruments in the patrolling and enforcement of state ideological norms as set out in the cultural policy documents and the legislative acts regulating freedom of expression discussed above.

The Sovremennik scandal resulted in an announcement ten days later, on 2 August 2021, that the Ministry of Culture's 'Civic Council' was being tasked with conducting checks on theatres to ascertain whether they were operating in line with the 'strategy for national security' ('Obshchestvennyi' 2021). As mentioned above, it was the 'Fundamentals of State Cultural Policy' that in 2014 described cultural policy as an 'inseparable part of national security' (Decree 808 2014). Nobody was sure what that meant at the time, whether it was just political posturing or would have practical consequences. Six years later, it was becoming clear what it meant for culture to be 'part of national security'. It meant a regime of denunciation censorship, whereby figures inside the cultural establishment or in the Ministry of Culture inform on transgressors to one of the state-financed 'enforcer' groups. A representative of the chosen 'offended' group then lodges an official complaint to a government ministry—usually the state prosecutor or Roskomnadzor (the mass media and information watchdog)—which then opens an investigation. At this point the case goes from being nominally non-state to state-led. Then, as demonstrated by countless high- and low-profile cases in recent years, notably including Serebrennikov's farcical trial described above, anything can be proven or disproven in a Russian court. Professional witnesses in the pay of the courts were simply employed to give evidence that the production or work in question had broken the law. This process was designed to give the illusion of a healthy civic sphere, in which good, duty-bound citizens take action autonomously to report offending works. In this model, non-state actors initiate the patrolling and enforcement of state ideological norms of their own accord, and the state merely reacts to events initiated and reported on by well-meaning groups of citizens. This procedure is important to keep up the appearance of the rule of law, backed by societal consensus.

The 2014 'Fundamentals of State Cultural Policy' document appeared to suggest that there would be a concerted promotion of national values and spiritual ties in the cultural sphere, as determined by the state. This was reaffirmed at the start of July 2021 when Putin published an updated version of the 'Strategy for the National Security of the Russian Federation', which included an expanded section on culture. It referred specifically to the harmful influence of swearing in public performances, and to the threat to national security from the 'westernization' of Russian culture (Decree 400 2021). When pressed on which theatres the Ministry of Culture's Civic Council would be checking, one member of the council said that it would take action when a particular production had come to its attention (Mongait and Treskunov 2021). This confirmed the new denunciation-based system taking shape. Given that complaints predominantly originated from state-sponsored pro-Kremlin groups such as Officers of Russia, and were targeted at the perceived liberal, oppositionally inclined theatres such as Teatr.doc, the Gogol Centre, the Meyerhold Centre, and the Sovremennik, it was fairly predictable which theatres would be most closely monitored for 'threats to national security' (i.e. anti-war messages, 'gay propaganda', swearing, etc.) in their productions. This became especially acute following the invasion of Ukraine in 2022 and the ensuing clampdown on any form of opposition to the war.

It was evident from the Sovremennik case that the mechanisms for policing culture were taking a more concrete, systematized form, with clear procedures in place for denouncing theatres and thereby pressurizing them to conform, self-censor, and stay within the safe zone of the norm, as dictated by state cultural policy and enforced by the Ministry of Culture and its acting agents. This tightening regulatory regime will likely be the defining feature of the conditions for contemporary theatre production in Russia in the years ahead, for as long as the current political regime remains in power. If keeping up appearances had been important to the regime before the invasion of Ukraine, the war left little room for anything other than conformity or silence. With many prominent theatre figures losing their jobs, fleeing the country, or even being arrested and put on trial, appearances no longer had to be protected because there was nothing left to protect. The emperor had well and truly revealed himself, but no one was laughing.

Notes

1 In Russia, the artistic directors of state-financed theatres are appointed either by the Ministry of Culture (which is a government department) or by the relevant regional cultural department, such as the Moscow Department of

Culture, depending on whose jurisdiction the theatre building falls under. Furthermore, state financing of theatres comes directly from the relevant government department, with no intermediary body, such as exists in the UK in the form of the Arts Council, for example. This means that the senior management of state-financed theatres are essentially state employees whose positions and salaries are dependent on ministerial approval.

2   During Kapkov's time in charge, a number of the capital's tired old Soviet-era theatres were overhauled in addition to the Gogol Centre, including the Sovremennik and the Stanislavskii Electrotheatre. This was alongside the renovation of public parks, libraries, and museums, and the launch of an ambitious urban regeneration programme to make Moscow into a modern European city.

3   These laws are, respectively: 'On the protection of children from information propagandizing the denial of traditional family values' (Federal Law N135-F3, 2013); 'On the improvement of legal regulation in the sphere of the usage of the Russian language' (Federal Law N-190238-6, 2014); 'On the counteraction of offences to religious convictions and feelings of citizens' (Federal Law N136-F3, 2013).

4   It later turned out that large sections of Medinskii's doctoral thesis had been plagiarized, but calls for him to be stripped of his degree were dismissed by the Kremlin as an attempt to discredit him.

5   For the video footage, see TV Rain (2019).

6   Iurii Itin was given a suspended sentence of three years' imprisonment and a fine of 200,000 roubles (c.£2,000), whilst Aleksei Malobrodskii was given a suspended sentence of two years' imprisonment and a fine of 300,000 roubles (c.£3,000). See Korniia (2020).

7   In November 2021, however, it was reported that Serebrennikov had paid off the entire debt of 129 million roubles collectively owed to the Ministry of Culture, as well as his personal fine, thanks to unnamed private donors. This enabled him to finally travel outside of Russia once more. See 'Serebrennikov edinolichno' (2021).

8   Medinskii was Minister of Culture for eight years, from 2012 until 2020, when he was replaced by Olga Lyubimova, who had served as head of film under Medinskii, and as such represented a continuation of the existing cultural policy.

9   *First Bread* emerged at the Lyubimovka Festival of Young Dramaturgy in 2017, where it was given a well-received rehearsed reading.

10 Tashimov is from a Tatar village in the Omsk region of Western Siberia and is a graduate of Nikolai Koliada's famous playwriting school in Ekaterinburg. Koc is a graduate of the Russian State Institute for Stage Arts in St Petersburg, as well as of Viktor Ryzhakov's master's programme in directing at the Moscow Art Theatre and the Meyerhold Centre.

11 Ryzhakov has directed productions of many of Vyrypaev's plays since their first collaboration on the latter's breakout work *Kislorod* (*Oxygen*), which premiered to great acclaim in 2002 in Moscow at Teatr.doc. See Chapter 7 ('Ivan Vyrypaev and the Abject') of Beumers and Lipovetsky (2009: 241–69).

12 Along with Ryzhakov, the other two to be dismissed were the aforementioned Aleksei Agranovich at the Gogol Centre, and Iosif Raikhelgauz, artistic director and founder of the Contemporary Play School. See 'Za odin' (2022).

13 That these organizations are state-funded is well known. Between 2011 and 2016, the All-Russian Social Organization 'Officers of Russia' received three Presidential Grants, as well as one grant from the National Charitable Fund, and one grant from the Ministry of Work. The organization's opaque financial structure makes identifying other significant income sources difficult. However, the resources at its disposal suggest that there is major additional financial backing behind it, with oligarchs and businessmen close to the Kremlin being the most likely sources. See 'Anatomiia' (2016).

References

'Anatomiia "Ofitserov": kak rabotaet odna iz samykh neprozrachnykh rossiiskikh organizatsii'. 2016. *BBC Russian*, 27 September

Belov, Kim, and Roman Super. 2015. 'Kirill Serebrennikov: "Eto dazhe khorosho, chto seichas nam plokho"', *GQ Russia*, 2 March

Beumers, Birgit, and Mark Lipovetsky. 2009. *Performing Violence: Literary and Theatrical Experiments of New Russian Drama* (Bristol: Intellect)

'Bravo "Nureevu", "Svobodu rezhisseru!"'. 2017. *Novaia gazeta*, 11 December

Curtis, J.A.E. 2020. 'Introduction: Recent Developments in Russian, Ukrainian, and Belarusian Drama', in *New Drama in Russian: Performance, Politics and Protest in Russia, Ukraine and Belarus*, ed. by J.A.E. Curtis (London: Bloomsbury Academic), pp. 1–20

Decree 400. 2021. 'O Strategii natsional'noi bezopasnosti Rossiiskoi Federatsii', 2 July <http://publication.pravo.gov.ru/Document/View/0001202107030001> [accessed 10 January 2022]

Decree 808. 2014. 'Osnovy gosudarstvennoi kul'turnoi politiki', 24 December <http://www.kremlin.ru/acts/bank/39208> [accessed 10 January 2022]

Diakonov, Valentin. 2013. 'Ministr i kirpich: Kul'turnaia politika', *Kommersant*, 16 October

Federal Law N135-F3. 2013. 'O vnesenii izmenenii [...] v tseliakh zashity detei ot informatsii [...] propagandiruiushchei otritsanie traditsionnykh semeinykh tsen-nostei', 29 June <http://www.consultant.ru/document/cons_doc_LAW_108808> [accessed 10 January 2022]

Federal Law N136-F3. 2013. 'O vnesenii izmenenii [...] v tseliakh protivodeistviia oskorbleniiu religioznykh ubezhdenii i chuvstv grazhdan', 29 June <http://www.consultant.ru/document/cons_doc_LAW_148270> [accessed 10 January 2022]

Federal Law N190238-6. 2014. 'O vnesenii izmenenii [...] v sviazi s sovershenstvovaniem pravovogo regulirovaniia v sfere ispol'zovaniia russkogo iazyka', 5 May <http://www.consultant.ru/cons/cgi/online.cgi?req=doc&base=PRJ&n=100743#Rm2a8uSkuDKWzvaL> [accessed 10 January 2022]

Freedman, John. 2010. 'Contemporary Russian Drama: The Journey from Stagnation to a Golden Age', *Theatre Journal*, 62: 389–420

Iablokov, Aleksei. 2013. 'V 2014 godu gosudarstvo vser'ez voz'metsia za kul'turu', *Vedomosti*, 11 October

Korniia, Anastasiia. 2020. 'Vynesennyi Kirillu Serebrennikovu prigovor udivil ekspertov', *Vedomosti*, 26 June

Latynina, Iuliia. 2017. 'Nichto za poslednee vremia tak ne vredilo Putinu, kak "delo Serebrennikova"', *Novaia gazeta*, 22 August

'"Meduza": SERB poluchaet den'gi ot MVD za "pomoshch" v raskrytii prestuplenii'. 2019. *Novaia gazeta*, 21 November

Molchanov, Arsenii. 2021. 'Chto proiskhodilo u Sovremennika vo vremia spektaklia', *RTVI*, 23 July

Mongait, Anna, and Semen Treskunov. 2021. '"Rech' idet o propagande LGBT, oskorblenii veteranov i netsenzurnoi leksike": Askol'd Zapashnyi—o tom, chto budet iskat' v teatrakh vo vremia proverki na natsbezopasnost', *Dozhd'*, 3 August <https://tvrain.ru/teleshow/utro_na_dozhde/askold_zapashny-535224/> [accessed 10 January 2022]

'Na teatr "Sovremennik" pozhalovalis' v prokuraturu iz-za "oskorbleniia veteranov" v monologe Akhedzhakovoi'. 2021. *Dozhd'*, 22 July <https://tvrain.ru/news/na_teatr_sovremennik_pozhalovalis_v_prokuraturu_iz_za_oskorblenija_veteranov_v_monologe_ahedzhakovoj-534452/> [accessed 10 January 2022]

Navalny, Aleksei. 2021. 'Ia khochu skazat', dorogoi moi sud, chto vash korol' golyi', *Ekho Moskvy*, 29 April [accessed 10 January 2022]

'Obshchestvennyi sovet pri Minkul'te proverit repertuar teatrov na sootvetstvie strategii natsional'noi bezopasnosti Rossii'. 2021. *Meduza*, 3 August

'Otmena "Nureeva": tri versii sluchivshegosia'. 2017. *BBC Russian*, 10 July

Parkhomovskaia, Nika. 2017. '2008–2012: Teatral'nye innovatsii v deistvii', *Teatr*, 32: 16–20

'Peskov ob"iasnil raznitsu mezhdu tsenzuroi i goszakazom v iskusstve'. 2016. *Meduza*, 25 October

Pomerantsev, Peter. 2015. *Nothing Is True and Everything is Possible* (London: Faber and Faber)

'Rezhisser fil'ma o Chaikovskom vernet 30 mln gosudarstvu'. 2013. *BBC Russian*, 19 September

'Serebrennikov edinolichno vyplatil summu v 129 mln rub. po isku Minkul'tury'. 2021. *Interfaks*, 12 November

Serebrennikov, Kirill. 2021. Instagram post, @kirillserebrennikov, 9 February

Sergeev, Igor, Roman Romanovskii, Aleksandr Vavilov, and Aleksandr Avtonagov. 2017. 'Kak rukovoditeli gosudarstvennykh teatrov platiat gonorary sami sebe', *Transparency International Russia*, 23 October

Shestakova, Anna. 2012. 'Chto takoe politicheskii teatr: Opros izvestnykh moskovskikh rezhisserov i khudrukov', *Teatr*, 8

Shpileva, Olesia. 2016. 'Rezhisser Maksim Didenko v Voronezhe: "Ia ne takoi uzh novator"', *RIA Voronezh*, 27 September

Solomonov, Artur. 2014. 'Samotsenzura igraet vse bol'shuiu rol'', *New Times*, 16 December

Tokareva, Marina. 2021. '"Ia zdes' uderzhan!": Aleksei Agranovich stal khudozhestvennym rukovoditelem Gogol'-tsentra', *Novaia gazeta*, 10 February

Trustrum-Thomas, Alex. 2020. 'From Stalinist Socialist Realism to Putinist Capitalist Realism: Tracing Cultural Ideology in Contemporary Russian Theatre', in *New Drama in Russian: Performance, Politics and Protest in Russia, Ukraine and Belarus*, ed. by J.A.E. Curtis (London: Bloomsbury Academic), pp. 53–68

TV Rain. 2019. *Zaderzhanie Pavla Ustinova, za kotoroe prokuror prosit 6 let*, online video recording, YouTube, 12 September <https://www.youtube.com/watch?v=LbkUA2bQE7E> [accessed 10 January 2022]

World Justice Project Rule of Law Index 2020. 2020. *World Justice Project*, 11 March

Yaffa, Joshua. 2020. '"They will destroy you": in Putin's Russia, How Far Can an Artist Go?', *Guardian*, 17 January

'Za odin den' moskovskie vlasti smenili rukovodstvo trekh teatrov—"Gogol' Tsentra", "Sovremennika" i "Shkoly sovremennoi p"esy"'. 2022. *Meduza*, 30 June

Žižek, Slavoj. 2012. *Less Than Nothing: Hegel and the Shadow of Dialectical Materialism* (London: Verso)

3
Risings and Cancellings: Implicit Censorship on a Free Irish Stage

ANNE ETIENNE AND LISA FITZPATRICK

a Bishop can make himself felt without showing himself
—Sean O'Casey (1956)

In opposition to its British counterpart, Ireland could boast both a national theatre and a stage free from official censorship in the early twentieth century.[1] Even following Irish independence in 1922, theatre—unlike publications and cinema—remained untethered by any centralized censorship system. However, the absence of apparatus does not equate to the absence of censorship, and Joan FitzPatrick Dean's taxonomy of stage censorship shows that the most pernicious interventions proved all the more effective because they operated outside of the law (2004: 27–32) and were motivated indirectly by a staunch Catholic ethos, if not directly by a prominent Church representative (2001). In this sense, O'Casey's comment cited in the epigraph to this chapter is apposite—a bishop need not be visible to be influential. In the twenty-first century, the influence of 'a Bishop' on artistic freedom has waned, but recent public events in Irish theatre conjure the image of levers that have functioned as mechanisms of exclusion. This chapter asks how the contemporary repertoire is shaped by exploring case studies through the lens of censorship, thereby attempting to identify contemporary agents of censorship in the Republic of Ireland (RoI) and Northern Ireland. In this way, we examine the strategies of censorship in programming and funding decisions across the island as

> implicit operations of power that rule out in unspoken ways what will remain unspeakable. In such cases, no explicit regulation is needed in which to articulate this constraint. The operation of implicit and powerful forms of censorship suggests that the power of the censor is not exhausted by explicit state policy or regulation. (Butler 1997: 130)

Anne Etienne and Lisa Fitzpatrick, "Risings and Cancelling: Implicit Censorship on a Free Irish Stage" in: *Theatre Censorship in Contemporary Europe: Silence and Protest*. University of Exeter Press (2024). © Anne Etienne and Lisa Fitzpatrick. DOI: 10.47788/DUMT2156

The examples chosen for this investigation include the #WakingThe Feminists (#WTF) campaign that offered vocal criticism of the Abbey's 2016 Centenary programme, which was almost devoid of women artists.² In 2022, the struggles of the theatre companies Aisling Ghéar in Belfast and Corcadorca in Cork to maintain the Arts Council funding essential to the delivery of their artistic programmes also offer a springboard to consider the operation of cultural norms and judgements of artistic value on the work of theatre artists across the island. This chapter explores the impact of these largely invisible forces of implicit censorship in three aspects of theatre in Ireland: gender equality, language, and regional representation.

Women writers and the 'national tradition'

The invisible or unofficial censorship of work by women has a long and complex history in Irish theatre practice and Irish culture more broadly. As Linda Connolly points out, Irish studies as a discipline has often overlooked Irish women's studies and the cultural focus on compelling metanarratives and on nation-building has tended to sideline women, whose lives and whose writing may prioritize domestic and private life (2004: 148). Connolly is one of a number of practitioners and scholars who, from the late 1980s, investigated and challenged the exclusion of women writers from the national canon. Eavan Boland's reflection on her experience as a woman poet in the Irish national tradition exposes some of the difficulties encountered by Irish women artists. Boland describes the Irish national tradition as 'constraining' and points to 'poetic ethics' as 'often the concealed agenda of a poetic tradition' (1987: 148). There is a problem in recognizing women poets, she argues, because women in Irish art tend to be emblematic and difficult to disentangle from the figure of Woman-Nation; the dominance of the Woman-Nation makes actual women invisible. Accusing Irish poets of 'evading the real women of an actual past [...] whose silence their poetry should have broken', Boland asks how 'real women with their hungers, their angers, endured a long struggle and a terrible subsistence [...] How then did they re-emerge in Irish poetry as queens, as Muses [...] That could happen only if Irish poets complied with the wishful thinking of Irish nationalism' (155). The apotheosis of this phenomenon is, perhaps, the original *Field Day Anthology of Irish Writing* (1990), which infamously excluded almost all women writers in pursuit of a national metanarrative.

The criticisms of the *Field Day Anthology* are significant because they are one of the earliest concerted responses to the 'Bishop', that invisible apparatus of censorship shaping what should and should not be included in the national repertory. The activist response to the *Anthology* is significant for bringing to public attention a burgeoning academic dialogue about the place of women artists in Irish culture. That issue is beyond the scope of this chapter, but is addressed in an interdisciplinary body of criticism (Meaney 1991 and 2010, Innes 1993, Sullivan 2002, Ryan and Ward 2004 Sihra 2007 and 2018, Leeney 2010, Hill 2019, Fitzpatrick and Hill 2022)—and in theatre such as Glass House Productions' ground-breaking *There Are No Irish Women Playwrights* in 1992–93. Glass House created a festival of readings of twelve plays by women writers in response to a bookseller who said there were no women playwrights. While the situation had improved by 2015, many of the same problems have persisted. In 2004, celebrating its centenary year, the Abbey Theatre, Ireland's national theatre, stoked controversy with its programme which excluded women from the main stage, and included just a one-night performance of Augusta Gregory's short comedy *Spreading the News* and a production of Marina Carr's *Portia Coughlan* in the Peacock Theatre—the studio space. This excision of women's voices from the main stage was ironically heightened by the theatre's staging of W.B. Yeats and Lady Gregory's *Kathleen Ni Houlihan* (1902), a powerfully political play in which Ireland is personified first as an old woman, and finally as a queen, rehearsing all of the Irish nationalist tropes of the Woman-Nation. Viewing the controversy from this juncture, it appears that the board of the National Theatre and then artistic director Ben Barnes were unaware of the gendered nature of the programming. The absence of women playwrights from the list was made invisible by its seeming to be a fact of nature. While there was some public debate on the issue in 2004 and afterwards, it appears to have had little lasting impact, since the centenary of the rising that led to the foundation of the Irish Republic, in 2016, was celebrated with another male-dominated programme at the Abbey Theatre. By 2015, however, when that programme was unveiled, a new generation of theatre scholars had emerged (Cathy Leeney, Anna McMullan, Melissa Sihra), several of them specializing in women's writing and in feminist performance more widely; and the advent of social media offered a platform for rapid and effective communication across Ireland and overseas. The Waking the Feminists movement was born under the hashtag #WTF.

#WTF

#WTF was initially an angry online response to the publication of the 2016 Abbey Theatre programme, titled 'Waking the Nation', on 28 October 2015. Within two days, there was vigorous discussion on Twitter; on 30 October, the theatre director Maeve Stone tweeted a reference to 'Waking the Feminists' as an ironic comment on 'Waking the Nation', and this was adopted as the hashtag for the protests. Designer Lian Bell quickly emerged as a key spokeswoman, rallying actors, designers, writers, and directors to challenge the male-dominated theatre sector and to demand meaningful change in a short space of time. Video footage from the #WTF event at the Abbey on 12 November, approximately a week after the programme was published, captures both the anger of the demonstrators and the lived experience of women theatre artists in Ireland. Three young actors assert that this is 'a conversation we've all been having, in private, in smaller sectors trying to make smaller change, and now finally it's reached a very big public forum' (O'Brien and Geraghty 2015). Actor Donna Dent discloses that, in twenty-seven years, she has only ever been cast in one play by a woman, has never worked with a female director, and has worked with only a very few female designers. Yet, she notes, stage management and crew are often female. She asks:

> How much talent have we lost to sexism? Why were we offered a debate, why aren't we being offered an apology? Because if any institution, let alone a National Theatre, something that's funded by the public, was homophobic or racist they'd be shot down, but sexism is still considered a petty crime. (Cited in O'Brien and Geraghty 2015)

#WTF offered a place for women (and men) to express their anger and frustration with the unrepresentative nature of Irish theatre, and particularly of the highest-funded, the prestigious Abbey, the first state-funded national theatre in Europe. The speed of the reaction and the numbers of male and female artists who responded indicates a previously publicly unspoken dissatisfaction with the status quo. The scale of the protest made it impossible to dismiss it as feminist troublemaking or a fringe concern. On 12 November 2015, the main stage of the Abbey hosted a passionate discussion in front of a packed house of artists and theatre-makers, scholars and critics, just two weeks after the story broke; tickets sold out in seven minutes, and the speeches were broadcast to crowds gathered in the street outside the theatre (Barry 2015). The event seated the thirty leaders of the protest on the stage, and invited women to speak and share their experiences as professional artists. While the focus was firmly on gender, writers from minority ethnic communities, queer writers, and working-class writers pointed out the intersectional nature of the discrimination and its impact on a national theatre that should be representing the diversity of the nation. Responding quickly, the Arts Council of Ireland pledged action, and within months had commissioned a report, titled *Gender Counts*, into the gender breakdown in Irish theatre over the preceding decade. Published in 2017, the report analysed gender in Irish theatre from 2006 to 2015, identifying 1,155 productions, and 9,205 individual roles. It focused on the top ten funded theatre organizations in the state to discover that the four highest-funded organizations had the lowest female representation, including the two largest Dublin theatres, the Abbey and the Gate. Overall, there was an inverse relationship between the amount of funding, and female representation: 'The gap to achieving gender parity ranges between 41 and 8 percentage points in the roles studied' but was greatest in the most prestigious roles and in the most prominent organizations

(Donohue et al. 2017: 7). The report included practical measures to be taken to actively address and change the situation.

Complicating this picture, retrospectively, were allegations that emerged first on Twitter during the #MeToo debate in 2019, about the behaviour of the long-time artistic director of the Gate Theatre. The #MeToo movement in Ireland was not directly related to #WTF. However, the discussions and investigations that #MeToo prompted revealed further layers of bias as contributing factors to discrimination against women theatre-makers on the island. The allegations against the Gate Theatre were subsequently investigated and published in the national press, the director resigned and retired, and the board of the theatre was disbanded. The case revealed long-time sexual harassment of female staff at the theatre, as well as incidents of harassment and inappropriate behaviour towards young and early career artists such as Grace Dyas, who first broke the story. This theatre was one of those identified in *Gender Counts* as having the lowest level of gender equality in its programming and hiring. These revelations and others led to the Irish Theatre Institute report *Speak Up: A Call for Change*, supported by the Arts Council (2021), which establishes the responsibility of employers to have appropriate training and policies in place to deal with bullying and harassment, including methods of monitoring and reporting violations. Overall, #WTF and #MeToo have motivated public and private reflections on working methods in the arts sector, bullying and harassment, and the urgent need for dignity at work for the most precarious employees.

Given this background of under-representation and of bullying, how might the concept of censorship illuminate the complexity of the situation? Why was (and is) the work of women writers being invisibly censored, especially on the main stages? What complex ideological and market forces underlie the decisions being made by dramaturgs, producers, boards of directors, and artistic directors, as they curate their repertory?

Nationhood and citizenship: a 'concealed agenda'

As seen in the instance of the Abbey Theatre and #WTF, a form of invisible and semi-conscious or even unconscious censorship appears to mitigate against women's full participation and recognition in the Irish theatre. Existing scholarship on this subject points insistently to the problem of the iconic Woman-Nation: if women are subsumed silently into the iconography of nationhood then moving, thinking, speaking female characters disrupt that easy identification. The influence of the Roman Catholic Church and its social teaching over many decades, particularly after independence, insistently associates women with the private, domestic, family sphere; and the 'stultifying social conditions' and 'atmosphere of stringent censorship [of publications] and moral rectitude' only exacerbated this (Pilkington 2001: 147).

The Church's authority also guided social attitudes that limited what respectable living women as well as female dramatic characters could do and say. Theatre is a public art, dependent on being out of the house and collaborating with men as well as other women; it was not regarded, historically, as a respectable career for a woman. Recent scholarship on the reclaimed interwar playwright Teresa Deevy has uncovered evidence of her influence on other writers, and her active engagement with at least one aspiring playwright, as well as her extensive professional networks (Kealy 2020; McCarthy and Kealy 2022). This involvement in public life, beyond the fact of writing itself, illustrates the significant social pressure mitigating against women's full participation in an artistic life in the theatre. Given the state's insistence on women's place in the home, and the concomitant dearth of support services for married women seeking to continue their careers, few women writers would have been able to continue working in theatre after starting a family.[3] It is therefore unsurprising that both male and female playwrights tend to position their female characters in the private world, and to reinscribe rigid gender stereotypes of feminine passivity. This often has the effect of reducing women characters to minor parts—mothers, wives, sisters, girlfriends of the main, male characters.

The impact of these factors is further intensified by the founding ambitions of the Abbey Theatre: 'to put on stage the deeper thoughts and emotions of Ireland' (Gregory 1913), which is cultural nationalism in action. The role of the theatre has been insistently framed in academic and critical discourse as a 'mirror up to nation' (Murray 1997) and as a means of 'cultivating a people' (Pilkington 2001), with theatre interpreted both as commentary on the progress of the state, and responsible for representing the 'nation' to itself. This is not only a historical phenomenon: cultural commentator Fintan O'Toole has argued repeatedly that the arts must intervene to make sense of Irish society, including the traumas of the 2010 financial crash and the uncovering of the abuses in industrial schools and Magdalene Laundries that came to light at the turn of this century. The arts in Ireland are understood to have a social and political responsibility linked to their representation of, and response to, the enactment of citizenship in the state both in the legislature and in the social practices of the population. It is a theatrical tradition very much concerned with identity.

In itself, such demands on the arts do not exclude women, as evinced by the success of artists like Garry Hynes, Louise Lowe, Caitriona McLaughlin, Lynne Parker, and many eminent writers and actors. But citizenship is a gendered concept, and women's citizenship is more tenuous than men's, all the more so when the discourses of nationalism and decolonization dominate. As the literal mothers of the nation, women occupy a particular role in nationalist ideology, where they are most often positioned as wives and mothers giving birth to the next generation of citizens, and thus to be defended by the male citizen soldiers, rather than as active citizens in their own right. As Enloe argues, women's engagement in politics and their critiques of colonial rule may well lead them to critique gender relations in their own culture, yet the mythic originary culture is very often a touchstone for nationalist and decolonizing actions. Therefore, there is frequently a process of silencing debates which are important to women (Enloe 1990: 60)—such as the debate about the 1937 Constitution, when women's protests were ignored (Luddy 2005). Alongside women being sidelined as citizens, women's art has also been sidelined as art for and about women, not for and about the nation: part of the often 'concealed agenda of a poetic tradition' as Boland terms it.

This can result in conscious or unconscious bias on the part of commissioning houses, literary managers, and artistic directors when making quality-based decisions about work to produce. Writing by women may appear to be insufficiently engaged with the major questions of the day; when challenged about the proposed 2016 programme, the Abbey's artistic director Fiach Mac Conghail replied: 'sometimes the plays and ideas that we have commissioned by and about women don't work out […] Them the breaks' (Twitter, 29 October 2015). It is difficult to imagine the same wording being used in a comment on theatre by and about men. The comment suggests that the work is ontologically out of the mainstream: by being by and about women, it is understood to be focused on a particular and non-normative category of citizens. At the initial launch of the programme, Mac Conghail had spoken about naming his programme 'Waking the Nation', the aspiration to interrogate the legacy of 1916 and reflect on how the nation has fared in the century since: 'We turned to writers like Sean O'Casey, like Sean P. Summers, David Ireland, indeed like Phillip McMahon to help us interrogate that' (2018). It is extraordinary but not surprising that Mac Conghail and his board assumed that a satisfying interrogation of the nation over a century could be achieved without women's voices, or indeed the voices of an increasingly diverse population.

Anecdotally, critics, authors, and theatre-makers have suggested that literary boards and artistic directors tend to assume that male characters are understood to interest everyone, while female characters are only of interest to women. Caroline Williams of Glasshouse Productions responds to an *Irish Times* review from 1991 that dismissed one of the company's shows as 'one for the Sisters' (Williams et al. 2001). And as Boland argues, men's writing about family and home life is interpreted metaphorically in the light of nationhood, while women's deployment of similar tropes is taken literally. If female characters in the dominant dramatic works are largely emblematic, or interpreted as such, then work that disrupts such interpretations may be judged as less good. Work by women—even when it is performed—is less likely to be remounted, published, anthologized, making it less available to the scholars, students, and theatre practitioners who would ensure its afterlife on stage in Ireland and internationally.

In response to #WTF, Fiach Mac Conghail attended the event on 12 November 2015 and acknowledged to the audience that the movement 'has presented a professional challenge to me as a programmer and has made me question the filters and factors that influence my decision making' (cited in Kelleher 2015). This was a retreat from his unfortunate first response, when he tweeted 'I don't and haven't programmed plays on a gender basis' (Kelleher 2015). His admission that the protests had caused him to reflect is a useful illustration of the invisibility of the gender imbalance on the Abbey's stage. When he took on the post of artistic director, Mac Conghail pledged to introduce affirmative action; but in fact during his tenure the number of Abbey productions of plays by women fell from 14% to 12.3%, against a national average of 20%. During Mac Conghail's tenure, a number of women playwrights turned their focus to the independent sector (Sonya Kelly, Deirdre Kinahan), or overseas (Stella Feehily, Nancy Harris, Ursula Rani Sarma), while long-established playwrights like Augusta Gregory and Teresa Deevy were overlooked, and Elaine Murphy's comedy *Shush* was explicitly marketed as a 'girls' night out' rather than a play that might speak to the contemporary nation. However, Mac Conghail can be credited for examining his preconceptions, and he is one of a number of artistic directors who were prompted to reflect upon their unconscious bias by the #WTF movement.

By late 2015, Mac Conghail had signalled his intention to resign the following year. The Abbey Theatre hired its new artistic directors from overseas—Neil Murray and Graham McLaren (National Theatre of Scotland)—and established a clearer set of guidelines to address equality and diversity on the stage.

The Abbey: new model, new protest

The new directors envisaged the national theatre as challenging 'assumptions around the words "national", "theatre" and "Ireland"', a driving concept aimed at redefining the workings of the Abbey and maybe our conception of it' (Abbey Theatre 2015).[4] Coming from the itinerant model of the National Theatre of Scotland and in the wake of the #WTF movement, their vision amounted to a promise for a national stage with a more inclusive programme that addresses issues of gender equality and of regional access to the theatre's productions.[5]

By 2019, a protest elicited an alternative picture of the changes effected at the Abbey: on 7 January, 312 actors and theatre-makers sent an open letter to Josepha Madigan (the Minister for Culture, Heritage and the Gaeltacht), the Arts Council, the board of the Abbey Theatre, and the *Irish Times*, expressing concern about the direction of the national theatre and the economic consequences of its break with the Irish literary canon (see O'Toole 2019). In the following weeks, more than 400 signatories put their names to the letter. That the artists chose to complain directly to the government at the same time as publicly via the *Irish Times* is reminiscent of the campaign led by George Bernard Shaw and his fellow writers against the Lord Chamberlain in 1907. However, they bypassed dialogue with the directors because their complaint concerned their diminishing employment and pay rates after two years of the new Abbey management, which prompts our examination of economic factors as forces apt to affect artistic programming.

At the root of the protest lies Murray and McLaren's increasing use of the Abbey as a receiving rather than a producing venue, which had dire financial repercussions for 'Ireland-based' actors:

> The changing artistic model of producing fewer in-house productions and presenting or co-presenting more has caused devastation amongst our ranks. Although the management's strategy of offering diversity to their own audiences is admirable in theory, it offers up several problems in practice. The National Theatre reducing its own production output means less diversity, and reduced employment, not more. There will not have been an Ireland-based actor in an Abbey Theatre production on an Abbey stage since *Jimmy's Hall* ended on 8 September 2018 until *The Country Girls* opens on 23 February 2019. That is five and a half months without an Ireland-based actor directly employed by the Abbey. (Abbey Theatre 2019b: 10)

The directors may well have translated their understanding of a contemporary, diverse Ireland into staging more recent plays, by hitherto shunned playwrights, working with new companies, and promoting gender equality. However, their programming decisions also responded to a financial deficit of €1.4 million inherited from previous seasons—a controversial amount later clarified by the board of the Abbey (Falvey 2019b): 'These losses were incurred by the programming model that the signatories' letter appears to advocate—a predominance of large-scale Abbey Theatre self-produced shows with little access for smaller independent companies and artists' (Falvey 2019a). In adopting a different model—which diminished the proportion of in-house shows in favour of co-presentations and associations—the Abbey initiated less onerous collaborations with (also funded) Irish artists, planned for reruns after the first year, and invited international productions that had proven box-office successes.[6] As a result, the letter's signatories acknowledged that, after two years of Murray and McLaren's regime, 'the institution [was] financially buoyant—and due congratulations for this' while protesting pay rates (Abbey Theatre 2019b: 10).

In terms of core funding, the Abbey receives the lion's share in Arts Council subsidies: from €6.1 million in 2017 to €7.5 million in 2022— these figures represent roughly 10% of the annual Arts Council budget, and 50% of the entire drama budget (Joint Committee 2019). Such substantial financial support befits the national theatre, but comes with conditions attached. In fact, Murray and McLaren's appointment and vision for the Abbey are arguably direct responses to the review commissioned by the Arts Council in 2014:

> It recommended a re-prioritisation of the Theatre's activities, to address a lack of touring and of community and education work, the under-involvement of visiting companies, and the under-utilisation of the Peacock Theatre as a space for artistic experimentation.
>
> In the period since, the Abbey has implemented the review's recommendations. In July 2015, the Board appointed Neil Murray and Graham McLaren as its Co-Directors, effective from July 2016, with ownership of the programme from January 2017. They were given a clear mandate to increase the activity levels of the Abbey, while maintaining financial sustainability. (Abbey Theatre 2019a: 2)

It seems unsurprising that 'he who pays the piper can have a very big influence on the tune' (Peter Hall cited in Thomas et al. 2007: 240) and, arguably, the stakes are higher in the case of the Abbey as a symbol of the nation. Yet the initial mission of the Arts Councils is to allocate public money to support artists rather than to influence programming decisions, or even to withhold funding. Such a punitive course had been taken in England in 1968 during the build-up to the private performance of Edward Bond's *Early Morning* at the Royal Court, which placed the Arts Council's action in the territory of censorship. More recently, in 1999, the Arts Council of Northern Ireland (ACNI) had withheld funding for DubbelJoint's production of *Forced Upon Us*, co-written by Christine Poland and Brenda Murphy (a former IRA prisoner), after making the unprecedented demand to read three drafts of the script—a procedure more watchful than even the Lord Chamberlain implemented in England until 1968. The ACNI claimed that their decision was based on artistic merit. However, the topic of the play (a nationalist perspective on the Royal Ulster Constabulary), and the fact that it provoked parliamentary questions about 'freedom of expression and political vetting of the arts' (McNamara 1999), leave little doubt that, in that instance, the ACNI acted beyond the remit of its function, as both drama expert and political censor, by axing the play's funding. The company folded a few years later.

In December 2022, Corcadorca closed its doors in Cork; in Belfast, Aisling Ghéar lost its annual funding in June 2022, appealed the decision unsuccessfully, and launched a judicial review. While these companies depend on different national budgets, they share in common not only the loss of annual funding but also their nomination in two categories of the Irish Theatre Awards in February 2023: whatever motivated the decision-making of the funding bodies, it appears unlikely to be caused by the artistic merits of the companies. On what grounds, then, does the Arts Council become a mechanism of exclusion rather than support?

Aisling Ghéar

From the perspective of the Arts Council, the first stumbling block revolves around the budget allocated to the arts, and comparatively Northern Ireland is the pauper, at only £5.44 per capita in 2022 against £10.35 in Wales (its closest comparator), and £25.90 in RoI. The situation has worsened because 'Government investment in the Arts has fallen by 30% in cash terms in the last decade from £14.1m to £9.5m', putting additional pressure on lottery revenue to complement—to the tune of one-third of the total budget—funding provided by the Exchequer (ACNI 2021: 4). In practice, this means that the ACNI has no choice but to implement austerity and such measures partly explain the relentless decrease in Aisling Ghéar's annual funding from £77,229 in 2013 to £62,818 in 2021–22.[7] However, at the same time, other organizations have seen their subsidies rise, signalling its priorities.[8]

Growing out of the Irish-language community in West Belfast, Aisling Ghéar was established in 1997 by author Gearóid Ó Caireilláin; artistic director Bríd Ó Gallchóir joined in 1998. Aisling Ghéar is the only Irish-speaking professional theatre company in Northern Ireland, holding as such a unique role in developing theatre in Irish and sustaining the Irish-language community and culture. Over twenty-five years, they produced and toured plays—including Brian Friel's *Translations* in a bilingual version, but also Marie Jones, Samuel Beckett, and Dario Fo in Irish—as well as children's shows and site-specific work.

In 2022, the ACNI failed Aisling Ghéar's application on two criteria: 'artistic excellence and creative innovation' and 'organisational capacity and governance'. Regarding the first criterion, *Minimal Human Contact*, written by Naoise Ó Caireilláin, had been part of Aisling Ghéar's Annual Funding Programme (AFP) bids two years in a row; what was seen by the ACNI as lacking creative innovation was justified by the fact that in 2020–21, the Covid-19 pandemic had closed the doors of all theatres and, in 2021–22, social distancing had dictated half-capacity in venues.[9] Regarding the second criterion, the company was denied funding because the minutes of the board meetings had not been submitted. As Bríd Ó Gallchóir explained, the production had to be postponed until 2022 because the company would be able to fill Smock Alley Theatre in Dublin and Cultúrlann in Belfast and to expect 100% box office returns due to the international popularity of Naoise Ó Caireilláin—aka Móglaí Bap of the hip-hop band Kneecap: 'the actual costs of the show are banking on box office, which often wouldn't be the case' (Ó Gallchóir 2022). The show's success and critical recognition vindicated the company's artistic excellence and creative innovation. In addition, the governance issue could have been resolved by a quick reminder, as tends to be the case with long-established companies and drama officers. In the end, Aisling Ghéar only received a 'soft landing' of £15,704 from AFP and £32,110 from project funding, a strand that the ACNI encouraged for future support and which, ironically, was awarded for *Minimal Human Contact* (Ó Gallchóir 2022).

Critics have described drama in Irish as precarious and underground (O'Leary 2017, Coilféir 2018, Huddleson 2023), a status amplified by the scarcity of theatre companies. In Dublin, Amharclann de hÍde, created in 1992, ceased operations in 2001; Aisteoirí Bulfin, an amateur group running since 1967, worked sporadically and has not produced a show since 2015. With Aisling Ghéar, the only professional Irish-language company remaining in Ireland is Fíbín, in the Gaeltacht. As 'the' Irish-language theatre company in the north of Ireland, Aisling Ghéar fulfils a pivotal function in bridging 'a recognised gap in the Irish language sector [:] the need to support individual artists working through the medium of Irish'—a commitment to promote Irish included in the Good Friday Agreement (Department for Communities 2022: 80). This concern is arguably reflected in the ACNI's inclusive vision of 'improving relationships between and within communities' and 'ensuring that everyone living here— regardless of social, economic, community or ethnic background—has the opportunity to access and engage fully with the Arts' (ACNI 2021: 6). And yet, by removing annual funding, the ACNI renders the company's standing more precarious and hinders audience engagement with Irish-language culture. But whose engagement? In the Republican newspaper *An Phoblacht*, Pam Brighton, co-founder of DubbelJoint, had already suggested in 1999 that the stark disparity in funding

> has an effect on the access to drama for people living in the working class areas of Nationalist West Belfast. To give such an excessive increase in funds to the Ulster Orchestra which most working class people will find boring demonstrates the elitist mentality of those Unionists and Castle Catholics who are attempting to sidestep the issues thrown up by the last thirty years. (Cited in Kelly 1999)

Brighton's point remains valid in terms of audience class division. In her study of *Forced Upon Us*, Helen Freshwater approaches the position of the Arts Councils in terms of a conflict of values: 'The funding body will necessarily experience a split between responsibility to the audience that receives the end product and the wider community whose tax contributions pay for the grants' (2009: 133).

It is hazardous and unfair to assign a political agenda to the ACNI's decision. On the one hand, the Irish government has identified potentially 'systemic' funding inequalities 'affecting [...] indigenous language/culture communities (Irish and Ulster-Scots)' as the Department of Communities expressed its support for more funding to be committed to culture in Irish (Department for Communities 2021). In that light, the ACNI's resolve to cut the core funding of a small theatre structure is tantamount to excluding a whole community from access to contemporary playwriting in Irish. In England, the governmental recognition of the country's multi-ethnic make-up and its concomitant inequalities had led the Arts Council to draft positive discrimination criteria about race into its funding applications. The tick-boxing exercise functioned as both an eye-opener and a funding proviso, making it clear that, in the 2000s, 'the arts should be instrumental in supporting public policy' (Freshwater 2009: 133). On the other hand, the ACNI's priorities do not address one particular department so that, according to Ó Gallchóir, its decisions are its own, grounded on the claim that it is apolitical. Maybe, like the Lord Chamberlain's readers who licensed *Fin de partie* before censoring *Endgame*, the ACNI's adverse ruling comes down to an individual blunder. After all, how else could they account for their announcement that the 'AFP of £13,012,490 will support the core and programming costs of those organizations who are *central* to the arts infrastructure in Northern Ireland today' (ACNI 2022, my emphasis) and reject the company's application five months before the passing of the much-awaited Identity and Language (Northern Ireland) Act 2022?

Corcadorca

One of the rare theatre companies to continue to receive annual funding outside Dublin, Corcadorca was founded in 1991 by artistic director Pat Kiernan to foster new Irish writing and explore the international canon in site-responsive productions. Like most companies at the time, Corcadorca initially developed with and around the work of a playwright—here, Enda Walsh—premiering *The Ginger Ale Boy* (1995) and *Misterman* (1999), and reaching national and international recognition with the touring of *Disco Pigs* (1996–98).

In the Republic of Ireland, the Celtic Tiger (referring to Ireland's exceptional economic growth from the 1990s to the mid-2000s) saw total state funding for the arts multiply between 1994 and 2008, the Arts Council's budget increasing from £13.3m (€16.5m) to €82m. Figures decreased with the recession but the closure of Corcadorca Theatre Company in 2022 concludes a year when the Arts Council retained a €130m provision. After thirty-one years of activity, Pat Kiernan bowed out: with Corcadorca's artistic programme growing against diminishing subsidies, he felt unable to apply for further funding. His is not a rare predicament. Many of the structures which started to receive annual funding in the 1990s ceased operation in the 2000s—for example, Storytellers and Calypso Productions in Dublin, Red Kettle in Waterford, Meridian in Cork, Island Theatre Company in Limerick, Bickerstaffe in Kilkenny, and Galloglass in Clonmel. But if we draw a funding map of Ireland, Blue Raincoat in Sligo and Druid in Galway remain the only theatre companies outside of Dublin to be awarded annual funding, which gives a regrettable impression that artistic development anywhere else does not merit a yearly programming budget. With the demise of Corcadorca, Cork lost in one sweep its only company and a hub that nurtured local and regional artists, thereby sustaining its theatrical ecosystem.[10]

In his foreword to the extensive Theatre Review carried out in 1995, the Chairman of the Arts Council exposed the funding dilemma at play when confronted with the flurry of new companies, plays, and theatre projects: 'to cut and concentrate, or dripfeed and starve' (Benson 1995). In monetary terms, the 2022 figures confirm the concentration on the Abbey, the Gate, Druid, and the Dublin Theatre Festival. The Arts Council has been loath to cut subsidies outright, even though, following the 1995 review, it completed 'the regrading of the 32 production companies receiving annual support'—a collapse which aimed to ensure that the money went to the artists rather than inflated administrative costs (de Valera 1998; see Meaney 1999). The successive plans rather exhibit a tendency to 'dripfeed' exacerbated by the recession and, from the 2010s, implemented by its privileging project funding over annual funding.

Corcadorca benefited for the first time in 1995 from a 'grant to organization', a 'project grant', and the now defunct Playwrights' Commission scheme.[11] From then on, their core annual funding steadily increased to an apex of €240,000 in 2008, dipped to €150,000 during the recession, and regained a tentative momentum in 2016. Those figures alone fail to give an adequate picture that would explain how the company eventually starved, as they would need to be evaluated against the budget requested by the company to sustain its running and production costs. In 2018, for instance, the Arts Council's annual funding of €180,000 showed a €10,000 decrease from the previous year and fell €30,000 short of the requested amount;[12] it also came with the warning shot that alternative funding streams may be best suited—this subtle push towards project funding was experienced by a number of companies.

Despite Corcadorca's track record, in 2018, the company's artistic standards and the strategic sustainability of its model ranked disappointingly when scored against the priorities set out in *Making Great Art Work*, the Arts Council strategy for 2016–25—a document informed by the Department of Arts' 'Value for Money and Policy Review of the Arts Council'. In its introduction, the strategy identifies the artist and public engagement as driving priorities (Arts Council 2015: 14). In examining Corcadorca's legacy in these areas, one may ponder that the vision of the strategy is not only to fund the arts but also to '[steer] their development'—a term that may capture positive connotations (such as encouragement of diversity) but hardly denotes neutrality (10).

Over the years, Corcadorca's critical and commercial appreciation varied yet, in 2018, the company received seven nominations in the Theatre Awards. Beyond such measures of artistic value, a major activity of Corcadorca was geared towards the artists: it launched the careers of playwrights Enda Walsh and Ray Scannell, actors Cillian Murphy and Eileen Walsh, and collaborated with new generations of artists such as Kevin Barry, Pat McCabe, Ailís Ní Ríain, and Éadaoin O'Donoghue. This impetus pertained to the establishment in 2011 of its Theatre Development Centre: located in the Triskel Arts Centre, the black box studio hosted a year-long programme of weekly residencies, which concluded every Friday with a public and free presentation of work-in-progress. The scheme was soon complemented by a mini-festival, SHOW, where sector professionals and audiences could sample the most honed productions.

Audience engagement encompasses quantitative measurement as well as societal considerations (spatial and demographic, inclusive of diversity). A wider spatial audience base can be achieved through touring, and it was therefore an expectation of the Arts Council for regional companies to achieve a national or international impact. However, after *Disco Pigs* (1996–98), Corcadorca toured very little: in 2016, their midsummer show *Request Programme* toured to the festivals of Galway, Kilkenny, and Dublin; in 2022, they brought Enda Walsh's *The Same* to the Irish Arts Centre in New York. For one, Kiernan preferred to expand his Cork audience, an audience that grew with the company—though not exponentially. Nonetheless, the primary concern for reaching audiences, and in particular audiences that would stay away from theatre venues (for social or geographic reasons), was a deciding object in creating a company that pioneered site-responsive theatre in the RoI: to bring drama to the audience and explore how the words resonate throughout the city. In 2020, rather than finding digital solutions to the restrictions implemented in response to the Covid-19 pandemic, their travelling show *Contact* offered performances to various socially distanced communities across the city. Furthermore, the site-responsive nature of their work often posed an inherent problem to touring, even more so as Kiernan's ambition lay in big theatre events: for instance, the run of *The Merchant of Venice*, a promenade production that—with the generous endowment of Cork European Capital of Culture—took thousands of spectators through the city in 2005.

The paradox may be articulated in the tension between the artistic vision and the expectations of the funding body: be ambitious—more productions, bigger audiences—but with less funding. This 'dripfeed' effect was experienced during their last promenade performance, Kevin Barry's adaptation of *Guests of the Nation*, in June 2022, when the production budget had dried up and props had to be purchased out-of-pocket by the creative team. In the end, as Kiernan contends, 'Simply we didn't have the resources to meet the demand to implement the strategies and policies of funding requirements' (Leland 2022). It is striking that the statement makes no reference to creative considerations: eventually the Arts Council's assessment that the company's working model (one artistic director and one manager) would not prove sustainable sounds like a self-fashioned prophecy, as the human resources were starved by the same administrative and goal-related demands required from much bigger organizations. Given its unique position within the theatre ecosystem in Cork, and by extension in Ireland, Corcadorca's closure leaves a 'devastating hole' that raises questions regarding the application of the Arts Council's artist- and audience-led engagement plan.

The operation of a largely unconscious 'concealed agenda' and its impact on women theatre-makers is an example of the workings of implicit censorship which marginalizes voices and creative works that disrupt settled assumptions and metanarratives. But addressing the issue requires more than adding more women's voices to the repertory. An annual programme has a limited amount of space, so the entire selection process must be examined if it is to reflect more closely the composition of the audience base and, in the case of the national theatre, the composition of the nation. This means revising assumptions about the audience's interests, including the assumption that men's writing is better and more interesting than women's, or that only people of colour will want to watch plays about visible minority communities, both of which are based on limited readings of artistic work. It also means revising assumptions about what makes a play or a performance 'good', and worth staging. What criteria are used to select O'Casey over Deevy, Summers over Kinahan, or Ireland over Gregg? This is not a question that criticizes the work of those male writers, but rather it seeks to critique a process of selection that is not transparent, and which appears to be significantly in thrall to an outdated conception of nationhood and citizenship as primarily masculine.

While the Abbey has the capacity to weather public controversies and the Arts Council's admonishment, other professional companies lack the infrastructure to draft policies and seek exterior financial sources that the Arts Council now insists upon as evidence that they do merit annual funding: this recalls the Thatcherite entrepreneurial approach to the arts. Having historically thrived, the artistic impact of Aisling Ghéar and Corcadorca has been thwarted rather than supported by the funding bodies. In amending the theatrical ecosystem, the Arts Council bodies perform an implicit censorship 'that works precisely through its illegibility', presiding over what will be shown allegedly on artistic merit (Butler 1997: 134). This becomes all the more suspicious when companies with a record of national and international regard fail on that score and when they have been filling a gap in the sector—in theatre in Irish, and in theatre in the south of Ireland. The Arts Councils work behind the scenes, like the infamous bishop, holding the power to silence not specific productions, but whole theatre companies. While the #WTF rising against the Abbey shed light on the systemic exclusion of women artists, the doors of small structures close in a deafening silence.

Notes

1. For further reading on theatre censorship from the turn of the twentieth century to the 1960s, see FitzPatrick Dean (2001 and 2004), McDiarmid (2005: 87–122), Arrington (2010), and Houlihan (2021: 125–62).
2. The slogan 'Oestrogen Rising' was visible on some placards, thus connecting the feminist protest to the Easter Rising.
3. The added complications of being unable to access family planning services into the 1980s, combined with a cultural preference for larger families, obviously heighten difficulties for women combining motherhood and work outside the home.
4. Murray and McLaren's motivation might best be expressed in the questions they raised about the Abbey in an interview for the talks series 'First Up': 'Is there a different way to do things at the Abbey? Is the Abbey ready for change? Does the Abbey want to change? [...] But also what was absent? Where were the women? What happened to that part of the story? How do we make that the new story? How do we reflect an Ireland that looks completely different to the Abbey's glory days' ('First Act' 2017).
5. The Abbey Theatre's Annual Review 2017 indicates attention to the issue of gender in relation to both the authoring and directing of productions.
6. The Abbey's Annual Reviews 2017 and 2018 show the board's satisfaction at the programme, which contained a number of shows previously presented in other Irish or international venues (the first of which, Walsh's *Arlington*, had premiered in 2016 at the Galway International Arts Festival): 'Abbey Theatre audiences responded very positively to the 2018 programme, and this was reflected in the continuing growth in the numbers attending' (Abbey Theatre 2018: 5).
7. Those figures were obtained on 18 January 2023 following an email query to the ACNI.
8. The AFP for the Lyric Theatre and the Ulster Orchestra rose from £970,000 to £1m, and from £1,780,000 to £2m, respectively.
9. This point on capacity was published in August 2021 in the Taskforce report: 'The reality is that a social distancing requirement, even at one metre, makes it is [sic] highly likely that many cultural venues and activities will be unviable' (Department for Communities 2021: 19).
10. This assertion needs nuancing: Graffiti is a long-established youth theatre company, and Brokencrow has been operating from three locations (Cork, Waterford, and Dublin) where its members reside.
11. The appellation of the core annual funding strand was adjusted as new AC plans were drawn up, ranging from 'grant to organization', and finally 'strategic funding'. Similarly, we have used the generic term 'project funding' to differentiate from core annual funding, but the current term used by the Arts Council is 'Arts grants'
12. Some figures were obtained from the published archives of the AC; others were accessed directly by Anne Etienne in her capacity as board member of Corcadorca Theatre Company. The Tesselate mentoring scheme, led by Corcadorca in collaboration with the Everyman Theatre and the Cork Midsummer Festival, was initially funded under the category of theatre resource-sharing support. In 2018, its cost was earmarked within the company strategic funding, which accounts for the actual decrease in funding.

References

Abbey Theatre. 2015. 'Future Directors of the Abbey Theatre Appointed', n.d.
—— 2018. *Annual Review 2018*
—— 2019a. 'DRAFT 2. Statement from the Abbey Theatre to the Joint Oireachtas Committee on Culture, Heritage and the Gaeltacht', 30 January, 1–6
—— 2019b. 'A Report by the Abbey Theatre to the Minister for Culture, Heritage, and the Gaeltacht, in Response to the Issues Raised in the Open Letter of 7 January 2019', n.d., Appendix 2: 10–12
ACNI (Arts Council of Northern Ireland). 2021. 'Response to the NI Executive, Consultation on the 2021–22 Draft Budget', 25 February
—— 2022. 'Arts Council of Northern Ireland Announces Annual Funding Programme Awards for 2022–23', 1 July
Arrington, Lauren. 2010. *W.B. Yeats, the Abbey Theatre, Censorship, and the Irish State* (Oxford: Oxford University Press)
Arts Council. 2015. *Making Great Art Work*, Arts Council Strategy (2016–25)
Barry, Aoife. 2015. 'Fury, Apologies, and Calls for Respect as Feminists Shake the Irish Theatre World', *The Journal*, 12 November
Benson, Ciarán. 1995. *Arts Council Theatre Review 1995–1996*
Boland, Eavan. 1987. 'The Woman Poet in a National Tradition', *Studies: An Irish Quarterly Review*, 76.302: 148–58
Butler, Judith. 1997. *Excitable Speech: A Politics of the Performative* (London and New York: Routledge)
Coilféir, Máirtín. 2018. 'Contemporary Theatre in the Irish Language', in *The Palgrave Handbook of Contemporary Irish Theatre and Performance*, ed. by E. Jordan and E. Weitz (London: Palgrave), pp. 135–49
Connolly, Linda. 2004. 'The Limits of "Irish Studies": Historicism, Culturalism, Paternalism', *Irish Studies Review*, 12.2: 139–62
de Valera, Síle. 1998. 'Funding of An Chomhairle Ealaíon: Motion'. *Seanad Debates*, Houses of the Oireachtas, vol. 154, no. 6, 18 February
Department for Communities. 2021. 'The Art of Recovery—Survive: Stabilise: Strengthen', *Report of the Culture, Arts, and Heritage Recovery Taskforce*, 9 August
—— 2022. 'Recommendations for an Irish Language Strategy', *Report of the Expert Advisory Panel*, February
Donohue, Brenda, et al. 2017. *Gender Counts: An Analysis of Gender in Irish Theatre 2006–2016* (Dublin: Arts Council / An Chomhairle Ealaion)
Enloe, Cynthia. 1990. *Bananas, Beaches and Bases: Making Feminist Sense of International Politics* (Berkeley: University of California Press)
Falvey, Deirdre. 2019a. 'Abbey Theatre Uproar: 300 Actors and Directors Complain to Minister', *Irish Times*, 7 January
—— 2019b. 'Abbey Controversy: Theatre to Review Lower Pay on Productions', *Irish Times*, 11 January
Field Day Anthology of Irish Writing. 1990. Edited by Seamus Deane. Derry: Field Day Publications
'First Act: Neil Murray and Graham McLaren Directors Abbey Theatre'. 2017. *Totally Dublin*, 3 April
Fitzpatrick, Lisa, and Shonagh Hill. 2022. *Plays by Women in Ireland 1926–1933: Feminist Theatres of Freedom and Resistance* (London: Methuen Drama)

FitzPatrick Dean, Joan. 2001. 'Irish Stage Censorship in the 1950s', *Theatre Survey*, 42.2: 137–64. https://doi.org/10.1017/S0040557401000072

——— 2004. *Riot and Great Anger: Stage Censorship in Twentieth-Century Ireland* (Madison: University of Wisconsin Press)

Freshwater, Helen. 2009. *Theatre Censorship in Britain* (London: Palgrave Macmillan)

Gregory, Augusta. 1913. *Our Irish Theatre* (New York: G.P. Putnam's Sons)

Hill, Shonagh. 2019. *Women and Embodied Mythmaking in Irish Theatre* (Cambridge: Cambridge University Press)

Houlihan, Barry. 2021. *Theatre and Archival Memory: Irish Drama and Marginalised Histories 1951–1977* (London: Palgrave Macmillan)

Huddleson, Richard. 2023. 'Brave New Worlds? COVID-19 and Irish-Language Theatre Produced under Lockdown in Northern Ireland', *Theatre Research International*, 48.1: 67–81. https://doi.org/10.1017/S0307883322000414

Innes, Catherine L. 1993. *Woman and Nation in Irish Literature and Society* (New York: Harvester Wheatsheaf)

Joint Committee on Culture, Heritage and the Gaeltacht díospóireacht. 2019. 'Abbey Theatre: Discussion', Houses of the Oireachtas, 30 January

Kealy, Una. 2020. '"Resisting Power and Direction": *The King of Spain's Daughter* by Teresa Deevy as a Feminist Call to Action', *Estudios Irlandeses*, 15: 178–92. https://doi.org/10.24162/EI2020-9406

Kelleher, Patrick. 2015. 'Waking the Feminists: Irish Theatre's Equality Debate', *University Observer*, 26 November

Kelly, Ned. 1999. 'Arts Council in Funding Bias Row', *An Phoblacht*, 15 February

Leeney, Catherine. 2010. *Irish Women Playwrights 1900–1939: Gender and Violence on Stage* (New York: Peter Lang)

Leland, Mary. 2022. 'Corcadorca, a Pioneer of Irish Theatre, Loses Its Uphill Struggle', *Irish Times*, 23 November

Luddy, Maria. 2005. 'A "Sinister and Retrogressive" Proposal: Irish Women's Opposition to the 1937 Draft Constitution', *Transactions of the Royal Historical Society*, 15: 175–95. https://doi.org/10.1017/S0080440105000307

Mac Conghail, Fiach. 2015. Twitter post, 29 October

———2018. *RTE Radio 1 News*, 28 October

McCarthy, Kate, and Una Kealy. 2022. 'Writing from the Margins: Reframing Teresa Deevy's Archive and Her Correspondence with James Cheasty, c. 1952–1962', *Irish University Review*, 52.2: 322–40. https://doi.org/10.3366/iur.2022.0570

McDiarmid, Lucy. 2005. *The Irish Art of Controversy* (Ithaca and London: Cornell University Press). https://doi.org/10.7591/9781501728693

McNamara, Kevin. 1999. 'Forced Upon Us', *Hansard*, House of Commons, vol. 337, col. 41, 1 November

Meaney, Gerardine. 1991. *Sex and Nation: Women in Irish Culture* (Cork: Attic Press)

——— 2010. *Gender, Ireland, and Cultural Change* (New York and London: Routledge)

Meaney, Helen. 1999. 'Arts Report Highlights Need for Change in Funding', *Irish Times*, 30 January

Murray, Christopher. 1997. *Twentieth Century Irish Drama: Mirror up to Nation* (Manchester: Manchester University Press)

O'Brien, Bryan, and Paula Geraghty. 2015. 'Waking the Feminist Event Takes Over the Abbey Theatre', *Irish Times*, 12 November
O'Casey, Sean. 1956 (1994). 'Bonfire under a Black Sun', in *The Green Crow* (London: Virgin)
Ó Gallchóir, Bríd. 2022. Interview with Anne Etienne, 5 August
O'Leary, Philip. 2017. *An Underground Theatre: Major Playwrights in the Irish Language 1930–80* (Dublin: UCD Press)
O'Toole, Fintan. 2019. 'If the National Theatre Is Not World Class or Keen on Ireland's Dramatic Canon, What Is It For?', *Irish Times*, 15 June
Pilkington, Lionel. 2001. *Theatre and the State in Twentieth-Century Ireland: Cultivating the People* (London and New York: Routledge). https://doi.org/10.4324/9780203207628
Ryan, Louise, and Margaret Ward. 2004. *Irish Women and Nationalism: Soldiers, New Women, and Wicked Hags* (Dublin: Irish Academic Press)
Sihra, Melissa (ed.). 2007. *Women in Irish Drama: A Century of Authorship and Representation* (London: Palgrave Macmillan). https://doi.org/10.1057/9780230801455
Sihra, Melissa. 2018. *Marina Carr: Pastures of the Unknown* (Cham: Palgrave Macmillan). https://doi.org/10.1007/978-3-319-98331-8
Sullivan, Moynagh. 2002. 'I Am, Therefore I'm Not (Woman)', *International Journal of English Studies*, 2.2: 123–34. https://doi.org/10.6018/ijes
Thomas, David, David Carlton, and Anne Etienne. 2007. *Theatre Censorship: From Walpole to Wilson* (Oxford: Oxford University Press). https://doi.org/10.1093/acprof:oso/9780199260287.001.0001
Williams, Caroline, Katy Hayes, Sian Quill, and Clare Dowling. 2001. 'People in Glasshouses: An Anecdotal History of an Independent Theatre Company', in *Druids, Dudes and Beauty Queens*, ed. by Dermot Bolger (Dublin: New Island Books), pp. 132–47

Part 2

Ghosts of the Past

Intervention 2

Censorship in Hungary: Comedy, Silence, and Subversion

ANDREA TOMPA

During the 2022 parliamentary election campaign in Hungary, each party was given exactly five minutes in the public media to present its programme (this practice was introduced in 2018). The Hungarian Two-Tailed Dog Party—a satirical opposition group which, with only 126,000 votes, failed to gain parliamentary seats—used its five minutes to deliver a satirical stand-up comedy performance ('Választás' 2022). In this sketch, Bruti—a stand-up comedian, musician, and supporter of the party—makes a series of ironic references to the current political climate during a supposed phone conversation with his wife. He mentions being in the television studio which 'we [i.e. the party] visit regularly' at the time of each election; the scene concludes with his departure from the studio: 'see you maybe in four years'. Within the five allocated minutes, the practice of censorship was thus held up for ridicule because opposition parties in Hungary usually have no access to the media. In the performed scene, a journalist—a woman wearing a red skirt and high heels—sits next to the male speaker, Bruti, sent by the party to represent it. The latter's sexist remarks to her imply that a woman's role on television is limited to looking feminine, rather than acting as a professional news reporter. It was a well-rehearsed sketch, a piece of playful subversion, which provided a moment of freedom and sardonic comedy.

But laughter, irony, and subversive responses to oppression and censorship are not regular features of public life in Hungary. Although the work of stand-up comedian Tibor Bödőcs—the country's most popular political stand-up artist, whose video titled 'Ruszkik, haza, család' ('Russians, home, family'), released in mid-March 2022, received 2.6 million views within six weeks—demonstrates the revival of political cabaret, criticism expressed in a playful or comic mode is rare.[1] We do not live in a culture of popular laughter (in the sense of Mikhail Bakhtin's understanding of counterculture): such subversive forms of resistance were highly repressed in the past, during the era of state socialism. Overidentification—that is, when certain ideas and forms of behaviour are taken seriously as a means to subvert them—is the principal mechanism of comic expression in contemporary Hungary. Such modes of comic performance have penetrated the wider public sphere and include subversive demonstrations such as the Peace March organized by the Two-Tailed Dog Party in 2018, which parodied the marches organized in support of Prime Minister Viktor Orbán.

Beyond the censorship of public media, following the victory of the illiberal populist party Fidesz in 2010, the government has silenced or threatened important printed and electronic media as well as radio: for example, the newspaper *Népszabadság*, the news website *Index*, and the radio station Klubrádió. Cultural institutions have experienced forms of indirect censorship: the centralization and creation of large-scale institutions led by hyper-powerful loyal leaders; the destruction of the independent arts field through demoralization and financial cutbacks; the corruption and lack of transparency in the appointment of artistic directors at national institutions; and the widespread nurturing of a culture of nepotism. Major democratic principles, such as decentralization, transparency of decision-making processes, mobility, equal access to public funds, and democratic competitions have long been corrupted, and many of them—like transparency of processes—have not been achieved in this country.[2]

When discussing the censorship and oppressive cultural policy processes that are both similar and very different in contemporary Hungary and Putin's Russia, I always emphasize that neither direct censorship nor violent interference in culture—that is, the direct closing of institutions, physical threats on cultural figures, aggressive interruptions of performances by police, banning of shows, all of which happened in Russia—is characteristic of Hungary; rather, censorship interventions have always been masked as legal and manifest themselves in the form of budget cuts, restructuring, and reorganizations. No performances were closed for political reasons, as has happened in Russia, and there are no specific topics banned. Hungary has always had a tradition of 'sloppiness': a chaotic, flexible, and complex modus operandi of censorship. Theatre censorship was regulated by law until 1867, but a more invisible interference with the artistic product has always been present, although there was no official institution of censorship during the state socialist era (Vince 2015). Since the elections of 2010, however, state interference with the arts sector has grown dramatically. In this intervention, therefore, I will reflect on practices of censorship in Hungary, and responses to these practices, from this date.

Theatre censorship

In 2017, the parliamentary National Security Committee discussed the national security threats posed by three individuals: stage director Árpád Schilling, and activists Márton Gulyás and Gábor Vágó. Gulyás is an award-winning political journalist, who curates the prominent YouTube channel Partizán, while Vágó is an investigative journalist and politician—he held a parliamentary seat for Hungary's Green Party, the LMP, from 2014 to 2018. However, the case of Schilling is unique: the internationally renowned director, political activist since 2010, and founder of the educational, community, and arts foundation Krétakör (Chalk Circle) was the only artist in Hungary to be identified by Szilárd Németh, the vice-president of both the National Security Committee and Fidesz, as representing a 'national security risk'. Schilling left the country the day after the elections in 2018, when Fidesz won its third government majority, but he continues to be a vocal critic of Orbán's regime on social media (though he is much less visible as an artist in Hungary since he left the country). The identification of artists and activists as enemies of the state was relatively uncommon in the past and was eventually discontinued: denunciations could lead to any form of legal and informal oppression, and the practice was abandoned due to the general national and international outcry provoked by the treatment of Schilling. As stated, Schilling left the country; Gulyás became a powerful independent journalist, and Vágó works in Brussels for the European Green Party.

There is a long history of theatre censorship in Hungary: from the 1950s, party newspapers flagged theatre productions as ideologically and aesthetically harmful; indeed, a style called 'denouncing criticism' was widely practised in the Eastern bloc, implemented by the Soviet newspapers in the 1930s when an author's work was (often anonymously) criticized from an ideological standpoint, resulting in the banning of the author. From 2010, such denunciations have re-emerged in pro-government media: articles, often authored anonymously, identify and deride certain performances as harmful, while emphasizing that state-/local government-supported institutions give space to (anti-government) propaganda. Two cases come to mind: the production of Gogol's *The Inspector General*, directed by Viktor Bodó in the largest theatre in Budapest, the Vígszínház (Comedy Theatre), just before the parliamentary elections in 2014; and *A bajnok* (*The Champion*), a play written and directed by Béla Pintér at the Katona József Theatre in 2016.[3] What attracted the attention of pro-government press workers were the political references, in the form of direct address, on the stage—a relatively recent phenomenon in Hungarian theatre after the state socialism era, which rejected overtly political speech in performances.[4] In both cases, the denouncing articles did not have a direct impact on the productions: the performances were continued, and nobody was dismissed. However, they drew the government's attention to the political shows of state-sponsored theatres, and the local government (whose mayor at that time was affiliated to Fidesz) attempted to demonstrate power through intimidation, to the extent that one of the directors was summoned to a hearing.[5]

Artistic directors, as well as leaders of state institutions more widely, tend to remain silent and do not enter into disputes with a media that is prone to character assassination. After *The Champion* was denounced, pro-government media questioned the legitimacy of Gábor Máté's appointment. The artistic director of the Katona Theatre had been hired by the Fidesz majority of Budapest's city council (all artistic directors of Budapest's city theatres are appointed by the local government): as an editorial in *Heti Válasz* put it on 24 April 2017, 'we will get rid of him again'. Another article in the same newspaper exposed and denounced sensitive issues in Máté's private life: although such gratuitous commentary can be expected from the tabloids, this rhetoric is now typical of mainstream pro-government media.

Indeed, in 2018, a further series of articles sought to denounce not just performances, but the artists themselves, targeting their political opinions and sexual preferences.[6] This damaging press was part of the *Kulturkampf*, exemplifying an intent not only to challenge and change the cultural elite, but also to denounce cases where artists who are vocal in their criticism of the government—established writers like Péter Nádas, György Dragomán, and János Háy, the singer Zsuzsa Koncz—are supported by government-funded institutions and foundations (through invitations, grants, and awards).

The aim of such articles was not only to silence and intimidate cultural actors, but also to participate in the formation of cultural policy within the Fidesz government. Few artists responded to these provocations: most affected writers tried to avoid having their name (and profession) disparaged in the media. Therefore, these violent, personalized verbal attacks often remained unanswered: even the organizations that hosted the artists often kept silent. In addition, a dramatic change took place in the leadership of the most prominent literary institution, the Petőfi Literary Museum: an Orbán loyalist, Szilárd Demeter, was appointed in 2019 and became very powerful, centralizing institutions and controlling huge budgets. At the same time, personal denunciations have continued, often directed at gay and trans artists, as the degrading language of the media intertwines with state-level homophobia.

There was significant international backlash when a collection of fairytales published by the LGBTQ organization Labrisz, *Meseország mindenkié* (Wonderland is for everyone)—to which I contributed a story—was publicly torn apart during a press conference by a senior far-right politician in 2020.[7] This destructive gesture—reminiscent of Nazi book-burning in 1933—had major consequences both in galvanizing solidarity nationally and internationally, but also in radicalizing Orbán's anti-LGBTQ policy and in bringing provisions against the LGBTQ community into law.[8] Finally, and though votes proved invalid, the referendum on so-called child protection held on 3 April 2022, the same day as the general election, aimed at backing up the anti-LGBTQ legislation passed in 2021: a major negative consequence of state-level hatred towards the LGBTQ community was a law that failed to distinguish between paedophilia and homosexuality, and banned 'propaganda' (in other words, LGBTQ content) for minors. State-level homophobia transformed LGBTQ people into primary enemies of the state.

It is important to note that this situation reflects the radicalization of Hungarian politics over more than a decade. Soon after the parliamentary elections in 2010, the director of the National Theatre, Róbert Alföldi, came to the attention of the Fidesz government. The removal of Alföldi from his position at the National was a number-one cultural policy objective of the far-right party Jobbik, whose representative deployed both antisemitic and homophobic language while attacking Alföldi in Parliament. At that time, Alföldi had not publicly come out as gay but it may be assumed that his sexuality, even more than the progressive, socially engaged, artistically high-quality theatre he was responsible for, triggered the fury of far-right politicians.[9] Despite personal attacks and criticism of his artistic programme, Alföldi managed to complete his mandate, and his final months at the helm of the theatre were celebrated with huge public support.[10] However, the type of hate speech to which he was subjected gradually became more oppressive as it was adopted and 'normalized' by mainstream politics and pro-government media.

Hungary often presents the image of a passive, apathetic country where there is little resistance to state oppression and the interference of politics in the arts. Yet there are frequent creative and effective responses to growing state control. Timothy Snyder, whose book *On Tyranny: Twenty Lessons from the Twentieth Century* (2017) offers a series of good practices in times of tyranny, notes that efforts are being made to defend democracy in my country—though maybe insufficiently. The practice of corporeal politics is collective and we have engaged with it: some demonstrations proved powerful and game changing, but others had no impact (such practices were also hit by the global disaster of the Covid-19 pandemic).

Demonstrations as responses to censorship were—at least in the theatre field—more typical during the first Orbán regime (2010–14), when the major Budapest theatres underwent radical changes: this was the case at the Új Színház (New Theatre) in 2011 and the National Theatre in 2013. The appointment of a radical far-right director, György Dörner, in the first case, and the significant state involvement in the appointment of the artistic director of the National in the second, provoked opposition from professionals and the public alike: in neither case did demonstrations lead to a change of the initial situation (Tompa 2017).

However, the demonstration held in December 2019 had a direct, positive influence on cultural policy when the government hastily withdrew a law targeting the destruction of the National Cultural Fund. The role of the National Cultural Fund is crucial in financing independent Hungarian culture and it is symbolic as an arm's-length, state-sponsored institution. Its liquidation would have been another step towards the centralization of cultural institutions, the threat of which alarmed cultural organizations and citizens. The most memorable speaker at this demonstration was Béla

Pintér, a writer-director-actor and independent leader of the Béla Pintér Company. When he stepped onto the stage, Pintér knew that the law had been withdrawn that morning—the Parliament was alarmed by the outcry from the artistic field and the planned large-scale demonstration—but he delivered his speech with humour and wry subversive overidentification. He asked the audience, in a tone of total astonishment: 'So, then, independent culture will not be completely eradicated?'

The Hungarian Theatre and Film Academy

The most effective silencing concerned the Hungarian #MeToo movement, at least at the level of cultural institutions. For the analyst Gábor Polyák:

> [i]n a cultural context, where the governing political elite clearly reflects, communicates and supports a subordinated role for women, the #MeToo has just the opposite effect to what it is aimed at. The victim [who spoke up] is humiliated for the second time by the environment and attitude. Those who support the victims in such an environment can't have an influence. (2021)

The first #MeToo testimonies came from the performing arts sector. As I have shown, the media in Hungary is subject to censorship and the state-funded theatres prefer to keep silent and avoid public debate. Those women who were brave enough to talk about their experiences were abandoned or harshly attacked in the press and on social media. Their testimonies were also wielded against specific theatres and institutions, politicians calling them 'places of harassment' which should be dismantled and closed down. For example, when Péter Gothár, a director at the prestigious Katona József Theatre and a teacher at the Hungarian Theatre and Film Academy, admitted to harassing a co-worker at the theatre, his predatory behaviour was used by the political authorities to justify an attack against both institutions.

The Academy is a 150-year-old state university that produced the most prominent Hungarian theatre and film artists and makers of the twentieth century. When attacks on the Academy began in the media, the 'critics' of the university deployed the usual discourse in the press: without offering a reasoned argument, a campaign of discreditation was launched. The main 'concern' was that teaching staff promoted 'ideologically based pedagogical activity' (Kovács 2020).[11] The discourse turned personal and involved mudslinging as the accusations against the 'old elite' intensified. A lengthy and painful process in the performing arts field ensued: the destruction of the Theatre and Film Academy had not begun at the time of the 2019 December demonstration, but a turning point was already evident.

The aggressive privatization of the Theatre and Film Academy in 2020 resembles a Russian-style clean-up of a historic and unique institution.

Other universities have been privatized in recent times and, in the last decade, other moments of conflict in the performing arts field have been followed by demonstrations and protests, but none was as long-lasting or involved as many participants (students, staff, and wider Hungarian society). The Academy was 'reformed' very quickly, in a process euphemistically called the 'change of institution model': the state thus placed the university in the hands of a foundation which cleaned up the old institution (more than two dozen professors and a hundred students left). The existing (old) leadership of the academy was excluded from negotiations between the state and the new management: Attila Vidnyánszky, who had already been appointed director of the National Theatre following Alföldi's tenure, became the head of the Academy's managing board in 2020.

For seventy days, from 1 September 2020 at the commencement of the new academic year, students occupied the Academy to resist the takeover. However, though the large international support, long-lasting outcry, and exemplary resistance of the students resonated in the country and internationally, it could not, in the end and after many months of occupation and resistance, save the institution. The occupation ended in mid-November due to pandemic measures.[12] Gradually, faculty members quit their positions. There was a divide between the 'old'—i.e. students and professors— and the 'new'—i.e. the board of the privatized university and its advocates, supported by the government. Such a schism emerged due to a lack of governmental will to restore peace, to mediate, or to negotiate. It was rather in the interest of politicians to create and deepen the crisis.

From September 2020, pro-government voices started to talk about a 'very serious international background power and network' with students being manipulated by professors (Vidnyánszky 2020).[13] As the linguist László Kálmán points out, this argument identifies Attila Vidnyánszky with the current 'soft Nazi' (*szalon názi*: Nazi of the saloon) rhetoric of the Orbán regime (Uj 2020). Any effort of the university to take part in the process of privatization was disregarded and all the leaders were overlooked. No representative proposed by the university was accepted onto the board. The decisions about the future operation of the Academy were taken by the government without consulting the university's rector and senate.

Those who left the Academy have found themselves in a marginal situation. Yet marginal situations are also creative ones: a free university has now been established based on an association of theatre academies abroad—German, Polish, Austrian—that confers diplomas on those who left the Hungarian Theatre and Film Academy (the staff members still volunteer their labour). However, this free university is expensive, while students in state universities pay no fees.

It is important to note that state cultural policy leaders and their supporters in the theatre viewed the privatization of the Academy as a 'real change of the system', thus trying to expropriate the rhetoric of the old socialist order (Vidnyánszky 2020). The phrase has been employed by representatives of the new political elite without pondering why a change of the system would be needed; what it hints at, though, is the idea that the old guard are the representatives of the elite before the social changes (in other words, they are representatives of the state socialism of the 1970s and 1980s). Tellingly, a key figure of the Academy, respected professor Gábor Székely, was discredited as an old communist. Another important event was the dismissal of the head of doctoral studies at the Academy: Professor György Karsai was dismissed for no justifiable reason. Karsai was critical of the reforms of the Academy, and was the target of an antisemitic comment from Attila Vidnyánszky, who declared in 2020: 'I will never be able to explain to György Karsai what a nation is, what a homeland is, what Christianity is, because he is incapable of accepting what I think. His thinking in this regard is exclusive and exclusionary' ('Elhatárolódást' 2020). This, however, demonstrates that the takeover of the Academy was very much about changing the elite, and not about changing a system.

State interference in the cultural field has a lengthy and painful history in twentieth-century Hungary, often threatening the freedom of artistic expression. But in the twenty-first century, the cultural struggles in the name of building an authoritarian, illiberal state have brought dramatic changes. No direct censorship can be detected in contemporary Hungary, but tools of silencing—often resulting in self-censorship—are detectable. The freedom of creative margins is more important today than at any point in the recent past.

Notes

1   In 'Russians, home, family', Bödőcs ridicules the pro-Putin Hungarian policy, Orbán's so-called peace policy, and the goverment's anti-migration policy, and mocks the Hungarian elections compared to China—'in China there is no democracy, but they consider elections important' (Bödőcs 2022).
2   Polyák (2019) as well as Polyák and Urban (2016) provide insights into Orbán's illiberal media policy and processes of censorship in Hungarian media since 2010.
3   More information on both productions and directors can be found, for instance, in Herczog (2021) and Avila (2015).
4   Both performances were reviewed by the (then) pro-government weekly, *Heti Válasz*. *The Inspector General* was accused of being part of the political campaign (the elections followed soon after the show opened); three Budapest city theatres and five independents were named as part of such a campaign and their shows reviewed: 'The degree of politicization varies, but in the case of productions based on sketches, it is not as if the artistic quality is important: the play merely provides a prop and a framework for the current political counter-parade. Those who don't want to do that should at least consider where they go to the theatre until the elections', wrote Noémi Sümegi in *Heti*

Válasz on 6 February 2014 (my translation). As for *The Champion*, Sümegi accused the authors of 'putting artistic freedom above the sanctity of privacy': in other words, putting on stage the private life of a certain (recognizable) politician (*Heti Válasz*, 24 March 2016; my translation).

5   Such hearings were never made public in the media; I had the opportunity to interview the artistic directors. Hearings are occasions where the political body expresses its views and expectations of a theatre, and demonstrates its authority and power.
6   I was identified as one of the 'frightened', meaning 'afraid of the Orbán regime'. Generally, these articles consist of lists of people who are grouped by their points of view, sexuality, or political affiliations (for example, liberal, anti-government, anti-Hungarian, belonging to certain sexual minority groups).
7   The English translation of the volume, *A Fairytale for Everyone*, was published by HarperCollins in 2022.
8   Unexpectedly, the book sold a large number of copies and was translated into more than ten languages; its project manager, Dorottya Rédai, was included in the 100 most influential people in *Time* magazine in 2021.
9   The Hungarian and international press commented on the personal and erroneous attacks against Alföldi. See Cohen (2011) and O'Quinn (2011 and 2013).
10 Further information on the attacks on Alföldi as well as the support he received between 2010 and 2019 may be found inter alia in Avila (2011) and Bozók (2017).
11 Attila Vidnyánszky, now the most powerful cultural policy leader, stated in a public radio programme: 'there is only one kind of training, based on a leftist liberal idea, and anyone who says that there is no ideological influence is lying' (Kovács 2020).
12 For a chronology of events, see 'Az SZFE' (2020).
13 Interviewed on a television news programme, Vidnyánszky referred to an international 'army' manipulating the students of the Academy ('Magyarország' 2020).

References

Avila, Robert. 2011. 'What Is a National Theatre? Robert Alfoldi Battles to Invigorate Hungary's Premier Stage with Visions of the Here and Now', *American Theatre*, 11 November, pp. 62–66
——— 2015. 'Hungarian Theatre and Its Government Inspectors', *American Theatre*, 9 April
'Az SZFE egyetemfoglalás története'. 2020. *Szabad Európa*, 1 December
Bödőcs, Tibor. 2022. 'Bödőcs: Ruszkik, haza, család', YouTube <https://www.youtube.com/watch?v=PJc-QRn-jaQ> [accessed 10 May 2022]
Bozóki, András. 2017. 'Nationalism and Hegemony: Symbolic Politics and Colonization of Culture', in *Twenty-Five Sides of a Post-Communist Mafia State*, ed. by Bálint Magyar and Júlia Vásárhelyi (Budapest and New York: Central European University Press), pp. 459–91
Cohen, Nick. 2011. 'Who Will Confront the Hatred in Hungary?', *Guardian*, 2 January

'Elhatárolódást vár a kulturális kormányzattól Vidnyánszky szavai miatt az SZFE'. 2020. *HVG*, 3 September

Herczog, Noémi. 2021. 'Béla Pintér and His Postmodern National Theatre', in *20 Ground-Breaking Directors of Eastern Europe*, ed. by Kalina Stefanova and Marvin Carlson (New York: Palgrave Macmillan), pp. 159–70

'The Hungarian Right and Artistic Taste'. 2011. *Hungarian Spectrum*, 26 May

Kovács, Blanka. 2020. 'Az SZFE szerint Vidnyánszky már alá is írta a dokumentumokat, amik felszámolnák az egyetem autonómiáját', *Mérce*, 29 August

'Magyarország élőben Vidnyánszky Attilával'. 2020. *Magyarország élőben*, HÍR TV, 4 September <https://www.youtube.com/watch?v=q83QV5G_JMU> [accessed 4 July 2022]

O'Quinn, Jim. 2011. 'Who's Winning Hungary's Truth-to-Power Standoff?', *American Theatre*, November, pp. 56–61

—— 2013. 'Hungarian Showcase 2013: Bipolar Politics and the Unruly Arts', *American Theatre*, 1 May

Polyák, Gábor. 2019. 'Media in Hungary: Three Pillars of an Illiberal Democracy', in *Public Service Broadcasting and Media Systems in Troubled European Democracies*, ed. by Eva Połońska and Charlie Beckett (London: Palgrave Macmillan), pp. 279–303

—— 2021. Unpublished interview by Andrea Tompa, 7 June

Polyák, Gábor, and Ágnes Urbán. 2016. 'Az elhalkítás eszközei. Politikai beavatkozások a médiapiac és a nyilvánosság működésébe', *Médiakutató*, 17.3-4: 109–23

Snyder, Timothy. 2017. *On Tyranny: Twenty Lessons from the Twentieth Century* (New York: Tim Duggan Books)

Tompa, Andrea. 2017. 'And the Winner Is... Appointing Artistic Directors in Hungary', *Polish Theatre Journal*, 1-2.3-4: n.p.

Uj, Peter. 2020. 'Kálmán László: Vidnyánszky nem a kisnyilasokkal, hanem a szalonnácikkal azonosította magát', *444*, 16 August

'Választás 2022—A Magyar Kétfarkú Kutya Párt 5 perce az M1-en'. 2022. YouTube, 23 March <https://www.youtube.com/watch?v=0X6ljMT57wk> [accessed 5 May 2022]

Vidnyánszky, Attila. 2020. 'A mi szakmánkban most kezdődik a rendszerváltás', interview by Rebeka Nóra Ádám, *Mandiner*, 8 September

Vince, Paál. 2015. *A sajtószabadság története Magyarországon 1914–1989* (Budapest: Wolters Kluwer)

4
Nothing New on the Eastern Front: Censorship in Contemporary Slovenia

DENIS PONIŽ

We often hear that censorship is a thing of the past and a feature of undemocratic regimes. It may be true that what we understand as traditional censorship—an explicit state mechanism of prevention and repression—is dead and only exists today as the subject of critical studies on cultural and other productions, be they religious, political, or philosophical (see Jovićević 2008: 79–86, Gabrič 2008: 63–77, Gabrič 2010: 171–88). Yet this has been substituted by a large number of sophisticated censorship procedures which, just like traditional censorship, attempt to modify texts and 'synchronize' them with the prevailing ideological models, eliminate 'disturbing' elements, and silence unwelcome criticism.

A common characteristic of traditional censorship is that the authors of literary and non-literary texts either would know or at least could guess what was liable to become the object of censorship, because they were aware of the censors' criteria: though limiting to the artist, censorship was explicit as it was based on written rules and prompted reports and correspondence. In this sense, state censorship differs from contemporary forms where the criteria are shifting, and censors are multiple and informal: contemporary modes of censorship are constantly adapting to the changing social, moral, political, and ideological demands of the ruling elite, and are often invisible as a result.

It is, of course, unwise to offer a universal definition of censorship, as we need to consider three interconnected variables that shape the field in which censorship, then and now, is constituted. First: who is censoring and why? Second: who/what is the object of censorship? And third: what are the forms and methods of censorship? Depending on the geopolitical and historical contexts, these questions present additional complexities for the researcher, as the experience and practice of (theatre) censorship in the twentieth century varied greatly in totalitarian and absolutist states compared to democratic countries. The majority of theatregoers know little about the context in which contemporary censorship takes place, and how past, traditional systems of censorship impact and influence censorious actions in the present. The legacy of the past is of particular importance in the case of Slovenia, which is the focus of this chapter.

The territory of present-day Slovenia, for longer or shorter periods in the past, was part of larger political entities or territories, each of which had its own system of state censorship.[1] Following the communist takeover in May 1945, censorship was no longer (officially) practised in Yugoslavia.[2] Formal, or traditional, censorship was replaced with informal, or 'invisible', censorship (Gabrič 2010: 173, Poniž 2010: 15). Invisible censorship was the characteristic and predominant form of censorship employed by the repressive authorities in commmunist Yugoslavia, and one that had a number of features. Authors never knew the rules of the game, since nowhere was it explicitly stated what was permitted and what was not, and an investigation could be initiated at any moment. As a result, they had to rely on their own sense of what was allowed and what was prohibited: in other words, they had to exercise self-censorship, which also tends to be invisible. Not only that, but the general public was unaware that individuals with no formal expertise of censorship within various institutions—the ideological commission of the Communist Party (both federal and in the republics), the secret police, writers' and other cultural associations—acted as censors. Most decisions about censorship measures were undocumented. Instructions on what should be banned were communicated verbally or by phone, from higher to lower levels, to those responsible for executing them. It is therefore practically impossible to reconstruct individual censorship processes. The best sources of information are the testimonies of those artists who were victims of this state-led invisible censorship (Lah 2012: 10–14). Only a few people, however, are willing to talk about their experiences with invisible censors. The word 'censorship' itself therefore acquires a magical quality: it was not uttered or used but was replaced with several euphemisms such as, indicatively, 'to prevent hostile propaganda', 'to protect the heritage of socialist revolution', 'to protect public morality', and 'to struggle against Western cosmopolitan decadence'.

Though informal, these censorship measures were nonetheless embedded within structures of communist power: party committees at all levels and the para-communist organization known in Slovenia as the Socialist Alliance of Working People (SZDL). Above all, they fell under the remit of various policing bodies: the civil political police, known as the State Security Administration (UDV or UDBA) from 1946 to 1966, and the State Security Service (SDV) from 1966 to 1990; and the military political police, known as the Counterintelligence Service (KOS) from 1946 to 1955, and the Security Administration (OB) from 1955 to 1990 (Poniž 2010: 15–16). While those censors were devoted party members, they had little or no knowledge about art and literature, Molière or Shakespeare, or Slovene artists and playwrights: most had only elementary education and, like all citizens, had to follow the instructions of the party in their daily lives (for instance, it was considered inappropriate to listen to jazz or rock and roll). Alongside the traditional preventive and repressive processes of censorship (checking manuscripts, bans on performances, trials of authors), these bodies employed a range of informal measures: the intimidation of dissident writers and others through unannounced interrogations, the clandestine searches of their homes and installation of eavesdropping devices, the confiscation of manuscripts, letters, and diaries, the surveillance of personal mail, threats to family members, the threat of losing a job, and even imprisonment as a result of the 'show trials' (trials of innocent individuals—'show trials' were imported into Yugoslavia from the Soviet Union in the years preceding the ideological divisions between Tito and Stalin in 1948) (Vodušek Starič 1992, Režek 2009: 30–32, Lah 2012: 7). These measures were so effective that traditional, and uncomfortably visible, processes of censorship became unnecessary and only rarely occurred in Slovenia (Dovič 2008, Gabrič 2008). In other republics of the 'second' Yugoslavia (1943–90), particularly Croatia and Serbia, traditional forms of censorship remained the norm (Vukelić 2012, Zrnić 2015).[3]

The absence of written rules and the arbitrariness of the censors, who employed different criteria for every text, visual arts piece, and music composition that came to their attention, led to absurd situations. For instance, the black comedy *Nečastivi na Filozofskom: fakultetu* (The Devil in the philosophical faculty, 1982) by Croatian playwright Ivo Brešan (1936–2017) fell victim to invisible censorship that prohibited its staging in Croatian theatres, but was produced (in uncensored form) in Slovenia, at Ljubljana's municipal theatre (1983). In the absence of censorship criteria, this discrepancy was likely the result of internal party struggles between the Republic's party leaderships and, within those, tensions between pro-Soviet and pro-Western factions. Something similar occurred with the plays of the Czech playwright (and later president of Czechoslovakia) Václav Havel. While Havel was imprisoned as a dissident and his plays and books were banned in his own country, theatre companies in Slovenia (and in other republics of Yugoslavia) produced them in prominent theatres (including the National Theatre in Ljubljana), despite the fact that Havel's plays also alluded to the secret police repression, violation of human rights, and privileges of the party nomenclature that existed in Yugoslavia as well (Poniž 2014). This example of leniency was motivated by the belief of the Yugoslav Communist Party that its regime was more humane and allowed more freedom than the Soviet bloc.

In the majority of cases, the informal operation of censorship in communist Yugoslavia was hidden from the public, thereby further ensuring invisibility. Secret censors (the civil and military police) conducted the majority of measures in such a way that practically no archival material remains, or it is so incomplete that very often it is impossible to reconstruct the course of events; above all, it is impossible to establish who ordered a specific censorship measure and who was responsible for putting it into effect.[4] The majority of repressive actions against the authors or creators of 'controversial' and 'hostile' articles, books, plays, and other works of art were not issued in written form but instead given verbally or by telephone, and not infrequently in the form of 'informal interviews' between those who were being censored and members of the secret political police (Pucci 2020: 56, Oset 2021: 12). In most cases, such 'informal interviews', which in reality were (more or less) veiled threats and psychological intimidation, proved to be effective: the targets of these interviews opted for self-censorship rather than risk becoming the object of increasingly severe repression and, eventually, ending up in court. Repressive measures meant that those affected did not dare discuss these 'informal interviews' even with their closest relatives; even after the end of the communist era, the majority of them did not have the courage to document the kinds of pressures and threats they had experienced.[5] However, it is possible, on the basis of the few surviving documents and testimonies of censored authors, to identify a number of typical patterns in the practice of censorship, which I will explore in the next section. These are interesting not only because they shed light on 'invisible censorship', but also because some of the practices employed by the single-party regime were carried over after its collapse into the contemporary period, as my case study will show. This chapter, therefore, approaches censorship as a supranational phenomenon and demonstrates that, despite the change in regime, the censorship climate in the 'second' Yugoslavia (1943–90) and in independent Slovenia since 1990 remains similar.

The 'second' Yugoslavia (1943–1990): patterns of censorship

The first pattern in the practice of censorship hinged on delegation, transferring the order to carry out a specific censorship measure from the ideological commission of the Central Committee of the Communist Party—the supreme censor—to lower levels of the party structure. These 'lower levels'—for example, municipal committees and committees at educational institutions—then acted in accordance with the current situation (in other words, more or less publicly), while also engaging local and, where necessary, republic-wide media (radio, television, newspapers) or their commentators, who launched attacks against the targeted individual. Through this chain, the initial order was transformed into actual measures eventually carried out by anonymous officials. The ideological commission of the Central Committee of the Communist Party was a de facto censorship authority that took most decisions on when it was necessary to prohibit publications and artistic events (above all, theatrical presentations and, in the last decade before the fall of communism, alternative punk and rock concerts)—the Chairman himself acting as final arbiter in cases of disagreement. Unfortunately, almost the entire archive of this commission in Slovenia was destroyed by senior officers of the secret police before the democratic changes that took place from 1989.

The second pattern was denunciation: every large enterprise and scientific, educational, or cultural institution had a person who was either employed by the secret political police or acted as its informant.[6] This individual kept a close eye on what was happening and would immediately raise the alarm with their superiors, who would then take action in various ways: most often by publicizing the fact that 'ideologically conscious working people' were unwilling to print a given work, or that the members of a given theatre company were indignant at having to perform a text which they considered to be 'hostile' propaganda. In most cases, no records were kept of such incidents, with the result that we can only rely on the rare testimonies of the individuals concerned and a few surviving documents.[7]

The third pattern was omission. This was possible in the predigital age, when a manuscript was written by hand or by typewriter. Cases are known of manuscripts—by writers seen as undesirable by the regime—mysteriously being 'lost' in the editorial office or even at the printing press.[8] There are also cases in which an author's manuscripts, correspondence, or diaries were simply stolen during the clandestine searches carried out in private dwellings by the secret police. People familiar with the operations of the secret police therefore left duplicates of their manuscripts in the safekeeping of trusted friends or kept them on their person at all times.

One of the rare documented forms of censorship consists of the lists of foreign literature (including newspapers and magazines) that appeared in almost every edition of the official gazette published by the Ministry of the Interior in each of the Yugoslav republics. It was a criminal offence to bring into the country such 'prohibited' literature, also referred to as 'hostile propaganda'—one of the many terms, reminiscent of Orwellian Newspeak, that was used by party leaders—and anyone caught doing so was sentenced to imprisonment. This process, and with it a one-year prison sentence, was experienced by the writer Drago Jančar: he returned from Austria with a book by the Slovene emigrant writer and priest Branko Rozman (who wrote under the pseudonym Tomaž Kovač); the volume, titled *V Rogu ležimo pobiti* (In Rog we lie shot), was about the mass extrajudicial executions of anti-communist soldiers who were returned to Slovenia by the British Army in May and June 1945 (the book was published during his exile in Argentina in 1968).

There were various reasons given for prohibiting books or other printed material, and the following were banned: criticism of the regime and its representatives, and reports by foreign correspondents on police repression, economic crime, corruption, and the persecution and imprisonment of dissidents. The situation was further complicated because censorship standards were constantly changing (Darton 2014: 233–47).

Independent Slovenia (from 1991): the end of theatre censorship?

After the fall of communism in Central and Eastern Europe (1989–91) and the break-up of Yugoslavia (1991–95), a new period began in which democratic norms and the associated, constitutionally guaranteed human rights and freedoms—such as those written into its own constitution by the newly independent Republic of Slovenia in 1991—eliminated all forms of institutional censorship, both explicit and implicit. The state apparatus and law enforcement bodies (police, public prosecutors) no longer involved themselves in questions of censorship, since freedom of speech and thought permitted the expression of a broad range of views on the past and the present. However, attempts to curtail free speech were taken over by other, mainly informal, groups in most cases linked to political parties or capital. Censorship passed from state to private entities and, in the process, was skilfully concealed behind concepts of ownership and editorial policy. The majority of publishing companies, media houses, and marketing organizations were privatized, which means that their owners were able to direct editorial policy and reject anything that was incompatible with their ideological disposition. It is, of course, almost impossible to prove whether this editorial policy also included censorship in the traditional sense of the word.[9]

Significantly more problematic is a similar form of censorship that is carried out by specific state or parastatal institutions when they commission research studies and expert reports, and place specific demands on those commissioned to carry them out. This category of attempted censorship also includes the demands placed by such state institutions on cultural and artistic organizations or individuals when commissioning specific cultural content from them. The season programmes of most theatres are approved by professional councils (consisting of theatre employees, but also of theatre experts, and local community representatives). As many members of these councils were active during the communist regime, they are accustomed to invisible censorship methods.

An illustration of contemporary censorship is to be found in the events surrounding the annual presentation of Slovene drama and the awarding of the Slavko Grum Award for best dramatic text, as investigated by Urška Brodar (2005: 167–90).[10] She argues that, since Slovenia's independence in 1991, the criteria for selecting the best dramatic text had become increasingly opaque and that, in some years, the winning play was not subsequently produced at the municipal theatre in Kranj, as is required by the regulations of the Grum Award:

> Following detailed examination of the data on the only festival of Slovene drama, I can only wonder at the questionable professionalism of the organization and functioning of Slovene Drama Week.

Selection criteria for plays and citations detailing the reasons for awarding the Grum Award are absent in the 1990s. Instead, the selection of plays and the reasons for awarding the prize are left to individual consideration, which cannot be verified anywhere. This apparently chaotic situation calls into question the value of the festival itself, and of the Grum Award. (Brodar 2005: 181)

I have undertaken my own analysis of the forty-three shortlisted plays—plays that did not win the Grum Award, or that did win it but were not produced—between 1990 and 1999.[11] In those ten years, only eighteen plays were performed and, among those that remained unproduced, at least twelve contained a sharp critique of Slovene social reality in the 1990s; in addition, and though no reason was given, none of the thirty-five plays in the competition received an award in 1997. The majority of the unproduced dramatic texts were written by young playwrights who offered critical reflections on the contemporary situation and the anomalies that accompanied the formation of the new state after 1991. Though it is perhaps unsurprising that the potential controversy of political drama would be monitored and avoided when awarding prestigious prizes, the absence of any documentation regarding the decisions of the jury renders any claim of censorship a mere hypothesis. I can posit with a considerable degree of certainty that at least some of these texts were censored, but proof remains elusive when invisible censorship is at play. As Brodar points out, no written documentation exists that could help us clarify the decisions by which certain prize-winning texts, despite their undisputed quality, remained unstaged, or why some plays which raised critical questions about the sociopolitical climate after 1991 did not receive the prize at all.

Case study: Prešeren Day—Mare Bulc and invisible censorship (2015–2016)

In Slovenia, 8 February is a national cultural holiday known as Prešeren Day in memory of the Romantic poet France Prešeren (1800–1849). The cultural programme accompanying the national celebration, during which the highest awards for artistic creativity in the past year are presented, always consists of a performance of some kind (recitals of poems, music, ballet, theatrical scenes, and, in recent decades, video projections), created each year by a different artistic director nominated by the Prešeren Fund Management Board (a highly prestigious appointment).[12] The selected director puts together a script for the performance—a kind of draft of the director's book, which provides a list of the artists due to participate as well as details of the staging/scenic elements that are fundamental to understanding how the performance will proceed. This book also contains the full text and musical score of every piece performed as well as references to choreography, video recording, and lighting effects; the length of each scene is also noted (the performance usually lasts an hour).

The members of the Prešeren Fund Management Board generally approve the script without major comment.[13] In 2015, Katja Pegan, the artistic director of Koper Theatre in the coastal town of Koper and a member of the board, proposed that the theatre director Mare Bulc should be in charge of the 2016 ceremony.[14] Bulc submitted a four-page draft of the director's book to the board, who unanimously approved it on 30 November 2015. The board's only comment—conveyed to Bulc in a phone call—was that there should be no barbed wire on the stage. Bulc had wanted to use barbed wire to symbolically draw attention to the migrant crisis, which was escalating at the time: his conceptual vision for the piece was clearly responsive to one of the most urgent crises in contemporary Europe. Insofar as the board modified the artistic integrity of Bulc's vision, this early intervention does amount to censorship. Nonetheless, Bulc agreed to the board's terms (Bulc 2020).

Bulc proceeded to develop a detailed director's book, comprised of two parts, that ran to twenty-seven pages. The first, 'ceremonial' part consists of the speech by the Chair of the Board, and so the director is only able to offer limited variations to elements of the set, visual effects, and sound. The second, 'artistic' part gives the director scope to elaborate an original creation. Bulc structured his piece around two elements: a critical view of the relationship between society and its attitude to culture; and the sense of cosmopolitanism arising from Prešeren's Romantic poetry—as evidenced in the seventh verse of his famous poem 'Zdravljica' ('A Toast'), the lines of which were co-opted as the text of Slovenia's national anthem in 1991 (Bulc 2021).[15]

Bulc submitted his completed director's book to the board at the beginning of January 2016, a month before the date of the celebration. On 12 January, he received an emailed reply sent from the private address of the secretary of the board—who is also an official at the Ministry of Culture:

> Mr Bulc, The Prešeren Fund Management Board has instructed me to inform you that it has revoked its decision on the selection of the stage director of the Prešeren Day celebration on 7 February 2016. (Bulc 2020)

This one-sentence email is unusual for two reasons. First, the wording gives no explanation as to why the board had 'revoked' its 'selection of the stage director', which would be expected in the case of such a radical and unexpected decision. Second, the email does not disclose who made this decision: the board had not convened since the end of November, when it had approved the director's draft book. This prompts a series of speculations: was the decision taken by the Chairperson of the Board, Professor Janez Bogataj, or were other members consulted—especially those who have theatrical expertise? Were any minutes drafted? (I received no reply from the Ministry of Culture to my written request to scrutinize the documentation from this case.)

The decision appears impractical, if not absurd, since it would be difficult for the board to find a new director in just three weeks, who would then not only have to prepare a script, but also choose a new team of collaborators (performers and technical staff), and rehearse.[16] Bulc raised similar concerns in his correspondence with the board and, on the following day (13 January), he received an email from Bogataj. This communication, which was once again forwarded to him via the secretary's private email address, nullified his dismissal:

> Dear Mr Bulc, permit me first of all to apologize on behalf of the Prešeren Fund Management Board for this disagreeable occurrence, the consequence of a lack of coordination and the poor flow of information. Things are now as they should be, and also as laid down by our statutes. I therefore invite you to attend a meeting of the Prešeren Fund Management Board at the Ministry of Culture at 12.00 p.m. on 15 January. I would request that at this meeting you present us with your detailed and final script for the national celebration. Thank you for your understanding. Best wishes, Janez Bogataj. (Bulc 2020)

The situation had changed overnight, but the only reasons given for this confusing state of affairs were, according to the email, 'lack of coordination and the poor flow of information'—which begs the question, coordination of what and which information? All of a sudden, the board was willing to hold a discussion with Bulc, which took place on 15 January at the Ministry of Culture. Immediately afterwards, Bulc received an email stating that the board approved the final version of the script, despite a few dissenting voices.[17] It appears that the whole 'operation' with emails was a case of coercion or pressure on the director to bend to the demands of the board. Although the script was approved, there were conditions attached. Bulc accepted the censor's interventions with a heavy heart, not only because he had put considerable time and effort into the work as a freelancer, but also because he did not want to disappoint the performers—Slovene and foreign artists—whom he had invited to participate in the project. He had to agree to the following amendments:

> The national coat of arms projected onto the screen above the stage must be in colour, not in black and white as envisaged by the director, and should not appear throughout the celebration but only at the start, while the national anthem was being played; the coat of arms should then be replaced by projections of individual portraits of the Romantic poet France Prešeren.[18]

This request is bizarre since no authentic portrait of the poet exists: all portraits of Prešeren were created after his death and are merely phantom images, more or less authentic approximations.

For the closing of the celebration, Bulc had planned to include an appearance by the rapper N'toko (Miha Blažič), known for his provocative lyrics that reflect on and address established culture as well as other social developments and problems regarding marginal groups (Bulc 2020). The official reason given for the cancellation of N'toko's appearance was that the rapper was still working on his piece and had not been able to submit a final text. However, it is likely that N'toko was too radical and provocative a choice for the majority of board members and the Slovenian cultural establishment, who have displayed more conservative tastes in the previous and subsequent celebrations:

> Instead of N'toko, there would be an appearance by the actress Pia Zemljič, the winner of a Prešeren Fund Prize in 2015, who would recite Prešeren's 'A Toast'—all eight verses. (Bulc 2020)

In this case, we can justifiably talk about censorship, since the majority of board members—if not all—knew who N'toko was and that the nature of his piece would be critical and provocative, but in accordance with the concept devised by the director and set out in his script: 'We live in a time that demands a comment, a statement from the artist!' (Bulc 2020). Evidently, such a conclusion to the celebration was not acceptable to the board—or at least to some of its members. As the director's book had already been approved, the requested changes clearly illustrate the board's censorious intent and actions.

The conclusion of this email is also noteworthy: the board—whether only the chairperson, or other members, remains unclear—'desires and recommends that all the previously unresolved issues should not be a reason to spread rumours'. The board clearly wished to keep its censorious activities secret to avoid controversy: if they were to become public and the media were to report on them, it would be impossible to conceal any longer the arbitrariness with which the board had interfered with the script.

Finally, another anomaly surfaced. Under Slovene labour law, a contract from a public authority must be carried out only when the contractor (in this case Bulc) has an undersigned contract. The contracts for the director and his team would ordinarily be drawn up in December, following the acceptance of the draft, and undersigned by the time the full script was completed. In this case, however, it was only when the board articulated their requests that Bulc and his team received their contracts. Because working for a public authority without such a contract is a violation for both sides, the board was in breach of the law as much as Bulc. This predicament can be read as yet another soft form of invisible censorship: on the one hand, it showed Bulc that the board did not fear being in breach, placing themselves somehow above the law; on the other hand, it hinted to Bulc that he would be found in breach if he did not carry out their requests, leaving him with very little choice.

Despite these instances of censorship, Bulc decided, in consultation with his co-workers, to continue as director of the ceremonial event. However, once the ceremony was over, Bulc retaliated by reading the following statement to the flagship television network of the state-owned broadcaster, RTV Slovenia:[19]

> The celebration was censored. Its artistic, original part. The ceremonial part is more or less determined in advance. They eliminated a number of key elements: they demanded a new set design (as a result of which the set designer left the project), dismissed one of the key performers, added a new compulsory artistic number, and so on. Even before this they tried to intimidate me by dismissing me as director.
>
> Despite having invited me at the end of November to direct the event, and having officially approved my original artistic commentary, after six weeks of work they dismissed me without any explanation. Twenty-four hours after that they re-engaged me, explaining that there had been a mistake. This 'game' of dismissal, the censorship that my team and I have been subject to, and the fear of an excessively provocative and exaggeratedly critical celebration are an indication of a total lack of confidence in autonomous artistic expression and critical reflection on the age we live in.[20]

Bulc's unexpected denunciation of the board's attempts to dismiss his artistic vision revealed its otherwise invisible actions. An article published in the *Slovenia Times* on 8 February (the day after the celebration) quotes the responses of Janez Bogataj, as well as the Culture Minister, to Bulc's public intervention:

> Other 'artistic expressions Bulc may have come up with' however belong in the experimental theatre or on the streets and not in the state ceremony, [Janez Bogataj] added.
> Culture Minister Julijana Bizjak Mlakar noted that the Prešeren Fund was in charge of the ceremony and had to ensure that state symbols were used in line with the law. ('Culture Day' 2016)

Surprisingly, perhaps, public opinion did not take the side of the director and his team; in fact, quite the opposite occurred. Bulc was subjected to personal attacks by newspaper columnists and described variously as an 'immature attention whore', a 'political agitator spitting on national symbols', and 'a chancer with psychological problems' (Vezjak 2016). The negative comments in the print and broadcast media were followed by a flood of similar comments on social media. Some of them expressed undisguised hostility towards Bulc, while others accused him of attempting to dishonour national symbols, the memory of Prešeren, and even the celebration itself. Yet none of the commentators questioned the significance and consequences of censorship. Such reactions from the public are also proof of the weakness of collective historical memory, which has quickly forgotten certain similar 'interventions' in artistic works and projects that were affected, in similar ways, by invisible censorship in communist Yugoslavia. Bulc's experience as director of the ceremony was not only marred by pressure (characteristic of invisible censorship) from the board and the media, but had further repercussions for his career: most visibly, he was blackballed from most venues and, as a freelance artist, was only given the opportunity to direct youth theatre for the next two years; his income declined rapidly as a result.

No one, with the exception of the philosopher and blogger Boris Vezjak, made any attempt to reflect on the direct references to *censorship* in the director's statement; although—as Vezjak points out in his blog—Bulc garnered some positive reactions (in the form of occasional letters from readers and viewers), the Association of Theatrical Artists—an organization, of which Bulc is a member, that combines the remit of trade union and consultative body—remained silent (Vezjak 2016). Even the theatre director Katja Pegan—the board member who had invited Bulc to direct the celebration—stated that 'Mare Bulc cannot be more important than the prize winners' and appeared wholly untroubled by the fact that she herself was part of a structure that had not only permitted the censorship of an artistic work but had also implemented it. As someone with a theatrical background, Pegan would know what such a radical intervention in an artistic project represents. It should also be added that, with the exception of Vezjak, no one commented on the fact that a classic process of censorship was taking place in a democratic country and that, unlike censorship processes in regimes where institutional censorship was the norm, no clear explanation was provided as to why such radical interventions into the substance of an artistic creation were necessary. The work in question was indeed critical, but by no means offensive to any individual or institution. Not only that, but it breached no ethical or moral standards and did not insult state institutions and their symbols. It appeared that the reflex that characterized the communist period—when the regime prohibited talking or writing about censorship on the grounds that censorship did not exist—had not died out (Wachel 2006: 178–83).

In what way does the 'old' censorship that prevailed in communist Yugoslavia differ from the 'new' censorship we have encountered since 1991, when Slovenia became an independent country? Not by much it seems. In the case of the Prešeren Day celebration, the difference is that Bulc was brave enough to break the silence and openly express how his artistic vision had been compromised. Revealing the background of such measures is to call censorship by its true name: the Prešeren Fund Management Board, which includes two representatives of the Ministry of Culture, tried very hard to prevent their actions from becoming public to ensure that their censorious intervention would pass unobserved—something that Bulc thwarted with his live televised statement.[21] The events described point to an old form of censorship in new guises—invisible censorship, something that was openly articulated at the time by only two individuals: Bulc and Vezjak.

Although many things changed after the fall of the Berlin Wall and the collapse of the totalitarian and repressive regimes that held sway in some European countries, vivid remnants of past regimes live on. The traditional Yugoslav model of invisible censorship has remained active in Slovenia. It still interferes in the lives of social groups and artists, in attempts to dictate what is appropriate. This may be linked to an important historical factor: because Slovenia did not perform the lustration, a considerable number of the 'old boys' are still in power. Their presence and influence enact a continuation with communist-dominated Yugoslavia that not only explains how invisible censorship defines Slovenia today, but also revivifies, for contemporary artists, previous forms of repression. However, and despite the climate of fear this creates, artists such as Bulc now have the courage to talk about the censorship they experienced. It is also possible to research and classify its technical processes, which allows us to identify it even when it is concealed behind unsubstantiated arguments.

Notes

1 From the nineteenth century onwards, the territory of present-day Slovenia has been part of Austria (until 1867), Austria-Hungary (1867–1918), the State of Slovenes, Croats and Serbs, which then became the Kingdom of Serbs, Croats and Slovenes, otherwise known as the Kingdom of Yugoslavia (1918–43), the second Yugoslavia (1943–91), and, from 1991, the independent Republic of Slovenia.

2 This was established in Paragraph 67 of the Constitution of the Federal People's Republic of Yugoslavia, adopted by the National Assembly of Federative Republic of Yugoslavia on 31 January 1946. In practice, censorship was administered by agitprop until 1952, and by ideology administrative committees from 1952 to 1971 (Poniž 2010: 12). Režek further suggests that 1953 to 1989 should be seen as one period which is defined 'alongside certain formal and semi-formal forms of censorship, by freedom of expression being restricted and governed primarily by self-censorship' (2009: 32).

3 Information can also be accessed in the private collection on state censorship which Zagreb prosecutor Iljko Karaman donated to the Croatian State Archives in 1992 <http://arhinet.arhiv.hr/details.aspx?ItemId=1_5683> [accessed 2 February 2022].

4   In 1989–90, 90% of the relevant files were destroyed by the secret political police. Other documents may have been preserved in court archives, but these will only be accessible after 2040.
5   In the entire period from the formation of an independent state of Slovenia to the present day, I have identified only two or three testimonies referring to self-censorship as a consequence of repressive pressures and threats.
6   My early experience working as a proofreader for a newspaper illuminates the paranoid atmosphere created by this system. All employees suspected one individual to be an informant, but the decision to print or not ultimately lay with the editor-in-chief. Later, after the disintegration of Yugoslavia, the name of this informant, who was a member of the secret police, was revealed—by which time, he had died.
7   One such story of attempted invisible censorship has been documented in *Global Insights of Theatre Censorship* (Poniž 2016: 95–108).
8   Vladimir Kralj (1901–69), theatrologist, university professor, and theatre critic, was interned in the Nazi concentration camp at Dachau in 1944–45. In the short-story collection *Mož, ki je strigel z ušesi* (The man who twitched his ears), he criticized the selfish behaviour of interned communists, amongst other things. As a result, the editorial office of the publishing house that was supposed to publish the book 'lost' the single copy of manuscript. Kralj had to write the collection all over again. It was finally published in 2007.
9   For further information regarding the processes of censorship via advertising in Slovene media, see Erjavec and Poler Kovačič (2010: 269–82).
10 The Grum Prize is also discussed in Šorli (2009), as well as in Wade (2007).
11 In those ten years, 275 plays were submitted, the majority of which did not meet the minimum standard for staging. For the years 1991, 1994, and 1996, the jury minutes are either missing altogether or are incomplete since they were not undersigned by the members of the jury.
12 The Prešeren Fund is a parastatal institution within the Ministry of Culture, consisting of members from various fields of culture. It is chaired by a distinguished figure from the field of culture or academia: in the period in question, the ethnologist Janez Bogataj, professor at the University of Ljubljana.
13 The most frequent complications have been with the budget for the celebration, when individual members of the management board have attempted to remove individual items on the grounds that certain elements are too expensive. Among the fifteen members of the Prešeren Fund Management Board, three to five have theatrical education or knowledge.
14 Mare Bulc (b. 1974) is an award-winning director and performer who graduated from the Academy for Theatre, Radio, Film and Television (University of Ljubljana). From 2003 to 2010, Bulc managed ‚No History', a group of international artists and, from 2010 to 2013, was art director of the experimental theatre Glej (Look) in Ljubljana. He has led several art projects, especially in the field of experimental theatre.
15 'God's blessing on all nations, / Who long and work for that bright day / When o'er earth's habitations / No war, no strife shall hold its sway; / Who long to see / That all men free / No more shall foes, but neighbours be' (translated by Janko Lavrin).
16 Bulc had been rehearsing with his team from the moment the script was approved, despite the fact that neither he nor the members of his team had received any kind of contract (Bulc 2021).

17 According to Bulc, some members were opposed to his script but they realized that it was impossible to appoint a new director in less than three weeks (2021).
18 Author's translation of a document in Bulc's personal archive. Article 9 of the Act Regulating the Coat of Arms, Flag and Anthem of the Republic of Slovenia and the Flag of the Slovene Nation, adopted on 20 October 1994, permits, in addition to the standard three-colour (red, yellow, and blue on a white background) coat of arms, the use of a black and white version (for example, in official documents). The Act regulating this exception is a by-law of Article 6 of the Constitution of Slovenia.
19 It may seem surprising that the state-owned broadcaster allowed Bulc's statement, but I can think of two possible reasons. First, the editorship for culture and art on national television was quite independent of political influence and, at the time, the relations between the editor and Prešeren's award board were rather strained. Second, the show was a live broadcast and any interruption would have made a worse impression than Bulc's short statement (especially since this statement was later criticized).
20 Bulc's statement was broadcast immediately after the end of the official celebration, in a special series of interviews with the leading figures who prepared the celebration.
21 There is no recording of the ceremony to be found in the archival database of TV Slovenia.

References

Brodar, Urška. 2005. 'Teden slovenske drame v Kranju in Grumova nagrada ali: kaj zmoremo Slovenci?', in *Dramatična in teatralna devetdeseta*, ed. by Urška Brodar and Denis Poniž (Ljubljana: Academy for Theatre, Film, Radio and Television), pp. 167–90

Bulc, Mare. 2020. Personal archive

—— 2021. Unpublished interview with the author, 27 June

'Culture Day Attracts Many, Ceremony Leaves Bitter After Taste'. 2016. *Slovenia Times*, 8 February

Darton, R. 2014. *Censors at Work: How States Shaped Literature* (New York: Norton)

Dovič, Marjan. 2008. 'Literatura in cenzura, resnica in strah', *Primerjalna književnost*, 31.3: 1–7

Erjavec, Karmen, and Melita Poler Kovačič. 2010. 'Nove oblike cenzure v slovenskem novinarstvu: oglaševalska cenzura', in *Cenzurirano: Zgodovina cenzure na Slovenskem od 19. stoletja do danes*, ed. by Mateja Režek (Ljubljana: Nova revija), pp. 269–82

Gabrič, Aleš. 2008. 'Cenzura v Sloveniji po drugi svetovni vojni: od komunističnega Index librorum prohibitorum do ukinitve "verbalnega delikta"', *Primerjalna književnost*, 31.3: 63–77

—— 2010. 'Cenzura gledališkega repertoarja v prvi in drugi Jugoslaviji', in *Cenzurirano: Zgodovina cenzure na Slovenskem od 19. stoletja do danes*, ed. by Mateja Režek (Ljubljana: Nova revija), pp. 171–88

Jovićević, Aleksandra. 2008. 'Cenzura in dramske strategije v jugoslovanskem gledališču (1945–1991)', *Primerjalna književnost*, 31.3: 237–49

Lah, A. 2012. *Slovenski književniki in književnice v komunističnih zaporih* (Ljubljana: Slovenski gledališki muzej)

Oset, Ž. 2021. *Udbovski učbenik Osnovni tečaj* (Šentjur: Ž. Oset Publishing)

Poniž, Denis. 2010. *Cenzura in avtocenzura v slovenski dramatiki in gledališču 1945–1990: Prvi del: Obdobje 1945–1964* (Ljubljana: Slovenski gledališki muzej)

—— 2014. 'Uprizoritev iger Václava Havla na slovenskih odrih do leta 1990 in njihova kritiška recepcija', in *Sto let slovenistiky na Univerzitě Karlově v Praze: pedagogové a vědci ve stínu dějin*, ed. by A. Jensterle-Doležel (Prague: Filozoficka fakulta Univerzity Karlovy), pp. 352–69

—— 2016. 'Who Was Afraid of Fernando Arrabal? *The Architect and the Emperor of Assyria* in Yugoslavia', in *Global Insights on Theatre Censorship*, ed. by Catherine O'Leary, Diego Santos Sánchez, and Michael Thompson (New York and London: Routledge), pp. 95–108

Pucci, M. 2020. *The Secret Police in Communist Eastern Europe* (Yale: Yale University Press)

Režek, Mateja. 2009. 'Cenzura v genih. Politična cenzura in fenomen samocenzure v Sloveniji/Jugoslaviji v obdobju komunizma/Censorship in the Genes', *Glasnik UP ZRS*, 13.6: 30–32

Šorli, Maja. 2009. 'The Internationalization of Slovenian National Theatre Between 1989 and 1996: The Seven Years of Pandur Theatre', in *Global Changes: Local Stages: How Theatre Functions in Smaller European Countries*, ed. by Hans van Maanen, Andreas Kotte and Anneli Saro (Amsterdam: Rodopi), pp. 428–459

Vezjak, Boris. 2016. 'Bulčeva cenzura ali ko žica zareže v jedro kulture', *In Media Res*

Vodušek Starič, Jera. 1992. *Prevzem oblasti 1944–1946* (Ljubljana: Cankarjeva založba)

Vukelić, Deniver. 2012. 'Censorship in Yugoslavia Between 1945 and 1952: Halfway Between Stalin and West', *Pecob's Paper Series*, 19: 9–52

Wachel, A.B. 2006. *Remaining Relevant after Communism: The Role of the Writer in Eastern Europe* (Chicago: University of Chicago Press)

Wade, Lesley Ann (ed.). 2007. *Slovene Theatre and Drama Post Independence: Four Plays by Slovene Playwrights* (Oxford: Peter Lang)

Zrnić, Dijana. 2015. 'Yugoslav Literature Under (Il)legal Censorship 1945–1990', *Law and Literature*, 28: 1–14

5
Un-Divine Comedy. Remains and Self-Censorship as Work-in-Progress in Poland

Agnieszka Jakimiak

> Regarding all the forms of hostility and downright hatred coming from the outside towards the yet unmade performance, we are making the decision to suspend the rehearsals of *Un-Divine Comedy* until the time when we are certain that the content of it serves as a basis of an important discussion, instead of being a reason for brawls, violence and aggressive behaviour towards the members of the ensemble of the Stary Theatre. (Stary management 2013)

On 26 November 2013, the management and acting ensemble of the National Stary Theatre in Kraków published a statement announcing that the production of *Nie-Boska komedia. Szczątki* (*Un-Divine Comedy. Remains*)—directed by Oliver Frljić and loosely adapted from Zygmunt Krasiński's 1835 play *Nie-Boska komedia* (*Un-Divine Comedy*) by Frljić in collaboration with dramaturgs Joanna Wichowska, Goran Injac, and myself—was postponed without any provision of an alternative date.[1] The production was due to premiere on 7 December 2013; prior to what amounts to a cancellation, the rehearsals had already been suspended by the Stary management for three days on 8 November.

This chapter investigates the reasons put forward by the theatre to justify both the suspension and subsequent cancellation of Frljić's production. I will analyse the decisions not as a response to 'hostility from the outside', but as an act of institutional self-censorship, thereby re-examining the notion of censorship and self-censorship according to the balance of institutional power and structural divisions that are present within a venue that is also a national structure. In the light of this institutional critique, I argue that the subject which applies self-censorship is not necessarily an individual in charge of an institution but may be understood as a collective institutional body. I will explore self-censorship as an 'inside job' undertaken by institutions to prevent the outside from interfering with their structure, but also as a tool which potentially replaces an institutional crisis with an 'artificial' one. By 'artificial' I mean a crisis that is self-imposed and self-provoked by an institution, but which—despite its origins—remains actual and is experienced as a crisis by those involved in the institution.

From January 2013, the managing director of the Stary Theatre was Jan Klata and the deputy director was Sebastian Majewski. To shed light on the final decision made by the management, I analyse the preparations for the performance, and the events and choices that led to the cancellation. *Un-Divine Comedy. Remains* has been extensively discussed in the Polish and international press and in specialist writings by outside observers, critics, and theoreticians (see, for instance, Niziołek 2013, Adamiecka-Sitek 2015). At the same time, following the cancellation of the production, all members of the acting ensemble at the Stary were advised by the management that, while their public statements could address the process of rehearsals, they should not discuss the cancellation itself. The only people entitled to share their opinion publicly were members of the creative team: dramaturgs Joanna Wichowska, Goran Injac, and myself; set designer Anna Maria Karczmarska; and director Frljić.[2] Therefore, while I refer to debates arising from the act of censorship in academic writings and in the press, I also focus on my experience of participating in the process and witnessing the chain of censorious decisions made by the management concerning this production.

Initial steps

On 8 October 2013, Oliver Frljić began rehearsing his new project at the National Stary Theatre in Kraków. The text for the performance—Krasiński's *Un-Divine Comedy*—was chosen by the management of the theatre and Goran Injac, who was then working as a curator of International Projects and Side Programmes at the Stary. Apart from Injac, no one from the management had previously had an opportunity to see a performance directed by Frljić. The decision to invite the Bosnian-Croatian director was based on Injac's recommendation and the recognition that Frljić had gained from his productions at international festivals such as Wiener Festwochen (*I Hate the Truth*, 2010) and Kunstenfestivaldesarts (*Damned Be the Traitor of His Homeland*, 2010). Frljić's focus on ruptures in national identities and politics as well as his interest in revisiting the most painful events in contemporary European history have fostered his reputation as a controversial theatre director who is unafraid of the political scandals stirred up by his productions. His work problematizes the unseen or concealed divisions in post-Yugoslav societies (*Zoran Đinđić*, 2012; *Alexandra Zec*, 2016), as well as those in Western European countries (such as *Balkan macht frei*, 2016 or *Hamletmaschine*, 2019 in Germany or Austria), and interrogates centres of symbolic power (such as the Catholic Church in *The Curse*, 2017).

Commissioning Frljić to direct a play was the first time the Stary's relatively new management employed a director from abroad. From the start, their appointment was regarded as controversial by some critics. At the beginning of the twenty-first century in Poland, Klata became famous for revising national myths and rewriting historic narratives. In 2005, the Theatre Institute in Warsaw organized a showcase of his works titled Klata Fest: this proved contentious because his early performances were characterized by a willingness to judiciously edit classical texts and recontextualize musical anthems associated with heroic events in Polish history, and frame them in anti-heroic narratives. Nevertheless, when Klata took over the position of managing director of the Stary, he was a well-established theatre director. From January to June 2013, Klata and Majewski introduced a programme that tackled national heritage and Polish myths. The decisions of the new management were praised by critics and audiences alike, and the 2013 season at the Stary—such as *Bitwa warszawska 1920* (*The Battle of Warsaw* 1920) by Monika Strzępka and Paweł Demirski—was well received (Kyzioł 2013, Mrozek 2013). Klata and Majewski's approach was described as 'un-mythologizing and purposefully misaligned'; it was also praised for 'provoking discussions, encouraging disputes' (Drewniak 2013, Gazur 2013).

Six months after their appointment, Klata and Majewski's decision to invite Frljić to direct at the Stary was understandable: Frljić was acclaimed as a director who openly challenges historical traumas, questions assumed narratives, and appropriates the position of those minority groups who are discriminated against in public discourse. Nonetheless, Frljić's productions remained largely unknown in Poland and only theatre professionals who attended international festivals were likely to have encountered his works. Information about Frljić was accessible to those who read international scholarship or theatre reviews but, as is the case with other theatre directors from former Yugoslav countries, his practice remained under-researched in Polish theatre studies. Yet theatre curators and managers in Poland were aware of the conflicts that Frljić's work had caused among audiences and critics. For example, when *Damned Be the Traitor of His Homeland* (2010) was performed at the Dialog Festival in Wrocław in 2011, one of the actors, Primož Bezjak, used his monologue, which was adapted for the context of each performance, to indict the Polish approach towards the Smolensk air disaster (2010) in which ninety-six people died, including the Polish president Lech Kaczyński.

According to Frljić, his work has been repeatedly attacked and subjected to acts of censorship and institutional self-censorship. When describing *Zoran Đinđić* (2012)—a performance about the motives and consequences of the assassination of the Serbian prime minister in 2003—Frljić stated:

'A lot of pressures were put on this production, and it was even stopped at one moment' (cited in Soszyński 2013). By 2013 most of the articles that covered Frljić's productions were focused on the controversial aspects of his work: the Dubrovnik Summer Festival introduced the guest performance of *Danton* as a work by 'the most provocative Croatian theatre director'; the Belgian Academy for the Future (CIFAS) advertised a workshop with Frljić labelling him 'one of the most innovative and controversial Croatian theatre director [*sic*]'; and Kunstenfestivaldesarts described Frljić as a 'theatre terrorist' ('Coming Soon' 2012, 'Oliver Frljić & Mladinsko Theatre' 2012, 'Oliver Frljić bientôt' 2013). The perception of Frljić's work as provocative should have alerted the Stary to the fact that his upcoming production in Kraków might also touch upon sensitive and problematic issues. After the cancellation of *Un-Divine Comedy. Remains*, the Stary was criticized for not doing enough to contextualize and understand Frljić's methodology and for ignoring its political, provocative, and inflammatory potential (Niziołek 2013).

Klata and Majewski applied for the position of directors of the Stary with a programme that was related to the heritage of the national institution. Its main objective was to comment on, question, and revise the legacy of the five most distinguished male theatre directors who had worked at the Stary in the past and contributed to its prominence in Poland. Each year of Klata and Majewski's management was to be dedicated to a different director: Konrad Swinarski, then Jerzy Jarocki, Tadeusz Kantor, Andrzej Wajda, and Krystian Lupa. Wajda and Lupa did not welcome the idea of providing a focus for a theatre season (Targoń 2017: 5–22). The proposal did not attract much support from theatre-makers or critics either, mainly due to its seeming arbitrariness and lack of clarity—the rationale for why those names were more significant for the Stary than others was never explained. In her assessment of the evolution of this initiative, Polish theatre critic Joanna Targoń points out that the initial plan was quickly dropped: 'In the 2014/2015 season the management discreetly backed off from the concept of thematic blocks—and rightly so, as the experience of the Swinarski Season proved that this attractive idea looked good only on paper while it did not work in practice' (2017: 16). The unsuccessful season Targoń refers to opened with Klata's production of *Damascus* (I will return to this dispute later), to be followed by *Un-Divine Comedy. Remains*.

'A flawed masterpiece'

Commissioning Frljić to tackle the heritage of Konrad Swinarski made sense as long as the aim of the management of the Stary was to examine the theatre's history, which, according to Klata, 'needs to be challenged and inspired not by those elements that are conservative and standardized, but by those that are dynamic, even sacrilegious' (cited in Cieślak 2012).

Swinarski, who had directed *Un-Divine Comedy* at the Stary in 1965, was one of the most famous and acclaimed theatre directors who spent his most productive and prosperous years there. After his death in 1975, and despite being labelled as a scandalmonger and provocateur during most of his artistic career, he almost immediately became a legendary point of reference for upcoming generations of theatre-makers. In her article on Swinarski's influence, Targoń refers to the process of mythologizing the director and argues that his legacy is a complex structure of inner contradictions and outer disputes:

> I am concerned that if Swinarski somehow materialized nowadays, he would be put in a tough situation. He would be called out on having a half-German mother who was a Volksdeutsch and a brother in the Wehrmacht, and some eager beavers would rub his nose in the fact that Swinarski desecrated his adaptation of *Forefathers' Eve* with notes in the German language. (2013)

Targoń implies that Polish biases against Germany—often exacerbated under conservative leadership—would affect the reception of Swinarski's work. Similarly, his approach towards religious content and Catholic imagery—often labelled as blasphemous—would not find many allies among supporters of traditional text-based theatre in the twenty-first century. Nevertheless, the narrative that was prominent at the Stary concerning Swinarski was much more focused on implying his greatness than exploring the subversive aspects of his work. A bust of Swinarski is still present in the upper foyer of the theatre, and its digital archives underline the existential aspects of his work rather than its social resonance and provocative impetus—the article on the Stary Theatre's website dedicated to Swinarski's legacy is revealingly titled 'Konrad Swinarski—A Moralist' (Litak 2011). Given the discrepancy between the reception of Swinarski during his lifetime and the more traditional turn that took place in the perception of his work following his death, the decision to tackle the legacy of one of Kraków's theatre legends was a potentially fruitful initiative.

Frljić's attention, however, focused not on the persona of Swinarski, but on the play that he was commissioned to adapt for the stage. In Krasiński's *Un-Divine Comedy*—a play canonized in Polish literature as the mysterious and multilayered work of a Romantic visionary—the plot is built on historic and conceptual tensions. Starting from the conflict between art and reality, Krasiński exposes a struggle between aristocracy and democracy, refers to the French Revolution, problematizes the idea of the Polish Romantic spirit, and concludes with an apology for providentialism. Nevertheless, out of the many ideological viewpoints that Krasiński sketches in his magnum opus, one remains particularly resonant for readers in twenty-first-century Poland—namely, the antisemitic frame of reference that is outlined in one of the sequences of the play:

> The crux of the matter is that this dramatic work is both canonical and profoundly embarrassing for Polish culture, on par perhaps with *The Merchant of Venice* in the western theatre canon. [...] In Krasiński's vision, in addition to the two feuding ideological camps profoundly devoted to their principles yet laboriously pushing the world towards a catastrophe, there is a tribe busying itself with destructive work alone, forever bent on annihilation of the Christian world. Krasiński refers here to Jews or, more precisely, the Neophytes (converts from Judaism): Jewish traitors, members of the old order presenting themselves as Christians, allies of Satan. (Adamiecka-Sitek 2015: 2)

Agata Adamiecka-Sitek's comparison with *The Merchant of Venice* seems even more apt as, among theatre-makers in Poland, Krasiński's play is perceived as extremely difficult to stage due to its antisemitism, which casts a shadow on *Un-Divine Comedy* as a whole and compromises the diagnosis of historical events presented by Krasiński.

Polish literary critic Maria Janion drew attention to Krasiński's ideological mindset in 1970 and more recently described *Un-Divine Comedy* as a 'masterpiece flawed by antisemitism' (Janion 2009: 119). For her, there was no ambiguity about the ideology that influenced and coincided with Krasiński's writing:

> Krasiński's antisemitism was nourished already in his childhood and early youth. General Wincenty Krasiński was publishing antisemitic comments in *On Jews in Poland*. His private tutor was Alojzy Chiarini, a retired professor of Eastern languages and the history of the Catholic Church at Warsaw University. Chiarini was instilling his young 'loving scholar' with ideas about the calamitous role of Marranos [Spanish and Portuguese Jews]. (1970: 133)

According to Janion, the catastrophic perspective depicted by Krasiński was deeply rooted in his conviction that Jews represent 'a destructive and subversive force that aims at undermining Christian order and inspires all revolutions' (134). For Krasiński, revolutionary movements were inherently evil and fatal. Janion does not question the significance and influence of *Un-Divine Comedy* as a literary document of a certain era, nor does she diminish its artistic potential; however, her comments attend to the problematic core of Krasiński's play and the difficulty of overlooking this in a staged adaptation.

All that remains from Swinarski's 1965 production of *Un-Divine Comedy* is an audio recording, a description of the performance, several reviews, and Swinarski's rehearsal script. From the start of the research and rehearsal process, Frljić scrutinized the antisemitic stance of *Un-Divine Comedy*. In addition to posing questions about the content of the play, the political situation in Poland, and working conditions in theatre institutions, Frljić engaged the dramaturgical team and the cast in focused research on the history of antisemitism in Poland and its resonance today.

Initially, the most inconclusive part of this exploration related to the figure of Konrad Swinarski. At the beginning of our research, Swinarski's approach towards antisemitic threads in *Un-Divine Comedy* remained unclear. Judging from the reviews and descriptions of the performance, Swinarski focused on the theatricality of the play and the conflict between aristocratic and revolutionary forces (Jabłonkówna 2001: 96–98). Most of the critics did not tackle the antisemitic tone of Krasiński's writing nor did they evaluate Swinarski's artistic response to the ideological background of the Polish Romantic writer (Mamoń et al. 2001: 99–102). Given the lack of critical discourse on antisemitism in the 1960s in Poland, the intervention of Jan Kott—one of the most significant Polish theoreticians and theatre critics—was in this context an exception. Kott directly addressed the antisemitic sequence of *Un-Divine Comedy* and analysed Swinarski's presentation of the converted Jews as devils:

> Swinarski tripped over these devils. It was not enough for him to present one [converted Jew] as a devil, he turned all Jews into devils. […] It is an extremely risky transformation. If it is to be taken seriously, it can mean only one thing: Satan is wielding Jews in order to destroy God's Church. (1966: 120)

For Kott, this directorial choice could easily be misread. Even if it was a result of taking a critical stance towards antisemitic stereotypes present in folk culture or of exaggerating clichés concerning Jews, such a procedure did not achieve its purpose, creating only a 'masquerade' (121). Evidence that could shed light on Swinarski's approach to staging remains elusive. Our research relied on archival material and, despite a thorough investigation, our attempts to sketch the reactions of the 1965 audience to a sequence in which Swinarski acknowledged the antisemitism of Krasiński's text were extremely limited. Fortunately, one member of the cast—Zygmunt Józefczak—had attended the premiere in 1965. Together with Frljić, we started to document his experience of the performance. As expected, the testimony of an eyewitness became important because it served as material for analysing the work of memory and ways of remembering theatre.

Autoethnography and development of conflict

In order to illustrate the process of rehearsals and its dynamics, I will refer to my personal experience of participation. At the start of the process,

Frljić established the focus of the production. Instead of creating a platform for theatrical fiction, he underlined the need to blur the borders between artistic fiction and non-fiction. A central point of reference for the actors was Philip Auslander's *Task and Vision: Willem Dafoe in LSD* (1997), which describes the acting method of Willem Dafoe. Auslander explores the methodology devised by the Wooster Group, where performers create personas who possess a double function:

> The performers' simultaneous creation and demystification of effects associated with conventional acting make their performance deconstructive of acting [...]: they place 'acting' under erasure. [...] The multiple, divided consciousness produced by doing something with the knowledge that it is being observed, while simultaneously observing oneself doing it, yields a complex confrontation with self. (1997: 42)

'Non-acting' does not involve suspending any of the performative tools that are at the disposal of actors; on the contrary, it relies on putting the performative urgency above the premise of creating a fictionalized matrix. In Frljić's theatre, actors usually perform under their own names, though on stage their actual identity is always put in question. Even if a performer states a radical point of view, it is not certain whether this opinion belongs to them: an ideological standpoint that is presented on stage is automatically transferred to the realm of fiction, narrative frame, and theatrical context. Frljić often refers to this uncertainty in stage representation and, in the case of *Un-Divine Comedy. Remains*, the contradictions implied by fictional and non-fictional aspects of stage presence were to become the primary modus operandi.

The gesture of giving theatre employees a platform to state (or dissimulate) their political agenda quickly manifested its complexity during the rehearsal process. Firstly, in order to create a realm of fiction that is manufactured from reality, a thematic framing needed to be constructed. Therefore, during the first stage of rehearsals we encouraged performers to engage in an atypical method of working: rather than supporting them with stimuli and opinions, we introduced the main themes of our research and asked everyone to propose ideas for discussions. These tasks were focused on the questions of antisemitism in Poland and in Krasiński's play, the resonance and meaning of Swinarski's performance, the engagement of the performers in political and social life in Kraków and in Poland, and their role on stage.

The cast of *Un-Divine Comedy. Remains* consisted of actors who had met or worked with Swinarksi, and actors who had never encountered him (since they were born after his death). This division was pre-planned: Frljić asked for a cast that included people who had performed in Swinarski's productions in the past, so that he could use their memory and experience to build a ground for a theatrical confrontation with the younger generation of actors. In rehearsals, the practice of remembering Swinarski resembled a ritual that consisted primarily in appealing to religious feelings. Swinarski was described by some members of the company as 'devotional' and his theatre as 'sacred'.

Despite the prominence and popularity of Swinarski's theatre, only one member of the cast—Zygmunt Józefczak—was able to bring first-hand information about the staging of Un-Divine Comedy in 1965 because he had attended the performance and had seemingly memorized many details from it. However, when asked about the sequence in which Jews are dressed as devils, he could not add anything to what we had read in the press. When the rest of the cast were asked whether they considered it possible that the performance might have included an antisemitic sequence, the actors who used to know Swinarski unanimously disputed this presumption.

The preparations for Un-Divine Comedy. Remains centred on the conflict between people participating in the project and the fracture between sentimentality towards the past and its contemporary revisions. As close as this attitude may seem to the agonistic theory of Chantal Mouffe, its practical execution rarely resulted in creating a platform for 'affirmation of difference' (1993: 2). On the contrary, the discussions concerning the legacy of Swinarski and Polish antisemitism led to seven members of the cast (out of eighteen) leaving the production—and as much as their decisions were approved by Frljić and inscribed in the process, their departure also proved that openly exercising an ideological conflict is not the most welcome methodology of work at the Stary Theatre.[3]

Multidirectionality and excluding problematic narratives

Frljić relied on creating a platform for the coexistence of historic narratives—one of them acknowledging that a highly praised classic text by Zygmunt Krasiński is at the same time a foundation for Polish antisemitism. Establishing this coexistence hinged on dethroning the interpretative frameworks that constituted the hierarchical structure of the institution.

In the view of Michael Rothberg's book *Multidirectional Memory: Remembering the Holocaust in the Age of Decolonization* (2009), collective memory does not need to be perceived as a realm of competitiveness, where one account is prioritized over another, and certain narratives are challenged to prove their accuracy or historical validity. His concept of multidirectional memory assumes that memory is 'subject to ongoing negotiation, cross-referencing, and borrowing; as productive and not privative' (Rothberg 2009: 32). Rothberg elaborates on the conflict between two narratives that is highlighted by Walter Benn Michaels. According to Michaels, the prevalence of Holocaust narratives in American commemoration may draw attention away from the history of systemic racism in the United States (Rothberg 2009: 28). For Rothberg, it is not a question of one narrative overshadowing another, but a possibility of creating a public sphere that he perceives 'as a malleable discursive space in which groups do not simply articulate established positions but actually come into being through their dialogical interactions with others; both the subjects and spaces of the public are open to continual reconstruction' (38). This 'continual reconstruction' was the main tool we used in analysing the legacy of Swinarski and, more importantly, of Polish antisemitism.

Competitive memories have been a crucial part of Polish discourse concerning Jews for a long time. The most vocal dispute of recent years is connected to the publication of Jan Tomasz Gross's book *Sąsiedzi: Historia zagłady żydowskiego miasteczka* (*Neighbours: The Destruction of the Jewish Community in Jedwabne, Poland*) in 2000. Gross investigates the case of a massacre committed by Polish civilians in Jedwabne in 1941. This investigation and its aftermath challenge the most widespread narrative concerning atrocities committed in Nazi-occupied Poland: namely, that Polish people were either rescuers or, in the worst case, bystanders who did not take an active part in murdering Jews. The omnipresence of this conviction became visible as a consequence of publishing *Neighbours*: apart from hostile attacks from conservative media (newspapers such as *Nasz Dziennik* and *Głos*) which accused Gross of slandering Poland, the non-conservative voices were also important in understanding the scale of the problem of historical denial. Adam Michnik, the editor of *Gazeta Wyborcza*—a liberal Polish newspaper—queried why the righteous should gain less recognition than the perpetrators and underlined that there are many Polish trees planted in the Avenue of the Righteous Gentiles at Yad Vashem in Jerusalem:

> Thanks to my choice, I am a Pole, and I am responsible to the world for the evil inflicted by my countrymen. [...] But I am also a Jew who feels a deep brotherhood with those who were murdered as Jews. From this perspective, I assert that whoever tries to remove the crime in Jedwabne from the context of its epoch, whoever uses this example to generalize that this is how only the Poles and all the Poles behaved, is lying. [...] A Polish neighbour might have saved one of my relatives from the hands of the executioners who pushed him into the barn. [...] For these people who lost their lives saving Jews, I feel responsible, too. I feel guilty when I read so often in Polish and foreign newspapers about the murderers who killed Jews and note the deep silence about those who rescued Jews. Do the murderers deserve more recognition than the righteous? (2004: 453)

A consequence of such binary thinking is the conviction that one historical narrative excludes another—that either we commemorate heroic Poles who rescued Jews during the Second World War, or we acknowledge Polish involvement in killing Jews. This lack of openness to 'continual reconstruction' was apparent during the rehearsals for *Un-Divine Comedy. Remains*. One of the repeated arguments during the discussions about Polish complicity in the Holocaust and Polish antisemitism concerned the number of Polish trees in Yad Vashem: 'How is it possible that Poles are antisemites, if we have the largest number of trees planted in Yad Vashem?' was one of the recurring questions posed by actors.

Instead of encouraging the narrative of Polish victimization during the Holocaust and the heroic actions of the Poles who rescued Jews, Frljić insisted that the dominant perspective in the performance should be the one that advocated for reconciliation and acknowledged the guilt and complicity in promoting antisemitic discourse in Poland. The narrative concerning brave citizens who were saving Jews was, in our perspective, widespread enough and did not warrant another platform. Creating a discourse in the spirit of multidirectional memory in this case oscillated around highlighting the viewpoint that was either absent or excluded and diminished in public debate. This motivated the decision to focus on the play's most problematic part and to treat it as a starting point for exposing the long-lasting affiliation of Polish culture with antisemitic prejudice.

In *Multidirectional Memory*, Rothberg analyses discourses that, instead of excluding each other, can benefit from one another: he claims that 'postcolonial studies can learn from the history of Jews and antisemitism in Europe in a number of ways', and vice versa (2009: 86). Two discourses that we tried to juxtapose in *Un-Divine Comedy. Remains* were parts of the same ideological and historical structure: the history and prevalence of Polish antisemitism is not far removed from the complicity of Poles in the extermination of Jews. At the same time, our purpose was not to implicate collective guilt, but rather to address the idea of the implicated subject. Rothberg's analysis enables us to apprehend our own entanglement in the infliction of harm on others; this approach does not assume that we are responsible for the harm but underlines our implication in it (2019: 1). In connection to the idea of the implicated subject, shared memory, and responsibility resulting from it, Frljić's intention was for the actors to begin the performance with a provocative statement. After a monologue from Zygmunt Józefczak—who, in a highly theatrical manner, described Swinarski's production, highlighting the conflicts between the aristocracy and revolutionaries and paying special attention to the scene with Jewish converts disguised as devils—the performer Anna Radwan delivered a confrontational speech:

> Ladies and Gentlemen, tonight we are not going to perform *Un-Divine Comedy* by Zygmunt Krasiński. Tonight, we are going to burn this play, as we think it is a disgrace for any national culture to have such a work canonized. It is a disgrace for Poland and for Poles to acknowledge an anti-Semite as one of the most important

Romantic poets. It is a disgrace that children learn at school hatred towards Jews. It is a disgrace that the Stary Theatre has such a play in its repertoire. It is a disgrace for us to participate in such a play. If Krasiński marks the top of Polish culture, it's better for it to not exist at all. Our performance is the beginning of the process of cleansing Polish culture from this artwork and works of this kind. Hate that founds our national identity needs to go away. That is why tonight we will try to performatively destroy *Un-Divine Comedy*, hoping that the next generations of Poles will not have to read this play or plays of this kind. (Jakimiak and Wichowska 2014)

This statement was followed by another declaration in which the actors, one by one, stated: 'From now on, I am not a Pole. From now on I am Jewish'. One of the actors, who did not want to declare this, commented: 'The director of this performance wanted me to state that I am not Polish, but Jewish. I will not do it.' Standpoints that openly conflicted with Frljić's ideological position were thus also integrated into the performance. This strategy was supposed to work as a performative twist and a mechanism that questions the constitutive power of statements spoken from the stage, but its main purpose was to undermine the process of creating a fixed identity for the actors on stage.

Frljić's strategy is based on the juxtaposition of elements that seem to be mismatched, incompatible, or conflicting. He aims to disrupt the continuity of meanings and hamper coherence. This approach stems from a presumption that statements constructed on stage do not create a consistent body of arguments. According to Frljić, political theatre has little to do with presenting and supporting one thesis: it is much more about creating a realm for discord and ideological plurality, and this involves experimenting with many theatre conventions at once. In *Un-Divine Comedy. Remains*, Józefczak's monologue was interrupted by Anna Radwan's speech, followed by a verbatim sequence in which actors presented their conflicting views about antisemitism in Poland and the rise of nationalism.

After the cue, 'From now on, I am not a Pole. From now on I am Jewish', the actors performed a parodic take on *Un-Divine Comedy*. In a choreographed scene, they recalled the symbols and themes that appear in the drama—such as the national anthem and the figure of the Virgin Mary—so that the fixed points of national reference/reverence became subverted or undermined. The Polish national anthem was sung in Russian or performed with the melody of Haydn's *Deutschlandlied*. Nodding to the set design in Swinarski's production (in which the altar was used as a place of marriage ceremony and then turned into a bed), the performers enacted the rape of a woman who was then crowned as the Blessed Virgin Mary, Mother of God, before giving birth to the Star of David on the altar—which was later transformed into a concentration camp. At the end of this sequence, the actors formed a cortège and participated in a confession, when they admitted the sins they had allegedly committed during the performance (the rape of the Virgin Mary, giving birth to a Jewish descendant, resigning from Polish identity). The edited scenes highlighted the production's cultural intertextuality by integrating references to classic episodes from Polish theatre—the concentration camp was a quotation from Grotowski's *Akropolis* (1962), while the choreography and the song that was used in the background ('My, pierwsza brygada' ['We Are the First Brigade']) referred to Kantor's *Wielopole, Wielopole* (1981). These productions have a very special place in the history of Polish theatre as they openly problematized the relationship between remembering and portraying the Holocaust.

Klata and Majewski insisted on attending a rehearsal and, on 8 November, they observed the approximately twenty-minute sequence described above. These scenes, which were chosen because they gave an indicative sense of the performance as a whole, caused a deep conflict between the creative team and the management, who put the production on hold.

Performance on hold

After their visit to the rehearsal room, Klata and Majewski called Frljić and his dramaturgical team to the director's office where they questioned the ideological and aesthetic direction of the production. The discussion was quickly overshadowed by a personal argument, in which Klata accused us of misrepresenting Krasiński's work, Swinarski's performance, and the Holocaust discourse. He claimed that in Polish theatre there had been many depictions of the debate concerning the Holocaust and tackling this issue once again was pointless, as was the idea of treating Krasiński's drama as a pretext for another discussion. He argued that the presented segment had little to do with Krasiński's play and that clearly none of us possessed detailed knowledge about the field of Holocaust representations in Polish art. By the end of the meeting, the disagreement between management and dramaturgical team was not resolved. Instead, the rehearsals were halted, and we were asked to await Klata's decision concerning the future of the production. On the next day, the actors tried to convince Klata that calling off the production was misguided and unwanted by the cast. Frljić had an additional meeting with Klata and, after a couple of days, the rehearsals were allowed to resume. Klata admitted to Frljić that he was put off by the aesthetic of the piece; however, he also claimed he understood the need to introduce a variety of theatre styles and methodologies at the Stary. On the following day, he came to the rehearsal room to apologize and to point out that, on an ideological level, the direction of *Un-Divine Comedy. Remains* was compatible with the theatre's perspective. He explained that the work should be focused on highlighting the most relevant and painful aspects of the political dispute over national identity and nationalism in Poland.

One week after Klata's intervention, on 14 November 2013, a group of spectators interrupted his production of Strindberg's *To Damascus*. During a sequence in which actors simulated sexual intercourse on stage, the group started insulting them, shouting, and whistling. Klata asked them to leave and the performance resumed. A couple of days later, the initiator of the protest, Stanisław Markowski, reignited the issue when he claimed that the protest was against Klata and Majewski's artistic direction of the Stary:

> We came to the conclusion that that's the last straw, it is no longer a national theatre. On this stage there should be place for plays that enrich the audience and don't just serve up scandal. Meanwhile, everything here has gone to the gutter. (Cited in Gąsior 2013)

Klata replied in the press that he was 'deeply embarrassed with the crass behaviour of a group of litigators' and that he and his co-workers were not going to 'bury their heads in the sand, [but] want to confront the audience that represents another point of view in a peaceful way' (Pawłowski 2013). The right-wing newspaper *Dziennik Polski*, which had waged a campaign against the management of the Stary since October 2013, condemned the gesture of the group as shameful and misguided (Kręskawiec 2013).

On 22 November 2013, *Dziennik Polski* published an article by its culture editor, Wacław Krupiński, about the upcoming production of *Un-Divine Comedy. Remains*. Though based on hearsay, it prompted Jan Klata to cancel the production:

> Two weeks before the opening, on the stage of Stary Theatre the conflict continues. Some of the actors are outraged by the method of using Krasiński's text. Actors who spoke about the reasons for leaving the production don't want their names to be mentioned. However, we know from unofficial sources that they did not want to participate in a piece that—allegedly—is a huge provocation and has nothing in common with the text of the playwright, nor with the staging of his tragedy that was realized on this stage in 1965 by Konrad Swinarski. [...] *Un-Divine Comedy* in [Frljić's] version is a total revision. For a month and a half, the performance has been rehearsed without a script. In the play there are no characters from the drama. Sentences that are said are a result of actors' improvisations on Polish antisemitism, allegedly present in Swinarski's staging. 'We haven't worked with the text of the drama even once, but we participated in consecutive provocations that were meant to found a thesis that the Polish nation was mutually responsible for antisemitism' one of the actors relates. (Krupiński 2013)

The description of the performance presented in *Dziennik Polski* was partly accurate: the rehearsals were based on improvisations, the script was written on a day-to-day basis, and a sequence of the performance depicted a staged debate in which actors implied Polish complicity in antisemitic discourse; we also worked with the argument—presented already in Jan Kott's review—that Swinarski's production might have included a scene that was antisemitic. The article then describes the 'fake reconstruction' of Krasiński's play and highlights the potentially outrageous fragments—such as singing the Polish anthem in Russian and with the melody of *Deutschlandlied*, and giving birth to the Star of David (Krupiński 2013). However, Krupiński pointedly excluded any context in order to stir up a sense of outrage. For instance, he articulated his disbelief concerning Frljić's critical view of Swinarski's performance based on the fact that 'this exceptional director worked with theatres from Israel and he surely wouldn't have been invited there if these presumptions concerning his art made any sense'. He also did not seem to know that some of the scenes he condemned belonged to an earlier part of the process and had already been cut out. The article includes a fragment of a monologue—which had not been retained in the final production (indicating that the source of the article was misinformed or biased)—in which actors who opted to stay in the company accused those who left of betraying the performance. Finally, Krupiński queries: 'What is it all about? Surely not about theatre'. The management of the Stary decided to suspend the production four days after the publication.

The backlash that characterized the theatre management's tactics in the face of this publication suggests that the journalist's arguments and fears were shared by Klata and Majewski. I was called in to Klata's office and accused of offending the major acting stars of the Stary and, together with Goran Injac, of being 'responsible for burning down the theatre'. This exaggerated metaphor implied that the institution had re-established its territory and redefined itself as an entity consisting of people who acted on its behalf—and neither I (commissioned by the theatre to work on the production) nor Injac (a full-time worker at the Stary) were considered a part of this institution. When the article was published, Frljić was in Belgium leading a workshop, two other dramaturgs were in Ukraine, and I was in Kraków conducting rehearsals for three days in Frljić's absence. No one from the Stary contacted me after the publication of the article by *Dziennik Polski*: I was offered no legal counselling by the theatre, nor any public relations advice to deal with the attack from the press or with further comments and questions posed by journalists from *Gazeta Wyborcza* and *Dwutygodnik*. When Injac returned from Ukraine, we were called in to the management's office together: Klata accused us of bringing somebody 'from the Balkans' to bad-mouth Poland and of offending great and significant stars of Polish theatre—such as Anna Polony and Jerzy Trela, who had decided to leave the ensemble after the publication of the article in *Dziennik Polski*. At a time of crisis, this breakdown of communications prevented us from engaging in further dialogue. As soon as Frljić returned from Belgium, Majewski called an informal meeting at a nearby café and told him and his creative team that Klata had decided to suspend the production.

The official statement published by the Stary addressed 'all the forms of hostility and downright hatred coming from the outside' as the reason for suspending the work on the production. Yet, the 'hostility' identified by the management did not come from the outside: arguably, this argument served as a pretext for reuniting the employees of the Stary by constituting an enemy from the outside—the invidious press, a group of aggressive protesters, malevolent discussions initiated by the inhabitants of Kraków, hearsay—that threatened the institution. What was announced publicly was the threat 'from the outside' while, within the institution, the element that was treated as a threat was the production of *Un-Divine Comedy. Remains*—this proved to be the first casualty of the crisis. In this light, the decision of the management of the Stary may be regarded as an 'inside job': an example of self-censorship by an institution that found itself in a position to justify its own unwillingness to challenge dangerous political and social stands, and its capitulation to reactionary sociopolitical critique.

Despite its antisemitism, *Un-Divine Comedy* is still perceived as one of the most important texts on revolution and historical dialectics, and its most problematic layer has not been openly confronted in Polish theatre beyond Frljić's rehearsal room at the Stary. While this aspect of Swinarski's staging remained widely ignored (apart from Kott's commentary), Frljić's open confrontation with the antisemitic elements of Krasiński's play and of Swinarski's interpretation resulted in the cancellation of the production.

Four years later, in 2017, Frljić directed *The Curse* in Teatr Powszechny in Warsaw—a controversial Polish play that remains highly critical of the Catholic Church and its ideological background. The performance, which attacked hypocrisy and the cover-ups of sexual misconduct among the representatives of the Catholic Church, was subjected to harsh attacks from right-wing journalists, government representatives, and rioters. The management of the Powszechny Theatre, knowing in advance that the performance might stir controversy, did not retreat to avoid the dispute; on the contrary, they sought to prepare the creative and acting team for the debate and upcoming ideological tensions. Without creating divisions among employees of the Powszechny Theatre, the subsequent crisis resulted in a public debate on the unlimited power that the Catholic Church holds in Polish society, and it did not affect the stability of the theatre, which was able to maintain integrity in the face of political upheaval. Compared to the events at the Stary, the production at the Powszechny contributed to a debate that reached beyond institutional self-reference. As a result of *The Curse*, multiple organizations dedicated to fighting violence and abuse inflicted by the Catholic Church became vocal and more visible, while any discussion concerned with tackling Polish antisemitism in theatre came to a halt after *Un-Divine Comedy. Remains*. By acknowledging their employees in the process and ideological agenda, the management of the Powszechny

Theatre avoided experiencing backlash on an internal level. At the Stary Theatre, the unfinished production was blocked when it tried to prove one of its initial premises—that mechanisms of exclusion and discrimination are institutionally and socially supported.

Notes

1 For the avoidance of doubt, references to *Un-Divine Comedy* in the chapter refer to Krasinski's play; references to *Un-Divine Comedy. Remains* refer to Frljic''s adaptation of Krasinski's play.
2 Actors participating in the project were instructed by the management to follow the official arguments given for the cancellation of the production. The dramaturgical team, together with the director and set designer, were not obliged by their commissioning contracts to represent the official arguments and—because we had already lost our commissioned job—we did not feel the urgency to defend the decision of the Stary Theatre. Given that the cancellation happened against our will to continue working on the piece, we openly expressed our opinion. Actors who were told by the management that they should follow the official position did not sign the statement that the creative team published with Oliver Frljić in which we named the decision as an act of censorship.
3 Most of the actors who left belonged to the 'older generation', but those who stayed did not belong to one specific age group—two of them were approaching their seventies, some were in their late forties or early fifties, and others were in their thirties. Therefore, it is difficult to draw an age-based division as far as ideological standpoints are concerned.

References

Adamiecka-Sitek, Agata. 2015. 'Poles, Jews and Aesthetic Experience: On the Cancelled Production by Oliver Frljić', *Polish Theatre Journal*, 1: 1–21

Auslander, Peter. 1997. *From Acting to Performance: Essays in Modernism and Postmodernism* (London and New York: Routledge)

Cieślak, Jacek. 2012. 'Pięć sezonów z mistrzami—rozmowa z Janem Klatą', *Rzeczpospolita*, 16 July

'Coming Soon: Premiere of the Provocative Play "Danton" by Frljić'. 2012. *JustDubrovnik*, 15 August

Drewniak, Łukasz. 2013. 'Stary Teatr, nowa rewolucja', *Dziennik Polski*, 15 July

Gąsior, Michał. 2013. 'Organizator protestu w Teatrze Starym zabiera głos: To była chałtura na granicy kiczu i perwersji. Nie mogliśmy milczeć', *NaTemat*, 16 November

Gazur, Łukasz. 2013. 'Stary Teatr, nowa rewolucja', *Dziennik Polski*, 15 July

Jabłonkówna, Leonia. 2001. 'Kościół boga czy czarta?', in *Krytycy o Swinarskim*, ed. by M. Katarzyna Gliwa (Katowice: Muzeum Historii Katowic), pp. 96–105

Jakimiak, Agnieszka, and Joanna Wichowska. 2014. 'Szkic spektaklu, którego nie było', *Didaskalia*, 119: 15–20 <https://didaskalia.pl/sites/default/files/content/attachments/szkic_spektaklu_ktorego_nie_bylo_119_0.pdf> [accessed 31 October 2022]

Janion, Maria. 1970. 'Wstęp', in *Nie-Boska komedia Zygmunta Krasińskiego*, ed. by Maria Grabowska (Wrocław: Zakład Narodowy im. Ossolińskich), pp. 7–255

────── 2009. *Bohater, spisek, śmierć: wykłady żydowskie* (Warsaw: W.A.B.)

Kott, Jan. 1966. 'Diabelskie wątpliwości', *Dialog*, 4: 117–24

Kręskawiec, Marek. 2013. 'Tajne przez jawne na widowni Starego Teatru', *Dziennik Polski*, 14 November

Krupiński, Wacław. 2013. 'Nieboska prowokacja w Starym Teatrze. Aktorzy rezygnują', *Dziennik Polski*, 22 November

Kyzioł, Aneta. 2013. 'Jak teatr mierzy się z najnowszą historią', *Polityka*, 27, 2 July

Litak, Anna. 2011. 'Moralista Konrad Swinarski', Cyfrowe Muzeum <http://www.cyfrowemuzeum.stary.pl/przedstawienia/osoba/757/swinarski-konrad> [accessed 2 November 2021]

Mamoń, Bronisław, Jarosław Iwaszkiewicz, and Zygmunt Greń. 2001. *Krytycy o Swinarskim* (Katowice: Muzeum Historii Katowic)

Michnik, Adam. 2004. 'Poles and the Jews: How Deep the Guilt?', in *The Neighbours Respond*, ed. by Antony Polonsky and Joanna B. Michnic (Princeton and Oxford: Princeton University Press), pp. 434–40

Mouffe, Chantal. 1993. *The Return of the Political* (London and New York: Verso)

Mrozek, Witold. 2013. 'Dzierżyński uwodzi w Krakowie—weekend oskarżeń w Starym Teatrze', *Gazeta Wyborcza*, 26 June

Niziołek, Grzegorz. 2013. 'Protest', *Dwutygodnik*, 121

'Oliver Frljić & Mladinsko Theatre'. 2012. Programme of Kunstenfestivaldesarts, *beursschouwburg* <https://www.beursschouwburg.be/en/events/kunstenfestivaldesarts-2012/oliver-frljic-mladinsko-theatre-damned-be-the-traitor-of-his-homeland/> [accessed 2 November 2021]

'Oliver Frljić bientôt'. 2013. CIFAS workshop announcement <http://www.cifas.be/en/workshops/oliver-frljic> [accessed 2 November 2021]

Pawłowski, Roman. 2013. 'Atak na teatr, krzyk z widowni. Klata zażenowany chamskim zachowaniem', *Gazeta Wyborcza*, 16 November

Rothberg, Michael. 2009. *Multidirectional Memory: Remembering the Holocaust in the Age of Decolonization* (Stanford: Stanford University Press)

────── 2019. *The Implicated Subject: Beyond Victims and Perpetrators* (Stanford: Stanford University Press)

Soszyński, Paweł. 2013. 'Divine Kraków, Un-Divine Comedy: Talk with Oliver Frljić', *Biweekly*, 42, November

Stary management. 2013. 'Kraków. W Starym Teatrze zawieszono próby nad "Nie-Boską Komedią"', 26 November <https://e-teatr.pl/krakow-w-starym-teatrze-zawieszono-proby-nad-nie-boska-komedia-a170391> [accessed 2 November 2021]

Targoń, Joanna. 2013. 'Taki teatr, jaki robił Swinarski', *Dwutygodnik*, 120

──────. 2017. 'Klata i po Klacie', *Dialog*, 9.730: 5–22

6

Opera Censorship in Europe: Production, Circulation, and Reception in a Transnational Market

ANDREW HOLDEN

The opera industry in historical context: implications for censorship

Many of the trends in theatre censorship discussed in this volume are common across performing arts genres. However, several conditions within lyric opera mark out its particular susceptibility to new forms of censorship, notably the relationship between music, text, and staging, and opera's strong history of transnational production, mediation, and circulation. The continuing dominance of a largely nineteenth-century canon, and its legacy of operatic tropes like orientalism, fuels negative perceptions of its relevance and accessibility, and makes opera a site of contest between 'traditional' and progressive interpretations (Newark and Weber 2020). Opera has, since its earliest days, been created and circulated in a transnational context which negotiated legal, institutional, and informal processes of censorship.[1] The most frequently discussed case study of opera's variegated treatment by official authorities is that of Giuseppe Verdi's career. Religious and political themes in his operas were subject to widely differing treatment by authorities across the pre-unification Italian peninsula, and elsewhere in Europe.[2] The history of Verdi's operas also highlights how authorities often viewed opera more leniently than spoken drama or literature.[3] However, even in a democratic country like the United Kingdom, new operas could still excite the ire of the Lord Chamberlain's censorship in the early twentieth century. Richard Strauss's adaptation of Oscar Wilde (using the German translation by Hedwig Lachmann) was initially banned until conductor Adrian Boult negotiated an acceptable staging of *Salome* (Rowden 2016). Even in the 1940s, Benjamin Britten's *The Rape of Lucretia* was compared by the English censor to D.H. Lawrence's *Lady Chatterley's Lover* when requiring changes to the libretto (Kildea 2013: 9–10).

After the Second World War, assumptions within Western European countries emphasized that 'universal' values of freedom of expression tended to undermine state controls across the spectrum of artistic practice and consumption, including opera—attitudes which spread east after the collapse of communism—despite the persistence of formal and informal censorship at national, regional, and local levels in many countries.[4] In the twenty-first century, the global circulation of opera has been transformed by multiple political, socio-economic, and technological trends. The opera business model in many European countries has been weakened by changing audience behaviour and declining public grants, with companies required to court private donors more assiduously and generate higher commercial income (Payne 2015: 17–30). One strategy to address these threats has been for major institutions to diversify income and audiences through an expanded global system of co-production and hires to share costs and enhance their profile.[5] This transactional circulation of productions, transplanting them between different cultural contexts, and often linked to political agendas of cultural diplomacy, frequently results in censorship of existing productions for aspects of sexual, moral, and political content to an extent not seen for over a century, and which might be unacceptable in native centres of production or funding. For example, gender norms, sexuality, and violence, cultural habits like smoking and tattoos, and the visual representation of naked flesh are policed in highly individual contexts as opera ecologies expand in regions like East Asia and the Middle East. Furthermore, in many countries where freedom of expression and artistic licence were previously expanding, for example the former Soviet bloc, restrictions are re-emerging, and opera practitioners find themselves once more in a culture war with public authorities.

The immediacy and unpredictability of digital reception and criticism also pose fundamental challenges for opera companies, practitioners, and audiences, which explode the boundaries between regulatory and critical control. Opera performance tradition since the mid-nineteenth century has privileged signifiers suggested by text and stage directions, and used established modes of storytelling (Abbate 1991, Penner 2020). Power structures in performance practice elevate this tradition alongside the authority of the conductor, and more recently the stage director, but these are incrementally being breached by more collaborative approaches to production, as well as performer and audience activism based on gender and ethnicity.[6] As I aim to demonstrate in this chapter, these structural innovations challenge existing concepts of censorship, in which a range of participants (such as singers, technical crew, and members of the public) have agency in processes that may mimic regulatory control, in pursuit of diversity and against cultural appropriation—for example, ethnocentric operatic tropes such as 'blackface' Otellos and 'yellowface' orientalism. Social media and the internet, amidst a wider political debate about cancel culture, have become increasingly dominant catalysts or even agents in these processes.

Towards a new theoretical model of opera censorship

The heterogeneity of these contemporary processes suggests that existing analytical frameworks of censorship need re-assessing. The 'new censorship' debate, beginning in the 1980s, reinvigorated theoretical concepts of censorship drawing on a range of different philosophical approaches, but with a strong emphasis on Foucault's constitutive model of power:

> What makes power hold good, what makes it accepted, is simply the fact that it doesn't only weigh on us as a force that says no, but that it traverses and produces things, it induces pleasure, forms knowledge, produces discourse. It needs to be considered as a productive network, which runs through the whole social body, much more than as a negative instance whose function is repression. (1995: 119)

Various scholars, including Richard Burt (1998), Judith Butler (1998), and Helen Freshwater (2004), have wrestled with the implications of deconstructing juridical definitions of censorship and an understanding which implies censorship's ubiquity or inevitability, elaborating different 'linear scales' between state repression and murder at one extreme and the constitutive or productive outcomes of informal or self-censorship at the other. However, when we try to apply them to real-world contexts involving the dynamic relationships between multiple agents—administrators and artists within an opera company, during the rehearsal process, and the digital activism prevalent in current culture wars—linear models feel inadequate. As Burt has argued, building on Foucault (1995), censorship involves both cultural legitimation as well as de-legitimation (1998: 17–18). This is particularly helpful when we look at how new agents within opera, notably for race equality and gender empowerment, are challenging existing performance traditions and the operatic canon.

I also refer to ethnographic approaches to performance and opera research pioneered by sociologist Paul Atkinson, who applies principles of organizational anthropology to the administration and production of opera, focusing on the negotiation and subtle modes of communication required within the rehearsal room (2010: 31–33).[7] This provides a more practical lens for viewing these organic instances of censorship in action. This chapter therefore uses a definition of censorship in opera which foregrounds the dynamic nature of the ecology of opera production, where censorship involves both exclusion/excision and inclusion/creation, often within the same act, through control of the process of opera's production and mediation. This complexity is being heightened by three factors around which my case studies are structured: opera's transnational circulation; the political reappraisal of the opera canon; and the expansion of potential sites of censorship from the performance (or publication) of the artistic work to casting and production, marketing, social media, and audience engagement. The case studies address fundamental questions about power and agency in opera production—who is involved and who is excluded in the transnational mobility of opera, and how we can use a more multivalent understanding of censorship to articulate how the negotiation of performance and communication of opera involves multiple agents.

A methodological challenge that requires acknowledgement is the barrier to fieldwork and data collection for researchers. Apart from those professionals at genuine risk of persecution or imprisonment, freelance artists are often unwilling to discuss openly instances in which they may have been subjected to, or even complicit in, acts of censorship during the production of opera. Similar motivations prevent many administrators or theatre employees discussing experiences that may involve reputational risk. Research for this chapter included interviews with artists and administrators (some requiring anonymity), and attendance at rehearsals and performances of case study productions.

Opera in Oman: exporting censorship or European cultural diplomacy?

My first group of case studies examines censorship within the transnational model of global opera production, through productions which circulate from theatre to theatre, in this example from Europe to the Middle East, with *Maria Stuarda* and *Aida* in Oman. These Omani productions demonstrate how European opera companies employ rhetorical strategies of cultural exchange and sensitivity to distance themselves from complicity in acts of censorship, acts which risk compromising the artistic vision of the production's creators, sometimes without their involvement or consent. The Royal Opera House in Muscat, which opened in 2011, was built by the Sultan of Oman. The Sultanate of Oman has been described by John Beasant (2014), writer and observer on the Middle East, as the most charming police state in the world. On Freedom House's scale for political and civic rights, it scores a lowly 23 out of 100, putting it within the category of countries which are considered 'not free' (Repucci and Slipowitz 2021). Journalists and protesters criticizing the monarchy or investigating corruption are regularly jailed, and internet freedom is heavily circumscribed. The creation of the opera house was part of the Sultanate's strategy to open up to the West and engage in cross-cultural exchange and dialogue. Yet its programming is tightly if indirectly approved by a board comprising three ministers and a member of the royal family which reports to the deputy prime minister. The opera house is run mainly by administrators and technicians from overseas. Rather than producing its own work, co-producing with other theatres, or hiring productions to be staged by a resident company, it invites foreign companies to bring productions to Oman including staging, cast, and technical crew, acting more like a receiving house than a producing theatre. Its first artistic director, Christina

Scheppelmann, subsequently general manager at Seattle Opera, came to Oman from the Teatro Liceu in Barcelona. She explains the theatre's perspective on programming by describing it as a process not governed by censorship, but by a sense of cultural sensitivity:

> [Those of us from a Western cultural tradition] have hopefully given up on colonising. It's cultural exchange. As you expand your reach you have to adapt. It is a different culture than ours and we are not there to homogenize cultures. When I had doubts [about how to programme works] I talked with my Omani colleagues, especially my brilliant female colleagues [...]. I employed criteria that I learned from them. (Scheppelmann 2019)

Scheppelmann compares the changes required of particular operas to the modifications that Japanese performers might make to simplify kabuki theatre for a Western audience: 'The changes would involve nothing drastic that would really change the actual story' (ibid.). The Omanis, according to Scheppelmann, like opera with a dramatic framework that relates to their local theatrical art forms and tradition of storytelling, most famously *A Thousand and One Nights*.

Maria Stuarda

Scheppelmann may disavow the term censorship, but a number of repertory operas are considered unprogrammable in Oman—notably *Tosca*. Puccini's opera was prominent on the list of operas discussed between ROH Oman and Welsh National Opera for WNO to take to Oman in 2013. As Isabel Murphy, former head of planning at WNO, recalls from the negotiations, anything with a strong religious theme, explicit sexual content, or inappropriate language was rejected (2019). Eventually, the chosen work was Donizetti's *Maria Stuarda*. Though both politics and religion feature in *Maria Stuarda*, Scheppelmann contends that *Maria Stuarda* resonated more with educated Omanis who had studied European literature and history, and appealed to their taste for stories of nobility and moral integrity.

Donizetti's libretto for *Maria Stuarda* by Giuseppe Bardari was drawn from Andrea Maffei's translation of Schiller's play *Maria Stuart*, in which Schiller invented a confrontation between Mary and Elizabeth. This scene in the libretto contains the fateful insult that Mary hurls at her cousin, '*vil bastarda!*', which led Donizetti's opera to become a victim of censorship on its first conception in 1834 (Act I.6, bar 267–70). With the opera banned by the Bourbon regime in Naples, Donizetti produced a sanitized version, *Buondelmonte*, using the same music, which the composer found highly unsatisfactory. Even when brought to the stage finally as *Maria Stuarda* in Milan in 1836, censorship stalked its production. Donizetti had made various musical changes to adapt the eponymous role for the voice of Maria

Malibran, as was common practice in nineteenth-century opera. He had also agreed to various textual and dramatic amendments to accommodate the Milan censor, including changing *'vil bastarda'* to *'donna vile'* and altering the confession scene when the stage direction indicates that Maria falls to her knees before Talbot, Earl of Shrewsbury, to ask her friends to pray for her, presumably considered an unregal posture before a subordinate (Act III.8, bar 195). Malibran herself clearly preferred the uncensored version, which she delivered at the premiere, leading the Milan police to close the production. The *'bastarda'* line continued to plague revivals of the opera, but Donizetti had little involvement except offering an alternative, for a Milan production in 1837, of *'bugiarda'* (liar) (Donizetti 1997: XLII–VII).

Following selection of the opera to be brought to Oman, the next stage of the process, common to both my Omani case studies, was for the Omani personnel to view a performance and send a list of changes required by the Royal Opera House, to staging and costume in particular. *Maria Stuarda* presented a range of different challenges in this regard. In 2013, WNO had originally produced the complete 'Tudor trilogy' of Donizetti operas including *Anna Bolena* and *Roberto Devereux*. The cycle shared a uniting design concept by British designer Madeleine Boyd, set in a nonspecific period drawing on references to both Elizabethan architecture and costume as well as contemporary fashion, including Vivienne Westwood. In Austrian director Rudolf Frey's production of *Maria Stuarda*, the stage was divided by two movable trucks, which represented each queen's world and could be read as different types of incarceration. Frey's concept involved several postmodern *Regietheater* glosses that distanced the action from any sense of its Elizabethan setting, for example Maria holding a gun and later smoking a cigarette while she waits for news of her impending fate in Act III. These images were excised not for the implicit disrespect to a monarch, according to Scheppelmann, but because it was thought the postmodern period interventions would not be understood by the local audience (2019). Maria was also required in the Welsh production to jump from the stage truck onto the stage floor. This was one of the actions that was excised for seeming 'unqueenly'. Scheppelmann acknowledges that depictions of regal authority would be sensitive in Oman: there is a 'strong hierarchy in the Arab world especially in the Gulf. If you're of higher standing or royal a certain behaviour is expected of you' (2019). Talbot's washing of Maria's feet in Act III.8, which had caused the Milan censor to intervene in 1836, was also restaged. This echo of the historical censorship of the opera invites a consideration of the censorship of canonical works as a type of palimpsest in which we glimpse echoes of previous acts of suppression, compromise, or self-suppression that ripple through contemporary and future readings of these timeless works. It may be impossible to erase these histories of censorship from the performance of problematic aspects of canonical works.

Perhaps incongruously, the immortal line '*vil bastarda*' was retained in Oman. However, one of the most arresting visual images of the production—a copper-effect leather breastplate bodice shaped like a female torso—was replaced by arm-covering sleeves and a red sash. The process for executing these changes illustrates again how artists involved in creating a work can lose agency through the production process as it operates in this type of international hire between opera companies. Neither the director nor the designer were involved in effecting these changes, partly for practical reasons as they were already working on other productions. However, neither felt comfortable with the way they were executed or the effects that were realized, for example the quality of the costume materials and fitting, or the effacement of the period distancing (Boyd 2019, Frey 2019). Common practice would give a freelance director or designer control or influence over changes for a revival or hire, but on this occasion the Omani hire of *Maria Stuarda* was considered a tour of the main run of the production, and the alterations were handled by WNO technical teams. Yet WNO also refutes any suggestion of involvement in a process of censorship. As Murphy describes it, 'the censorship was done [in Oman] before they chose *Maria Stuarda*' (2019). These perspectives may not be reconciled and highlight the highly contested nature of judgements about what constitutes censorship and who controls the 'editing' of artists' work.

Aida

My second Omani case study is Teatro Regio di Torino's 2015 production of Verdi's *Aida*, directed by William Friedkin, responsible for Hollywood films including *The French Connection* (1971) and *The Exorcist* (1973). His staging was avowedly traditional in maintaining the setting in ancient Egypt, and was specifically created to celebrate the latest refurbishment of the Museo Egizio in Turin, the most important Egyptian museum collection outside Egypt. Carlo Diappi's sets specifically referenced the collections in the Museo Egizio. The genesis and performance tradition of *Aida* in relation to its Egyptian setting, and the degree to which it exhibits orientalist tropes, has an extensive literature relevant to the sexual and racial aspects of the staging under consideration here.[8] This case study again illustrates the complex interplay between different motivations for censorship, including the cross-cultural circulation of the production and progressive concerns about racist tropes.

In Italy, the act of blacking up white singers and actors, 'blackface', sits alongside Black singers being cast in principal roles, and has been little challenged until very recently. In the inaugural Turin performances of this production, the first-cast Aida and her father, the Egyptian king Amonasro, were sung by African Americans Kristin Lewis and Mark S. Doss. They were supported by choristers and actors who were blacked-up as African Ethiopians. The second-cast Aida and Amonasro, Anna Pirozzi in Turin and Ambrogio Maestri in Oman, were white and given make-up darker than their own skin, but less extreme than that given to the chorus and actors. Apart from Aida herself, Ethiopians were depicted as savage or uncivilized. Extensive reworking of the costumes was carried out following consultation with ROH Oman, which operated different standards depending on the character's gender and prominence. Principals' costumes, notably for Amonasro, were lengthened to cover the knees and arms, as well as that of the hero general, Radames. Costumes for both Aida and her nemesis, the princess Amneris, had their necklines raised to cover the cleavage. The only exception was made for Aida herself, who was allowed to show bare arms. For the chorus and actors, no bare limbs, female cleavage, or male chests were allowed to be visible, consistent with the cultural norms in Oman where, for example, men may not wear short trousers on the street, although swimming costumes are acceptable on the beach.[9]

According to Scheppelmann, during the process of negotiation with the Teatro Regio:

> I asked about the dancers' costumes not slipping down or kissing or intimate touching—it's not just religion, their cultural norms are different, we are not the measure of all things. For them it can be perceived as borderline prostitution. There was discomfort about seeing skimpily dressed dancers, and men in skintight leggings. You have to respect the differences in how things are perceived. (2019)

Crucially for this production, transparency and the impression of nudity were prohibited, so golden leotards were created for the dancers in the triumphal scene, and for the priestesses' dance in Act I, white equivalents were worn under the existing veiled costumes. These changes were made by the Regio's own wardrobe department, and their team considered them aesthetically more successful than those required for the 'Dance of the Moorish Slaves' in Act II, where brown body suits given to the dancers, combined with existing black wigs and brown make-up, produced an effect of very crude blacking-up.

Opera in the new European culture wars

The Teatro Regio *Aida*'s use of blackface in Oman also raises another issue: opera's travails in the gathering culture war between progressive approaches to opera production—encompassing movements for diversity and equality—and defenders of traditional performance practice, which such movements challenge. Already in the 1990s Burt observed, not uncontroversially, that a rhetoric of diversity risks reinscribing a censorious logic of exclusion (1994: xv). More recently, North American attitudes to gender and racial politics have gradually permeated Western Europe. The historic censoring or ghettoizing of Black voices in a few designated Black or exoticized roles has been partially eroded. The question of representation has now widened to encompass the operatic canon, what stories are excluded, and how the core repertoire addresses issues including race, patriarchy, and sexual violence. *Regietheater* approaches to opera staging have long outraged more conservative audiences. In the social media age, these have even generated a hyperactive Facebook group, Against Modern Opera Productions (AMOP), which polices productions across the world for crimes against what it considers the composer's original intentions, pitting adored conservative heroes like Franco Zeffirelli against its bêtes noires, notably Catalan director Calixto Bieito. The vitriol expressed by AMOP's followers spills over into direct abuse of individuals on social media who express what AMOP consider to be heretical views on opera production. Musicologist Mark Berry, in conversation with Eli Zeger, has established that the membership of the German-language AMOP group has a significant crossover with membership of PEGIDA, the far-right anti-Islam movement—cultural conservatism correlates in this case with a political programme to exclude Muslims from European society (Zeger 2017).

Crises of self-censorship

Unlike the situation in countries like Oman, operating an official system of censorship analogous with nineteenth-century practice in Europe, opera in the West is struggling to navigate its way through the hyper-polarized atmosphere of cancel culture, triggering, and identity politics in the transnational context of its production. Productions of two very different operas in 2006 and 2015 illustrate how *Regietheater* approaches to the reinterpretation of opera have toppled opera companies into crises of self-censorship in the midst of new social and cultural environments. In 2006, Hans Neuenfels' production of Mozart's *Idomeneo* at the Deutsche Oper in Berlin placed severed heads of religious prophets—Christ, Muhammad, and Buddha—on stage alongside the classical god Neptune, whose wrath directs the action of the story. The figurative representation of the decapitated Muslim prophet was bound to be particularly controversial and had aroused disquiet among some Muslims when the production was first staged in 2003. By 2006, in the wake of the furore over the Danish publication of cartoons satirizing the Prophet, the German security services notified the theatre of an anonymous threat. Neuenfels reportedly refused to excise the scene from the production and the theatre's management, led by Intendant Kirsten Harms, took the decision to withdraw the planned revival of the production. Political and artistic outrage at this restriction of free speech in Germany was intense, reaching even to Chancellor Angela Merkel, a well-known melomane. Subsequently a revised security analysis revealed no concrete threat and the decision was reversed (Dempster and Lansey 2006).

Conversely, when Damiano Michieletto's production of Rossini's *Guillaume Tell* was produced at the Royal Opera, Covent Garden in 2015, protests were first raised, during and following the dress rehearsal, about the action in the Act III ballet. Ballets in French grand opera were obligatory divertissement in the nineteenth century, but Michieletto took the libretto's stage direction, '[the German] soldiers force the Swiss women to dance with them', to an extreme conclusion by staging a simulated gang rape by the male chorus of one of the female villagers (performed by a dancer), whom they stripped naked. Some women reported feeling extremely upset at this depiction of sexual violence, with one engaging Kasper Holten, the Covent Garden artistic director, in email correspondence in which changes to the scene were posited alongside stronger warnings about the production's content (Lebrecht 2015, Rogers 2015). The company strenuously defended the director's intention to use the scene to depict the horror of war. However, audience reaction to the scene on opening night involved aggressive booing and protests, reflected in the critical reaction to the production which was almost entirely condemnatory (Ashley 2015, Thicknesse 2015). The negative responses encompassed both gender-based objection to the perceived gratuity of the sexual violence and conservative opposition to progressive 'realist' interpretation of canonical opera, sometimes heard from the same witnesses.[10] Following the reaction to the premiere, the extent of the nudity and the choreography were adjusted but the scene was retained.[11] Three years later, the production was revived by the Teatro Massimo in Palermo, with only limited booing of the director at opening night (almost de rigueur among conservative Italian audiences in response to any reinterpretation of a canonical work by an Italian composer) but no wider protest (Imam 2018). Both critical and audience reaction to the aesthetics of *Regietheater* in these productions points towards a shift in terrain where perceived offence against liberal principles, for example protecting the interests of minorities, or campaigns against gender-based violence become the driver for forms of censorship and self-censorship.

Italy's attitude towards blackface was finally challenged in 2019 by the American soprano Tamara Wilson in yet another production of *Aida*. Cast as Aida for some of the Arena di Verona's long run of summer performances, Wilson objected to the use of blackface: 'I don't want to be a cog in the wheel of institutional racism. I won't wear blackface anymore or wear the costume given to actresses until now [to simulate Black arms]' (Florio 2019). She negotiated with the company a modified form of make-up, only to withdraw from the performance due to ill health. She was replaced by another of the sopranos in the run, Uruguayan Maria José Siri, who used the original blackface make-up (ibid.). Another Italian soprano, Anna Pirozzi, who had sung Aida in the Teatro Regio production, also sang in the 2019 Verona production, and posted to Facebook—the week before Wilson's case reached the media—a timelapse video of being blacked-up as Aida. For Wilson it was a lesson learned: 'I was naïve. I should have found out that for this production they would require me to wear blackface' (ibid.). She found little support from her peers in Italy. Placido Domingo, conducting the performances at Verona, commented that he had always worn blackface for Otello and was made up with 'almond eyes' for Calaf in Puccini's *Turandot*, and that 'the text should be respected' (di Peluso 2019). Nonagenarian director Pier Luigi Pizzi argued: 'it's not racist to ask singers to follow the directions of Verdi' (ibid.). Meanwhile, Fortunato Ortombina, head of Venice's Teatro alla Fenice, attempted a more reductionist explanation of racial characterization and casting by arguing that 'if, for example an African American singer was cast as Manon Lescaut, she wouldn't be made-up as white. But only because it's difficult to lighten her skin. The opposite, though, one can do' (ibid.). It would have been easy to observe that occasions for whitening Black singers in Italy were vanishingly rare, considering that few had ever been cast in roles beyond those designated as Black in the libretto.

Deracializing *Porgy and Bess* in Hungary

Hungary has long been the crucible of the conflict between progressive liberal values and authoritarian conservatism in Europe, and the cultural politics of its far-right government under newly re-elected prime minister Viktor Orbàn have now also extended to the racial politics of opera. In 2018, the Hungarian State Opera produced Gershwin's *Porgy and Bess*, a milestone work in countering the lack of Black representation in opera when it was composed in 1935, which the Gershwin Estate insists be performed by a predominantly Black cast. The continuation of this rule has been challenged even in the USA, on the questionable basis that Black representation on the stage has sufficiently progressed that colour-blind casting should now extend also to this work (Tommasini 2002). Moreover, despite the opera's claims to portrayal of an authentic part of the African American experience, its all-white team of creators—combined with representations of race within which traces of minstrelsy are clearly visible—make it a problematic piece even for African Americans who appreciate its musical and dramatic strengths (André 2018: 85–119).

Yet Hungarian Opera's defiance of the Gershwin Estate put the work at the centre of the government's rhetoric claiming double standards on human rights by the liberal West, and its own domestic agenda of creating an ethnically homogenized white nation in which Roma, Black, and Muslim people are ostracized. On his appointment, the company's general manager Szilveszter Ókovács had flirted with more progressive programming including the stage musical of *Billy Elliot*, the story of the Durham boy who defies the narrow cultural confines of the former mining community in which he lives to become a ballet dancer. Considered an incitement to homosexuality by the government, the production was curtailed and thereafter Ókovács toed the regime line, including a season devoted to Christianity in opera (Balogh 2019). The director of the Hungarian

Porgy and Bess, András Almási-Tóth, outlined his reinterpretation of the opera in a YouTube marketing video:

> I have taken the plot out of its original settings. It revolves around people who have no homes but desire for the promised land. It is not the reality only of those who have lost their homes during Hurricane Katrina, but everyone's reality in a situation like this due to religious or social relationships. This piece has almost disappeared from the world of opera for the well-known legal restrictions. Now we have a sort of non-replica production because we don't need to have an all-Black cast. This way the story may get new dimensions. (2018)

Notwithstanding the fact that *Porgy and Bess* has far from 'disappeared from the world of opera', this rhetorical effort to deracialize the opera's narrative could not mask the racist ideology underlying official cultural policy.[12] The Hungarian Opera used the bizarre tactic of requiring white singers to sign a declaration that they 'identified' as African American. At the same time, Ókovács condemned the Gershwin Estate rule as 'racist and politically incorrect' and asked rhetorically, 'What colour is "black" on the Pantone scale? [...] One of Barack Obama's grandparents was "white", do you think it would be right if he performed in *Porgy and Bess*?' (Balogh 2019). As Valencia James—Barbadian dancer, artist, and activist, who worked for ten years in Hungary—commented on the episode, the Hungarian regime's co-option of the racist victim label for white Hungarians is part of the far-right strategy of emptying racism of any meaning, linked to structures of power which allow one culture to dominate another (James 2019). For Black performers such as James, *Porgy and Bess*'s reinterpretation outside its original setting should not be undertaken by whites, particularly those engaged, as in Hungary, in marginalizing their non-white communities.

The silencing of Black voices in global opera

The historic exclusion and censoring of Black voices and bodies on the operatic stage has progressively been challenged in the seven decades since *Porgy and Bess*'s creation, and the first Black singers were permitted to sing on the main stages of European opera houses, albeit in very limited roles, from the late 1950s. However, continuing lack of opportunity has been further highlighted by Black artists in the wake of the George Floyd murder in the USA on 25 May 2020. In a Facebook Live discussion, 'Lift Every Voice', hosted by Los Angeles Opera on 5 June 2020 as part of its response to the Black Lives Matter movement, several Black artists, led by soprano J'Nai Bridges, catalogued the myriad ways in which their off-stage experience in opera was as damaging to their opportunities and well-being as issues around casting. They pointed to the lack of diversity in management, among directors and donors, as well as racist interactions with audiences and donors. Morris Robinson, a bass who as well as being a regular performer at the Metropolitan Opera has sung in major theatres across Europe, summed up his experience:

> I walk around every opera rehearsal I've ever been to guarded [...] cognisant of the fact that my interaction needs to be very public, in front of everyone, and very innocuous, such that all doubts, all potential images, are eradicated [...] In 20 years, I've never been hired by a Black person; I've never been directed by a Black person; I've never had a Black C.E.O. of a company; I've never had a Black president of the board; I've never had a Black conductor [...] I don't even have Black stage managers. None, not ever, for 20 years. (Borne 2020)

Consequently, in addition to the historic and continuing censoring of Black artists, many feel compelled to self-censor their professional behaviour in order to conform. Such lack of diversity off-stage is replicated across Europe, even in those countries where addressing lack of diversity is built into national and organizational policy and funding, such as the United Kingdom.[13] In 2019, Paris Opera appointed a new general director, the German Alexander Neef, who most recently had been leading both Canadian Opera Company and Santa Fe Opera. He attracted opprobrium from right-wing commentators for commissioning a report on diversity from historian Pap Ndiaye and rights activist Constance Rivière, which recommended wholesale audit and revision of practices at the company and ballet school, including elements of repertoire. The authors also advocated wider structural changes in education at conservatoires, echoing similar research by Arts Council England on classical music education in the UK (Arts Council England 2021). The authors of the Paris report denied that their recommendations on repertoire and performance practice amounted to censorship (Chaudon 2021). Yet the editor-in-chief of *Le Monde*, Michel Guerrin, accused Neef of 'taking the Paris Opera down the road of runaway self-censorship by artists and programmers to avoid trouble' ('La France' 2021).

Similar controversy regarding racial tropes within opera engulfed Scottish Opera in 2021 when its production of John Adams' *Nixon in China* was nominated for a prestigious Sky Arts award. The pressure group BEATS (British East & Southeast Asians in the Screen & Stage Industry) accused the company of whitewashing its production with white singers in Chinese roles and suggestions of yellowface make-up. Colour-conscious casting, according to BEATS, should be used, and pan-Asian casting where actors of specific national heritage were unavailable (BEATS 2021a). This was not the first UK instance where claims of racist tropes impacted on the staging of a contemporary work—as opposed to the reinterpretation of canonical works like *Madama Butterfly*. In 2017, Music Theatre

Wales's (MTW) staging of *The Golden Dragon*, a new opera by Hungarian composer Peter Eötvös, provoked negative criticism with an all-white cast in a 'tragicomic' opera about the experience of Chinese immigrants, set in a 'pan-Asian restaurant' (Farrington 2019). MTW initially rejected the criticism through social media, arguing that 'the singers play a variety of roles, genders and nationalities; two air hostesses are played by burly men; a cricket is played by a tenor, an ant by a mezzo and a small boy by a grown woman [...] Quite deliberately, there is no realism'. This unleashed vociferous responses from Asian artists and campaigners, leading to the cancellation by the Hackney Empire Theatre of its performance of the opera (ibid.).[14]

This experience was forefront in the mind of Alex Reedijk, General Director of Scottish Opera, when the publicity images for its Sky Arts award nomination prompted an outcry from BEATS (Reedijk 2021). Working only from two images published on Twitter—one of Mao, ageing and ill, sung by Marc Le Brocq, the other of the ballet sequence 'The Red Detachment of Women'—BEATS accused Scottish Opera of having used yellowface make-up and having indulged in 'white-washed' casting (BEATS 2021b). In a statement, they argued for 'colour-conscious casting' in order to tackle the historic and continuing exclusion of artists of colour on the stage, and described the casting of white artists in 'non-white' roles as a 'regressive' perpetuation of this exclusion. Conversely, they recommended that pan-Asian casting, even of different nationalities to that of a character's own, should be made in preference to casting white artists in any East or Southeast Asian roles (BEATS 2021a). The management of Scottish Opera felt they had strong grounds to defend the production from these accusations, particularly as the 'twitterstorm had been started by people who hadn't even seen the production' (Reedijk 2021). The staging had been removed from a specifically Chinese setting following the critical response to the original performances (Maddox 2020). The company denied that the published images were evidence of yellowface make-up. They could point to the mixed casting among the principal singers (including Black baritone Eric Greene as Nixon and South Korean soprano Hye-Youn Lee as Madame Mao). However, Reedijk recognized that, through social media, these arguments were difficult to make and would 'pour more petrol on the firestorm' (Reedijk 2021). As a result, the company withdrew from the Sky Arts award nomination. Reedijk reflected that this caused 'a lot of internal pain as some staff took it very personally. A sense of injustice permeated the corridors' (ibid.). The company also received negative feedback from core supporters who accused them of cowardice and self-censorship. More positively, this episode focused the company's thinking about equality, diversity, and inclusion (EDI) themes; policies and procedures were revised; checklists developed for productions to ensure EDI compliance; and the company pledged to listen more to the views of cast members. A plan to revisit *Butterfly*—the company's first production in 1962—was paused while they considered how it might be staged appropriately and by what creative team.

Nixon in China therefore stands as an example of how complex censorship processes are currently operating in opera—censorship extends beyond the performance itself to impact the rhetorical tools of the theatrical world including a company's image and brand, and its use of social media and audience communication. Meanwhile, one form of censorship—the self-cancellation of promotion of the opera through an award—is conceded under pressure to address another form of censorship—the historic exclusion of non-white artists. A measured reflection by the Royal Opera House's artistic director, Oliver Mears, attempted to put a marker in the stand against reductionist, literal approaches to casting, while arguing for 'greater diversity across the board' (2022). Time will tell where such nuanced strategies will lead.

My analysis demonstrates that censorship is not one process or a linear action between two forces, the artist and 'authority'; nor is it solely a binary qualitative scale between censoring and not censoring. In opera more than elsewhere, there are many forces at play in what we might term a matrix of censorship, operating in multiple dimensions. Furthermore, in the context of the reinterpretation of opera and its relevance to new audiences and minority groups, many artists and equality campaigners argue that censorship may be an important and justifiable tool, particularly in countering the ongoing silencing of excluded voices. Yet evident risks are appearing as the megaphone power of social media has an amplifying effect across the industry, which many others believe chills creativity and artistic freedom, or simply abandons cherished performance traditions and repertoire. Opera companies are, undoubtedly, struggling to mediate between these impulses.

Notes

1. A country-by-country survey of stage censorship in the nineteenth century can be found in Goldstein 2009; Walter 2016 explores the relationship between censorship and the transnational nature of the opera industry in the nineteenth century. For further examples of the persistence of informal censorship, see Holden (2022): 174–7, and Izzo (2015).
2. Giger (1999) discusses the treatment of Verdi's mid-career operas in Rome; Chusid (2012: 78–81) suggests how Verdi's compositional strategy was driven by the need to create a convincing staging despite the censorship of religion; Körner (2018) questions assumptions about the officiousness of Austrian imperial censorship in its Italian provinces.
3. Piazzoni (2000: 173) quotes Italian censors' approval of the musical setting of *La forza del destino* despite the immorality of the text adapted from a Spanish play. Montemorra Marvin (2001) explores similar reactions towards Verdi's operas among the examiners of plays working for the Lord Chamberlain's

Office in London, and how their concern was focused more on the printed English translation of the Italian libretto rather than the original being sung.
4   O'Leary et al. (2016) provide a wide survey of these twentieth-century trends across Europe. My own research (Holden 2005) sets the end of the Lord Chamberlain's role in theatre censorship in England in the context of the wider regulation of public morality.
5   The increase in co-production has received little scholarly attention but as a strategy it has been examined at a local level in Italy in Mariani (2007).
6   On the development and state of *Regietheater* or 'director's opera', see Risi (2019) and André (2018).
7   A similar approach has been applied from a dramaturgical perspective in McKechnie (2014).
8   For the literature on *Aida* and exoticism, see Said (1993), Locke (2005), and Guarracino (2010).
9   One member of the production team compared the process to bringing a ballet gala to the neighbouring, stricter emirate of Bahrain in 2018, where the choreography of classical ballet did not offend local sensibilities, but publicity posters outside the theatre had to be photoshopped to cover up the ballerina's shoulders and lengthen her skirt to the knee (this information was disclosed to the author from a private source).
10 For example, by one audience member speaking at Oxford Brookes University's 'Opera and Violence' conference, 11 September 2018 <https://obertobrookes.com/2018/10/08/conference-report-oberto-2018-opera-and-violence/> [accessed 1 April 2022].
11 This information was disclosed to the author from a private source.
12 According to the OperaBase website—which holds a database of international opera productions—there were twenty-nine productions of *Porgy and Bess* outside the United States in the period 2011–21.
13 Since 2020, Arts Council England has been setting 'stretch targets' for its regularly funded organizations to address continuing lack of diversity. See Brown (2020).
14 Farrington (2019) has published a detailed chronology of this case study. For further background on the efforts of the artists involved to secure diversity in casting, see Rogers and Thorpe (2014).

References

Abbate, Carolyn. 1991. *Unsung Voices: Opera and Musical Narrative in the Nineteenth Century* (Princeton: Princeton University Press)

Almási-Tóth, András. 2018. '*Porgy and Bess* press conference', YouTube, 23 January <https://www.youtube.com/watch?v=kDcPsNADVL8&t=21s> [accessed 20 August 2021]

André, Naomi. 2018. *Black Opera: History, Power, Engagement* (Urbana: University of Illinois Press)

Arts Council England. 2021. 'Creating a Fairer and More Diverse Classical Music Sector for England'

Ashley, Tim. 2015. '*Guillaume Tell* Review: Sex, Violence and Protracted Booing', *Guardian*, 30 June

Atkinson, Paul. 2010. *Everyday Arias: An Operatic Ethnography* (Lanham: Altamira Press)

Balogh, Eva S. 2019. 'The Racist Gershwins and the Open-Minded Hungarians', *Hungarian Spectrum*, 12 April

Beasant, John. 2014. *Oman: The True-Life Drama and Intrigue of an Arab State* (London: Mainstream Digital)

BEATS. 2021a. 'BEATS Statement on Colour-Conscious Casting in Opera', n.d. <http://wearebeats.org.uk/> [accessed 6 September 2021]

BEATS. 2021b. 'BEATS Statement Regarding Scottish Opera's *Nixon in China*', 11 June <www.wearebeats.org.uk> [accessed 1 April 2022]

Borne, Joshua. 2020. 'Opera Can No Longer Ignore Its Race Problem', *New York Times*, 23 September

Boyd, Madeleine. 2019. Unpublished interview with the author, 10 June

Brown, Mark. 2020. 'Arts Bodies Threatened with Funding Cuts over Lack of Diversity', *Guardian*, 18 February

Burt, Richard (ed.). 1994. *The Administration of Aesthetics: Censorship, Political Criticism and the Public Sphere* (Minneapolis: University of Minnesota Press)

—— 1998. '(Un)Censoring in Detail: The Fetish of Censorship in the Early Modern Past and the Postmodern Present', in *Censorship and Silencing: Practices of Cultural Regulation*, ed. by Robert C. Post (Los Angeles: Getty Research Institute for the History of Art and the Humanities), pp. 17–42

Butler, Judith. 1998. 'Ruled Out: Vocabularies of the Censor', in *Censorship and Silencing: Practices of Cultural Regulation. Issues & Debates*, ed. by Robert C. Post (Los Angeles: Getty Research Institute for the History of Art and the Humanities), pp. 247–59

Chaudon, Marie-Valentine. 2021. 'L'Opéra de Paris s'engage pour la diversité', *La Croix*, 8 February

Chusid, Martin. 2012. *Il Trovatore: The Quintessential Italian Melodrama* (Rochester: University of Rochester Press)

di Peluso, Marianna. 2019. 'Domingo sull'Aida nera', *Il Corriere di Verona*, 28 July

Dempster, Judy, and Mark Lansey. 2006. 'Opera Cancelled over a Depiction of Muhammad', *New York Times*, 27 September

Donizetti, Gaetano. 1997. *Maria Stuarda: Tragedia Lirica in Two Acts by Giuseppe Bardari, Historical Introduction by Elizabeth Hudson* (Milan: Ricordi)

Farrington, Julia. 2019. 'Music Theatre Wales/The Golden Dragon', *Index on Censorship*, 15 May

Florio, Felice. 2019. 'L'Aida nera è razzista?', *Open Online*, 27 July

Foucault, Michel. 1995. *Power/Knowledge: Selected Interviews and Other Writings 1972–77*, ed. by Colin Gordon (Harlow: Pearson)

Freshwater, Helen. 2004. 'Towards a Redefinition of Censorship', in *Censorship and Cultural Regulation in the Modern Age*, ed. by Beate Müller, Critical Studies: Volume 22 (Amsterdam and New York: Brill), pp. 225–45

Frey, Rudolf. 2019. Email to the author, 1 June

Giger, Andreas. 1999. 'Social Control and the Censorship of Giuseppe Verdi's Operas in Rome (1844–1859)', *Cambridge Opera Journal*, 11.3: 233–65. https://doi.org/10.1017/S0954586700005061

Goldstein, Justin (ed.). 2009. *The Frightful Stage: Political Censorship of the Theatre in Nineteenth-Century Europe* (New York: Berghahn)

Guarracino, Serena. 2010. 'Verdi's *Aida* across the Mediterranean (and beyond)', *California Italian Studies Journal*, 1.1: 1–18

Holden, Andrew. 2005. *Makers and Manners: Politics and Morality in Post-War Britain* (London: Politico's Publishing)

────── 2022. 'From Heaven and Hell to the Grail Hall via Sant'Andrea della Valle: Religious Identity and the Internationalisation of Operatic Styles in Liberal Italy', in *Italian Opera in Global and Transnational Perspective: Reimagining Italianità in the Long Nineteenth Century*, ed. by Axel Körner and Paulo M. Kühl (Cambridge: Cambridge University Press), pp. 167–91

Imam, James. 2018. 'Damiano Michieletto's controversial *Guillaume Tell* resurfaces in Palermo', *Bachtrack*, 25 January

Izzo, Francesco. 2015. 'Censorship', in *Oxford Handbook on Opera*, ed. by Helen M. Greenwald (Oxford: Oxford University Press), pp. 817–39

James, Valencia. 2019. 'My Response to the Hungarian White-Washed *Porgy and Bess*', *valenciajames* blog, 3 May <https://valenciajames.com/2019/05/03/my-response-to-the-hungarian-state-operas-white-washed-porgy-and-bess/> [accessed 30 November 2022]

Kildea, Paul. 2013. 'On Ambiguity in Benjamin Britten', in *Rethinking Britten*, ed. by Philip Rupprecht (Oxford: Oxford University Press), pp. 3–19

Körner, Axel. 2018. 'Che il pubblico non venga defraudato degli spettacoli ad esso promessi: The Venetian Premiere of *La traviata* and Austria's Imperial Administration in 1853', *Verdiperspektiven*, 3: 93–109

'La France prend le chemin d'une autocensure galopante des artistes et des programmateurs afin d'éviter les ennuis'. 2021. *Le Monde*, 10 January

Lebrecht, Norman. 2015. 'An Open Letter from Kasper Holten on William Tell', *Slipped Disc* blog, 1 July. https://slippedisc.com/2015/07/exclusive-an-open-letter-from-kasper-holten-on-william-tell [accessed 7 September 2023]

Locke, Ralph P. 2005. 'Beyond the Exotic: How Eastern is *Aida*?', *Cambridge Opera Journal*, 17.2: 105–39. https://doi:10.1017/S0954586705002004

McKechnie, Kara. 2014. *Opera North: Historical and Dramaturgical Perspectives on Opera Studies* (Bingley: Emerald Publishing)

Maddox, Fiona. 2020. '*Nixon in China* Review—A Gripping Human Drama', *Guardian*, 22 February

Mariani, M.M. 2007. 'Coopetition as an Emergent Strategy: Empirical Evidence from an Italian Consortium of Opera Houses', *International Studies of Management and Organization*, 37.2: 97–126. https://doi.org/10.2753/IMO0020-8825370205

Mears, Oliver. 2022. 'Beyond Blackface and Yellowface: How Opera Can Address Prejudice', *Guardian*, 14 June

Montemorra Marvin, Roberta. 2001. 'The Censorship of Verdi's Operas in Victorian London', *Music and Letters*, 82.4: 582–610. https://doi.org/10.1093/ml/82.4.582

Murphy, Isabel. 2019. Unpublished interview with the author, 4 June

Newark, Cormack, and William Weber (eds). 2020. *The Oxford Handbook of the Operatic Canon* (Oxford: Oxford University Press)

O'Leary, Catherine, Diego Santos Sánchez, and Michael Thompson (eds). 2016. *Global Insights on Theatre Censorship* (New York and London: Routledge)

Payne, Nicholas. 2015. 'Trends and Innovations in Opera', in *The Business of Opera*, ed. by Anastasia Belina-Johnson and Derek B. Scott (London: Routledge), pp. 17–30

Penner, Ninna. 2020. *Storytelling in Opera and Musical Theatre* (Bloomington: Indiana University Press)
Piazzoni, Irene. 2000. *Spettacolo, istituzioni e società nell' Italia postunitaria 1860–1882* (Roma: Archivio Guido Izzi)
Reedijk, Alex. 2021. Unpublished interview with the author, 5 October
Repucci, Sarah, and Amy Slipowitz. 2021. 'Freedom in the World 2021: Democracy under Siege', Freedom House, Annual Report
Risi, Clemens. 2019. 'Opera in Performance: "Regietheater" and the Performative Turn', *The Opera Quarterly*, 35.1-2 (Winter–Spring): 7–19. https://doi.org/10.1093/oq/kbz013
Rogers, Amanda, and Ashley Thorpe. 2014. 'Interview with Daniel York, Actor, Writer, and Director and Anna Chen, Writer, Performer, and Broadcaster', *Contemporary Theatre Review*, 24.4: 496–503. https://doi.org/10.1080/10486801.2014.946922
Rogers, Catherine. 2015. 'Shock Factor'. *Opera Div* blog post <https://operacat.tumblr.com/post/122857938113/shock-factor> [accessed 6 September 2021]
Rowden, Clair. 2016. *Performing Salome, Revealing Stories* (London: Routledge)
Said, Edward. 1993. 'The Empire at Work: Verdi's *Aida*', in *Culture and Imperialism* (London: Vintage), pp. 111–31
Scheppelmann, Christina. 2019. Unpublished interview with the author, 31 May
Thicknesse, Robert. 2015. 'The Real Shame of the Royal Opera House's "Guillaume Tell"', Rhinegold Publishing, 3 July
Tommasini, Anthony. 2002. 'All-Black Casts for *Porgy and Bess*? That Ain't Necessarily So', *New York Times*, 20 March
Walter, Michael. 2016. *Oper: Geschichte einer Institution* (Stuttgart: J.B. Metzler and Kassel: Bärenreither)
Zeger, Eli. 2017. 'Rage and Cringe: On Against Modern Opera Productions', *VAN*, 10 August

Intervention 3

The Tenacity of Tradition: Performativity in the Dutch Black Pete Controversy

Lonneke van Heugten

Each year in October, many young children in the Netherlands begin to anxiously anticipate the arrival of Sinterklaas (Saint Nicholas) with his troupe of helpers called Pieten (Petes). Televised nationally, these characters arrive halfway through November by steamboat, supposedly from Spain, at a different harbour city each year. The ensuing parade attracts thousands of spectators as the 'good holy man' dressed up in a red bishop's costume with a mitre and a long white beard is carried along on his white horse, Amerigo, and the Petes hand out sweets from jute bags. Once the annual children's festivity has begun, the theatrical figures of Nicholas and his Petes are omnipresent in Dutch public life. Hundreds of Dutch municipalities organize parades. The adventures of Nicholas and his 'helpers' are reported daily in the *Sinterklaas News* (*Saint Nicholas News*) on the national television station, NTR. There are activities for kindergarten and elementary school children such as dressing up in the Petes' costumes, learning the songs, and making drawings. Images and decorations of Saint Nicholas and the Petes are prevalent in commercials, advertisements, supermarkets, and bakeries. There are even children's movies and theatrical productions about the adventures of these characters. For young children, anticipation is built from finding small gifts in their shoes on the morning of 5 December, supposedly delivered through the chimney by the Petes who are therefore deemed to be 'black as soot'. The culmination is the *pakjesavond* (gift-giving eve) on the night before 6 December, the anniversary of the death of the original Saint Nicholas of Myra, which is deemed to be his birthday. Then, in the privacy of family homes, as well as in schools and even workplaces, 'surprises' are exchanged, disguised gifts with poems mocking the receivers. This tradition is ceremoniously accompanied by Saint Nicholas songs and sweets.

Lonneke van Heugten, "The Tenacity of Tradition: Performativity in the Dutch Black Pete Controversy" in: *Theatre Censorship in Contemporary Europe: Silence and Protest*. University of Exeter Press (2024). © Lonneke van Heugten. DOI: 10.47788/CYXY9391

Often seen as a distinctive national tradition, the Saint Nicholas feast was part of the Dutch inventory list of UNESCO Intangible Heritage. However, in the summer of 2022, the version of the tradition upheld by *Sint Nicolaas Genootschap* (the Saint Nicholas Society) was removed from this list on ethical grounds (KIEN 2022), as it included a highly controversial element: namely, Zwarte Piet (Black Pete). The traditional version of the feast is still widely performed and defended to this day: the Black Pete character is played mainly by white adults, who cover their faces in black make-up, put on curly black wigs, and sometimes red lipstick. The parallels with racist characterizations in blackfacing and minstrel shows in the United States seem evident. Furthermore, the cartoonish Black Pete figure on the packaging of commercial products, wrapping paper, books, posters, and political cartoons was and sometimes still is a golliwog-like caricature. In 2019, the nationally televised *Saint Nicholas News* and the arrival parade replaced the black face paint of the performers with smudges of soot, but the controversial blackfacing continues to be donned and defended in many private and public spheres. The tenacity of this tradition is even more remarkable as critiques of the appearance of Black Pete emerged in the media as early as the 1920s, and intensified into activism from 2011. Since then, the Saint Nicholas preparations, parade, and feasts are accompanied by a parallel tradition of protest and debate.

While voices of critique have been unheard, silenced, or denied existence for decades, those who continue to defend and perform the racist stereotype of Black Pete often accuse objectors of censoring 'their' tradition. There are complex cultural politics at work in this reversal of censor and censored. This intervention delves into the performativity and theatricality of censorship in this tenacious tradition-turned-controversy. As the Saint Nicholas tradition is celebrated similarly in Belgium, and exists in many different iterations all over Europe, this is not just a local issue. Moreover, the analysis of the tenacity of Black Pete may shed light on the controversial elements in many other traditions.[1]

Cultural politics of a performative image repertoire

Generally, Black Pete's outfit is called a Moorish costume, but it cannot be traced to any single historical fashion. That the figure is a descendant from the Moors in the seventeenth century is often used as an argument for the non-racist nature of Pete.[2] This bypasses the performativity of images and narratives that circulated in the time of teacher Jan Schenkman's children's book, *Sint Nikolaas en zijn knecht* (*Saint Nicholas and His Servant* [1850]), which was supposedly the first depiction of the saint with a Black Pete and popularized it (Meertens Instituut 2018). While some sources suggest a chronological, emancipatory evolution to Pete, such as on the Dutch news site NOS (2016), the Sinterklaas tradition jumps vertically and horizontally through time and space, borrowing, discarding, reviving, and transforming images, objects, customs, and rituals from diverse contexts. Traditions do not traverse endlessly into the past, as echoed by Foucault: 'What is found at the historical beginning of things is not the inviolable identity of their origin; it is the dissension of other things. It is disparity' (1996: 142). As the tradition is diverse and has continuously changed through religious, pedagogical, political, and consumerist influences, there is no defining 'fact' that can uncover a 'truth' about Pete.

If there is an origin to the figure, it may be the Germanic myth of Odin's thunderous Wild Hunt across the sky, with dead souls dragging anyone who saw them to the underworld. In Austria and other Germanic countries, Saint Nicholas is still accompanied by Krampus, a hairy black devilish figure with a gold chain, sticks, a bell, and a bag to take bad children to the underworld. Presumably under Christian influences, the celebration of Sinterklaas in the Netherlands instead features the saint as a singular embodiment of both the frightening and the friendly tropes of the punisher and gift-giver. Sometimes he even appears with clattering chains, demanding to know if children have behaved themselves (Boer-Dirks 1993: 8). When or how the figure of Black Pete became physically part of the Sinterklaas tradition is unclear. He may have been based on a Black servant playing the role of *Pieter-me-knecht* (Peter-my-servant) on Sinterklaas's Eve in a wealthy Italian merchant's home in Amsterdam in 1828 (Helsloot 2011). A German collection of stories, in Dutch known as *Piet de smeerpoets* (Pete Greaser), may have been another inspiration, with a story about white boys who were dipped in ink by 'old Niklas' for teasing a Moorish boy, making them 'more black' than their victim (Nijssen and Smits 2003: 101). Or Black Pete may have been based on an enslaved child in a painting from 1687 (Kruijt 2013). The dress of Black child servants in several paintings seems to refer to that of a commedia dell'arte harlequin. Again, the original harlequin's outfit may also have derived from the patchwork clothes of the enslaved. During the first organized and televised 'arrival' of Sinterklaas by steamboat in Amsterdam in 1934, he was accompanied by white Spanish noblemen and seven Black Petes: one blackfaced 'Headpete' and six 'Helperpetes' who were Surinamese men, supposedly sailors from the harbour, although their motives for participating remain unknown (Hoving et al. 2005: 252, NOS 2016). In this event, Dutch colonialism and Black Pete are performatively linked. The characterization of Pete has changed over time: from a scary, Krampus-like figure with a stick and bag to take children to Spain, to childish, silly, and clownesque, to more contemporary friends or employees of old Saint Nicholas.

The myriad influences culminate in an image repertoire that has inspired the changing tradition up to the present day. Instead of inoculating the tradition against racism, the multiplicity of associations strengthens the recurrence and performativity of racist stereotypes. This is exemplified by the change in Pete in the 1980s. Brightly coloured outfits, big red lips, and golden earrings were suddenly introduced. These changes *could* be a reference to the devilish Krampus figure's bright red tongue and gold chain. Not coincidentally, these changes in appearance happened after the independence of Suriname in 1975, when many Surinamese moved to the Netherlands. Some Black Petes even donned an exaggerated Surinamese accent.

Black Pete can draw from racist theatrical mechanisms in minstrelsy shows and incorporate gestures and accents from different minorities. As Hobsbawm and Ranger (1983) explain, the inventiveness of traditions means they can be both subject to and complicit with interests of power. Conversely, this adaptability and political performativity also means an emancipatory tradition is possible, one that can change the everyday imagining of community by drawing from more hopeful image repertoires. Facing the contingency of tradition and the role it has come to play in our societies is part of accepting notions of flow and uncertainty in relation to imagining community, instead of holding on to the illusion of a cultural 'structure' (Appadurai 2006: 600).

The misfiring of critique

In 2015, a United Nations report on the elimination of discrimination in the Netherlands expressed concern that Black Pete was 'sometimes portrayed in a manner that reflects negative stereotypes of people of African descent' (CEDAW Committee 2015: 4)—a legacy of 400 years of Dutch imperialism and its role in slavery.[3] Similarly, the national Children's Ombudsman in 2016 declared that, according to the Convention on the Rights of the Child, the future consequences for children should be considered (Kinderombudsman 2016). Bullying, exclusion, and discrimination have been associated with the prominence of Black Pete: for example, children of colour are called Black Pete when they are teased by white peers. In contrast to these reports, a television survey in 2018 showed that 80% of 40,000 respondents did not consider Black Pete racist (van Vliet and Kester 2018: 4). Since the annual survey in 2013, the number in favour of change has grown gradually from 11% (van Vliet 2017: 3) but stagnated at 32% in 2018 'in reaction to the hardening of the public debate' (van Vliet and Kester 2018: 2–3). In 2018, the panel approached Dutch Antillean and Surinamese people to participate in the survey for the first time (780 of 40,000 respondents), of whom 73% perceived Black Pete as racist, and six out of ten reported that they or someone in their family had been discriminated against by behaviour associated with the character (van Vliet and Kester 2018: 2).

While the Black Pete figure has been critiqued for many decades, it has only slightly adapted to educational and societal shifts. One explanation for the tenacity of the tradition lies in its implicit promotion of a central, though problematic, national self-image. Gloria Wekker calls this the paradox of 'white innocence': a continuous construction of 'an innocent, fragile, emancipated white Dutch self [...] versus a guilty, uncivilized, barbaric other' (Wekker 2016: 15). The tradition allows for the Netherlands to assume a position of neutrality, naivete, or even victimhood that ignores its own troublesome historical roles in the slave trade, colonial oppression, and the Second World War. In order for this construction to persist, racialized and ethnicized others are approached through modes of 'forgetting, glossing over, supposed color blindness, an inherent and natural superiority vis-à-vis people of color, assimilating' (ibid.). As a result, addressing structural racism and discrimination threatens this national self-image and is often met with public denial, outrage, and even threats of violence.

In the case of Sinterklaas, it is the unrelenting work of activists, especially from 2011, that has made the controversy a visible (counter)part of the annual tradition. The largest of such movements began as an art project: 'Black Pete is racism' was launched on Keti Koti, the Remembrance Day of the abolition of slavery, on 1 July 2011, by the Black activist poet Jerry Afriyie—also known as rapper Kno'ledge Cesare—and the poet and artist Quinsy Gario. They made headlines when they were arrested for wearing T-shirts with the slogan at the arrival of Sinterklaas in Dordrecht. From this project, the movement 'Kick Out Zwarte Piet' ('Kick Out Black Pete', henceforth KOZP) emerged in 2014, with Afriyie taking the lead. In 2021, Afriyie called for 'hope and inspiration from small steps' because change is 'a marathon, not a sprint' (Meershoek 2021). With the increasing awareness of racism in the Netherlands sparked by the deaths of Mitch Henriquez in The Hague in 2015 and George Floyd in 2020, and the resulting Black Lives Matter demonstrations, political parties and local authorities began turning to KOZP to learn to fight racism and discrimination. The KOZP movement has disrupted the stream of dominant narratives and created space for other voices to be heard. It has borne the brunt of police suspicion, arrests, hate, and threats of violence against the peaceful protests. Now, the demonstrations have achieved a mainstream status and the public debate about how to deal with Black Pete cannot be denied or laughed off. Judith Butler's notion of performativity as simultaneously foreclosing and producing subjectivity is at work (2009: iv): to stick one's head out is to receive hate, so that many do not dare to broach the discussion or their experiences of racism, and simply declare that 'enough has been said'.[4] This stultifies the emergence of new subjectivities. As for KOZP, it has produced the online Black Manifest (Stichting Nederland Wordt Beter et al. 2021), which—Afriyie hopes—will lead to more impactful changes than the mostly symbolic anti-racism efforts of the 1980s.[5]

Theatrical complicity

In an analysis of the Sinterklaas tradition as a 'theatrical event', Peter Eversmann focuses on the theatrics, the rite-of-passage, and the role-playing as positive, creative acts that build community and shape Dutch society. Even the rite-of-passage aspect, when a child inevitably learns that the Saint and Pete figures are fictional, is seen as a productive 'traumatic experience' which makes the tradition 'a binding factor that is experienced and defended as typically Dutch' (2007: 290). This perspective adds to our understanding of the tenacity of Black Pete. However, positing theatricality as a neutral mechanism obscures the exclusionary politics involved in this shaping of Dutch national identity. Writing in 2007, Eversmann mentions the Black Pete tradition only briefly, relegating it to a period in the 1980s and 1990s when experiments were carried out with different colours of face paint, after which the Petes were 'back to black' (294), as if this were a naturalized theatrical element of the tradition. Theatricality can be complicit in the policing of imagined communities through culture. The focus on roles, conventions, and historicity constructs a division between those who are 'in the know' and those who are not. Both implicit rationalizations and humour can work in this way. Two examples elucidate this.

In November 2014, the two 'head Petes' who organized the Sinterklaas parade in Amsterdam resigned. They published a letter in the national newspaper, *De Volkskrant*, in which they stated that 'being Black Pete was a dream' (van Konijnenburg and Graafland 2014). They felt the discussion should be about 'the real cause of the dissatisfaction and the different worldviews of those who are for and against'. Changing the 'symbol' would only polarize the conversation. Moreover, they contended that politics should not be involved with the 'content' and that they were very skilled at staging the 'fairytale' as 'an artform' and not as a 'marketing-like facade without layers'. As they put it: 'The feelings about tradition and racism may be justified, but the factual underpinnings often turn out to be a lot more complicated and not always correct'.

The letter thus stages the organizers of the festivities as knowledgeable and rational, and those who object as irrational and emotional. This in itself is a reinscription of a privileged position in society. It dictates who is and is not allowed to change the national tradition, performatively producing a division of who counts as part of 'the' Dutch people. The letter offers an example of how theatrical notions of Black Pete as 'just a fictional character' often surface in public debate, implying critics simply misunderstand the conventions. Theatricality can thus serve to cover up the real-life implications of racism instituted by a tradition that continually recycles racist stereotypes.

This mechanism of 'white innocence' is prevalent in governmental politics. It allows for humour as an affective cultural political tool to support the image of a nation that is predominantly white. This was, for example, demonstrated in 2014, when Prime Minister Mark Rutte stated in his weekly press conference: 'Black Pete is Black and I can't change that' (NOS 2013). One year later, in response to a question from a foreign correspondent, he reiterated this view, adding jokingly that 'his friends in the Dutch Antilles' were happy during Sinterklaas because 'they don't have to paint their faces. But when I'm playing Black Pete, I'm trying to get the stuff off my face for days' (NOS 2014). Rutte's misplaced joke illuminates the paradox of 'white innocence', at once eclipsing and exhibiting racism. In 2020, in a debate in the House of Representatives on the subject of the Black Lives Matter demonstrations in the Netherlands, Rutte said he had changed his mind: 'In a few years almost no Petes will be black' (NOS 2020). He added, however, that it is 'No use for the government to force people to let go of a symbol'. He also admitted that racism happens in the Netherlands, but that he did not want to use the term 'institutional racism'. He later explained that with such 'very complicated sociological debates', 'you would lose a large part of the population' (NU.nl 2020). His clarification exposes his populist approach of catering to a majority. The unwillingness of the prime minister to take everyday racism as a serious matter for politics is performative in that it furnishes forth the national image of 'white innocence'.[6]

Both examples—referring to Black Pete as purely fictional and the use of humour in politics—downplay racism and implicitly frame those who object as irrational and not being in-the-know. Thus, Black Pete functions to police who may be seen and heard as having political agency, as Jacques Rancière (1999) has theorized, and determines who may shape society as a whole. Those who object to Black Pete expose the contingency of what is presumed to be common sense, which creates anxiety. In the Netherlands, with its consensus culture (the polder model), the notion that the consensus may be wrong cuts painfully to the core of this delicate enmeshment of culture and politics. Right-wing parties capitalize on this mechanism.

Tradition as a far-right fairytale?

In November 2021, KOZP contacted the mayor of Volendam, Lieke Sievers, about organizing a protest at their Sinterklaas arrival parade. The activists' plan foundered when the mayor announced that the parade would be cancelled as a measure to stop the spread of Covid-19. However, on 14 November, members of KOZP saw video footage of two unofficial parades that had taken place unexpectedly in the village: one of a traditional Saint Nicholas with Black Petes and one, surprisingly, of Thierry Baudet, the leader of the right-wing party Forum for Democracy, playing Sinterklaas.[7] These events spurred KOZP to organize their own protest on 4 December, a day before the official Saint Nicholas feast. Forum for Democracy's and KOZP's performances illustrate how theatricality is used to arbitrate censorship.

First, the slickly staged and edited YouTube video (Forum voor Democratie 2021) begins with Baudet walking through Amsterdam, declaring: 'I'm going to buy presents for the children because the Sinterklaas celebration has been cancelled by Kick Out Black Pete'. Baudet then meets the other performers, they buy presents in a shop, and he is fitted with the characteristic Saint Nicholas beard: 'Let's go to Volendam!' In the video of the small parade, Baudet as Saint Nicholas is flanked by Black Petes and blonde women in sailor costumes. The people they meet in the streets are greeted in traditional fashion, hands are shaken, presents and sweets handed out, and photos taken. The upbeat YouTube video shows a caption explaining that the original parade had been cancelled due to 'absurd corona-measures'. While Baudet presents himself as the saviour of innocent fun for children, he also performs the populist dream of being the saviour of Dutchness itself. In the comments section of YouTube, viewers express their 'love' for Baudet, the children, the *oer-Hollands* (ur-Dutch) tradition, and the country. Others declare they experienced 'chills' of emotion (meaning they felt touched), praise the 'fun' and 'funniness', and declare Baudet 'a hero' who is a 'pillar' for a 'broken nation'. Sara Ahmed (2004) has theorized how the cultural politics of emotion work through circulation. Through declarations of love, the affect of hate starts to adhere to different events, groups of people, and narratives that threaten that which is loved. Staging the need for protection of an imagined Dutch community of white Sinterklaas-lovers, Forum for Democracy stimulated hate towards KOZP as well as the state (which is repeatedly associated with cancel culture and the 'absurdity' of the coronavirus measures). This hate was put on display in the following event.

On 4 December 2021, a day before the Saint Nicholas feast, KOZP responded with a protest in Volendam. It was registered as a live video on the 'Black Pete is Racism' Facebook page (Nederland Wordt Beter 2021): protesters gathered at the Volendam street market chanting 'Volendam be ashamed', 'Festival for everyone', and 'Festival for children'. They carried signs and banners with messages such as 'Away with Black Pete' and 'Black Pete is racism'. The police blocked angry onlookers but could not prevent them from throwing objects. The protesters retreated through the market to their buses, besieged by fireworks, tomatoes, eggs, fish, and cigarettes. A traffic cone was thrown and cracked the windshield of one of the buses. Meanwhile, the Facebook Live chat was filled with both praise and death threats directed at the protesters, and jokes about the Volendammers being 'inbred'. As the protesters were boarding the bus, and as it drove off, inhabitants intermittently stopped shouting and throwing and started smiling and waving in silence.

This collective gesture is striking in that it reverses the welcoming of the boat of Saint Nicholas and the Petes. It shows how the repertoires of an imagined 'we' are embodied through the annual practice. No direction is needed, no signal is given; in this case, theatricality, the being-in-the-know of theatrical roles and rules, produces a racist, xenophobic gesture of waving goodbye in a symbolic enactment of the oft-heard 'If you don't like it, leave' argument, which implies that those who object are 'not from here'.

Getting unstuck

Despite undeniable but slow changes, the figure of Black Pete recurs in the annual Dutch Sinterklaas tradition. Its tenacity can be explained as a mechanism to perpetuate white innocence and deny institutional racism, hindering the healing of collective societal traumas. Theatricality is deployed in the denial of the potential for Black Pete to carry any racist connotations. However, the perspective of performativity demonstrates how both the performance of the blackfaced character and the discourse of its suggested innocent nature implicitly censor those who point out the fallacies in the presumed consensus over the tradition, as well as the specific Dutch national self-image it promotes.

Playing the character can—even unintentionally, but nevertheless with real-life consequences—draw from and performatively revive racialized stereotypes from a vast image repertoire. It is not only sticky in the sense that many associations can be stuck to it. It also contains a political stickiness. The theatrical means of humour (Rutte in his public speech), and the staging and filming of a 'fake' but real Sinterklaas parade (Forum for Democracy), have sidelined the experiential racist dimensions of Black Pete. As long as the Black Pete figure tenaciously remains, it can be abused by xenophobic and extremist right-wing politicians. Understanding the political performativity and specific mechanisms of controversial traditions is therefore central to getting 'unstuck' in the Netherlands, but also in other countries where the tenacity of tradition is an issue.

Notes

1. For instance, blackfacing is common in the Three Kings tradition in the south of the Netherlands, as well as in Germany and Spain, and racist stereotypes are also performed by the golliwog-style logos on some Spanish coffee brands.
2. In a televised debate in 2011, Emeritus Professor of Cultural History Herman Pleij made an exemplary remark denying racism by arguing that Black Pete was not based on the history of slavery but on the Moors. He argued that the character had been 'completely adapted to current times' and 'is now a ridiculous figure', superior to the 'stuffy' Saint Nicholas ('Zwarte Piet' 2011).
3. I have analysed the framing of discourse around censorship and argued for a critical perspective on the notion of Dutch tolerance in *Theatre as a Vortex of Behaviour in Dutch Multicultural Society* (van Heugten 2013).
4. This reaction occurs on both sides of the debate. See, for example, Eeuwijk and Rensen (2017).
5. Besides intensified activism and the Black Lives Matter movement, it is important to mention the cumulative work of social actors such as invested individuals, foundations, and scholars who have been combating inequality and racism for decades through education, publications, and events.
6. In 1984, Philomena Essed, a Dutch anthropologist whose parents were Surinamese, published an extensive study called *Everyday Racism*. In reaction,

public discourse was quickly flooded with voices denying such experienced realities existed.

7 As yet, the mayor has not made clear whether these alternative, unannounced parades had been granted a licence (Teillers 2021).

References

Ahmed, Sara. 2004. *The Cultural Politics of Emotion* (Edinburgh: Edinburgh University Press)

Appadurai, Arjun. 2006. 'Disjuncture and Difference in the Global Cultural Economy', in *Media and Cultural Studies: Keyworks*, ed. by Meenakshi Gigi Durham and Douglas M. Kellner (Malden, MA: Blackwell), pp. 584–603

Boer-Dirks, Eugenie. 1993. 'Nieuw licht op Zwarte Piet: een kunsthistorisch antwoord op de vraag naar de herkomst van Zwarte Piet', *Volkskundig Bulletin*, 19: 1–35

Butler, Judith. 2009. *Excitable Speech: A Politics of the Performative* (New York: Routledge)

CEDAW Committee. 2015. 'Concluding Observations on the Nineteenth to Twenty-First Periodic Reports of the Netherlands', CERD/C/NLD/CO/19-21, 28 August

Eeuwijk, Jop, and Frank Rensen. 2017. 'Geschiedenis van de Zwarte Piet-Kritiek', *Historiek*

Essed, Philomena. 1984. *Alledaags racisme* (Amsterdam: Sara)

Eversmann, Peter. 2007. 'The Feast of Saint Nicholas in the Low Countries', in *Festivalising!: Theatrical Events, Politics and Culture*, ed. by Temple Hauptfleisch, Shulamith Lev-Aladgem, Jacqueline Martin, Willmar Sauter, and Henri Schoenmakers (Amsterdam and New York: Rodopi), pp. 281–98

Forum voor Democratie. 2021. 'Thierry Baudet gaat op pad als Sinterklaas!', YouTube <https://www.youtube.com/watch?v=rfKteuAUa9o> [accessed 10 December 2021]

Foucault, Michel. 1996. 'Nietzsche, Genealogy, History', in *Language, Counter-Memory, Practice: Selected Essays and Interviews*, ed. and introduced by Donald F. Bouchard (Ithaca, NY: Cornell University Press), pp. 139–64

Helsloot, John. 2009. 'Is Zwarte Piet uit te leggen?', in *Sinterklaas Verklaard*, ed. by Willem Koops, Madelon Pieper, and Eugenie Boer (Amsterdam: Uitgeverij SWP), pp. 77–85

—— 2011. 'De oudst bekende naam van Zwarte Piet: Pieter-mê-knecht (1850)', *Newsletter Meertens Instituut*

Hobsbawm, Eric, and Terence Ranger (eds). 1983. *The Invention of Tradition* (Cambridge: Cambridge University Press)

Hoving, Isabel, Hester Dibbits, and Marlou Schrover (eds). 2005. *Cultuur en migratie in Nederland: veranderingen van het alledaagse 1950–2000* (Den Haag: Sdu Uitgevers)

KIEN [Kenniscentrum Immaterieel Erfgoed Nederland]. 2022. 'Stichting Sint & Pietengilde uitgeschreven uit Inventaris Immaterieel Erfgoed Nederland'

Kinderombudsman. 2016. 'Zwarte Piet vraagt om aanpassing', 30 September

Kruijt, Michiel. 2013. 'Geen twijfel: "Zwarte Piet stamt af van kindslaven"', *Volkskrant*, 23 October

Meershoek, Patrick. 2021. 'Na 10 jaar actie tegen antizwart racisme heeft Jerry Afriyie de wind in de rug, maar: "Er is nog geen buit in zicht "', *Het Parool*, 25 June

Meertens Instituut. 2018. 'Vragen over Zwarte Piet'

Nederland Wordt Beter. 2021. 'Facebook Zwarte Piet is racisme'

Nijssen, Robert, and Guus Smits. 2003. 'Sinterklaas—altijd anders', in *1993–2003*, ed. by Rob Nijssen, Guus Smits, and René Toonen (Sint Nicholaas Genootschap Nederland), pp. 96–103

NOS. 2013. 'Rutte: Piet is nou eenmaal zwart', 18 October

—— 2014. 'Rutte krijgt vraag over Zwarte Piet', 23 March

—— 2016. 'Hoe Zwarte Piet veranderde, van pageknecht tot roetstrepen', 30 September

—— 2020. 'Rutte: ik ben anders gaan denken over Zwarte Piet', 5 June

NU.nl. 2020. 'Rutte legt uit waarom hij niet spreekt van institutioneel racisme', 4 June

Rancière, Jacques. 1999. *Disagreement: Politics and Philosophy* (Minneapolis: University of Minnesota Press)

Stichting Nederland Wordt Beter, the Black Archives/New Urban Collective, and Black Queer & Trans Resistance NL. 2021. Kick Out Zwarte Piet <https://zwartmanifest.nl/> [accessed 10 July 2022]

Teillers, Frederique. 2021. 'Geen officiële sinterklaasintocht in Volendam, wel twee verrassingsstoeten met onder anderen Thierry Baudet als Sinterklaas: "Hij deelde cadeautjes uit"', *Noord Hollands Dagblad*, 15 November

van Heugten, Lonneke. 2013. *Theatre as a Vortex of Behaviour in Dutch Multicultural Society*. Berlin: Tectum Verlag

van Konijnenburg, Frans, and Bram Graafland. 2014. 'Zwarte Piet zijn was een droom, nu stoppen we ermee', *De Volkskrant*, 17 November

van Vliet, Lisette. 2017. 'Onderzoek: Zwarte Piet', *EenVandaag*, AvroTros, 22 November

van Vliet, Lisette, and Jeroen Kester. 2018. 'Onderzoek: uiterlijk van Zwarte Piet', *EenVandaag*, AvroTros, 15 November

Wekker, Gloria. 2016. *White Innocence: Paradoxes of Colonialism and Race* (Durham, NC: Duke University Press)

'Zwarte Piet, Racistisch of Niet?'. 2011. *Debat op 2*, KRO, 3 December

Part 3
Staging Taboos

Intervention 4
Racialized Censorship in the Age of Culture Wars

ROAA ALI

In the UK, 'culture wars' have increasingly become a frequent infiltrator of political, media, and cultural discourse (Policy Institute 2021). The more contested term of 'cancel culture', which purportedly refers to the cancelling, or silencing, of those who have a prominent public profile in response to comments or cultural texts deemed discriminatory, is having a potent impact on the concepts of creativity, freedom of speech, and social justice. Although cancel culture has been employed by the left and right of the political and ideological divide, of late, it has been effectively appropriated and weaponized by the right to create draconian political and cultural measures that aim to curtail racialized and marginalized voices.

In this intervention, I argue that while cancel culture is a tool employed to redraw ideological fault lines, there is a danger that a more nefarious version could be sanctioned by the state to censor racialized and marginalized voices. In recent years, two theatrical examples stand out as a worrying development regarding censorship in the arts: the National Youth Theatre's cancellation of the play *Homegrown*, by Omar El-Khairy and Nadia Latif, and the obfuscation of the production of LUNG Theatre's *Trojan Horse*. Both touch on racialized religious minorities and their freedom of expression. The censorship strategies at work in these cases is a product of direct state interference in the case of *Homegrown*, and indirect instrumentalization of the state's policing of the arts in the case of *Trojan Horse*—both relating to the controversial Prevent Strategy in the UK (Holmwood et al. 2020). These examples will be examined as I investigate censorship and the weaponizing of cancel culture as a way of silencing racialized voices connected to an agenda that maintains white privilege, if not supremacy; this agenda is also invested in policing and, at times, in criminalizing racialized sections of society.

What is cancel culture and woke culture?

Gaining traction initially as an accountability measure manifesting in the 'calling out' of public figures via social media platforms, cancel culture has become an increasingly contested asset in the culture wars era. Cancel culture in its ideal application was understood to address imbalances of power but is steadily being weaponized precisely against those whom it was meant to empower. Media studies scholar Meredith Clark traces cancel culture practices in social media to their origin from resistant practices rooted in 'Black vernacular tradition' that have been misappropriated by social elites. She argues that '[p]oliticians, pundits, celebrities, academics, and everyday people alike have narrativized being canceled into a moral panic akin to actual harm, adding a neologic twist on the origin of the practice by associating it with an unfounded fear of censorship and silencing' (2020: 89). Within the discourse of cancel culture, 'wokeness' or 'being woke' is another assailed ideological position that references awareness of and advocacy for social justice, but it is now widely perceived as a pejorative term (Policy Institute 2021).

Bart Cammaerts argues that '[w]oke is intrinsically tied to black consciousness and anti-racist struggles' (2022: 5), but has been 'weaponised by the right, deturning it from its initial meaning in the struggle for civil rights into an insult used against anyone who fights fascism, racism and other forms of injustices and discrimination as well as to signify a supposed progressive over-reaction' (6). The 'abnormalisation', to borrow Cammaerts's term, of vocal public indignation against racist, sexist, and LGBTQ-phobic views is adopted by right-wing political discourse and action. The former UK Cultural Secretary Oliver Dowden had championed several measures aimed at combating what he terms 'painful woke psychodrama' (cited in Mason 2022). If culture wars tell us anything, it is that culture is fundamentally important. Cancel culture and woke culture tell us, perhaps, that political and ideological wars are nowhere more fiercely contested, fought, and won, than on the terrain of culture, of which theatre is a pillar.

Playwright Tom Stoppard has proclaimed that 'cancel culture eroded free speech' (2021). Other prominent figures in the theatre industry have alleged that cancel culture could 'wipe out comedy' (Razzall 2021). One might ask: whose free speech, and has it really been eroded? And which jokes are being scrutinized and who is the target? The aspiration for social justice mostly championed by those who are marginalized (e.g. Black and ethnically diverse, LGBTQ, women) is often purposely devoid of context and exploited to generate a panic mode over an alleged threat to freedom of expression. Thus, those who are the butts of the original joke often become more marginalized within the discussion.

A deeper analysis of high-profile cases of alleged cancel culture shows that what is produced is a pseudo-narrative of who has a voice, who is allowed to speak, and ultimately who is silenced. Take, as an example, *The Family Sex Show* (2022) at Bristol's Tobacco Factory, produced and co-created by Josie Dale-Jones, which aims to depict under-represented bodies and is an educational piece about body image and sexuality. The show was cancelled even before it was staged due to moral outrage by right-wing campaigners (Dale-Jones 2022). *The Family Sex Show*, according to Dale-Jones, was meant for everyone, including children above the age of five if accompanied by an adult. To the campaigners who organized a petition on Citizen Go, a platform 'believed to have links with extremist hard-right Christian groups in the US' (ibid.), the show was akin to 'grooming', and the performers faced abusive and violent threats. In this instance, the silencing of progressive views on gender and sexuality was effected by a section of the political spectrum that mobilized online, using 'words and ideologies that are rooted in queerphobia, racism, fatphobia, ableism, misogyny and transphobia,' as Dale-Jones puts it.

The silencing of racialized voices

I argue that the backlash against woke culture and its cancel culture effect is an indignant reaction against those who have newly acquired a platform and activated their agency in direct opposition to white supremacy. This defensive posture is pregnant with racial undertones. In a case that ignited much public debate and intense social media activity, three ethnically diverse writers received a barrage of racial abuse when they called out a white writer for what appeared to be racist tropes in her recent book. Authors Sunny Singh and Chimene Suleyman, and journalist Monisha Rajesh, criticized author Kate Clanchy for employing ableist as well as 'anti-Semitic and anti-black tropes' (Rajesh 2021) in her 2019 Orwell Prize-winning book *Some Kids I Taught and What They Taught Me*. Rajesh evidences her critique by citing extracts from the book, which clearly show a reliance on racist stereotypes, and explains how quickly the narrative changed on social media from holding Clanchy accountable to targeting her ethnically diverse critics with abuse. Rajesh observes: 'It's a familiar pattern: pointing out racist language is labelled "aggressive" and "instigating a pile-on"' (ibid.). She describes the fierce silencing, racism, and effective cancelling that the three racialized writers had to endure:

> A group of white women authors pointedly demeaned Singh, Suleyman and me as 'activists' who were 'attacking' Clanchy. Pullman [Philip Pullman, former President of the Society of Authors] suggested we were looking for offence and likened us to Isis and the Taliban, a comment which came as the three of us were already under a coordinated racist attack from the 'alt-right' which targeted our emails and social media. (Rajesh 2021)

After months of controversy, Clanchy parted ways with her original publisher, Picador, but it was quickly announced that independent publisher Swift Press has acquired the book and reissued a version of it with the controversial sentences and tropes removed (Flood 2022). Speaking to the generally presumed right-wing magazine *Spiked*, Clanchy declares 'no one is safe from the woke mob', professing her victimization at the hands of an aggressive 'outrage mob' (cited in Williams 2021). In similar vein, Cammaerts observes that 'a self-asserted victimhood, that is, from a position of dominance and privilege, is expressed; reversing the perpetrator into a victim and turning the victim into a perpetrator' (2022: 11).

This case exemplifies how cancel culture works in effect to undermine and censor ethnic voices in the service of white privilege. With a public campaign to defend Clanchy, the controversy amplified publicity for the book, which was reprinted, while the three ethnically diverse authors who publicly criticized her suffered relentless abuse and attempts to silence them in the name of alleged free speech and expression. The backlash against those who speak up against racist, LGBTQ-phobic, and sexist discourse, especially if championed by Black and ethnically diverse people, is illustrative of the discontent with the redistribution of power that such critiques produce. The backlash represents anger, and at times disbelief, that those who had little power and agency have the audacity to use their voice against those with more power and visibility; and a way to govern and police their discourse.

Cancel culture seems to focus on blocking or circumscribing the platform that a public figure or celebrity uses; it is less likely focused on the cultural text produced. This is an important distinction because the text exists, is not censored, and can circulate freely. What is affected is the temporal limitation placed on the creator and the consequent tendency to self-censor, which creators may develop for fear of being cancelled. That temporal limitation might eventually evaporate completely with time or generate the necessary promotion for works that are purposely premised on publicly courting controversy. If we compare this with the censorship of *Homegrown* and *Trojan Horse*—both touching on racialized, religiously minoritized subjects and their freedom of expression—the issue of whose 'cancelling' is enforceable and sanctioned by the state becomes clearer: the racialized voices who tend to explicitly confront racist and nationalist state-sponsored discourse are the ones that are unceremoniously cancelled into silence.

Contemporary theatre and censorship of the marginalized

Today, outright official censorship in theatre is assumed to be a feature of the past. Instead of the traditional and overt state-sanctioned censor, censorship nowadays has morphed and is enforced '[n]ot by governmental interference but by stifling effects of commercial, economic, and social forces' (Carlson 2012: 32). That is why it was all the more shocking when *Homegrown*, a British play co-created by two British Muslim authors/performance practitioners—playwright Omar El-Khairy and director Nadia Latif—was cancelled in August 2015, days before its scheduled premiere at London's National Youth Theatre (NYT). El-Khairy was approached in 2014 by NYT to develop a play that would treat the issue of alleged radicalization in schools in the wake of the so-called Trojan Horse scandal. The latter is a controversy well documented in *The Trojan Horse Affair* podcast (Serial Productions and *New York Times* 2022) about an alleged 'Islamic plot' to infiltrate schools in Birmingham, UK (Shackle 2017). The 'plot' was later proven to be greatly exaggerated—if not entirely fabricated—and it was capitalized upon in a political response that was misguided at best, and at worst Islamophobic. The *Guardian*'s Samira Shackle (2017) explains how many regarded the Trojan Horse Affair as 'confected scandal promoted by rightwing newspapers, the product of a climate in which all British Muslims are viewed with suspicion, and complex questions about faith and integration are reduced by politicians and the media to hysterical debates about terrorism'. The scandal and its politicization are the subject matter of *Trojan Horse* (2018), developed by playwrights Helen Monks and Matt Woodhead of LUNG Theatre.

In discussing censorship in these two cases, it is important to understand how Muslims in Britain are racialized, minoritized, and securitized in ways that make their censorship possible in an age where official censorship in theatre has all but disappeared. Muslims in the UK have been 'demarcated by a discourse that connotes them with alarm and security tension, and another that disadvantages them' (Ali 2018: 375). This discourse has both led to and been aggravated by the emergence of anti-radicalization policies such as the Prevent Strategy, which is part of the UK government's counterterrorism strategy and purports to 'stop people becoming terrorists or supporting terrorism' (Cm 8092 2011: 6). The Prevent Strategy 'has been increasingly challenged for reinforcing Islamophobic prejudices through racialized practices of surveillance on primarily Muslim communities' (Sian 2017: 2). In practice, it has sanctioned the securitization of Muslims, implementing racialization as a mode of identification of those alleged potential terrorists and a mode of execution for the Prevent programme, where many deradicalization initiatives target the culture of Islam (Sian 2017). Prevent represents a threat to creative freedom and expression in the UK, and one might question 'whether a regression in how the state engages with the arts is acceptable or should be tolerated' (Ali 2019).

The Prevent Strategy and its material and cultural impact is the context for both *Homegrown* and *Trojan Horse*. Playwright El-Khairy wanted to create a performance that explored the context of radicalization and Islamophobia through young people's perspectives as they negotiate their identity. The play was conceived as an immersive site-specific performance with up to 112 cast members. The NYT, as the commissioning and producing venue, approved the script and appointed Nadia Latif as a director. The co-creators describe what ensued:

> [e]xactly halfway through the process, the NYT came in to see rehearsals for the first time. They left full of praise and with a number of helpful suggestions. That night, we received an email from the NYT telling us that *Homegrown* was cancelled. There was no warning, no consultation and no explanation—indeed, they even attempted to prevent us from entering the building the next morning when we came to collect our things. All our attempts at meeting with the NYT have been delayed and then cancelled. (El-Khairy and Latif 2017: 13–14)

This put a stop to the making of the play, leaving it an incomplete attempt and the play still unproduced to this day. Although the script was later self-published by the co-creators (in 2017), the performance was censored by the NYT without clear justification after they attended a rehearsal. Marvin Carlson asserts '[s]ince performance is the expected realisation of a dramatic script, no play is more effectively and totally silenced than one denied any opportunity to be offered to an audience' (2012: 31). The media reporting that followed the cancellation created further reputational damage through incendiary headlines that labelled the play an 'Isis play' (Denham 2015) with an 'extremist agenda' ('*Homegrown*' 2015), despite the fact that journalists had not seen the play or read the script. A Freedom of Information request revealed that the NYT artistic director, Paul Roseby, sent an email to the Arts Council in which he admits to having consulted the police, who raised concerns about the play (Hemley 2015). The co-creators claim that they were told about a meeting between the NYT and the police in the first week of production without knowing who instigated the meeting, and that,

> [t]he police wanted to read the script, attend the first three shows, plant plain clothes policemen in the audience and sweep daily with the bomb squad. When we protested these measures, asking why the police felt the need to get involved, we were quickly told that the police had no power of ultimatum; and the issue was never raised again. (El-Khairy and Latif 2017: 13)

What transpired in this incident of censorship was multilayered, from the NYT's obfuscation of its reasons for cancelling the show to police pressure and inflammatory media reporting on the case. What is clear, though, is that the play fell foul of the redlines taped around discourses of Islam, radicalization, racialization, and minoritized identity, which became securitized by the Prevent Strategy. The most nefarious coded explanation of the cancellation came from the NYT, who accused the creators of not meeting their artistic 'standards' ('Controversial Islamic State Play' 2015).

Casting doubt on the ethnically diverse creators—who are already under-represented in the collective—as a way of shifting focus from the real reason behind the cancellation is harmful to them. The vision and artistic ability of the creators were praised by established theatre critic Lyn Gardner, who commended the script as 'gloriously authentic, snapping and crackling with the sense of young people thinking out loud about who they are, freely voicing their experiences and perceptions of the world' (2017). She acknowledges the difficult conversations presented in the play as something that audiences might disagree on, but states that *Homegrown* 'opens up a proper grownup debate about attitudes and opinions that often go unspoken and remain hidden' (ibid.). It is thus evident that the cancellation of *Homegrown* curtails what is already a deeply provisional and conditional sphere of cultural production and representation for British Muslim creators.

In a less direct and confrontational mode, playwrights Helen Monks and Matt Woodhead, creators of the LUNG Theatre production of *Trojan Horse* in 2018, faced numerous forms of censorship, including those that were self-inflicted and socio-economically imposed. The play was developed in response to the Trojan Horse controversy where the Muslim community became further circumscribed amidst accusations of failing multiculturalism; it was conceived as a documentary piece compiled from more than 200 interviews with ninety people narrating the lived experience of representatives of the community, from pupils to teachers, councillors, and government officials impacted by the affair. However, the research and development of the play was constrained by the culture of Prevent, and an air of alienation or inadmissibility towards minoritized narratives, which might have been deemed problematic for theatres wanting to otherwise 'play it safe'.

The playwrights found their interviewees, especially young adults, reluctant to express themselves freely, choosing instead to self-censor and/ or keep their identities anonymous 'out of fear directly induced by Prevent' (Ali 2019). Monk proclaims that it was 'the first time that it felt like a rebellious act of defiance to be putting voices on stage' (cited in Ali 2019). The fact that it takes a 'rebellious act' to represent particular racialized and minoritized voices on stage is evidence of the perilous terrain of free speech when racialized subjects are involved, and an indictment of the cultural milieu that tolerates the fettering of these voices. In fact, forms of indirect censorship that faced *Trojan Horse* included the purposeful act of distancing and alienation that several theatre companies practised against this play and its creators. Monk explains: 'Other venues [excluding Leeds Playhouse, which was supportive] that we normally have really strong relationships with have said that this is not the project for them and distanced themselves from the project and I think this is the culture of Prevent—it is easier to not get involved in the discussion' (cited in Ali 2019). It was only after the play won a Fringe First Award and the Amnesty International Freedom of Expression Award that it was welcomed in theatre spaces that had previously kept their doors uninvitingly shut. Here, indirect censorship manifests in more insidious ways because it often remains invisible.

These two examples show how both overt and covert modes of censorship work in practice in the UK's theatre scene. The fact that both plays sought to stage rarely represented Muslim voices, often racialized in the institutionalization of Prevent, yet faced attempts to silence them should be cause for concern. The censoring of racialized and minoritized voices can often be tolerated, if not encouraged, when these voices confront cultural, nationalist, and securitized ideals upheld by whiteness.

The debate over 'freedom of expression' in hyper-politicized culture wars is divided according to uncompromising ideological frameworks, each claiming to be on the unjust receiving end of cancel culture. However, the case studies of the Clanchy affair, *Homegrown*, and *Trojan Horse* show that cancelling is a tool of censorship most ferociously applied against those racialized and minoritized voices outspoken in their criticism of state-approved Islamophobia and racism, and to a lesser extent those who speak on their behalf. In the case of Clanchy, social and literary capital was used to silence three ethnically diverse women protesting against racism in an award-winning book. *Homegrown* demonstrates how direct censorship in the UK seems to be reserved for those racialized and religiously minoritized who dare challenge a state-sanctioned discourse on nationalism, race, and religious freedom. In the case of *Trojan Horse*, economic and commercial pressures worked to silence the narratives of the racialized subjects in the play. In the fury against cancel culture's alleged impact on free speech, one wonders whose voice and whose agency are upheld and whose silencing is legitimized. The next time public controversy erupts over a cancel culture incident, it is wise to read between the lines and decipher how racism, LGBTQ-phobia, and sexism can all operate in overt and covert ways in the name of alleged 'free speech' that only seems to be 'free' by proxy of white privilege.

References

Ali, Roaa. 2018. 'Homegrown Censored Voices and the Discursive British Muslim Representation', *Research in Drama Education: The Journal of Applied Theatre and Performance*, 23.3: 373–88. https://doi.org/10.1080/13569783.2018.1474095

――― 2019. 'Prevent in the Arts: A Threat to Creative Freedom and Expression', *Discover Society*, 4 September

Cammaerts, Bart. 2022. 'The Abnormalisation of Social Justice: The "Anti-Woke Culture War" Discourse in the UK', *Discourse & Society*, 1–14. https://doi.org/10.1177/09579265221095407

Carlson, Marvin. 2012. 'Modes of Censorship, Strategies of Silencing', in *Out of Silence: Censorship in Theatre & Performance*, ed. by Caridad Svich (Roskilde: EyeCorner), pp. 27–32

Clark, Meredith D. 2020. 'DRAG THEM: A Brief Etymology of So-Called "Cancel Culture"', *Communication and the Public*, 5.3–4: 88–92. https://doi.org/10.1177/2057047320961562

Cm 8092. 2011. *Prevent Strategy*, June <https://assets.publishing.service.gov.uk/government/uploads/system/uploads/attachment_data/file/97976/prevent-strategy-review.pdf> [accessed 2 September 2023]

'Controversial Islamic State Play Cancelled before Opening Night'. 2015. *BBC News*, 5 August

Dale-Jones, Josie. 2022. 'Cancel Culture? My Play was Shut Down by Rightwing Activists before It Even Opened', *Guardian*, 10 May

Denham, Jess. 2015. 'Isis Play *Homegrown* Sparks Censorship Debate after NYT Cancels It for "Quality Reasons"', *Independent*, 5 August

El-Khairy, Omar, and Nadia Latif. 2017. *Homegrown*. London: Fly Prates

Flood, Alison. 2022. 'Kate Clanchy's Controversial Memoir Reissued by Independent Publisher', *Guardian*, 1 February

Gardner, Lyn. 2017. 'Shut Down but Not Silenced: Isis Play *Homegrown* Demands to Be Staged', *Guardian*, 8 March

Hemley, Matthew. 2015. 'Revealed: The Unseen NYT Email That Shut Down Isis Play *Homegrown*', *Stage*, 3 September

Holmwood, John, Helen Monks, and Matt Woodhead. 2020. 'Writing Justice/Performing Injustice: Reflections on Research, Publicity, and the Birmingham Trojan Horse Affair', *Civic Sociology*, 1.1. https://doi.org/10.1525/001c.12089

'*Homegrown*: NYT Scrapped Play over "extremist agenda"'. 2015. *BBC News*, 4 September

Mason, Rowena. 2022. 'Tory Party Chairman Says "Painful Woke Psychodrama" Weakening the West', *Guardian*, 14 February

Policy Institute. 2021. 'Woke, Cancel Culture and White Privilege—How the UK's Culture War Debate Is Evolving', 12 May <https://www.kcl.ac.uk/news/woke-cancel-culture-and-white-privilege-how-the-uks-culture-war-debate-is-evolving> [accessed 28 June 2022]

Rajesh, Monisha. 2021. 'Pointing Out Racism in Books Is Not an "Attack"—It's a Call for Industry Reform', *Guardian*, 13 August

Razzall, Katie. 2021. 'Maureen Lipman: Cancel Culture Could Wipe Out Comedy', *BBC News*, 22 December 2021

Serial Productions and *New York Times*. 2022. 'The Trojan Horse Affair: A Mystery in Eight Parts', *New York Times*, 3 February

Shackle, Samira. 2017. '*Trojan Horse*: The Real Story Behind the Fake "Islamic Plot" to Take Over Schools', *Guardian*, 1 September

Sian, Katy. 2017. 'Born Radicals? Prevent, Positivism, and "Race-Thinking"', *Palgrave Communications*, 3.1: 1–8. https://doi.org/10.1057/s41599-017-0009-0

Stoppard, Tom. 2021. 'Sir Tom Stoppard: "Cancel culture has eroded free speech"', *Newsnight*, BBC, 6 August

Williams, Joanna. 2021. 'Kate Clanchy: No One Is Safe from the Woke Mob', *Spiked*, 12 August

7

Images of Protest: Religion, Theatre, and Censorship

CHRIS MEGSON

Fontaine: Is that all you saw?
Censor: There wasn't much else to see.
Fontaine: Because your eye stops at the image.
Censor: Most people's would.
Fontaine: Because they've lost the ability to see.

(Neilson 1998: 257)

In Anthony Neilson's play *The Censor* (1997), the eponymous character engages in a series of discussions with a pornographic filmmaker called Miss Fontaine, who has submitted her latest work for his invigilation. Fontaine, in the hope of reaching a wider audience for her distinctly uninhibited brand of erotica, seeks to reassure the Censor that her new film is freighted with meanings beyond the cavalcade of sex acts that are depicted in it. For her, the Censor's perspective on her work—he insists early on that the film must be cut quite drastically before it can be released—is overly literal and seemingly oblivious to the wider resonances and metaphoric associations which, she asserts, are also present in the film. In her conversation with the Censor excerpted in the epigraph above, Fontaine implies that, because his eye 'stops at the image', he has thereby 'lost the ability to see'. Over the course of the play's fourteen scenes, Fontaine attempts to seduce the Censor with the aim of deepening his perception and appreciation of the film. Neilson's achievement is to challenge spectators in the theatre—just as Fontaine challenges the Censor—to look beyond superficially shocking imagery on stage in order to apprehend the unusual but profound—in Neilson's words—'love story' (cited in Marmion 2002) at the heart of his drama.

Neilson's focus on shocking theatrical images and the contrasting, sometimes opposed, responses they solicit from spectators is highly resonant in the context of this chapter, which explores the representation of religion, and specifically religious images, on stage as a catalyst for censorial practices in twenty-first-century European theatre. In the following analysis,

I identify religion as a volatile site of contestation and protest, and a lens through which debates on freedom of expression in theatrical performance have been brought into focus. In the first part of the chapter, attending primarily to the British context since 2000, I consider some examples of individual and institutional self-censorship motivated by 'sensitivities' about references to Islam and the representation of Muslim lives on stage; in this section, I also discuss several productions that were the target of protests, led by evangelical Christian groups, on the grounds of perceived blasphemy in their treatment of biblical stories and religious iconography. In the second part, I examine some of the scholarly reappraisals of theatre censorship, published in the early 2000s, which explore, in particular, two high-profile case studies: the cancellation of Gurpreet Kaur Bhatti's *Behzti* at the Birmingham Rep in 2004, and the withdrawal of Mozart's opera *Idomeneo* at the Deutsche Oper in Berlin in 2006. A shared preoccupation of this scholarship is the advocacy for greater dialogue between practitioners, scholars, and audiences on problematic issues of stage representation, especially in contexts where performances on religious themes might, or are likely to, cause offence. The final part of the chapter considers a case study—the Italian theatre director Romeo Castellucci's production of *Sul concetto di volto nel figlio di Dio* (*On the Concept of the Face, Regarding the Son of God*) from 2010. Given the multiple protests that have erupted in various European countries over the past two decades against perceived blasphemous representation on stage, I draw attention to Castellucci's conceptualization of images in theatre, and his oft-stated resistance to their literal or monolithic interpretation. In the performance of *On the Concept*, a large-scale, close-up fragment of a Renaissance painting of Christ is riven and then resurrected on stage. This aspect of the production triggered outrage and violent protests from some religious groups, particularly when it was performed in Paris. I discuss Castellucci's defence of the theatrical image as a vital and necessarily ambivalent element of performance-making that is, crucially, always resistant to fixed and foreclosed interpretation.

'Extreme sensitivity'

The hostility towards the representation of religious subject matter in theatrical performance has deep historical roots but—whether in the past or present—belies broader negotiations of power and entrenched ideological agendas. The issue of religion—perhaps more than any other—remains controversial. The reasons for this are varied but pertain to the wider geopolitical climate in Europe that has been shaped by several seismic and interlinked events including the large-scale jihadi terrorist attacks in several countries from the early 2000s; the national security concerns arising from the proliferation of fundamentalist religious creeds and networks; the pressure on European states, institutions, and populations to respond to multiple refugee crises; and the ascendancy of divisive and sectarian nationalist and populist political movements. Steve Nicholson, in remarks published in 2016, contends that 'Religion is perhaps the most obvious area of extreme sensitivity where writers and theatres now may feel compelled to restrict what they say—to self-censor (which is always the aim of censorship)' (231).

Such 'extreme sensitivity' was evident in British theatre in the first decade of the new century following the London terrorist bombings of July 2005 and, two months later, the publication of satirical cartoons featuring the Prophet Muhammad in the Danish newspaper *Jyllands-Posten*, which triggered a wave of international demonstrations and riots. In October 2005, a production of Christopher Marlowe's *Tamburlaine the Great* opened at the Bristol Old Vic. A scene in the play—described by the theatre's then artistic director Simon Reade as 'unnecessarily inflammatory' (cited in Merritt 2005)—depicts Tamburlaine burning a copy of the Koran. David Farr, who directed the production, amended this scene so that Tamburlaine burns the holy books of all faiths, not just the Koran, in a gesture symbolizing the military leader's frustration with all religious creeds. Farr's decision attracted the criticism of Marlovian luminaries such as Royal Shakespeare Company director Terry Hands, and the historian and biographer Charles Nicholl. In defence of his position, Farr wrote a piece for the *Guardian* newspaper stating that the amendment had been made by him 'for purely artistic reasons', without any pressure from the Bristol Old Vic or the Muslim community: his thematic focus was on the play's philosophical content and he wanted to avoid creating a performance that indulged the usual 'shields and shouting masquerade' (2005). Whatever the reasons for Farr's directorial choice, it was interpreted by several commentators as an act of capitulation and self-censorship on the part of the theatre, albeit one that raised important questions about the adaptation and interpretation of classic plays, particularly when those plays are likely to offend modern values and sensibilities. A nuanced perspective was put forward by Stephanie Merritt of the *Guardian*, who pointed out that, while artistic subordination to religious intolerance is unwelcome, 'that is not the same as saying that classic texts can never be updated' (2005).

A more unambiguous example of theatrical self-censorship took place a few months later, in early 2006. In an interview published in 2010, the playwright Richard Bean disclosed that he had self-censored his work on several occasions, most notably when—in the aftermath of the Danish cartoons controversy—he removed several references to the Prophet Muhammad from his comedy about a prison riot, *Up on Roof*, staged at the Hull Truck Theatre. Bean claims that the theatre 'was just utterly scared shitless' (cited in Nathan 2010) by these references because of Hull Truck's proximity to the large Muslim population of Bradford. With some hesitancy, Bean agreed to amend his text, but he also decided to consult his fellow playwrights at the Royal Court Theatre in London for advice about this incident. According to his account of this meeting with his peers, Bean's concerns appear to have received a somewhat mixed reception:

> I was trying to work out if I had the strength to make a fuss. And then [the playwright] Caryl Churchill stood up in the meeting. The only bit I remember is that she said, 'You should be writing about how Muslims are oppressed throughout the world' and she turned around and walked out. I've never spoken to her since, and I won't ever again. (Cited in Nathan 2010)

Bean is no stranger to protesters calling for the withdrawal of his work—his 2009 play *England People Very Nice* provoked what was described as the first on-stage protest in the history of the National Theatre for its representation of racial stereotypes ('On-Stage Protest' 2009)—but, nonetheless, Churchill's alleged response demonstrates the intensities of feeling, as well as the differences in political view, that can arise from even small-scale alterations to a script. In a wide-ranging article published in 2009 on the emergence of what he terms 'the new censorship', the playwright and writers' advocate David Edgar contends that *Up on Roof* 'can be seen as another example of a growing and predictable trend to self censorship' in British theatre (593).

The cancellation of *Homegrown* in 2015 further illustrates the 'extreme sensitivity' of engaging with Islam and the lived realities of Muslim citizens in British theatre at the present juncture. *Homegrown* was commissioned by the National Youth Theatre (NYT) as an immersive site-specific performance at a school in North London, with a cast of 112 young people. The project focused on the urgent issue of radicalization in British Muslim communities and sought to counter gratuitous media sensationalism by representing the experiences of Muslim teenagers. Directed by Nadia Latif, the show was pulled by NYT artistic director Paul Roseby shortly before its opening preview on the grounds of poor quality and concerns about safeguarding. The cancellation of the play prompted accusations that the NYT was subordinating its repertoire to questionable government security priorities. As the creative team of *Homegrown* put it in an open letter published on the website of Index on Censorship: 'PREVENT and CHANNEL—[the government's counterterrorism and deradicalization] programmes [...] are creating an environment in which certain forms of questioning, let alone subversion, of the given narrative pertaining to radicalisation or extremism can be closed down' (Index on Censorship 2015).[1] Sean Gallagher, an editor at Index on Censorship, argues that the controversy around *Homegrown* exemplifies Britain's increasingly 'risk-averse culture' (cited in Mahmoud and Zitout 2017). However, he also acknowledges that the challenges faced by theatre directors in such difficult contexts can trigger an inadvertent slippage into censorial practice: 'when you are looking at risk assessment, and you are weary [sic] of everything that could possibly go wrong, you need to take steps to protect yourself and in that situation you can quickly find yourself almost unwittingly entering a censorious space' (2017).

In the past two decades, censorial pressures on theatre-makers have been activated and intensified by high-profile protest campaigns led, most pronouncedly, by groups affiliated to conservative Christianity. A widely reported case in the British context is Richard Thomas and Stewart Lee's *Jerry Springer: The Opera*. Initially conceived for the fringe venue Battersea Arts Centre in 2001, and subsequently staged at the National Theatre in 2003, the production transferred into the West End and was televised on BBC Two in January 2005. The piece is a surreal parody of the infamous American talk show hosted by the charismatic presenter-turned-international-icon Jerry Springer, in which Springer seemingly descends into hell where, in a state of hallucination, he encounters various religious figures. In their respective accounts of the show, both Ivan Hare and Elizabeth Schafer itemize the elements of the production that stoked the ire of evangelical Christians, including the depiction of Christ wearing a nappy, the camp flippancy of the dialogue, and the choral chanting of 'Jerry Eleison' in place of the traditional 'Kyrie Eleison' of Christian liturgy (Hare 2009: 297, Schafer 2019: 57–64). The production was fiercely opposed by the advocacy group Christian Voice, whose supporters put pressure on the BBC to abandon its plans to broadcast the show. The group also published the home phone numbers of BBC executives, picketed theatres during the production's national tour, and handed out leaflets with the occasional help of members of the far-right British National Party (O'Keefe 2006). Although the BBC broadcast of the production went ahead, the protests achieved a measure of success: several regional theatres refused to receive the show, and the high street stores Sainsbury's and Woolworths stopped selling DVDs of the production in fear of the furore (Lee 2006, Edgar 2009: 583, Appignanesi 2016: xvi). In a strategic escalation of the campaign that generated yet more media coverage, the national director of Christian Voice, Stephen Green, launched a private prosecution against the then director general of the BBC, Mark Thompson, and the producer of the show, Jon Thoday, accusing them of broadcasting blasphemous libel. The case was refused at the City of Westminster Magistrates' Court and, in a curious denouement following on the heels of this debacle, the government subsequently passed legislation in 2008 removing the common law of blasphemy and blasphemous libel from British statute (Hare 2009).

The charge of blasphemy appears frequently in the protest discourse of religious groups in their condemnation of theatre. Such an accusation was levelled at the Reduced Shakespeare Company's *The Bible: The Complete Word of God (Abridged)*, an irreverent but warm-hearted lampoon of biblical stories performed, in a bracingly rambunctious style, by an American trio of latter-day vaudevillians. On its tour of England in the late 1990s, there was occasional religious picketing of the performance and, in 1998, Harlow Playhouse in Essex was threatened with a private prosecution for blasphemous libel (Thomas et al. 2007: 238–39). When the production reached Northern Ireland, it was withdrawn from Newtownabbey's Theatre at the Mill, near Belfast, 'amid accusations of blasphemy' (Ferguson 2014). The decision to withdraw the show was taken by the Borough Council's artistic board after they received no less than eight 'complaints from individuals and church leaders', although— apparently—'more [complaints] were made by email and verbally to DUP [Democratic Unionist Party] councillors' (ibid.). The DUP claimed it was not an instrumental factor in banning the show, but political opponents stated that pressure from the party had forced the hand of the artistic board. Following negative publicity, the decision was overturned and the sold-out performances went ahead (McDonald 2014). One of the local councillors who supported the decision to cancel the show remarked that 'People have a right to believe what they wish but people have a right not to be mocked' (cited in Ferguson 2014). The statement is, of course, inaccurate—there is no ineluctable human right not to be mocked—but the tangible sense of grievance that percolates this comment proves the validity of Michael Thompson's wider observation on such cases: 'censorship is exercised ostensibly in defence of the national or community interest, protecting a social and discursive order deemed to be more valuable than freedom of expression' (2016: 260).

In the 2010s, the most notable example of a European theatre production buffeted and silenced by religious protests is, arguably, *Golgota Picnic* by Argentinian playwright Rodrigo García in collaboration with the musician Marino Formenti. *Golgota Picnic* offers a visually arresting critique of capitalism and a meditation on the incarnation and crucifixion of Christ, filtered through a part-scurrilous and part-sensuous deconstruction of Christian iconography: the piece features prolonged sequences of nudity and memorably chaotic scenography. The performances of the show in France and Poland attracted voracious media coverage. There were Catholic protests in Toulouse, while in Paris, Jean-Michel Ribes, the director of the Théâtre du Rond-Point where the piece was performed, received death threats (Chrisafis 2011). Three years later, when the production was due to open in Poland in 2014, Archbishop Stanisław Gądecki of the diocese of Poznań, in tandem with the right-wing Law and Justice party, mobilized to ban the show from the renowned Malta Festival Poznań because of its alleged blasphemy. In his letter to the festival director Michał Merczyński, Gądecki's rhetoric appears to condone the forceful street protests against the production:

> We are therefore dealing not only with the offending of religious feeling mentioned in our Constitution, but also with a provocation aimed at desperate people who see no other possibility than to take

some actions to finally put an end to being humiliated, and enduring mockery at the things which for them are most valued and sacred. (Cited in Płoski and Semenowicz 2014: 60)

As with *The Complete Word of God (Abridged)*, 'mockery' is an intrinsic component of the charge of blasphemous injury in this case. Despite a measured and detailed rebuttal from Merczyński, and despite counter-demonstrations, vocal opposition to the ban from artists, civic leaders, and public figures, and the publication of the play as an act of solidarity, the production of *Golgota Picnic* was withdrawn from the festival because of the threat to public safety.[2]

In her insightful analysis of contemporary independent theatre in Poland, Joanna Ostrowska notes that an informal coalition of the Catholic Church, right-wing political groups, and football fans has disrupted theatrical performances and put pressure on the prosecutor's office: 'They do not use legal instruments to do this, but instead orchestrate protests targeted at particular performances' (2016: 122). The sort of situation that Ostrowska describes was precisely exemplified in the city of Warsaw, where hostile crowds attempted to bar audiences from entering the theatre TR Warszawa to watch *Golgota Picnic*. Within such maelstroms of anger and propaganda, Ostrowska discerns the emergence of a 'new type of censorship—uncontrolled, ideologically driven, in most cases employing an imprecise article of the penal code which refers to an "offence against religious feeling"—[and] it is a sign of growing influence of the Catholic Church' (ibid.).

The examples of *Tamburlaine*, *Up on Roof*, and *Homegrown* evidence the 'extreme sensitivity' involved in, respectively, staging an act of Islamophobia in the revival of an early modern play, referencing the Prophet Muhammad in a contemporary comedy, and addressing the important topic of jihadi fundamentalism and its impact on Muslim youth in a fractious context of heightened security and intensifying surveillance. These productions also demonstrate a range of prohibitive practices in British theatre over a ten-year period from 2005, ranging from self-censorship, whether individual or institutional, to the sudden cancellation of performances. Meanwhile, *Jerry Springer: The Opera*, *The Bible: The Complete Word of God (Abridged)*, and—in continental Europe—*Golgota Picnic* were each accused of blasphemy—a word defined in all of these cases as injurious and humiliating mockery of the objects of Christian religious belief. These three productions were subjected to protests led by conservative Christian groups and clerics, sometimes in loose alignments with far-right political affiliates, resulting in public demonstrations, actual or threatened prosecution, and intimidation of audiences. The justifications put forward for prohibitive and censorial actions in these instances are varied but encompass the protection of young people from harmful content, the protection of theatre personnel from harassment and other forms of violence, the protection of (as Thompson puts it) 'national or community interest', and the protection of 'religious feeling'.

The landmark cases of *Behzti* by Gurpreet Kaur Bhatti at the Birmingham Rep in 2004, and Mozart's *Idomeneo* at the Deutsche Oper in Berlin in 2006, are discussed in several scholarly publications on theatre censorship that began to emerge around the time of these controversies. As I will show, a number of commentators discerned in these two incidents an opportunity to think anew, and perhaps more comprehensively than hitherto, about contemporary censorial practices in the context of religious protests, as well as the role of theatre in an increasingly fractious and polarized public sphere.

Contexts of crisis: *Behzti* and *Idomeneo*

Helen Freshwater's 'Towards a Redefinition of Censorship' (2004) exemplifies the re-evaluative scholarship on the subject of theatrical prohibition that was published in the early 2000s. Her chapter offers a purview of censorship theory and a broad critique of the Foucauldian (or constitutive) paradigm of censorial practice. More precisely, Freshwater notes the problems that inhere in the constitutive model, in which censorship is understood as 'a process, realised through the relationships between censorious agents, rather than a series of actions carried out by a discrete or isolated authority' (2004: 225). While the notion of constitutive censorship usefully foregrounds the networks of social relations within which censorship incubates and operates, it also tends to exclude the experiences of those directly impacted by it (2004: 233). Moreover, Freshwater holds that constitutive theories of censorship implicitly stymie the prospects of political resistance: 'If censorship is everywhere, unavoidable and ineluctable, then it is hard to believe that it is possible to intervene to counter it' (2004: 241). What emerges from her writing is the need for robust and in-depth evaluations of the sociopolitical and cultural contexts in which censorship arises: 'Conclusions about censorship should surely be provisional, rather than fixed; plural, rather than singular; time and site-specific, rather than universal' (2004: 242).

In retrospect, Freshwater's intervention is prescient in at least two respects. In the years following the publication of her chapter, as cases of controversy and protest on religious issues began to multiply, a number of theatre scholars published analyses—often in response to the productions cited above—that, firstly, focused on the experiences of those directly impacted by censorship, and, secondly, argued for a more inclusive and potentially transformative public dialogue on free speech and artistic representation. One example of this scholarship is Janelle Reinelt's article 'The Limits of Censorship', published in 2007, in which she observes that religion has become a lens for debates on freedom of expression in part because of the controversies making headlines at that time, notably in France and Britain, on 'the Muslim practice of wearing headscarves'

(2007: 6). Expressing her unease at the ubiquitous use of the word 'censorship', Reinelt makes the following appeal:

> I have been at pains to suggest the complexity of events that have sometimes been labelled censorship of one sort or another in order to urge artists and scholars to take up the challenge to participate deeply in thinking about and discussing, even struggling over, the best way to realize the value of freedom of expression while maintaining a consideration of competing values, intensely important within given concrete contexts. (2007: 13)

Like Freshwater, Reinelt presses the importance of locating censorship cases in 'concrete contexts', and 'thinking about and discussing' different perspectives on 'competing values'. As part of her analysis, she refers to an example of stage performance in Germany that illustrates what can transpire in the absence of meaningful dialogue or wider consultation on controversial or provocative production choices; for Christopher Balme, meanwhile, this incident demonstrates 'the incendiary power of blasphemous images on a global scale' (2014: 135).

In autumn 2006, Mozart's opera *Idomeneo* was performed at the Deutsche Oper in Berlin, directed by Hans Neuenfels. The production included an epilogue in which the severed head of the Prophet Muhammad was placed on a chair (along with the heads of Neptune, Christ, and Buddha). Given that the Danish cartoons controversy had erupted only a few months before, and on the basis of anonymous threats of violence, the police warned the theatre management of an 'incalculable risk' (Balme 2014: 131) to performers, theatre staff, and audiences should the performances take place. In consequence, Kirsten Harms, the artistic director of Deutsche Oper, called a press conference in September announcing the cancellation of the show. The decision of the opera house to, in effect, self-censor provoked widespread condemnation, including from the German Chancellor Angela Merkel, and the production was eventually reinstated. Balme clarifies that *Idomeneo* had, in fact, premiered in 2003 but critical reaction to it then had overlooked the inflammatory content of the epilogue: in the period between 2003 and 2006, the uproar over the Danish cartoons had generated a much more febrile atmosphere (2014: 134). In his assessment of the incident, Balme, like Reinelt, criticizes the tendency of theatre artists and indeed politicians to co-opt religious images as if they can be airily and summarily detached from their real-world contexts: 'The political reaction to the *Idomeneo* affair, the almost total disregard for religious arguments, demonstrated a spectacular failure of the translation processes needed to mediate between political, religious and artistic public spheres' (2014: 138).

In March 2006, a few months before the irruption of the *Idomeneo* controversy, David Edgar presented a paper on censorship at 'Gagging', a conference held at the University of Hull. What is notable about this intervention is that Edgar acknowledges his own ambivalence on the issue of religious protests against theatre because he sees in the public discourse on censorship a disproportionate amount of critique levelled at disadvantaged and racially minoritized groups. He notes, for instance, that 'the free speech lobby concentrate on Muslim (and Sikh) protesters, and pay little attention to years and years of attempts by Christians to suppress images of which they disapprove' (2009: 593); likewise, he also makes the point that Sikhs and Muslims, in contrast to Christian groups, 'have only been concerned to protest against images of things they regard as sacred' (ibid.). Edgar argues that the vicious cocktail of media misrepresentation and stereotyping of Muslim lives, repressive government policies, and the disdainful comments from politicians on Islamic dress have created a situation where, perhaps with some justification, 'Muslims see the publication of the Danish cartoons not as the exercise of a right but as the prelude to a pogrom' (2009: 593–94). Turning his attention to theatre, Edgar reflects on Gurpreet Kaur Bhatti's *Behzti* in 2004. The production was cancelled after its first performance at the Birmingham Rep because of objections and demonstrations outside the theatre by members of the local Sikh community, who condemned the depiction of a rape in a scene set in a gurdwara. As the protests escalated, Kaur Bhatti received death threats and went into hiding. The actions of the theatre's management were criticized by some industry professionals such as Lisa Goldman, the former artistic director of the Soho Theatre, who argued that the cancellation of *Behzti* 'sent shock waves through British theatre and pushed back the cause of free artistic expression' (2016: 83). Although the production of Kaur Bhatti's play enraged some—mostly male—members of the Sikh community, it also gave expression to the neglected experiences of Sikh women. As such, *Behzti* sits squarely within the Birmingham Rep's laudable tradition of staging challenging subject matter of interest to its diverse local communities. In a context of clashing and opposing perspectives, it is imperative, Edgar concludes, 'to assert the importance of free expression for the marginalized and the excluded, and to defend and protect fiction's right to portray, to explain, to represent, to shock, to inspire, and to imagine' (2009: 597).

Behzti galvanized extensive media debate and scholarly reflection on the wider implications of the case (Freshwater 2009). In her comments on the incident, Goldman also raises an important wider question: 'How does a theatre decide whether to "consult" with people from a community represented on stage? Indeed, should it ever?' (2016: 83). Such a query echoes Reinelt's earlier remarks on the need to establish a more comprehensive dialogue between theatres and their local stakeholders. As Reinelt points out, the Birmingham Rep attempted to hold discussions with members of the Sikh community to discuss *Behzti* before its production, but, despite this, critical questions still remain: 'Did they do enough? [...] Would it perhaps have been better to start with a tour of the play to community centres in Sikh and other Asian communities, then move it into the Rep's buildings? Was this even considered, and would it have been an appropriate consideration?' (Reinelt 2007: 10). The remarks on *Behzti* and *Idomeneo* from Reinelt, Balme, Edgar, and others attend carefully to the concerns of religious groups but they also seek to adumbrate the role of theatre in the contemporary public sphere, and to advocate for a more robust and sustained dialogue between theatre-makers and their (prospective) audiences.

The final section of this chapter focuses on the production and reception of Romeo Castellucci's *On the Concept of the Face, Regarding the Son of God*. The disruption of its performance in Paris has become a landmark case of interventionist religious protest against theatre. As I will discuss, several scholars have argued that the involvement of the police on the opening night of the performance in Paris reflected negatively on theatre as a space where dissent can be expressed and even celebrated; in so doing, they have queried Castellucci's seeming unwillingness to engage more sensitively with his vocal religious critics. However, it is also important to acknowledge Castellucci as a practitioner who has sought repeatedly to defend the autonomy of images in theatre, and the autonomy of theatrical space as a realm of metaphor that is separate from the real world. His defence of *On the Concept* therefore stands as a riposte to those, including religious protesters, who insist on definitive or fixed interpretations of images on stage.

Castellucci: 'the images are looking at you'

On the Concept was first performed by the company Socìetas Raffaello Sanzio in July 2010 at the Theater der Welt in Essen, Germany, and was subsequently staged at the Spill Festival at the Barbican, London, in April 2011, at Avignon's Opéra-Théâtre during the Avignon Festival in July that year, and at Paris's Théâtre de la Ville in October, as part of an international tour. It was directed and designed by Romeo Castellucci and featured music from his long-time collaborator, Scott Gibbons.

The visual field of this production is dominated by a large, close-up fragment from the Renaissance portrait titled *Christ Blessing* (1465) by Antonello da Messina, which is visible upstage. The painting is renowned for its evocation of Christ's searching, meditative gaze which is aimed directly at the viewer or, in this production, the audience in the auditorium. In her discussion of *On the Concept*, Sandra D'Urso observes that 'Each of the three parts [...] seems to evoke the Christological themes of sacrifice and persecution' (2013: 39); the 'three parts' of the piece also correspond to the theological trinity of 'Father, Son, and Holy Spirit'.

The first scene takes place in a modern domestic setting and features an aged and ailing father (performed by Gianni Plazzi), who is infirm and unable to control his bowels, and his adult son (Sergio Scarlatella), who endeavours to support him and give comfort. The repetitive actions on stage—a forensic choreography of physical decrepitude—underline the centrality of the mortal and vulnerable body in this performance. The unflinching depiction of bodily vulnerability, despite the intense fictional world-building of his productions, is a long-standing element of Castellucci's theatrical method that is referenced by him in an interview: 'The truth of the body becomes inscribed quite precisely in the fiction of the spectacle' (2004: 20). In the second scene, in a marked change of tone and rhythm, da Messina's portrait of Christ is assailed by a boy, who is soon joined by other youngsters; together, they hurl grenades at the image. In the third and most controversial sequence, dark viscous liquid resembling excrement begins to suppurate and pour from the right eye socket of da Messina's portrait. The drenched canvas is torn and ripped with knives and blowtorches. The words 'You Are My Shepherd'—an echo of the opening words of Psalm 23—become visible in lettering behind the damaged canvas; subsequently, the word 'Not' appears in between the words 'Are' and 'My', thus introducing an element of religious doubt or denial into the textual fragment. Finally, towards the end of the scene, the image of Christ's face is restored in a light projection.

The disparate and paradoxical elements of the production—the infirmity of the father, the inconsolable son, the youths with grenades, the degradation and eventual revivification of the portrait, the literal and thematic conjugation of the excremental and the sublime, and the affirmation and then disavowal of the biblical text—create a vertiginous constellation of psychosocial associations. In his detailed study of stage lighting in the performance, Yaron Abulafia states that, for him, 'the experience is so poetic that the mind drifts from one association to another in search of a settling meaning' (2016: 165).

According to Dorota Semenowicz, in the productions of Socìetas Raffaello Sanzio 'the primary instrument of constructing [a] new world is an image' (2016: 2). In similar vein, Gabriella Calchi Novati, in her assessment of the company's work, goes so far as to describe Castellucci and his collaborators as 'prophets of a new dramatic religion based on the absence of the incarcerating Word' (2009: 58). The images that are curated and created by the practitioners of Socìetas Raffaello Sanzio carry pronounced archetypal valences—in other words, they 'do not aim at the spectators' rational reasoning but at their unconscious' (Calchi Novati 2009: 62). In a platform discussion conducted by Joe Kelleher and Flora Pitrolo at the University of Roehampton in 2020, Castellucci elaborates his conception of theatrical images and the means through which they interpellate the spectator:

> When it works, you have the impression that the performers, the performance, are looking at you. You feel naked, without protection, in front of an image. So the images are looking at you. The

impression is that you know from the beginning this image, and the image knows you: it's an encounter. [...] What I do is to prepare the stage, objects, things, in order to evoke, call in a way, an image that already exists. [...] I combine, I combine endlessly—that, yes. But the images belong to everyone. (Castellucci 2020)[3]

In language that is redolent of Carl Jung's work on archetypes in the field of analytical psychology, the theatrical image for Castellucci is both personal and impersonal, specific and—he argues—universal: 'the images belong to everyone'. What is more, and once again adopting a Jungian concept, he holds that images are freighted with shadows: 'There is always an image that you don't know what it is, it is the shadow of the image' (cited in Castellucci et al. 2007: 225). In other words, images on stage are always incomplete and unknowable—their meaning and impact depends on the psychological projections and other associations brought to the theatrical 'encounter' by individual spectators. As Abulafia puts it: 'The power of the image in cognition, and its influence on our imagination, depends on the associations of the spectators and the semiotic drift in which they engage' (2016: 176).

Abulafia's phrase 'semiotic drift' conveys precisely the intended affective power of images in Castellucci's theatre: the performance extends an invitation to spectators to freely associate the interpretations they attribute to the images—including religious images—that are evoked or presented on stage. The image of Christ is 'an image that already exists' before its co-option in *On the Concept* (that is, da Messina's portrait pre-exists the performance, and images of Christ's face are ubiquitous globally); indeed, the image of Christ is a foundational archetype familiar to all and, in this sense, 'belong[s] to everyone'. However, in his commentary on the performance, Balme makes the point that religious images are distinctly hyper-real 'because they require by definition a different frame on the part of the viewer' (2015): in other words, for a religious believer, the sacred image is itself a locus of faith, not an inert or indeterminate floating signifier in a fictional realm of signs. It is the theatrical recontextualization of the religious image in *On the Concept*, as well as the degradation of da Messina's portrait in the process of performance, which galvanized protesters against the production.

The protests in Paris, in October 2011, were led primarily by Catholic groups. Demonstrators tried to prevent spectators from entering the Théâtre de la Ville and a relatively small group stormed the stage on the opening night and unfurled a banner with the slogan 'Christianophobia—it's enough!' The police were summoned and, in total, more than 200 people were arrested. Attending to the wider social context of the production, D'Urso notes that the Paris protests coincided with the tumultuous Arab Spring, the global 'Occupy' anti-austerity movement, and the brutal police response to student demonstrations at the University of California,

Davis (2013: 36). She argues that, due to the involvement of the police, 'what ensued [at the Théâtre de la Ville] was something that in the end looked much more like a scenography of the police state, evidenced in any number of the Occupy events, than like a democratic reckoning with dissent' (2013: 43). Balme makes the similar point that the protesters' views should not be ignored: 'But were not the protestors themselves theatre critics too, of a more corporeal kind?' (2015).[4]

The on-stage invasion on the opening night was, from Castellucci's perspective, an intrusion on theatre's differentiated status from the real. In an interview conducted in 2012, he commented:

> When a viewer intrudes on the stage, as happened to us in Paris during [*On the Concept*], the performance is broken because of the element of reality trespassing in another world, that of the performance. [...] Reality possesses no instruments to read itself, so it has to resort to metaphor, and a metaphor is a system of images. (Cited in Semenowicz 2016: 155, 156)

Castellucci's view is that since the protesters did not see the performance, they did not encounter its constitutive images; as such, the protests have no credible foundation. He explains that some religious people, in fact, defended the production, and he states that an encounter with his work can impact audiences in unpredictable ways: 'For instance, in Athens we staged it during social upheavals and many viewers interpreted the father's excrement as a legacy to which the next generation are doomed. In short: the young have to clean up after the old' (cited in Semenowicz 2016: 163).

In her article on what she calls the 'meta-affective' image in the work of Socìetas Raffaello Sanzio, Bryoni Trezise observes that 'the transformation of perception incurred by the work emerges from the interpolation of the twin paradigms of theatre and performance, of "fake" and "real", and, more precisely, the *felt effect* of their coincidental enactment' (2012: 213). In other words, Trezise notes that Socìetas Raffaello Sanzio invariably—and in various ways—subject what is 'fake' and 'real' to scrutiny and put these categories in an equivocal and imbricated relation in performance. Taking up this point, D'Urso argues that this indeterminacy is intensified and problematized in productions that feature religious images: 'For the fundamentalist Christians, only one meaning can be attributed to the face of Christ and that is that the image participates in the actual presence of divinity, and any violence done to the image is tantamount to an attack on the person of the divine' (2013: 42). The protests in Paris reflect, therefore, two different conceptions of the religious image on stage. The 'semiotic drift'—to borrow Abulafia's phrase—that characterizes the 'encounter' with images in Castellucci's ambiguous work is tantamount to blasphemy for the Christian believers outside the Théâtre de la Ville, some of whom stormed the stage in defence of the religious image's sanctity and 'one meaning'.

Religion remains a topic of 'extreme sensitivity' in the twenty-first century and its representation in theatre has triggered, across European nation states, demonstrations and accusations of blasphemy—defined as the subjection of religious images, narratives, or beliefs to satirical or scatological diminution. In response to numerous high-profile incidents of street protests and coordinated campaigns, theatre scholars have sought to address the problem of escalation by advocating for both a more robust understanding of the contexts in which censorial practices arise, and a more substantial dialogue between theatre-makers and audiences about provocative subject matter. Romeo Castellucci, however, takes a different view. At the start of the chapter, I noted that Anthony Neilson's play *The Censor* locates the censorial impulse and resulting dialogical impasse in an unwillingness or inability to acknowledge the ambiguous, associative, or metaphoric qualities of artistic images. Perhaps more than any other living theatre director, Castellucci champions theatre as an arena for compelling, and sometimes controversial, image production that is separate from the quotidian real world. He conceives of images in theatre, including carefully co-opted images of religious provenance, as intrinsic, archetypal, even primordial elements of meaning-making that can be revaluated in and through performance: in this respect, images on stage invoke the contemplation and 'semiotic drift' of spectators, as if returning their gaze. For Castellucci, the wider implications of theatrical image production reside in such collective scrutiny: as he puts it, '[t]he political potential of theatre lies in the fact that it forces us to be attentive' (cited in Semenowicz 2016: 160). Attentiveness is an active process through which differences of view, whether on religious belief or other divisive issues, can be acknowledged and perhaps even reconciled. The call for attentiveness, as spectators, theatre-makers, and citizens, is likely to become even more pressing in the years ahead.

Notes

1 An extract from the play was read at the Conway Hall, London, in March 2017 as part of 'The Inconvenient Muslim'—an event to launch the publication of *Homegrown* organized by Index on Censorship. For further analysis of the *Homegrown* controversy, see Roaa Ali's contribution to this volume.
2 For a detailed account of *Golgota Picnic* in Poland, see Płoski and Semenowicz (2014).
3 I am grateful to the organisers for generously providing me with access to a recording of this event.
4 Lara Shalson makes a similar point in her remarks on the protests against the performance of Brett Bailey's *Exhibit B* at the Waterloo Vaults, London, in 2014: such protests 'raised the question of who is included within the theatre's public' (2021: 35).

References

Abulafia, Yaron. 2016. *The Art of Light on Stage: Lighting in Contemporary Theatre* (Abingdon and New York: Routledge)
Appignanesi, Lisa. 2016. 'Foreword', in *Global Insights on Theatre Censorship*, ed. by Catherine O'Leary, Diego Santos Sánchez, and Michael Thompson (New York and London: Routledge), pp. xiii–xvi
Balme, Christopher. 2014. *The Theatrical Public Sphere* (Cambridge: Cambridge University Press)
—— 2015. 'In Extremis: Theatre Criticism, Ethics and the Public Sphere', *Critical Stages/Scènes critiques*, 12 (December)
Calchi Novati, Gabriella. 2009. 'Language under Attack: The Iconoclastic Theatre of *Socìetas Raffaello Sanzio*', *Theatre Research International*, 34.1 (March): 50–65. https://doi.org/10.1017/S0307883308004239
Castellucci, Claudia, Romeo Castellucci, Chiara Guidi, Joe Kelleher, and Nicholas Ridout. 2007. *The Theatre of Socìetas Raffaello Sanzio* (Abingdon and New York: Routledge)
Castellucci, Romeo. 2020. 'Art, Performance and the Act: Conversation with Romeo Castellucci', in conversation with Joe Kelleher and Flora Pitrolo, University of Roehampton, Surrey, UK, 19 February
Castellucci, Romeo, et al. 2004. 'The Universal: The Simplest Place Possible', translated by Jane House, *PAJ: A Journal of Performance and Art*, 26.2 (May): 16–25
Chrisafis, Angelique. 2011. 'Catholics Protest Against "Blasphemous" Play in Paris', *Guardian*, 8 December
D'Urso, Sandra. 2013. 'On the Theology of Romeo Castellucci's Theatre and the Politics of the Christian "Occupation" of His Stage', *Theatre Research International*, 38.1 (February): 34–46. https://doi.org/10.1017/S0307883312000971
Edgar, David. 2009. 'From the Nanny State to the Heckler's Veto: The New Censorship and How to Counter It', in *Extreme Speech and Democracy*, ed. by Ivan Hare and James Weinstein (Oxford: Oxford University Press), pp. 583–97
Farr, David. 2005. 'Tamburlaine Wasn't Censored', *Guardian*, 25 November
Ferguson, Amanda. 2014. 'Outrage as DUP Pressure Closes Bible Spoof Play *Complete Word of God*', *Belfast Telegraph*, 24 January
Freshwater, Helen. 2004. 'Towards a Redefinition of Censorship', in *Censorship & Cultural Regulation in the Modern Age*, ed. by Beate Müller, Critical Studies: Volume 22 (Leiden: Brill), pp. 225–45
——. 2009. *Theatre Censorship in Britain: Silencing, Censure and Suppression* (Basingstoke: Palgrave Macmillan)
Goldman, Lisa. 2016. 'Silence One Story and Another is Born: Experience of Censorship in Iran and the UK in 2010', in *Global Insights on Theatre Censorship*, ed. by Catherine O'Leary, Diego Santos Sánchez, and Michael Thompson (New York and London: Routledge), pp. 79–92
Hare, Ivan. 2009. 'Blasphemy and Incitement to Religious Hatred: Free Speech Dogma and Doctrine', in *Extreme Speech and Democracy*, ed. by Ivan Hare and James Weinstein (Oxford: Oxford University Press), pp. 289–310
Index on Censorship. 2015. 'Creative Team Behind *Homegrown* "Deeply Shocked" at Cancellation', 13 August <www.indexoncensorship.org/2015/08/statement-homegrown-creative-team-reacts-cancellation/> [accessed 13 July 2022]

Lee, Stewart. 2006. 'Christian Voice Is Outside, Praying for Our Souls', *Guardian*, 15 February

McDonald, Henry. 2014. 'The Bible—The Show Goes On in Belfast', *Guardian*, 29 January

Mahmoud, Osha, and Islam Zitout. 2017. '"Homegrown": The Play That Exposed Limit of UK's "Risk Averse Culture"', *Middle East Eye*, 21 March

Marmion, Patrick. 2002. '"What I do is a bit odd"', *Guardian*, 13 May

Merritt, Stephanie. 2005. 'Artists Must Always Risk Offending', *Guardian*, 27 November

Nathan, John. 2010. 'Censorship is Back on the British Stage', *Prospect*, 19 March

Neilson, Anthony. 1998. *Plays 1* (London: Methuen Drama)

Nicholson, Steve. 2016. 'Not Recommended for Licence: British Theatre Censorship under the Lord Chamberlain', in *Global Insights on Theatre Censorship*, ed. by Catherine O'Leary, Diego Santos Sánchez, and Michael Thompson (New York and London: Routledge), pp. 221–33

O'Keefe, Alice. 2006. 'BNP Members Join Christians to Halt "Jerry"', *Observer*, 22 January

'On-Stage Protest at "Racist" Play'. 2009. *BBC News*, 2 March

Ostrowska, Joanna. 2016. 'Hide and Seek: Selected Stratagems of Polish Independent Theatre Companies', in *Global Insights on Theatre Censorship*, ed. by Catherine O'Leary, Diego Santos Sánchez, and Michael Thompson (New York and London: Routledge), pp. 109–23

Płoski, Paweł, and Dorota Semenowicz (eds). 2014. *Golgota Picnic in Poland: An Account of the Events May–July 2014*, translated by Arthur Barys et al. (Malta Foundation)

Reinelt, Janelle. 2007. 'The Limits of Censorship', *Theatre Research International*, 32.1 (March): 3–15. https://doi.org/10.1017/S0307883306002471

Schafer, Elizabeth. 2019. *theatre & christianity* (London: Red Globe Press)

Semenowicz, Dorota. 2016. *The Theatre of Romeo Castellucci and Socìetas Raffaello Sanzio: From Icon to Iconoclasm, From Word to Image, From Symbol to Allegory* (New York: Palgrave Macmillan). https://doi.org/10.1057/978-1-137-56390-3

Shalson, Lara. 2021 (2017). *theatre & protest* (London: Bloomsbury Methuen Drama)

Thomas, David, David Carlton, and Anne Etienne. 2007. *Theatre Censorship: From Walpole to Wilson* (Oxford: Oxford University Press). https://doi.org/10.1093/acprof:oso/9780199260287.001.0001

Thompson, Michael. 2016. 'Conclusion: The Power of Theatre', in *Global Insights on Theatre Censorship*, ed. by Catherine O'Leary, Diego Santos Sánchez, and Michael Thompson (New York and London: Routledge), pp. 259–67

Trezise, Bryoni. 2012. 'Spectatorship that Hurts: Socìetas Raffaello Sanzio as Meta-affective Theatre of Memory', *Theatre Research International*, 37.3: 205–20. https://doi.org/10.1017/S0307883312000879

8
Religion and Politics: Silencing Greek Theatre in the Twenty-First Century

OLGA KOLOKYTHA, YULIA BELINSKAYA,
AND MATINA MAGKOU

Censorship is a means to exercise politics and power, and it is affected by the sociopolitical context in which it occurs (Müller 2004: 19–20). As the tools, scope, actors, and even the purpose of censorship may vary depending on the given country and time frame (Green and Karolides 2014), the study of censorship necessitates situating it within a specific historical context and communicative paradigms (Bunn 2015: 28). In the arts, as Tasos Zembylas (2014) argues, contested issues are related to social configurations, so an event that is regarded as a public offence in one country might not be conceived as such in another geographic, political, and social environment. Censorship does exist in twenty-first-century Greece and, although the traditional expression of censorship in the form of preventive and prohibitive measures has diminished, other forms have developed (Ziogas et al. 2008). Although censorship committees were abolished in 1986, censorship practices have continued, especially in the arts (Bozoni 2019).

This chapter examines theatre censorship in Greece post-2010, when the country suffered the effects of the financial crisis. We will identify and map the association of censorship with conditions of crisis and explore how direct and indirect processes and mechanisms of censorship operate in the domain of theatre. Our methodological approach draws on the literature on censorship in the cultural sector, and we focus on three examples of contemporary theatre censorship. Two of these plays were produced in the capital, Athens—*Corpus Christi* in 2012 and *I isorropia tou Nash (The Nash Equilibrium)* in 2016—and the other—*I ora tou Diavolou (The Hour of the Devil)* in 2017—in Thessaloniki, the second-largest city in the country. All three plays were censored for religious or political reasons and triggered protests, riots, threats, and arrests. We have selected these case studies for three reasons: firstly, they highlight the use of censorship for political and religious, rather than artistic, reasons; secondly, they showcase a dimension of censorship that denotes an instrumentalization of theatre for political purposes to serve the ulterior motives of different pressure groups; and thirdly, they illustrate censorship cases that took place during the Greek financial crisis, which started in 2009 and lasted almost a decade, thus illuminating the relationship between the two.

Following a theoretical consideration of the relation of censorship to artistic expression, this chapter offers a brief historical overview of censorship in Greece in order to provide a context for our analysis, and to reflect on the impact of the financial crisis in accentuating sociopolitical conditions and dynamics. Those conditions help to illuminate the motivations for the censorship of our case studies: in particular, we highlight the role of politics and the Church in instigating and pursuing censorship in the theatre post-2010. In so doing, we situate censorship as an act with political, rather than artistic or ethical, motives (for discussion of the artistic and ethical motives behind censorship, see, for example, Chapters 2 and 3 of Houchin 2009).

We used semi-structured, in-depth interviews with Greek theatre professionals—artistic directors, actors, and producers—to gain first-hand insight from those who are experiencing and are influenced by such phenomena.[1] We asked our interviewees about their perception of censorship in Greece, the conditions of censorship in theatre, the influence—if any—of the financial crisis on censorship, and their opinions on the particular censorship examples we analyse in our chapter. We aimed to conduct approximately ten interviews as our purpose was not to draw representative responses, but rather to obtain information on the attitudes and viewpoints of stakeholders on theatre censorship in the 2010s, especially because of the currently limited literature on the topic. We encountered, however, significant challenges in securing interviews with theatre professionals. This we attribute partly to the difference of the term 'censorship' in the Greek context—where the word tends to denote regulatory or state censorship rather than other forms—and partly to the sensitivity of the topic, which involves tackling issues, such as the rise of the extreme right and the role of the Church, that are not easy to discuss openly in a formal interview context. In the end, we managed to conduct five interviews. Our standard consent form offers anonymity to avoid deducing any information about the interviewed person, which was important to secure those interviews, hence our use of the non-specific term 'interviewees' in this chapter. We have not included direct quotes as an extra measure to ensure anonymity, but the contribution of our interviewees is apparent in the sections on 'The role of the financial crisis' and 'Theatre censorship in the 2010s: case studies'. In addition to the interviews, we investigated selective press coverage of the time to highlight these events and indicate the range of media responses. These are by no means the only cases of censorship in Greek theatre post-1986, although we have not been able to identify aggregated data on the number of plays that were censored since 1986 for comparative purposes.

The different faces of censorship

Censorship 'has become a common-sense catchword', as Janelle Reinelt argues (2007: 3), and is nowadays used as an umbrella term that commonly describes all forms of regulation and restriction of freedom of expression. Traditional censorship is defined as a form of control to maintain power regardless of the nature of the censorship—whether it refers to moral, political, or ethical dimensions—in the form of straightforward regulatory intervention mostly by the state or the church (Müller 2004: 4). The approach described by Müller does not restrict such interventions to the state or the church, but rather to the actors who operate that function within the given regulatory framework (2004: 12). A narrower definition, which reflects the liberal or traditional conception of censorship, attributes censorship to repressive forces applied by the state to violently intervene in processes of free communication (Bunn 2015). Neither definition, however, considers cases of self-censorship, when the censor and the censored are the same, or cases of censorship exercised by audiences in the form of protests.

New Censorship Theory, which is primarily rooted in the works of Michel Foucault on power and knowledge, shifts the focus from the state and the church to a combination of actors and bodies that form and disseminate discourse (Bunn 2015). This includes private institutions and the creators themselves in the form of self-censorship: 'a book might not be published because it is judged to have no market value in the "free marketplace of ideas"; in fact, it might not even be written' (Reinelt 2007: 4). New Censorship Theory sees censorship as a *process* of constantly changing norms and discourses rather than a simple set of practices (Freshwater 2004), and describes censorship as unavoidable: 'Rather than acting merely as a repressive force employed to curb communication, censorship is regarded as an integral element of communication' (Müller 2004: 7). Since there is no absolute freedom of expression, communication is affected by norms and discourses that can have a censorial character (Müller 2004). Censorship can exist within communication networks and often requires the 'quasi-consensual' participation of the actors (Bunn 2015: 40).

A clear, and historical, distinction is usually made between 'regulatory' or 'state' censorship and a 'structural' or 'constitutive' censorship (Müller 2004), meaning that, in contrast to direct acts of silencing, structural censorship is seen as heterogeneous and takes into consideration not only various actors but sociocultural contexts and norms, morals, and taboos that already exist in the community (Freshwater 2004). Moreover, structural censorship could also be seen as a productive rather than restrictive force, contributing to the formation of language and aesthetic values—an idea that is attributed to Michel Foucault and Judith Butler and discussed in O'Leary (2016: 2). The new, broader view on censorship includes the repressive forms alongside less direct practices that could be exercised by a range of actors and institutions (Bunn 2015). Even though New Censorship Theory has been criticized due to 'the risk of equating very different forms of control by confusing censorship with social norms affecting and controlling communication' (Müller 2004: 9), it provides a framework to the cases discussed in this chapter by broadening our understanding of censoring actors and the roots of censorship, and by putting societal and political factors such as the financial crisis into perspective.

Censorship and artistic expression in Greece

When it comes to artistic expression, censorship can occur not only before but also after production, and sometimes at both stages: 'A performance is closed or forbidden, a script is edited to remove offensive material, a television station is shut down, a certain press is forbidden to publish' (Reinelt 2007: 4). This may be exercised by an authority, or censorship may take the form of self-censorship. The pressure from minorities or religious organizations, often in the form of threats of violence, can lead to the disruption or cancellation of performances for reasons of public safety (Reinelt 2007).

In the twentieth century, censors feared theatre had 'the capacity to eradicate the boundaries between classes and genders, instigating political and sexual anarchy', and that actors, directors, and playwrights were able to disrupt existing power relations and establishments (Houchin 2009: 4). New Censorship Theory can be encountered in theatre, 'a medium subject to a wide range of political, institutional, professional, and economic interventions', where restrictions may come from various sources and take multiple forms other than straightforward repressive governmental control (Thompson 2012: 94). The political ideology that relies on conservative morals might perceive the fictional theatrical space, given its immediacy and proximity to the audience, as a place of significant threat: 'the conservative community fears artists, particularly theatrical artists. […] They fear that these artists will teach the faithful to imagine new systems, rewrite laws, and overturn the old order' (Houchin 2009: 2).

According to Vicky Karaiskou, 'art censorship in Greece since the establishment of the new Greek state in 1830 has been formulated in relation to the ideological patterns of national identity' (2011: 274). In order to represent the 'higher values' and the concept of 'nation', the fine arts in nineteenth-century Greece were shaped by the ideological patterns of Greek nationalism, reflecting the 'glory of antiquity' in political, social, and aesthetic senses (Karaiskou 2011: 275). Karaiskou points out the censoring role of art criticism, alongside self-censorship in the arts, and argues that the formal and informal art critics of the Romantic tradition aimed to glorify 'Greekness', heroism, morality, and religion.

Freedom of expression has been protected in Greece since the establishment of the Greek Constitution in 1975 as a fundamental human right in a democratic society. In contemporary Greece, modern art has been viewed as posing social danger (Karaiskou 2011). Theatre censorship in the country has a long history of upholding tradition, classical art, and conservative aesthetics (Van Steen 2014) and cases of artistic censorship occur regularly (Papanikolaou 2018). As popular art forms with significant appeal to the public, theatre and cinema have therefore been subjected to both state and non-state/atypical censorship practices (Petsini and Christopoulos 2018: 17). The current state of censorship in Greek culture cannot be studied in isolation from the country's historical context. After the end of the Second World War, Greece was torn apart by a civil war (1946–49) polarizing Greek culture and bringing ideological confusion (Tsichla 2019). A particularly interesting period with regard to censorship, however, is that of the military junta regime.[2]

From 1967 to 1974, the military dictatorship was in power, bringing the discourse of national identity into art. Dictatorial regimes are characterized by a 'more or less straightforward relationship between oppression imposed on political life and despotism enforced on cultural life' (Arvaniti 2015: 355). During the period of the dictatorship, the list of banned books contained more than a thousand items, mostly political in nature (Van Steen 2014: 97). Theatre had to officially comply with the national ideology and the junta regime made stage censorship a priority, realizing there were underlying dangers in theatre's topicality and immediacy (Van Steen 2014). Starting in April 1967, all theatre plays were censored by the junta if they were perceived to contain 'military references, references to fascism, revolutions and popular uprisings, subversive or communist ideas, pornography, homosexuality, and material that cast a slur on the nation, the Orthodox Church, the king and the government' (Asimakoulas 2005: 93). Censorship practices included not only rejecting scripts submitted to censorship committees for inspection before premiering the performances, but even after the play was running. Changes made by the actors during performances could affect the meaning and connotation of the play, so actors, directors, and theatre managers were held responsible for any such 'violations'; and if a theatre had to close down because of such incidents, theatre managers had to continue paying artists and staff (Van Steen 2014: 109). There were several tactics of evading the censors, such as, for example, using the family as a metaphor for the dysfunctional power dynamics of the state (94).

State censorship, which intended to ban any form of artistic expression that was considered dangerous for the state ideology, was expanded by the dictators into a system of preventive measures aimed to constitute a 'nation-wide change of mentality' (Van Steen 2014: 96). The junta used regulation put in place from the late 1930s to the mid-1940s, but which had not been used since. The instruments included, for instance, firing directors and actors at the National Theatre, establishing a Committee for the Control of Theatrical Works, and exercising censorship on both the text of the plays and the dress rehearsal. Control was exercised not only by the junta regime's different (smaller) committees; artistic teams and performers also had to check each other so that, during performances, there were no alterations to the approved text and its tone, a situation that created difficult dynamics among colleagues (Van Steen 2014: 108).

Although the junta regime ended in 1974, there have been many examples of censorship afterwards that showcase the difficulties contemporary art in general has been facing in the country. According to Penelope Petsini and Dimitris Christopoulos, 'censorship is the epitome of the violation of the right of free expression not as an accident, but as a symptom of power relations. To deal with censorship, we must delve into the core of these relations with regard to their historical depth as well as their political penetration' (2018: 19). The cases of censorship that occur in a modern democratic regime should not be considered as isolated cases, but rather as consequences of the processes deeply rooted in a variety of historical and societal factors.

In terms of artistic freedom, Panagiota Papanikolaou identifies 'several interventions in recent years in many artistic fields: from visual arts to drama and cinematography' (2018: 13). During the junta regime, theatre was officially censored by the then government because of its appeal to the public as a popular form of culture; for the same reason, censorship continued afterwards, though it was then conducted differently. Nowadays, censorship may not take place officially but on an individual basis, depending on whether the meanings conveyed by a play offend religious or partisan political organizations, official or otherwise, and other pressure groups.

The role of the financial crisis

The financial crisis, visible already in 2008, initiated a series of austerity measures in the form of additional taxes as well as reduction of wages and pensions, and had severe consequences such as unemployment and a severe 'brain-drain'—the migration of skilled workers abroad because of the high unemployment in the country (Lees and Alfieris 2019). The large-scale arrival of refugees in the mid-2010s, when Greece operated as a transition route and then host country, also confronted Greek citizens with questions of coexistence with refugees, religious diversity, and racism. It is not a coincidence that the rise of both Golden Dawn (Greece's extreme right-wing party) and the Greek Orthodox Church has been accentuated during the crisis—which, apart from an economic crisis, also became a crisis of values. Golden Dawn, in particular, attained fifth position in the elections of June 2012, with strong parliamentary representation during that period (Lees and Alfieris 2019: 47).

Our interviewees observe that the financial crisis in Greece resulted in the intensification of political competition and argue that, during the crisis, there has been a decisive claim for power from different groups within society. A logic of two poles—left and right—is historically present in the political life of Greece and has constantly been a field of ideological conflict. Next to the dichotomy between left and right, religion is another topic that has polarized public opinion in Greek society in recent decades. The Greek Orthodox Church plays a paramount role in Greek internal politics and has traditionally been a powerful actor exercising its influence mostly inside the Greek Orthodox temples, although in recent times it has also gained ground outside them, in the public sphere.

Theatre censorship in the 2010s: case studies

Corpus Christi, written by Terrence McNally in 1997, was staged in Athens in 2012 in a production directed by Laertis Vasiliou; *The Nash Equilibrium*, also staged in Athens, was based on a combination of texts by various writers and directed by Pigi Dimitrakopoulou in 2016; and *The Hour of the Devil* by Fernando Pessoa was directed in 2017 in Thessaloniki by Giorgos Apostolopoulos. While all plays met with public protests, in the case of *Nash*, in particular, not only did audience members react with hostility to the production, but there were also reactions by artists, culture professionals, and the board members of the National Theatre against censorship and the decision of the theatre's artistic director, Stathis Livathinos, to stop the production before its scheduled end date.

Corpus Christi (2012)

In October 2012, the theatrical group Artisan planned the first Greek staging of McNally's *Corpus Christi*—a play that had already received an outraged response from religious groups in the USA in 1998 when it was first performed. Directed by Laertis Vasiliou and based on a translation by him and Vasia Panagopoulou, the adaptation of the play reconsidered and reconstructed the story of Jesus and his twelve disciples, situating it in the Greek context. Jesus is presented as a leader and Judas as a man attracted to him, while the play follows the life of Jesus from his birth in a motel on the Greek Highway to his school adventures and his Crucifixion. Through the developing relationship of Jesus and his disciples, the play presents the lives of those thirteen young men in a context of love, affection, ambition, and betrayal. *Corpus Christi* triggered riots outside the Chitirion Theatre (a private theatre venue in Athens staging independent productions) from the day it opened.

The production took place in 2012, a year marked by two major political developments: the election of New Democracy, the Greek right-wing party, in government at the time of the production, and the rise of the far-right Golden Dawn party and its entry into Parliament after the elections (Bournazos 2016). Religious fanatics and members of Golden Dawn were at the forefront of reactions against the production with riots, threats, protests, and verbal and physical attacks carried out against audiences who attended the performance (Naftemporiki 2012). The Holy Synod of the Greek Orthodox Church had, earlier that year, disapproved of the play, labelled it as blasphemous and defamatory of Jesus ('Apodokimasia' 2012), and called on the faithful to reject it (Tsolakidou 2012). The special forces of the Greek police, MAT (Units for the Reinstatement of Order), were positioned outside the theatre, after members of the production team notified the police and the electronic crime squad that the stage director had received anonymous threats on social media ('Theatro Chitirio' 2012). The riots were so intense that McNally himself wrote to the producers to express his support, stating that 'another theatre would not have endured so much, but with all the blasphemy that they attribute to the performance, is the real message of the play lost? Is it possible that a play that was written to talk about love, ends up causing so much hatred?' ('Katevike' 2012). After three weeks of trying to perform the play amidst constant protests, mockery, and attacks against the artists, the production was discontinued to protect the artists, theatre staff, and audience (Rigopoulos 2012). In their statement, Vasiliou and Panagopoulou thanked those who supported the production and expressed their concerns about the state 'numbly watching the forces of darkness acting' ('Katevike' 2012). However, some of our interviewees note a different perspective regarding the role of the state in this incident. The presence of police units guarding the theatre where the production was taking place appears to be an expression of the modern role of the state, safeguarding the terms of public dialogue, in the framework of which it acted *against* the threatened censorship of the production.

The incidents in front of the Chitirion Theatre were reported in the national and international media, the latter underlining the role of the church rather than the state:

> The Greek Orthodox Church, its huge wealth unscathed by the crisis, is in no rush to condemn its clerics for siding, condoning, instigating and participating in acts of violence and disrespect against immigrants, homosexuals and people who challenge their view of what being Greek and Orthodox entails. (Baboulias 2012)

In contemporary Greece, religious censorship forms the lion's share of all censorship cases (see Ziogas et al. 2008, Tsichla 2019). Theatre pieces have often been targets of various religious organizations: for example, the production of Andrew Lloyd Webber's famous musical, *Jesus Christ Superstar*, was subjected to violent protests by religious fanatics in Athens in 2018 (Tsichla 2019). The Greek Orthodox Church has frequently had problematic relations with art and culture: one instance of this is the effort to excommunicate Nikos Kazantzakis (one of the greatest Greek writers and a nine-time Nobel Prize nominee, whose work deals with religion, spirituality, and the questioning of fundamental Christian values) which was rejected by the Ecumenic Patriarch Athenagoras. The Orthodox religion has been closely related to the forming of Greek national identity, which adds a political significance to its role and sustains the close connections between the church and the state (Fokas 2020: 103). The majority of Greece's native-born population are baptized into the Greek Orthodox Church, which sees itself and is regarded by a large majority of Greeks as the guardian of Greek identity and traditions. Until the early 2000s, the Orthodox religion was affirmed on all Greek identity cards, and the plans of the then government to change this led to major opposition from the Church. Archbishop Christodoulos initiated a campaign to collect signatures against the intention of the government, and public demonstrations were organized by the Church in Athens and Thessaloniki. These initiatives gave the Church the opportunity to step outside the temples—its traditional sphere of influence—and acquire the characteristics of an organized group intervening in the public sphere. At the time of the *Corpus Christi* production, the Church inaugurated the new premises of its radio station ('Apodokimasia' 2012), which demonstrates the ambition and level of its involvement in the public sphere.

The Nash Equilibrium (2016)

In 2016, *The Nash Equilibrium*, at the Experimental Stage of the Greek National Theatre, a small venue of 140 seats, was cancelled during its run. The piece was based on Albert Camus's play *The Just Assassins* (1949)—which deals with moral issues associated with murder and terrorism, and is based largely on historical terrorists—as well as on excerpts from the book *I mera ekeini: 1,560 ores stin entatiki. Mia martiria gia to diko mas Guantanamo* (*On That Day: 1,560 Hours in Intensive Care. An Eyewitness Account of Our Guantanamo*) by Savvas Xiros (Kakouriotis 2018), published in 2006. Xiros was a key member of 17 November (17N), a far-left, Marxist, and anti-imperialist terrorist group active in the 1980s and 1990s in Greece, and disbanded in 2002 after the arrest and trial of many of its members; Xiros is currently serving a multiple life sentence in jail. The book documents the days of his hospitalization and interrogation at the Evangelismos Hospital in Athens after his arrest. The play was devised by the director Pigi Dimitrakopoulou and her team: the performance touched upon justice, vigilantism, value systems, and contemporary Greek history (National Theatre 2016).

The play was perceived to be highly political due to its subject matter and its creation at the National Theatre. For these reasons, the piece received extensive coverage from the media and provoked harsh reactions. It was criticized for 'glorifying convicted killers' (Maltezou 2016), especially by the group of relatives of terrorist victims named Os Edo (which can be translated as 'Enough is enough'), who issued a statement lambasting the piece for 'purifying the terrorist act' (Ioannidis 2016).

The choice of the National Theatre to stage the production was described as 'an insult to the memory of the victims of the terrorist organization 17N' by Kyriakos Mitsotakis, New Democracy's leader and then Leader of the Opposition in Parliament (Ioannidis 2016). It should be noted that New Democracy and 17N have a troubled connection since Pavlos Bakoyannis, the parliamentary leader of the New Democracy party in the Hellenic Parliament who was shot dead outside his office in 1989 by the 17N, was the husband of Dora Bakoyannis, the sister of Kyriakos Mitsotakis. The news of Bakoyannis's assassination sent shock waves through Greek society, as the liberal politician was a moderate who called for unity on the political front.

The play premiered on 15 January and was scheduled to have a total of eleven performances, a number not unusual for the Experimental Stage. Pressured by public outrage, as well as the threats to cause physical harm to the artists, audience, and staff of the theatre, the artistic director of the National Theatre, Stathis Livathinos, decided to cancel the final four performances, out of a total of eleven. This in turn triggered a wave of reaction from the artistic world and the general public, and a wider debate about artistic freedom and the contribution of such works 'to understanding and offering not an alibi, legitimation and heroism to violence and terrorists, but answers to critical and long-lasting questions' (Kasimeris 2016). Prodromos Tsinikoris and Anestis Azas, the managers of the National Theatre's Experimental Stage, expressed their support for Livathinos's decision to protect audiences, staff, and the overall operation of the theatre by shutting down the production (Ioannidis 2016). In contrast, the National Theatre's board members issued a statement saying that, although they understood the difficult situation Livathinos was in, they believed the production should conclude its scheduled performances. They defended the theatre's position as a place of 'free expression and free dialogue':

> some people want to throw us into a deep conservatism and even at a time when everything self-evident around us is collapsing. Common sense is now disappearing. If an artist talks about a subject and researches it, does it mean that he [sic] embraces it? Since when are there taboo subjects in the arts? (Ioannidis 2016)

As our interviewees also argue, the case of *The Nash Equilibrium* highlights how political considerations result in censorship. Besides the content of the play itself, one of the main points of controversy was that such a play was staged at the National Theatre of Greece, a state-funded organization. The Greek cultural landscape historically favoured a strong connection of culture with politics: Greek cultural policy has been scarce and fragmented (Kolokytha 2022), characterized by a lack of long-term vision and strategy (Koutsobinas 2007), a narrow and elitist perception of culture constrained in the space between cultural heritage and support for the arts, and a clientelistic system (Tziovas 2017). Our interviewees acknowledge that the duality of power as well as the intense polarization between left and right, both strong characteristics of the Greek political scene, are visible in the cultural sector; they thus attribute a political character to the repertoire of cultural organizations in Greece, particularly the publicly funded ones.

In this case, the government's reaction could be described as neutral. The statement issued by the Ministry of Culture and Sports on the same day that Livathinos decided to stop the performances reflected that '[blind] reactions that don't deal with the specific content or the purposes of a performance make impossible any sober depiction of the work of art and any substantial public debate both about the memory of the victims and the phenomenon of uncontrollable violence' ('"Katevainei"' 2016). However, the Ministry underlined that it had neither the authority nor the intention to intervene in the repertoire of public theatres and described as sad and worrying the fact that the National Theatre had to cancel the final performances of this play under the pressure of threats (ibid.). It is quite unusual for the Ministry of Culture to either intervene or issue statements in such circumstances, so this highlights the political character this case of censorship had amassed.

In addition to the political storm caused by the National Theatre's decision to create the play, with the two major political parties using the play as a field of debate, giving a voice to Xiros through publicly mounting his work, showcasing his ideas, and acknowledging him as an author was perceived as a scandalous insult to the victims of terrorism on an ethical level. The play's creator and director, Dimitrakopoulou, hoped that

> no one would want to go back to the time of the Junta, when scripts and theatrical texts were stamped on every page by the Censorship Committee. The fact that I was not 'censored' in 2016 was considered a mistake, and the fact that I used a book by a member of an organization that was dismembered 14 years ago, at least criminal. ('Dilosi' 2016)

Her comment brought to the surface historically sensitive issues relating to freedom of expression in Greece, and particularly the spectre of the preventive censorship practices during the junta period.

The Hour of the Devil (2017)
A year later, in October 2017, riots took place outside the Aristoteleion Theatre in the centre of Thessaloniki for two consecutive days, when

religious fanatics and nationalist groups holding Greek flags and religious icons tried to interrupt the performance of *The Hour of the Devil* a week after its premiere (Vasvani 2017). The play is an adaptation by Grigoris Apostolopoulos, who also directed the piece, of a story by Fernando Pessoa, which puts the Devil into conversation with a woman, Maria: the drama explores and unveils their contrasting attitudes and presents questions of Good and Evil, and Life and Death. *The Hour of the Devil* premiered on 11 October 2017 for a total of ten performances; it had previously been performed in 2015 in Thessaloniki, but there were no protests at that time (Vasvani 2017).[3]

According to the protesters, the play depicts and glorifies the Devil as Christ's brother and mocks the Holy Cross, the Lord's Prayer, and the Virgin Mary. Two people were arrested by the police and were given a suspended sentence of four and six months' imprisonment, respectively, for participating in violent protests ('Thessaloniki' 2020). The lead actor, George Chraniotis, highlights the climate and repercussions of the events in an online interview, noting how protests made people sceptical about seeing the performances, with some deciding not to attend, and pointing out the impact of censorship on the relationship between artists and audience:

> We are going back to medieval practices, and it no longer seems funny to me, because I learnt that some people did not come to the performance because they were afraid of the religious and nationalist organizations which were outside the theatre. ('Eksallos o Chraniotis' 2017)

What makes the Thessaloniki case noteworthy is that it took place outside the capital of the country. Although Greece has a rich tradition of theatres in many regional cities, some of which mount unconventional, contemporary pieces, it seems that most cases of censorship take place in Athens—a paradox, given the popular belief that regional areas are bastions of conservatism. Our interviewees note the abundance of theatres and the concentration of political forces in the capital, which makes different groups keen to exercise power there. Censorship is a helpful instrument for them to exercise political pressure, and to acquire new, or confirm their existing, political power.

According to the late Stavros Tsakirakis, lawyer and professor of constitutional law, it is not a coincidence that religions which are powerful within a society attempt to censor works of art that they perceive to be blasphemous (2008). He argues that the dominant role of the Greek Orthodox Church, and its position at the forefront of protests and censorship against works of art, damages its status, causes problems to artists, hinders the development of art, and defames the country worldwide (Tsakirakis 2008: 96). As censorship practices are interlinked with and denote power relations, it is not by chance that, in places where the political parties and the church are powerful actors, cases of censorship are initiated and pursued by them.

Censorship cases such as these highlight how different groups seek to use social influence to reinforce their political power and incorporate forms of protest that can cause physical harm. To that extent, theatre censorship in Greece is a result of an appropriation and a targeting of culture for political purposes by different pressure groups. The cases examined in this chapter show that in contemporary Greece, theatre censorship is related to extreme political positions and beliefs, and rooted in political and religious frameworks. The ideological polarization of left and right, and the increasing power of the Greek Orthodox Church, lie at the centre of these three controversies. The financial crisis has intensified polarization in society and thus made censorship more acute as it has fortified the conditions that generate it. These conditions also include the display of power by political parties and the church.

Most importantly, these case studies denote an instrumentalization of theatre for ideological purposes which derives from the polarization in internal politics, an increased influence of the church on the public sphere, and the appetite for power of both. None of the arguments used to censor the three plays were concerned with the artistic merit of the respective pieces, but rather with their perceived impact and influence against actors seeking power within Greek society. To that extent, theatre censorship in Greece since the 2010s has become a tool in the quest for political power, and the protests against immoral and offensive performances have been recuperated for political purposes.

Ziogas et al. (2008) identify the reluctance of Greek society and the state to accept, acknowledge, or at least tolerate what they find ethically or politically repulsive, as factors that contribute to the marginalization of the issue of censorship in public discourse; they also highlight the need to investigate censorship in the cultural sector and identify the underlying reasons why it has not been part of a wider conversation. We contend that censorship in the arts in Greece is an issue that deserves further attention and research, particularly in relation to the parallel socio-economic developments in the country which create the conditions that feed it.

Notes

1   The interviews were conducted by one of the researchers affiliated with the Department of Communication at the University of Vienna, and the process was approved as part of the Department's institutional ethical review of research projects.
2   For a discussion of theatre censorship during the junta, see, for example, Van Steen (2014) and Arvaniti (2015). In Greek, the collective volume edited by

Petsini and Christopoulos (2018) includes two chapters on the subject of theatre censorship, written by Evdokia Delipetrou (pp. 19–26) and Stratis Bournazos (pp. 203–11).

3 Research into the 2015 performance has not yielded any information that could explain why it elicited no protest then.

References

'Apodokimasia tou theatrikou ergou Corpus Christi zita i Iera Sinodos'. 2012. *Kathimerini*, 7 June <https://www.kathimerini.gr/society/3541/apodokimasia-toy-theatrikoy-ergoy-corpus-christi-zita-i-iera-synodos/> [accessed 27 September 2021]

Arvaniti, Katerina. 2015. 'Dictatorship and Theatre: The Seven-Year Junta and the Performances of Greek Tragedy at Epidaurus', *Logeion*, 5: 355–71

Asimakoulas, Dimitris. 2005. 'Brecht in Dark Times: Translations of His Works under the Greek Junta (1967–1974)', *Target*, 17.1: 93–110. https://doi.org/10.1075/target.17.1.06asi

Baboulias, Yianis. 2012. 'Greece, in 2012: Fascists Beating Up People while the Police Look On', *Guardian*, 12 October

Bournazos, Stratis. 2016. 'Corpus Christi kai "Geron Pastitsios". Katastaltiki logokrisia, kratos kai Akrodeksia', in *I Logokrisia stin Ellada*, ed. by Penelope Petsini and Dimitris Christopoulos (Athens: Rosa Luxemburg Foundation Greece branch), pp. 203–11

Bozoni, Argiro. 2019. 'Gnwstes kai agnwstes istories logokrisias stin Ellada mesa apo ena leksiko', *The TOC*, 26 February <https://www.thetoc.gr/politismos/article/gnwstes-kai-agnwstes-istories-logokrisias-stin-ellada-mesa-apo-ena-leksiko/> [accessed 29 September 2021]

Bunn, Matthew. 2015. 'Reimagining Repression: New Censorship Theory and After', *History and Theory*, 54.1: 25–44

'Dilosi tis Pigis Dimitrakopoulou gia tin "Isorropia tou Nash"'. 2016. *Athinorama*, 28 January <https://www.athinorama.gr/theatre/article/dilosi_tis_pigis_dimitrakopoulou_gia_tin_isorropia_tou_nash-2511955.html> [accessed 21 September 2021]

'Eksallos o Chraniotis me tis antidraseis gia tin parastasi "I ora tou Diavolou"— "Den einai asteio, einai mesaionas"'. 2017. *Newsit*, 19 October <https://www.newsit.gr/topikes-eidhseis/eksallos-o-xraniotis-tis-antidraseis-gia-tin-parastasi-ora-tou-diavolou-den-einai-asteio-einai-mesaionas/2261122/> [accessed 27 August 2021]

Fokas, Effie. 2020. 'Religion and Human Rights in Greece', in *Global Eastern Orthodoxy: Politics, Religion, and Human Rights*, ed. by Giuseppe Giordan and Siniša Zrinščak (Cham: Springer), pp. 101–24

Freshwater, Helen. 2004. 'Towards a Redefinition of Censorship', in *Censorship and Cultural Regulation in the Modern Age*, ed. by Beate Müller (Leiden: Brill), pp. 225–45

Green, Jonathon, and Nicholas J. Karolides. 2014. *Encyclopedia of Censorship: New Edition*. (New York: Infobase Publishing)

Houchin, John H. 2009. *Censorship of the American Theatre in the Twentieth Century* (Cambridge: Cambridge University Press)

Ioannidis, Sakis. 2016. 'I "Isorropia" pou ksekikose antidraseis', *I Kathimerini*, 31 January <https://www.kathimerini.gr/society/847752/i-isorropia-poy-xesikose-antidraseis/> [accessed 27 August 2021]

Kakouriotis, Spiros. 2018. 'Isorropia tou Nash', in *Leksiko Logokrisias stin Ellada*, ed. by Penelope Petsini and Dimitris Christopoulos (Athens: Kastaniotis), pp. 367–73

Karaiskou, Vicky. 2011. 'Art Censorship as Art Criticism: Fighting the Sacrilegious and Protecting the "Shell"', in *Greek Research in Australia: Proceedings of the International Conference of Greek Studies, Flinders University*, ed. by M. Tsianikas, N. Maadad, G. Couvalis, and M. Palaktsoglou (Adelaide: Flinders University Department of Language Studies), pp. 274–88

Kasimeris, Yiorgos. 2016. 'Einai o Savvas Xiros iroas?', *Huffington Post Greece*, 27 January <https://www.huffingtonpost.gr/giorgos-kasimeris/-_3822_b_9086178.html> [accessed 10 February 2022]

'"Katevainei" i parastasi tou Ethnikou "Isorropia tou Nash"'. 2016. *Kathimerini*. 28 January <https://www.kathimerini.gr/society/847482/katevainei-i-parasta-si-toy-ethnikoy-isorropia-toy-nash/> [accessed 16 February 2022]

'Katevike i parastasi Corpus Christi sto Chytirio'. 2012. *News 247*, 1 November <https://www.news247.gr/politismos/theatro/katevike-i-parastasi-corpus-cristi-sto-chytirio.6177950.html> [accessed 25 September 2021]

Kolokytha, Olga. 2022. 'Crisis as Change: New Paradigms in Cultural Policy. The Case of Greece', in *Accomplishing Cultural Policy in Europe: Financing, Governance and Responsiveness*, ed. by Chris Mathieu and Valerie Visanich (Oxon: Routledge), pp. 71–86

Koutsobinas, Theodore T. 2007. 'Greek Cultural Policy after the 2004 Summer Olympics', *The International Journal of the Arts in Society*, 2.1: 165–71

Lees, Christopher, and Antonis Alfieris. 2019. 'Racist Discourse in the Years of the Greek Financial Crisis: Evidence from the Greek Press', *Journal of Greek Media & Culture*, 5.1: 45–67

Maltezou, Renee. 2016. 'Greek Theater Lowers Curtain on Political Violence Play as Censorship Row Builds', *Reuters*, 1 February

Müller, Beate. 2004. 'Censorship and Cultural Regulation: Mapping the Territory', in *Censorship and Cultural Regulation in the Modern Age*, ed. by Beate Müller (Leiden: Brill), pp. 1–31

Naftemporiki. 2012. 'Epeisodia gia tin parastasi Corpus Christi', *Naftemporiki*, 12 October <https://www.naftemporiki.gr/story/362214/epeisodia-gia-tin-parastasi-corpus-christi> [accessed 25 September 2021]

National Theatre. 2016. 'Isorropia tou Nash tis Pigis Dimitrakopoulou Apo 15 ews 31 Ianouariou stin Peiramatiki Skini—I' <https://www.n-t.gr/el/news/?nid=1802> [accessed 16 February 2022]

O'Leary, Catherine. 2016. 'Introduction: Censorship and Creative Freedom', in *Global Insights on Theatre Censorship*, ed. by Catherine O'Leary, Diego Santos Sánchez, and Michael Thompson (New York and Abingdon: Routledge), pp. 1–23

Papanikolaou, Panagiota M. 2018. 'The "Silence" of the Sculptures: Censorship Phenomena in Contemporary Greece. Open-Air Sculpture and Historical

Remembrance Monuments', *International Journal of Arts and Humanities*, 4.2: 9–16

Petsini, Penelope, and Dimitris Christopoulos. 2018. 'Isagogi: i logokrisia os krisi nomimopiisis—i elliniki periptosi', in *Leksiko logokrisias stin Ellada*, ed. by Penelope Petsini and Dimitris Christopoulos (Athens: Kastaniotis), pp. 13–19

Reinelt, Janelle. 2007. 'The Limits of Censorship', *Theatre Research International*, 32.1: 3–15

Rigopoulos, Dimitris. 2012. 'Pro-voles', *I Kathimerini*, 2 November <https://www.kathimerini.gr/culture/472133/pro-voles-558/> [accessed 07 July 2022]

'Theatro Chitirio: epithesi ston politismo me ergaleio tin vlasfimia'. 2012. *TVXS*, 5 October <https://tvxs.gr/news/ellada/epithesi-ston-politismo-me-ergaleio-tin-blasfimia> [accessed 20 November 2021]

'Thessaloniki: poines filakisis gia ta epeisodia stin "Ora tou Diavolou"'. 2020. *Ethnos*, 3 February <https://www.ethnos.gr/greece/article/86430/thessalonikh-poinesfylakishsgiataepeisodiasthnoratoydiaboloy> [accessed 15 February 2022]

Thompson, Michael. 2012. 'The Order of the Visible and the Sayable: Theatre Censorship in Twentieth-Century Spain', *Hispanic Research Journal*, 13.2: 93–110

Tsakirakis, Stavros. 2008. 'Techni, thriskeia kai logokrisia', in *Opseis logokrisias stin Ellada*, ed. by Yannis Ziogas, Leonidas Karampinis, Yannis Stavrakakis, and Dimitris Christopoulos (Athens: Nefeli), pp. 91–96

Tsichla, Markella. 2019. 'The Freedom of Expression under Assault in Contemporary Greece: Instances of Prohibition and Public Courts', *International Journal of Education and Social Science*, 6.6: 15–22

Tsolakidou, Stella. 2012. 'Police Arrest Golden Dawn MP for Theater Protest', *Greek Reporter*, 12 October <https://greekreporter.com/2012/10/12/golden-dawn-religious-protest-stops-play/> [accessed 16 February 2022]

Tziovas, Dimitris. 2017. 'From Junta to Crisis: Modernization, Consumerism and Cultural Dualisms in Greece', *Byzantine and Modern Greek Studies*, 41.2: 278–99

Van Steen, Gonda. 2014. *Stage of Emergency: Theater and Public Performance under the Greek Military Dictatorship of 1967–1974* (Oxford: Oxford University Press)

Vasvani, Lemonia. 2017. '"I ora tou Diavolou": ti lene gia tis antidraseis Hrysidou kai Aristoteleion', *Typosthes*, 19 October <https://www.typosthes.gr/thessaloniki/142583_i-ora-toy-diaboloy-ti-lene-gia-tis-antidraseis-hrysidoy-kai-aristoteleion> [accessed 15 February 2022]

Zembylas, Tasos. 2014. 'Contested Issues in the German-Speaking Literary Field', in *Kunst und ihre Öffentlichkeit*, ed. by Dagmar Danko, Olivier Moeschler, and Florian Schumacher (Wiesbaden: VS-Springer), pp. 365–86

Ziogas, Yannis, Leonidas Karampinis, Yannis Stavrakakis, and Dimitris Christopoulos. 2008. *Opseis logokrisias stin Ellada* (Athens: Nefeli)

9

Booing and Banning: Freedom and Prohibition in Spain's 'National Fiesta'

DUNCAN WHEELER

Bullfighting, like theatre, has historically been the scourge of political and ecclesiastical authorities, actors and matadors exerting fascination whilst operating at the fringes of respectability. In the twenty-first century, however, what was once known as the 'national fiesta' is considered by an increasing number of Spaniards to be an anachronistic bloody spectacle, as disreputable as the theatrical arts have become respectable as an elite cultural activity that bestows kudos on the players and audiences alike. Tales of dwindling popularity have, however, been exaggerated. The 10,872 seats in the bullring of the provincial city of Jaén sold out in under two hours for the reappearance of the world's leading matador, José Tomás, on 12 June 2022—the police have launched a criminal investigation into touts selling tickets at exponentially inflated figures (Donaire 2022). No twenty-first-century Spanish theatre practitioner generates expectation on this scale, the closest equivalent being one- or two-night residencies by performance artist Angélica Liddell—the limits of the comparison are put into sharp relief when she plays multiple dates and tickets only sell out on the night if at all. More generally, about twice the number of tickets for corridas as for theatrical productions are sold each year in Spain. The country's largest and most important bullring, Madrid's Las Ventas, programmes a month of consecutive corridas in May/June for the San Isidro fair, in which upwards of 20,000 spectators attend each night.

At a time when abolitionists chant 'It's not culture, it's torture', the taurine community increasingly seeks respectability through association, listing the roll call of cultured aficionados such as Francisco de Goya, Pablo Picasso, or the playwright and dramatist Federico García Lorca. Conversely, for the internationally renowned Liddell, a licensed heretic of the Spanish and Catalan stage, bullfighting constitutes a welcome dose of authenticity and integrity in an artistic landscape in which most theatre practitioners 'prefer to amass rights and die from mediocrity' (Liddell 2021: 37). In her play *All That is Left is for You to Die in the Plaza*, she addresses Juan Belmonte (1892–1962), a matador who committed suicide on finding retirement unbearable and haunted by the absence of his arch-rival, Joselito, who was mortally gored in 1920. Liddell dedicated the play to Rafael de Paula (b.1940)—a prodigious Gypsy bullfighter with a tumultuous personal life, imprisoned in 1985 for hiring two thugs to beat up a footballer he believed to be having an affair with his wife—with 'infinite love'. Despite never having attended a corrida in person, Liddell subscribes to Lorca's description of them as the most cultured festivity in the world, the antithesis of the infantilized and infantilizing woke agenda, in her opinion a 'neo-totalitarianism which may appear *soft* but which has disastrous consequences, plagued with camouflaged censorship disguised as liberty and progress, invisible and digested like baby porridge' (85–86). The censorial turn, be it real or perceived, has, more generally, resulted in the bullfighting lobby gaining some unexpected allies. In February 2022, for example, the Juan Belmonte Institute launched 'Conversations in the Catacombs' at Casa Patas, a now defunct flamenco bar in Madrid, with a round-table debate on cancel culture featuring Edu Galán, a journalist for the satirical magazine *Mongolia* (the closest Spanish equivalent to *Private Eye*, which nearly went into liquidation following a lengthy libel case against them by retired matador José Ortega Cano).[1] At the sold-out event, Galán stated: 'I rebel against those who say to me that people who go to watch the bulls are psychopaths and those who don't aren't lovely people'; a representative of the Juan Belmonte Institute went a step further: 'We created this public platform to ask for help in protecting bullfighting, but we have now come to realize that it is tauromachy that protects society'.[2]

Drawing on ethnographic research and socio-historical contextualization, the aim of this chapter is to critically interrogate the discourse of liberty in relation to taurine identity politics, contemplating the extent to which conversations surrounding censorship in bullfighting are translatable to other fields of (cultural) life. Mimicking the triptych structure of a corrida, I have divided my argument into three sections.[3] In the first, I explore the theatrical dimension of bullfighting alongside the interest shown in the ritualized performance by some theatrical practitioners. During the Franco dictatorship (1939–75), a period of significant censorship of theatre, it was frequently claimed that bullrings were the most democratic spaces in Spain as audiences had the right to challenge authority. Examining the validity and consequences of this claim provides the context for, in the second section, a consideration of how, especially in the wake of the Catalan prohibition in 2011, defences of Spain's 'national fiesta' have increasingly been framed in relation to freedom, attending a bullring equated to exercising a democratic right. The third and final section examines the correlative to this logic amongst taurine audiences who have rarely felt or been compelled to maintain the kind of aesthetic distance now considered de rigueur in most theatrical spaces.

A theatre of life and death

If the birth of modern-day celebrity culture in the British context can be traced back to the Georgian stage (see Zanardi 2012), a similar process took place in eighteenth-century Spain when bullfighting ceased to be an exclusively aristocratic practice and matadors of often humble beginnings became national treasures. The pageantry of the corrida and the bullfighter's outfits subsequently provided suitably exotic fare for operas, most famously Bizet's *Carmen* (1875). Aficionados and practitioners of opera often respond positively to the aesthetics of the corrida (Plácido Domingo was, for many years, a regular in bullrings around Spain), whilst top matador Enrique Ponce premiered *Crisol* (Crucible), a synaesthetic spectacle incorporating classical music, flamenco, Picasso-inspired paintings, and suits of lights in Malaga in 2017 (Wheeler 2018: 7–8). Numerous theatre practitioners have also taken an interest in the lingo and exercise of bullfighting. For the purposes of making actors prioritize bodily action over vocal expression (in his view an error of most theatre schools was to do the reverse), Jerzy Grotowski implemented the following exercise in his teaching: 'The actor is a bull and Grotowski the bullfighter with a red pullover that he had found somewhere. The actor must attack while singing' (Grotowski 1969: 151). The Argentine writer, director, and actor Ricardo Bartís observed:

> A friend of mine who loves corridas often speaks to me of something, a movement, that he calls a cross: the bullfighter cannot move and in this situation instead of avoiding the bull, he tries to cross him. He thinks: 'I am nearing him, but I shouldn't avoid the cross, the possibility that he kills me. I have to kill or be killed'. The comparison is perhaps slightly extreme, but it seems to be that there are some actors who, deliberately avoiding any possibility of risk, no longer cross the bull. (2013: 224)

As Bartís intimates, a fundamental difference between the theatrical and the taurine experience resides in the fact that, in the former, unlike the latter, the simulacrum of death is a means as opposed to a literal and figurative end. According to Jessica Goodman:

> Any stage death […] is also a non-ending, a fact of which any individual audience member—whether witnessing it for the first or the fifty-first time—must be aware. What looks like resolution, and closure, especially in the context of classically influenced tragedy, leaves something unresolved. There is an uneasy sense that the ending is false: quite literally only theatre. (2022: 3)

Even in Portugal, and in recent years in Ecuador, where it is prohibited to kill the bull in public view (a stipulation which lets the audience but not the animal, who will be slaughtered in camera, off the hook), genuine death is a—and arguably the—principal attraction involved.

The literal translation of 'matador' into English is 'killer of bulls', and they are contractually obliged to dispense with their enemy. For this reason, the police are always present in Spanish bullrings to arrest any matador who, for whatever reason, does not fulfil his legal duty of killing the bull within a stipulated period of time. Corridas are theatricalized forms of mass entertainment in which the non-human protagonist almost invariably dies (bulls are very occasionally pardoned on the say-so of the president, a figure appointed as the official voice of authority in any corrida, if their performance is deemed exceptional) and, to borrow a phrase from the French philosopher and aficionado Francis Wolff, 'only he who risks his own life can kill the esteemed animal' (2013: 70). In the words of the poet Francisco Brines, this is a dramatic performance, 'painful and enjoyable at the same time for the bullfighter, involving the sacrifice of an innocent victim who rebels from his position of free-will, a symbol of man in his final and undeserved destiny' (cited in Marzal 2010: 14). *Controversia del toro y el torero* (Controversy of the bull and the bullfighter), a 2006 play by the Catalan dramatist and aficionado Albert Boadella, depicts a journeyman matador who ends up in the infirmary after being caught by the bull in his farewell corrida. The injured bullfighter avers: 'The encounter between man and beast is not a circus because the bullfight, like a priest delivering mass, has no wish to distract those in attendance' (2011: 110). Lorca and Liddell both envisage the bullring as a sacred place in which values cast aside by the (post-)modern world are embodied and enacted. As far as she is concerned:

> In a period of decline such as our own, of pallor in all the arts, which refuses to recognise life in death, or ecstasy, or mystery, or the tragic, I refer back to [Ramón María del] Valle-Inclán, a personal friend of Belmonte's: 'If our theatre had the temblor of bullfighting it would be wonderful. If it had known how to transport that aesthetic violence, it would be a heroic theatre like the *Iliad*.' (Liddell 2021: 73)

In the time that Lorca and Valle-Inclán were writing their plays, objections to bullfighting predominantly related to the dangers to the physical well-being of matadors (nineteenth-century defenders typically made a point of higher casualty rates and injuries amongst boxers) and the negative effects on the audience, who they argued would be better advised dedicating themselves to work and spiritual concerns than working themselves into a collective frenzy.

If, on the one hand, the aestheticism of bullfighting has been used to defend its cultural credentials and its edifying potential for practitioners and audiences alike, growing awareness over animal welfare has raised concerns over the extent to which the pageantry and ritual on display disguises the violent reality of what is actually taking place on the sand below. Whilst taurine literature talks in epic terms of the matador and audience being heroic in their willingness to look death in the eye, the use of a red cloth (white cloths are often used to guide the bulls backstage) that adds spectacle and diminishes the visibility of blood is just one instance of how the suffering of the animal is systematically underplayed.

For abolitionists, this is a tragedy. Whilst some of the claims made by aficionados (for example, that fighting bulls have a privileged lifestyle until they arrive in the ring) could be marshalled to establish an argument that the aesthetic pay-off trumps the ethical costs, the overarching defence more habitually assumes that any moral objection to the corrida is in and of itself proof of aesthetic illiteracy. This position is analogous to literary theorists for whom, in Terry Eagleton's description, 'real-life tragedy is a metaphorical deviation from an ontological priority. For a host of exponents of tragic theory, there can be no more shameful naivety than confusing tragedy in art with tragedy in life' (2003: 14). In other words, 'tragedy is a technical affair, quite different from run-of-the mill calamity' (15). For aficionados, the possibility of genuine tragedy in the ring is sufficient justification to dismiss detractors as puritanical philistines.

It is a commonplace of taurine debates for matadors to say nobody loves bulls like they do. Following a near-fatal goring in Mexico by 'Navegante' ('Navigator')—fighting bulls are always given names—the matador José Tomás published a book in which, alongside other aficionados, including Nobel Prize-winning Peruvian author Mario Vargas Llosa, he addressed the potentially homicidal beast. Emerging from a coma, Tomás claims to have had visitations from 'Navegante' in his hospital bed:

> At first, to be honest, it didn't amuse me. But, as the weeks went by, I forgot my anger, we began to open up, we talked and became pals [...] That animal, who wanted to take my life away in Aguascalientes, is the very same one who helps me live the fullest life I know. (Tomás et al. 2013: 23, 26)

The Seville-born Salvador Távora (1930–2019) decided to retire from bullfighting after being tasked with killing the animal that had fatally gored horseback bullfighter Salvador Guardiola in 1960, because he realized that his desire to take revenge by executing the beast was an irrational and unfair response.

Távora went on to apply his taurine knowledge and background to theatrical and musical performances which, much like Lorca before him, fused popular culture and high art, transcending the folkloric image of flamenco and bullfighting promoted by Spain's tourist industry under the Franco dictatorship. In 1985, recreating a bullring on the theatrical stage,

Piel de toro (Bull skin) employed the corrida as a metaphor for Spain's character and history, incorporating characters resembling iconic figures such as General Franco. In 1996, his company premiered an original take on Bizet's *Carmen*, emphasizing the taurine scenes with large-scale performances in bullrings that incorporated a horseback bullfighter facing a live animal. When Távora sought to stage the production in Barcelona's Monumental bullring, the Catalan regional government withheld a licence because, in their view, the public killing of a bull for entertainment was only permissible within the specific context of a corrida but could not legally be incorporated into an opera. Through Catalonia's Supreme Court, Távora successfully petitioned for the decision to be revoked, as well as his right to receive compensation, based on the constitutional right to freedom of expression.

Távora and the taurine lobby won the battle but lost the war: bullfighting was subsequently prohibited by the Catalan regional government, and the final corrida featuring José Tomás and Catalan bullfighter Serafín Marín (who would later stand as an MP for the Spanish nationalist, far-right Vox party) was staged in front of a sold-out audience at Barcelona's Monumental bullring in September 2011. The Madrid-based Constitutional Court subsequently dictated the prohibition as illegal: according to their ruling, it did not fall under the jurisdiction of the Catalan government to ban a cultural form of expression protected by the 1978 Spanish Constitution. Theoretically, corridas could once again be staged in Catalonia but, thus far, no impresario has dared do so—attempts to stage a one-off benefit for the victims of the 2017 Islamic terrorist acts did not get beyond the initial discussion stage. In Catalonia, as elsewhere in Spain, bullfighting aficionados are frequently dismissed as the cigar-smoking anachronistic relics of the Francoist dictatorship. The prohibitions and persecutions to which the taurine lobby feel they have been subjected over recent years have, nevertheless, led them to appropriate the lexicon of freedom and democracy used by the oppositional left under the dictatorship, and depict their opponents as totalitarian.

To ban or not to ban

In recent years, the town of Tordesillas (where in 1494 Spain and Portugal divided the newly discovered lands outside of Europe between them) has become the bête noire of the animal rights movement for the Toro de la Vega—an annual event in which a bull is chased by hundreds of lancers, before accredited horsemen stab it to death. Following the partial ban (the bull could only be killed in camera), I travelled to the town (of fewer than 10,000 inhabitants, thirty miles from the regional capital of Valladolid) in 2017 to witness the effects of the prohibition during the town's annual festivities. I discovered medieval tradition being defended in surprisingly modern terms. In a castle just outside Tordesillas where Queen Joanna the Mad was imprisoned by her relatives in the early sixteenth century, a banner proclaimed 'Liberty, Tradition, Democracy'. Locals were incensed by the lack of public consultation, and believed the ban was the result of foreign agitation. For them, this was reminiscent of the Franco era, when local festivities were suppressed by the state. In the main square, thousands of teenagers—many of whom wore T-shirts deploring censorship—congregated for a lantern show celebrating the bullfighting tradition. I spoke to a number of the older people who had organized the festivities for decades. They proudly boasted of breaking the law in the 1960s (see Wheeler 2017: 45).

With the appointment of Manuel Fraga as Minister of Information and Tourism in 1962, censorship under Franco began to be tentatively relaxed in many areas. More politically charged plays were performed by Spanish playwrights and translated from other languages (see Wheeler 2020: 87–150, O'Leary and Thompson 2023). As regards bullfighting, however, new legislation replacing earlier laws dating from 1930 (which had not been updated since) were brought into force on 15 March 1962 and exerted far more state control than had hitherto been the case (Vizcaíno Casas 1962: 346). There are two principal explanations as to why bullfighting was treated as an exception amid the general trend for liberalization. First, the increasing importance of tourists for the Spanish economy led Fraga to centralize control over previously local activities such as Holy Week celebrations (Afinguénova 2021: 56–76). This was exacerbated in the case of bullfighting due to concerns about foreigners being offended by barbaric practices. Hence, for example, the Toro de la Vega was prohibited and the prizes for matadors were changed—successful performances are to this day rewarded with the bull's ears and, very occasionally, the tail, but the tradition of rewarding an exceptional performance by hacking off the dead animal's hoof was outlawed. Secondly, the anachronistic Franco regime increasingly justified its continued existence in a rapidly modernizing Spain with the claim that it had brought peace and prosperity to the nation. On the one hand, bullfights, like football, had arguably become the opium of the people, often programmed on May Day in an attempt to divert attention from workers' strikes. Conversely, comic corridas were also often used to mock figures of authority and, it was feared, might exacerbate class tensions.

Whilst there have been aficionados and professionals from across the political spectrum, bullfighting is a vertical as opposed to horizontal profession (in terms of everything from the prices of tickets to the reference to the star matador's supporting team as 'subalterns') and readily dismissed as the reactionary relic of a bygone age. On returning from New York in 2014 to take up the editorship of *El Mundo* newspaper, hardly a bastion of left-wing politics, David Jiménez registered his shock at a ceremony at the Palace Hotel in which Miguel Ángel Perera was named matador of the year: 'The evening brought together a Spain I thought no longer existed. A mixture of retired bullfighters, aristocrats with stretched skin, fading folkloric stars, landowners with large herds of cattle and representatives of high society, almost invariably with long greasy slicked back hair' (2019: 135–36).

Aficionados nevertheless waste few opportunities to maintain that the bullring was an oasis of democracy and contestation during the dictatorship: if, for example, a president was perceived to be too generous or mean with the awarding of ears, they could be booed. In reality, similar claims were already made in the nineteenth century when, to counteract the negative view that Spaniards were distracted from critical thinking and positive action by the bread and circus of bullfighting, defenders, as Adrian Shubert notes, 'presented it as a badly needed locus of contact between the classes', an example of proto-democratic coexistence in a society deemed to have a liberal deficit by its European neighbours (Shubert 1999: 142). Entrance was, of course, reserved for those who could afford a ticket, although the range of prices in Las Ventas, far more than in provincial rings in fact, has traditionally been fairly reasonable with the cheapest seats now costing less than a trip to the cinema. There are here some obvious parallels with Athenian theatre. In David Kawalko Roselli's words:

> While slaves, women, and metics were present, they could never constitute the same percentage of the total audience as they did of the total population. Although they were thus underrepresented in the theater, those non-citizens who were in the audience actively participated in a powerful group exercising much authority that was viewed as operating on both a cultural and political level. (2011: 197)

In the cultural wars of contemporary Spain, the anti-bullfighting lobby is often too quick to ridicule aficionados as the last bastion for reactionaries with no place in a twenty-first-century democracy. This impression is bolstered by the patronage of the new far-right xenophobic anti-feminist Vox party, whose leader Santiago Abascal is often accompanied on the campaign trail by matador Morante de la Puebla. Defenders of the 'national fiesta', for their part, preclude any genuine debate on its future by dismissing all potential objections out of hand as instances of puritanical censorship. As a result, it is virtually impossible to have a serious debate on such an emotive subject that has been weaponized by politicians across the ideological spectrum. In a populist gesture designed to reclaim frequently single-issue voters back from Vox, Isabel Díaz Ayuso, the president of the regional government of Madrid from the right-of-centre Partido Popular (People's Party [PP]), authorized a bullfighting festivity despite Covid restrictions in Las Ventas on 2 May 2021, two days before the elections. This proved to be a smart tactical move, as was her campaign slogan, 'Communism of Liberty', a recycling of Cold War clichés which resulted in her victory and the departure of her principal rival, Pablo Iglesias—the leader of anti-austerity Podemos who had called for a referendum on the future of bullfighting, which he believed to be a barbaric practice—from the forefront of politics (Wheeler 2022).

In Lucía Lijtmaer's diagnosis of contemporary Spain, 'The snowflake has become the new object of ridicule replacing the "disgusted of Tunbridge Wells"' (2019: 45):

> The statement that political correctness is leading us by the hand to a new age of puritanism appears on a daily basis in the media. Caricatures of the *ofendidito*—the US figure of the snowflake rendered in bad Spanish—and of the feminist neo-puritanism are a conservative invention that emerge from a new notion of the public sphere as oppressive, ever more 'correct', more emotional, less rational. (70)

Some of the activities of animal rights activists on social media have, admittedly, provided artillery for the taurine lobby to present their opponents as potentially dangerous, irrational beings. Bullfighters and their families have taken legal action against social media users who have referred to them as murderers in the wake of the fatal goring of matadors Víctor Barrio and Iván Fandiño in 2016 and 2017, respectively. There can be no excuse for the death threats received through social media by Adrián, an eight-year-old with cancer who dreamt of becoming a bullfighter. Such instances show the dangers of allowing free speech free rein. However, the reductive equation of free speech with democracy, and prohibition with dictatorship, has enabled the taurine lobby to depict itself as a bulwark against the new puritanism, thereby turning the conversation away from the animal cruelty that underpins the corrida.

In August 2021, two bulls killed in the Gijon bullring were named 'Nigeriano' (Nigerian) and another 'Feminista' (Feminist). The inclusion of Morante de la Puebla on the bill gave this the look of a deliberate provocation, but it was probably a coincidence. Fighting bulls inherit names from their mother, so these monikers will have been handed down from previous generations rather than having been thought of afresh. That said, exceptions have been made in the past. The first bull faced by the legendary Manolete as a fully fledged matador in 1939 had been baptized 'Comunista' (Communist) under the short-lived Second Republic (1931–36). Such a name was anathema following General Franco's victory in the Civil War (1936–39) and 'Communist' was diplomatically renamed 'Mirador' (Viewer).

In twenty-first-century Asturias, socialist mayor Ana González declared that a line had been crossed with the insensitive naming of the slayed animals, and that the municipal bullring would henceforth be used for concerts and other cultural activities, but not corridas. An open letter by bull-breeder and president of the Fighting Bulls Association Victorino Martín was a gift to satirists, claiming the decision was comparable to the destruction of religious artefacts by fundamentalists: 'The Taliban, much like the Mayor of Gijon, forget that neither the Buddhas of Bamiyan nor the bulls belong to them, but are rather common heritage of mankind' ('La Fundación' 2021). Something of an echo chamber, the bullfighting lobby often struggles to understand how it is perceived from the outside whilst also being plagued by internal battles. The same image of the Taliban has, curiously, been applied to the demanding audiences of Las Ventas. For journalist Rubén Amón,

> Liturgically speaking, it is the most orthodox public and least forgiving with the bullfighter, in the same way in which it is the least festive. They approach the bullfighter with reservations and hostility, even more so if they are a star matador. Madrid is the only bullring in the world where music isn't played in the final third, when the bullfighter faces the bull alone in the ring. The only bullring where the most vocal aficionados are known by name or their nicknames. The hardness is a reflection of Las Ventas's idiosyncrasy. Its Neo-Mudéjar style has ended up generating a fundamentalist symbology. As if it were a great mosque or the great madrasa which determines the dogma. (2021: 162)

The most orthodox spectators are located in Stand Seven, the area of the cheaper Sun Side located closest to the presidential box and in the area of the ring where the bulls are piqued. Some of its most famous inhabitants have become well-known figures within and beyond the ring, honoured with obituaries in the national press. The legend began with Luis Pelayo Bruna, alias 'El Ronquillo', a taxi driver from Madrid, whose criticisms and suggestions from the front row of Stand Seven have often been said to have inspired matadors Manolete (1917–1947) and Luis Miguel Dominguín (1926–1996) to deliver their finest performances in Madrid. El Ronquillo's final utterance in the ring prior to his death was in 1970 when he shouted 'a right pair of pensioners' to Antonio Bienvenida (1922–1975) and Dominguín. His present-day heir is 72-year-old Faustino Herranz, alias 'El Rosco', an ex-deputy mayor for United Left who now votes for Unidas Podemos despite their opposition to bullfighting. In September 2021, vociferous voices from Stand Seven demanded to know how and why Victorino Martín had brought such lacklustre bulls to the world's premier bullring. From his position in Stand Eight, in the shaded section, the breeder and president of the FTL seated alongside his family shouted back, 'I'll bring whatever bulls I fucking want'. Such a hostile exchange embodies the libertarian ethos of the corrida taken to its (il)logical extreme.

To boo or not to boo

Susan Bennett suggests that '[a] performance can activate a diversity of responses, but it is the audience which finally ascribes meaning and usefulness to any cultural product' (2007: 156). In summer 2020, the possibility of televising corridas staged without an audience was raised, but greeted at best with lukewarm enthusiasm. For Simón Casas, the impresario of Las Ventas: 'The audience is an essential actor within the fiesta's dramaturgy: in their absence, what we would be left with would be closer to an abattoir than the grandeur of the fiesta's staging' (cited in Pérez 2020). Even in non-Covid times, the act of filming corridas divides opinion: Morante de la Puebla is prone to quoting Rafael de Paula's aphorism that 'The Holy Spirit doesn't appear on the television', whilst adding: 'The commentators should keep their mouths shut more. It is the only artistic activity in which criticisms occur during the act of creation. In flamenco or painting, it's done afterwards' (cited in Muñoz 2018). When asked about his favourite audiences, Curro Romero—a legendary matador like Morante de la Puebla and Rafael de Paula, infamous for switching between inspired and disastrous performances—reputedly replied: 'The best public is the one for the tennis, because of their silence'. Grotowski's claim, that it takes just one spectator to make a performance, does not translate to the bullring (1969: 32). Whilst, as Bennett argues, spectators are generally 'trained to be passive in their demonstrated behaviour during a theatrical performance, but to be active in their decoding of the sign systems made available' (2007: 206), audiences in bullrings hark back, in multiple respects, to the classical world in which, to quote Erik Gunderson, 'the spectacle of the arena has a specular effect which makes a new spectacle of its own observers, revealing and determining them through their relationship to the image of themselves produced by their relationship to the arena' (1996: 116). If provincial bullrings are vibrant with triumphalist festivities, Madrid's season of corridas often seems closer to an examination than entertainment. Many season-ticket holders rush from work to attend a month's worth of consecutive corridas in which they expect a matador to hold their own in front of a bull and a discerning audience as effusive in their praise as in damning criticism.

On 27 May 2022, the euphoria surrounding a triumphant career-breakthrough performance by rising star Ángel Téllez was heightened by the fact that it came following a week of under-par performances, which had reached a nadir on the previous evening with Morante de la Puebla dodging cushions thrown into the ring from the stands of a full house united in indignation.

In Greek festivals, '[w]hile the ten judges were separated from spectators through both the selection process and their seating, the judges were also part of the audience watching (and evaluating) the performances in the theater' (Roselli 2011: 28). The president in a bullring is responsible for granting the trophies, but theirs is not the only or even the final word. When, for example, Rafaeillo delivered a career-best performance in Madrid in 2007 but lost out on ears through not making a clean kill, the matador from Murcia consoled himself with the respect from the audience:

'I am overjoyed by the repercussion of the efforts I made in Madrid, and by the recognition of the most demanding aficionados in Stand Seven who gave me a standing ovation, filling me with an inner sense of joy' (cited in Ojados 2007). Although the rule is not always adhered to, the regulations stipulate that presidents should abide by a majority petition from the audience, indicated through the waving of white handkerchiefs, for the granting of the first ear. Unprofessional decisions, perceived or real, by presidents are routinely mocked. In the provincial ring of Palencia in August 2021, José María Manzanares indicated his incredulity at the president granting him two ears but only one to his fellow matador Julián López, 'El Juli', by only holding one aloft in his victory lap. In May 2019, the occupants of Stand Seven in Las Ventas were disgusted at the president awarding two ears to Miguel Ángel Perera: they created a petition to have him dismissed and carried banners into subsequent corridas proclaiming 'Out of the Presidential Box'. During the 1990s, one of El Rosco's closest associates, Salva, sought police protection after his repeated complaints about corrupt and corrupting practices resulted in a baseball-bat-wielding thug turning up on his doorstep (Galiacho 2010).

In an anthology of taurine criticism, theatre and bullfighting critic Javier Villán included one of his own articles, about a disastrous corrida in Madrid held in 1994:

> If they throw the occupants of Stand Seven out of Las Ventas, gagging or violently expelling them, the result will be the gagging or violent expulsion of dissidents or anyone who protests per se […] The truth is that Madrid still marks the difference. But let nobody be deceived or attempt to deceive us: a few corridas like the one we witnessed yesterday or the recent fiasco with the Moura bulls, and Las Ventas will lose its status. And if Las Ventas loses its status, then we will have entered in tauromachy's Age of Tin Art. (2006: 392)

Spanish taurine audiences can be as harsh as their theatrical counterparts tend to be generous, where standing ovations and extended curtain calls are the norm. Irrespective of one's ethical concerns, there can be no denying that Spain has, in quantitative and qualitative terms, a richer tradition of taurine than theatrical criticism. For Belmonte: 'Bullfighting is one of the few activities in Spain that enjoys the luxury of having at its disposal a perfected critical apparatus. There exists a greater theory and doctrine of taurine art than can be found in relation to visual, musical or literary art' (Chaves Nogales 2012: 374). Theatre scholars in Spain have no equivalent to the remarkable Cossío encyclopaedia, commissioned by the philosopher José Ortega y Gasset, whose first volume appeared in 1943. Whilst bribery has been rife amongst some bullfighting critics and publications in the Hispanic world, taurine criticism remains far more professionalized than theatrical criticism in twenty-first-century Spain. Major newspapers have specialist critics on the payroll, whose chronicles are published in the cultural (not the sports) section.

The emergence of the Stand Seven phenomenon was an arguably necessary corrective given the triumphalism that took hold in many aspects of Spanish life in the aftermath of Franco's victory in the Civil War. Three of a total of only eleven tails to have ever been cut in Las Ventas were done so during the so-called Liberation corrida of May 1939. Taurine publications such as *El Ruedo* remarkably attributed greater generosity amongst audiences in the 1940s not to the general climate of triumphalism in dictatorial Spain—reviews of productions at the recently opened National Theatres were, for example, almost universally positive—but rather to a rising number of female spectators. A recurring blind spot of audiences in Spanish bullrings and theatres has been the insistence that ensuring a firm divide between culture and politics is not in and of itself a political gesture. In August 2016, I was present at the Bilbao bullring when the disgraced emeritus king Juan Carlos visited the Basque Country's biggest city for the first time during its annual summer fair—most of the audiences around me applauded his arrival whilst a few odd boos were criticized for their intolerance. Flags calling for the release of political prisoners in the Basque Country, unveiled from time to time in Pamplona and Azpeitia bullrings, are typically criticized by other spectators. The only time I have witnessed booing in a Spanish theatre occurred when watching a 2019 production of the early-twentieth-century *zarzuela* (light opera) *Doña Francisquita* directed by Lluis Pasqual. Objections, which occurred on most nights of the run, related not to quality but rather to the perceived liberties taken with the approach. The first catcalls came when a surtitle announced that the action would be taking place on a 'television set', although the audience was appeased with some 'typical' images of a woman with castanets on the big screens. This was, however, a mere temporary reprieve. Subsequent mentions of censorship in reference to a 1960s television adaptation of the *zarzuela* which, the on-stage characters speculate, might be watched at home by Franco was greeted with vociferous protests from the twenty-first-century audience. If the meta-framing device and changing of time period irritated the audience, the inclusion of political references into the ostensibly apolitical world of the *zarzuela* was seen as a profanation. On the night I attended, arguments broke out between spectators demanding the actors and director respect their art and audience, with others responding that it was disrespectful to interrupt the performance.

If we accept that the audience's right to protest forms an important part of both the taurine spectacle and the critical apparatus surrounding the industry, then surely critics and the occupants of Stand Seven cannot, unlike all other constituents of the corrida, be immune from criticism? Catcalls and booing are not necessarily about retaining the purity of the spectacle, and can respond to the base instincts of the mob. In the nineteenth century, the ultimate disgrace for a breeder was for dogs to be released on a bull that showed insufficient bravura. Frequently inebriated audiences became intoxicated by this violent spectacle, and often used the slightest pretext to call for an action theoretically reserved for special cases.

Audiences can be more deadly than bulls, and Joselito's fatal goring in 1920 was arguably prompted by spectators demanding the notoriously brave matador take ever more risks. That said, Belmonte responded to a rhetorical question of his own making—'Who says the masses have no conscience?'—with a diagnosis of the prevailing situation of the time:

> As a result of the death of Joselito, bullfighting audiences fell victim to a curious phenomenon of collective remorse. I could observe at that point that amongst the spectators at the corridas arose an exaggerated fear and a jealous care for the life of bullfighters. For a certain period, there was in the bullrings a strange nervous tension. The public was more scared than the bullfighter. (Chaves Nogales 2012: 323–24)

This rarely occurs in Las Ventas, where demanding audiences believe risk to be a necessary but not sufficient condition of a successful performance (unlike in most other rings, reckless gestures or continuing with an injury does not greatly increase the chance of receiving an ear).

The caustic comments directed towards star matadors are illustrative of the continued tension between the notions of bullfighting as bread and circuses or as art: I have witnessed Francisco Rivera (a staple of ¡Hola! magazine following his marriage into nobility) and Andrés Roca Rey, the current number-one box office draw, berated for theatrical flourishes with shouts of 'This isn't a television set' and 'Madrid isn't a circus'. In their self-proclaimed quest to police the sanctity of the corrida, to retain its tragic essence, the occupants of Stand Seven have stood accused of self-promotion and even putting lives at risk. In June 1983, the fourth bull caught Curro Vázquez in a potentially lethal manner. As he was carried out to the infirmary, the matador's manager, Enrique Bojilla, went round to shout at the occupants of Stand Seven, accusing them of ordering him to take unnecessary risks (Vidal 1983). The vociferous aficionados refused to apologize or admit their error, even on being booed from aficionados located in the more expensive seats. In the words of Amón, the biographer of Curro Vázquez: 'They were in the wrong, but evidence of their mistake did not provoke any sense of repentance, not even with the pool of blood left behind by Curro Vázquez's thigh, completely destroyed by the bull, visible from the stands' (Amón and Cano 2005: 123).

Vázquez was a father-figure to Amón, and a mutual animosity between the writer and the occupants of Stand Seven has persisted to the present day. He has referred to them on the radio as 'pissed off and fundamentalist aficionados' who constitute a 'turbo-inquisition'. Their response was to come to Las Ventas armed with a banner proclaiming 'Out of the plaza, Rubén Amón'.⁴

Despite such vitriolic exchanges, the behaviour of bullfighting audiences rarely translates into physical violence. The behaviour of British football hooligans in the 1980s undermined calls for Spain's entry into the European Economic Union in 1986 to be made conditional on prohibition of the corridas, however much some foreigners considered them to be an affront to civilized values. Hardly a model of tolerance or mutual respect—the right to be heard is rarely equated with the responsibility to listen—the behaviour of human participants in the corrida does not so much constitute a model of democratic coexistence as a manifestation of the limits of this slippery political model as a panacea in a world in which, to borrow a phrase from John McGrath, 'every crime a nation can commit is excused by false claims to democracy' (2002: 133). Complex and often contradictory discourses surrounding freedom and censorship will hardly settle debates on this tragic form of artistic expression, irrespective of the frequency with which such notions are evoked by those eager to have the last word and silence the voice of others both within and beyond the plaza. Bullfighting, whether we like it or not, remains a contested political and cultural act.

Notes

1 Following the death of his wife, folkloric superstar Rocío Jurado, Ortega Cano's much-documented problems with alcohol (footage of him drunkenly singing and giving speeches at a wedding are Spanish YouTube sensations) worsened and he ended up in prison for manslaughter after he drunkenly crashed his car. Spanish libel laws are far stricter than in the UK and the USA, and *Mongolia* was fined heavily for cartoons that mocked Ortega Cano for his plastic surgery and drunkenness.
2 See Fundación del Toro de Lidia (2022) for a recording of the debate in Spanish.
3 Sometimes described as a tragedy in three parts, a corrida consists of picadors, banderilleros, and the matador's killing of the bull.
4 For more information about this, see Amón (2019).

References

Afinguénova, Eugenia. 2021. 'State of Crucifixion: Tourism, Holy Week, and the Sacred Politics of the Cold War', in *Rite, Flesh, and Stone: The Matter of Death in Contemporary Spanish Culture*, ed. by Antonio Córdoba and Daniel García-Donoso (Nashville: Vanderbilt University Press), pp. 56–76

Amón, Rubén. 2019. 'Rubén Amón indulta a los ultras del tendido 7: "Identifica al aficionado cabreado y fundamentalista"', Onda Cero https://www.ondacero.es/programas/mas-de-uno/audios-podcast/opinion-masdeuno/indultado/ruben-amon-ultras-7-cobro-toros_201906045cf625590cf2d5c138bb47a7.html [accessed 2 September 2023]

—— 2021. *El fin de la fiesta* (Madrid: Penguin Random House)
Amón, Rubén, and Juan Luis Cano. 2005. *Pasa un torero: Curro Vázquez desde dentro* (Madrid: Espasa Calpe)
Bartís, Ricardo. 2013. *Cancha con niebla: teatro perdido* (Buenos Aires: Atiel)
Bennett, Susan. 2007. *Theatre Audiences: A Theory of Production and Reception*, 2nd edn (Abingdon: Routledge)
Boadella, Albert. 2011. *Controversia del toro y el torero/La cena*, ed. by Milagros Sánchez Arnosi (Madrid: Cátedra)
Chaves Nogales, Manuel. 2012. *Juan Belmonte, matador de toros* (Madrid: Alianza)
Donaire, Ginés. 2022. 'La reventa dispara los precios de las entradas para la reaparición de José Tomás en la plaza de toros de Jaén', *El País*, 2 April
Eagleton, Terry. 2003. *Sweet Violence: The Idea of the Tragic* (Oxford: Blackwell)
Fundación del Toro de Lidia. 2022. 'Conversaciones en la catacumba: alrededor de la cancelación', YouTube, 26 January <https://www.youtube.com/watch?v=_eUEeuFzBiA> [accessed 24 March 2022]
Galiacho, Juan Luis. 2010. 'La voz del tendido siete', *El Mundo*, 9 May
Goodman, Jessica. 2022. 'Introduction: Death on Stage: A Never-Ending Ending', in *Last Scene of All: Representing Death on the Western Stage*, ed. by Jessica Goodman (Cambridge: Legenda), pp. 1–9. https://doi.org/10.2307/j.ctv33b9p7v.5
Grotowski, Jerzy. 1969. *Towards a Poor Theatre* (London: Methuen)
Gunderson, Erik. 1996. 'The Ideology of the Arena', *Classical Antiquity*, 15.1: 113–51. https://doi.org/10.2307/25011033
Jiménez, David. 2019. *El director* (Madrid: Libros del K.O.)
'La Fundación Toro de Lidia compara a la alcadesa de Gijón con los talibanes por prohibir las corridas'. 2021. *Huffington Post*, 20 August
Liddell, Angélica. 2021. *Solo te hace falta morir en la plaza* (Segovia: La Uña Rota)
Lijtmaer, Lucía. 2019. *Ofendiditos: sobre la criminalización de la protesta* (Barcelona: Anagrama)
McGrath, John. 2002. 'Theatre and Democracy', *New Theatre Quarterly*, 18.2: 133–39. https://doi.org/10.1017/S0266464X02000222
Marzal, Carlos (ed.). 2010. *Sentimiento del toreo* (Barcelona: Tusquets)
Muñoz, Lorena. 2018. 'Reflexiones de Morante sobre el bombo, los veterinarios y la televisión', *ABC*, 26 September
Ojados, Francisco. 2007. '"Me cabreó pinchar en los dos toros cuando ya tenía la puerta grande"', *La verdad*, 1 June
O'Leary, Catherine, and Michael Thompson. 2023. *Theatre Censorship in Spain, 1931–1985* (Cardiff: University of Wales Press). https://doi.org/10.2307/jj.21995504
Pérez, Rosario. 2020. 'El arte de ver toros sin público: entre palmas y pitos', *ABC*, 2 May
Roselli, David Kawalko. 2011. *Theater of the People: Spectators and Society in Ancient Athens* (Austin: University of Texas Press)
Shubert, Adrian. 1999. *Death and Money in the Afternoon* (Oxford: Oxford University Press). https://doi.org/10.1093/oso/9780195095241.001.0001
Tomás, José et al. 2013. *Diálogo con Navegante* (Barcelona: Fundación José Tomás)
Vidal, Joaquín. 1983. 'Cogida muy grave de Curro Vázquez', *El País*, 3 June
Villán, Javier. 2006. *La crítica taurina: antología* (Madrid: Marenostrum)

Vizcaíno Casas, Fernando. 1962. *Suma de la legislación del espectáculo* (Madrid: Santillana)

Wheeler, Duncan. 2017. 'Diary', *London Review of Books*, 13 July, p. 45

—— 2018. 'Crucible: Art, Bulls and Music', *The Oxford Magazine*, Nought Week, Hilary, pp. 7–8

—— 2020. 'Censorship', in *Following Franco: Spanish Culture and Politics in Transition* (Manchester: Manchester University Press), pp. 87–150

—— 2022. 'Our Man in Madrid: Bullfighting Enters the Political Arena', *Political Quarterly*, 93.2: 326–35. https://doi.org/10.1111/1467-923X.13126

Wolff, Francis. 2013. *Seis claves del arte de torear*, trans. by Juan Córdoba (Barcelona: Bellaterra)

Zanardi, Tara. 2012. 'National Heroics: Bullfighters, Machismo and the Cult of Celebrity', *Journal for Eighteenth-Century Studies*, 35.2: 199–221. https://doi.org/10.1111/j.1754-0208.2012.00497.x

Intervention 5

Play on the Periphery: Irrational Queerness as Resistance to Censorship in Gestalta's Shibari Performance Art

HANNAH PROBST

It is a warm evening in early September somewhere in Berlin Friedrichshain. Just an hour ago I was waiting outside in a somewhat dilapidated courtyard; now I am sitting cross-legged on an orange pillow, shoeless in my tie-dyed socks, leaning against the low wall behind me in the warm light of the colourful paper lanterns that decorate the room. In front of me, a group of young people are sitting on yoga mats. Earlier, they had been speaking to one another excitedly in various languages; now, however, they are silent, because we are all staring at the open, half-lit space in the middle of the room, where a person is hanging from the ceiling.

We are in a BDSM art studio that has been transformed into a kind of theatre space to accommodate tonight's performance. The target audience of the event is queer—tickets have been limited to 'LGBTQIA+ and Friends'—and the performers are two shibari teaching artists, newly employed by the studio after moving to Berlin in the post-pandemic time. A large part of the audience consists of their friends, colleagues, and students. Tonight marks the first time since the beginning of the Covid-19 pandemic that a gathering of this size has been able to take place in this space, and the atmosphere is appropriately emotional. Many of the people in the room with me today have travelled from various corners of the world to gather for this special occasion. While the majority are based in Europe and the UK, some have come from as far as Japan, and many made their first connections with one another through online gatherings produced by the studio within the past year. As the studio's co-owner welcomes us into the space with some opening remarks, a recording of one such virtual meeting is projected onto

---

Hannah Probst, "Play on the Periphery: Irrational Queerness as Resistance to Censorship in Gestalta's Shibari Performance Art" in: *Theatre Censorship in Contemporary Europe: Silence and Protest*. University of Exeter Press (2024).
© Hannah Probst. DOI: 10.47788/NMMG9395

the wall behind them, depicting a kaleidoscope of Zoom-windows in which queer artists located all over the world engage in various bondage exchanges while a musician in the centre of the screen provides background music, uniting their separate improvisations with a mutual sonic underscoring. The isolation of the pandemic has been difficult, the studio's co-owner shares with us, but the strong connectedness of this community has helped it remain resilient: 'We made art,' they say reverently, gesturing at the screen behind them and addressing the room full of low-lit, glowing faces, 'and we survived.'

Queer survival and shibari may at first glance seem an unlikely association. A Japanese form of rope bondage known for its distinctive aesthetic and wide range of styles and applications, especially as a visual artistic medium, shibari and its aestheticized representations are more often relegated to the realm of stylized pornography than described as a relational, community practice. And yet it is despite (or perhaps because of) this unusual association that I would like to examine the piece which we experienced together that night—staged for the community by the British, Berlin-based rope artist Gestalta—as a specific performance of not only queer survival, but of queer resistance in the face of a certain brand of intra-queer censorship. Specifically, I am interested in what the particularities of shibari as a practical medium, with its focus on the body and history of sexualized stigmatization, combined with the aesthetic and social dimensions of the theatrical situation, with its staging devices and co-creative community of observers and observed, might offer for a reading of Gestalta's piece as a performative exploration of relational queer subjectivity. The performance challenges dominant notions of what queerness should look and feel like, thereby resisting the informal censorship of queerness performed by assimilationist queer social movements. How do queer shibari artists stage their bondage practice in their own community spaces? What relationships to sexuality, materiality, and power are navigated in these performances, and how are they mediated to their audiences? What embodiments of queerness do they explore, interrogate, or assert in doing so, and how do these embodiments resist the censure of queerness imposed by increasingly dominant assimilated queer subject positions? And finally, in performing this resistance, what insights might they offer the rest of us about queer survival under heteropatriarchy?

Queer assimilation and the rational

Answering these questions first demands a brief assessment of the precarious position of queer BDSM in the context of the ongoing assimilation debate within queer communities throughout Europe and North America. The decades-old argument goes something like this: as dominant heteronormative society gradually adjusts to allow more queer people access to power through institutions such as marriage and the family, still others remain marginalized (Weiss 2008, Huber 2013). Where proponents of liberal rights-based activism see increased agency in social integration, its opponents see increased censorship of queer embodied practice as a result of intensified state surveillance and informal social control, causing a deepened Othering of those queer people whose needs they do not address or whose methods of embodying their queerness are deemed too perverse for the mainstream.

I read this process as the construction of an assimilated queer subject position that is organized around the nuclear family, characterized by self-discipline, mind–body dualism, and an essentialized understanding of queer identity as inherent and immutable, and is finally supported through the co-construction of its irrational, non-disciplined, perverted, and pathologized queer Other. Both Michel Foucault's theories on governmentality (Foucault 2009) and the German philosophers Gernot and Hartmut Böhme's historical-anthropological examination of the eighteenth-century emergence of Kantian rational subjectivity (Böhme and Böhme 1985) prove useful in constructing such a reading. Foucault uses governmentality to not only identify the science of governing developed by the visible apparatus of the state, but also—more importantly—to describe the diffuse efficacy of power by way of the self-governance of (un)willing individuals through their active participation in the very organizational systems that allow the state's apparatus to maintain its control over the social order (a diffusion of power that is particularly mediated, for example, through the adherence to institutional structures such as the organization of societies into families). Similarly, Böhme and Böhme describe a regime of self-imposed discipline required for the transformation of the eighteenth-century individual into a rational subject, requiring individuals to cast out the 'inauthentic' and 'irrational' aspects of themselves (associated with qualities such as femininity, nature, and undisciplined bodily impulses) in a violent act of self-harm which Max Horkheimer and Theodor Adorno famously called the 'inflict[ion of] terrible injuries' still 'repeated in every childhood' in *Dialectic of Enlightenment* (2002: 26). Where Böhme and Böhme identify the construction of an irrational—and consequently pathologized—Other as a necessary step in the constitution of rational subjectivity, the self-governance (or, to paraphrase Horkheimer and Adorno, the self-mutilation) required to create this pathologized Other operates similarly to the upwards-facing—that is, self-imposed—dimensions of governmentality outlined by Foucault. Read together, these theories suggest an intrinsic relationship between informal social control in the form of self-censorship and the construction of subjectivity. To what extent do prevailing assimilationist ideas of queer subjectivity rely on the self-discipline or self-mutilation of queer communities from our own irrational Others, and to what extent are we doing the disciplinary work of the state for it, through our willing participation in its ordered domination?

'No Kink at Pride': (ir)rational queer subjectivity and intra-community censorship

One cultural site that illustrates this process is the increasing opposition to the inclusion of queer cultural practices deemed too sexual or perverse, such as visible kink, in public queer events like Pride. Advocates of this movement, recently christened 'No Kink at Pride' by tongue-in-cheek internet activists, argue that the inclusion of BDSM in public queer spaces harms their family-friendliness and forces unwilling onlookers to participate in the sexual relationships of strangers, reproducing rhetoric historically used against visible homosexuality towards new targets within their own communities. One recent opinion piece written by a USA-based author contends:

> Kink and BDSM are not sexual orientations, but rather sexual preferences. An orientation is innate and immutable. A preference can change. [...] [T]he former is about *who* you love, and the latter is about *how* you have sex. The struggle for lesbian, gay, and bisexual equality [...] has never been about our sex lives. (Baker-Jordan 2021)

Putting the historical revisionism and reductive identity politics of such statements aside, this argument constructs an assimilated and disciplined rational queer subject that defines itself through contrast with an irrational Other. By drawing a clear boundary between 'sexual orientation' and 'sexual preference', the author understands queerness not as constituted through socially encoded, yet decidedly embodied action—as queer theorists have argued since Butler (1990, 1993)—but as an 'innate and immutable' central quality of a rational individual, distancing itself from public signifiers of sex and sexuality while further pathologizing queer people and queer repertoires that do not fit into its framework. Here, queer subjectivity is located neither in the body nor in community relationships, but in the innate centre of the self-governing, static, and neatly categorized individual, reflecting the model of rational subjectivity as described by Böhme and Böhme: an innate and immutable cerebral 'soul' maintaining steadfast discipline over its irrational and pathological natural impulses, represented by its 'body' and/or embodiments (1985: 9–24; see also Böhme 1983: 113–25).

As such, the censorship of queer embodied practice advocated by the author is intrinsically linked to a specific ideology of queer subjectivity; it follows that an examination of the dominant storytelling of what queerness *is* must always be read in relationship to what it claims queerness *is not*, or *should not be*. The constitutive potential of performed action, furthermore, makes queer performance an especially interesting site at which to observe this interplay between subject construction and censorship of queer expression. Viewed in this way, movements such as 'No Kink at Pride' represent the attempt to censor members of their own community in response to a threat—namely, fear of the lasting impacts that the public performance of queer embodied practices such as BDSM might have on the constitution of assimilated queer subjectivity, jeopardizing the comfortable, governable position in the social order it seeks to defend at the expense of those it pathologizes. Such movements, I argue, can and should be regarded as efforts of intra-community cultural censorship, operating with the perfidious objective to maintain dominance over the constitutive (re)enactment of queer identity in social space.

Queer shibari performance artists resist this curated design of queer subjectivity by embracing queerness in all its irrationality as an embodied, libidinal, and relational practice. I argue that, by engaging policed and abjectified queer cultural practices in defiance of reigning informal censorship, these artists create utopian spaces where they can collectively assert performances of queerness that fall well outside the governable ideal: trans and non-binary, kinky and material, embodied and fluid, and above all else, grotesquely perverse. In doing so, they develop strategies of critical resistance to hegemonic queer subjectification, defying the informal censorship of the prevailing assimilationist narrative, and reasserting their queerness not as an essential internal characteristic, but as something that is 'done' by material bodies in relation to one another. In Gestalta's untitled piece, this is achieved through dramaturgies of touch, affect, and desire, through the subversive appropriation of power and hierarchy, and the troubling of subject–object relationships that assert themselves through an intentional ambivalence. It is this ambivalence which ultimately provides the largest threat to the censorship of 'irrational' queerness attempted by assimilationism. I want to use a critical framework of 'play' to attempt to find a language for this ambivalence, describing its influence on both the embodied practice of queerness as negotiated through shibari practice *and* the aesthetic mediation or communication of this embodiment to an audience in the performance context. What happens to queer subjectivity when we think about queerness as a playful practice, and what can shibari teach us about the defiant potentials of embodying queerness as play?

Queerness as play in shibari performance: relational subjects and (re)structured realities

Let us return to the studio and to the person hanging from the ceiling. The performance begins with slow, ethereal music as the performers enter the room: Gestalta, a non-binary person with dark hair and loose clothing, leads a second performer, a non-binary person wearing a white dress and a blindfold, carefully through the audience to the cleared space in the centre of the room, where a few red ropes and other objects lie bundled together beneath a hanging horizontal bamboo beam. Gestalta gently guides their partner to their knees and kneels across from them. Then, they begin to bind them: tying first their hands in front of their chest, then their hair into a ponytail which they carefully attach to the bamboo beam. Their movements are fluid and masterful as they gently move their partner through the space with a sly curiosity, and the movements of the model (the person being tied) respond completely to the non-verbal instructions given by the rigger (Gestalta, the person doing the tying). Through the slow addition of more bindings, the model's body is gradually transformed into a visual artwork that flows from shape to shape until it is finally fully suspended from the bamboo beam, where it swings gently back and forth as Gestalta and their audience observe from below. The performance is interspersed by short caesuras like these, which serve as visual tableaux and allow the rigger to engage in check-ins with their model, which they execute through quick moments of physical touch—such as playful bops on the nose—to which the model responds with a giggle or a nod. The sequence is tender and formidably technical, and I feel that I am encountering an incredible intimacy, made palpable by the tension I notice in my own body as I watch.

The dramatic action, if you will, of this performance is driven by touch and affective response. Both main 'narratives'—the visual transformation of the tied body and the staged relationship between the performers—are driven forward by physical contact, between the human bodies on the stage and the object bodies of the ropes, the bamboo, and other items (among them stones and ice cubes) that are incorporated into the hanging installation. This emphasis on touch not only highlights the materiality of the performers' bodies but also centres their relationality to one another and to the physical world. Despite their varying degrees of agency, all human and object bodies in the sequence are reliant on their material connection to the others for the performance to succeed. As such, the action is driven not through the negotiation of conflicts between individual actors, but through the collective work of material bodies which derive their agency entirely from their relationships to one another. Further, as the model's body is twisted into grotesque shapes, it becomes both alienated from its human subjectivity and juxtaposed with the non-human objects that hang beside it, at once an act of objectification *and* humanization as its uniquely human qualities are underscored (for example, when the model reacts to the physically challenging situation through sounds and small adjustments). Thus, the model becomes both subject and object at once, opening a spectrum of tension between 'human' and 'matter', which locates subjectivity not in the control of the rational mind over the body, but in the material, conscious bodymind.

The relational, embodied queerness that is explored here posits a form of queer subjectivity that cannot exist as an individual—as it is fully dependent on interaction with other bodies, both human and object, to gain agency within the dramatic logic of the performance—and, further, flourishes in the troubling or even near-collapse of boundaries between self and other, person and thing. The capacities of touch and affect to blur constructed delineations and material boundaries have been well examined by researchers across disciplines: one example is queer Disability Studies scholar David Serlin's use of Eve K. Sedgwick's famous description of touch as 'mak[ing] nonsense out of any dualistic understanding of agency and passivity' (Sedgwick 2003: 14) to describe touch as fundamentally queer, being 'infused with complexities of performance, affect, and desire that confound categories of sexual orientation and gender' (Serlin 2012: 146). By focusing on touch, these performers take advantage of the materiality of shibari as a medium to stage their own relationality—to one another and to the material world in which they operate—in a way that at once reaffirms and blurs the boundaries between them. If we are to view the material dynamics of this sequence as having implications for the exploration of queer subjectivity, much like Serlin asserts, this ambivalence becomes a playful exploration of the limit—where does one thing end and another begin?—that continues to flow through the performance's beats without ever arriving at a static resolution. Queerness as explored in this sequence is a collective, experimental process of exploring boundaries and negotiating the in-betweens—in other words, a process of 'play', of performed improvisation within and around given structures between challenge, subversion, and affirmation of them.

I read this playful articulation of queerness as a direct counter-narrative and a powerful affront to the censorship imposed on queer expression by assimilationism. The sequence directly refutes the Kantian paradigm of rational subjectivity by shifting its aesthetic focus from the supposedly sovereign *individual*, neatly boundaried away from and placed in disciplined control of its physical surroundings, to the dynamic ambivalence of the ever-to-be-renegotiated material *relationships* between people and things. In doing so, the artists' subjectivities—or, much more, the mutual subjectivity generated through this constant process of exchange and the blurring of the boundaries between them—appears not as a categorical characteristic derived from a disciplined and inherent 'essence' of self, but as a product of their deliberate, embodied action. Their queerness is dynamic, performatively constituted by their bodies in space, and—because it is contingent on its relationality—deliberately fragile, always in becoming and all too easily altered by the slightest change in its physical environment. By enacting their performance in the space provided by the studio, the artists demonstrate their own agency in choosing how to express their queerness despite the social pressures imposed on them by the cultural censorship of the mainstream queer respectability politics outside. They reaffirm their power to performatively construct their queerness as embedded in the grey areas between their moving bodies and the objects with which they remain in constant interaction. By choosing to (re)generate their queerness through play, then, they directly threaten rational queerness and assimilationist censorship: both through their reclamation of queerness as *action* (rather than innate and immutable identity) and through the complex ambivalence produced by their performance of queerness as an ever-changing, non-definable material relationship, defying the categorical organization required by cultural censors to govern and discipline queer identity.

Of course, 'play' within the context of BDSM also carries another connotation, namely the pre-negotiated enactment of specific scenarios between partners in assigned roles, often—but not always—incorporating sexual exchanges. As anthropologist Margot D. Weiss has shown, the similarities between BDSM-play and so-called theatre can be controversial amongst practitioners: while some view their 'play' as a fictional game, others take it very seriously, viewing their 'roles' as constructive of their social realities. Weiss consequently defines 'play' as liminally operating in a system of tensions between 'work–play, act–meaning, lifestyle–identity, real–pretend' that 'negotiates and renegotiates relations between self and other in terms of collective belonging [...] Play is recreational (something pleasant, not work) as well as re-creational (productive of new worlds or relations)' (2006: 230, 238). Furthermore, it is within the structural framing of 'play,' Weiss argues, that BDSM-players are able to experiment with power, hierarchy, and violence safely, even allowing minoritarian subjects to subversively re-enact violent scenarios of their own oppression in a framing that, in a crucial difference to violence in everyday life, affords them the agency of choice even as they perform their own loss of control (Weiss 2001).

Shibari performance, through its ostentatious staging of an intimate physical power exchange, certainly operates as 'play' in this sense, both in its ambivalence as a theatricalized but nonetheless very materially 'real' sequence, and through its controlled staging of power, pain, and grotesque abjectification. There is a moment near the beginning of Gestalta's performance where I am directly confronted with this ambivalence. The model is on their knees, their hands still tied in front of them, their hair tied above and backwards to the bamboo beam. I watch as Gestalta reaches into their mouth and begins to tie a red sewing thread to their tongue. Suddenly, the model makes an audible sound in reaction to the painful invasion. I am shocked—I don't know what I was expecting, but I certainly was not ready to *hear* them! Suddenly, the moment feels excruciatingly personal. I feel smacked with the truth that there is no clear separation between 'reality' and 'fiction' in this space; I just heard a real person make a real sound in response to a real tactile stimulus. To what extent am I currently bearing witness to an actual intimate relationship, and to what extent am I simply watching a rehearsed performance, staged by two professional teaching-artists for a paying audience? The rigger proceeds to tie an ice cube to the end of the red thread, and the weight pulls the model's tongue down and out of their mouth. They continue to vocally respond to the sensation, and the rigger watches them carefully, caressing their face in a short check-in moment. Then, Gestalta removes the blindfold from the model's eyes, revealing completely white contact lenses. The resulting tableau—white, quasi-demonic eyes; opened mouth with a bound, lolling tongue; hair tied backwards and hands tied forwards—is painful, disturbing, and grotesquely bewitching.

Here, the objectification of the bound model—their transformation into a grotesque, not entirely human, yet simultaneously all-too-human *something*—is accomplished through an explicit performance of the power dynamic between the two performers: Gestalta is in the clear position of power as their model becomes the direct object of its execution. The relational subjectivity established by the performance thus depends on a significant transfer of power and an enormous transfer of trust between the performers, to which the entire community of onlookers is made in equal parts complicit and reverently beholden. This sequence deliberately embraces the 'darker' aspects of BDSM, which are used by the cultural censorship movement to justify its exclusion from public queer life. Moreover, in relying on precisely these aspects to intensify the stakes of the performed relationship, the exchange casts them as irreplaceable cornerstones of the queer subjectivity produced by this relationship in the context of the performance. In its brazen celebration of the perverse, the taboo, and the pathologized, the performance thus at once celebrates the abject as a site of desire, is productive of profound physical intimacy, and appropriates power, even violence, in a way that I read as highly subversive. These artists do not seek to erase the human experiences of power, pain, and dehumanization, nor do they seek to deny the association of sexual desire with these experiences—despite the extensive histories of suppression expressed through medical pathologization (Lin 2016) and social marginalization (Hansen-Brown and Jefferson 2022) associated with this aspect. Instead, they utilize the subcultural queer community space provided by the studio to explore the potentials that structured play with these elements in a controlled setting can offer in testing the limits of human movement and sensory experience, and in generating trust and emotional intimacy. An intimacy which is generated between the performing partners, to be sure, but also within the community of onlookers bearing witness to this vulnerable exchange.

In this way, 'play' once again emerges as a method of exploring embodiments of queerness that derives its efficacy precisely from its performative ambivalence. The combined dynamics of the performed sequence, with its testing of physical and social limits within a controlled framing, and its aesthetic communication to the audience, with its blurring of the boundaries between 'real' and 'not real', 'performer' and 'role', open a crucial liminal space somewhere in between absolute fiction and social reality. It is within this ambiguous 'play' space that a boundary-testing exploration of queerness is made possible while still retaining its performative power to influence the 'real world'. As such, Gestalta's performance perfectly rides the line between 'recreational' and 're-creational' play in the sense that Weiss describes.

It is this remarkable tendency of queer shibari performance art to open this unique in-between space that I read as especially well suited to developing methods of critical resistance to the censorship of hegemonic queer subjectification. Working collectively within their own community space on the peripheries of mainstream society, these artists experiment with and playfully assert ways of *doing* their queerness that resist the censorship imposed by assimilationism; they provide an option for queer survival under heteropatriarchy that refuses to comply with the governable, rational individual subjectivity it champions and preserves queer cultural repertoires it seeks to exclude or repress. The irrational queer subject developed by these performers is squarely embedded in its relationships to its community, to its partners, and to the material world of which it is part. Because subjectivity is negotiated through action, queer performance and its relationship to censorship—what is and is not shown, what can and cannot not be done—must be treated as a crucial battleground for the unlimited articulation of queerness: acts are censored because we know about the constitutive power that acts can have. To censor queer cultural practice is to censor queer embodiments is to censor the very (re)articulation of our queer subject positions themselves. To practise queerness as play, then, is to practise the ever-changing, fluid, inclusive practice of challenging power and resisting categorization, to recast our queer bodies and desires as tools of destabilizing critique that deny order, embrace mess, and celebrate the joyful, community practice of making art, surviving, and relentlessly pursuing the limits of the spaces in between.

References

Baker-Jordan, Skylar. 2021. 'BDSM and Kink Don't Belong in Pride Celebrations. This Is Why', *Independent*, 25 May

Böhme, Gernot. 1983. '7. Vorlesung: Der Leib', in *Anthropologie in pragmatischer Hinsicht: Darmstädter Vorlesungen* (Frankfurt a.M.: Suhrkamp), pp. 113–25

Böhme, Gernot, and Hartmut Böhme. 1985 (1983). *Das Andere der Vernunft: Zur Entwicklung von Rationalitätsstrukturen am Beispiel Kants* (Frankfurt a.M.: Suhrkamp)

Butler, Judith. 1990. *Gender Trouble: Feminism and the Subversion of Identity* (New York: Routledge)

—— 1993. *Bodies That Matter: On the Discursive Limits of 'Sex'* (New York: Routledge)

Foucault, Michel. 2009 (1978). 'Lectures Four and Five', in *Security, Territory, Population: Lectures at the College de France, 1977–1978*, ed. by Michel Senellart, trans. by Graham Burchell (London: Palgrave Macmillan), pp. 87–134

Hansen-Brown, Ashley A., and Sabrina E. Jefferson. 2022. 'Perceptions of and Stigma Toward BDSM Practitioners', *Current Psychology*, 26 April. https://doi.org/10.1007/s12144-022-03112-z

Horkheimer, Max, and Theodor Adorno. 2002 (1944). *Dialectic of Enlightenment*, trans. by Edmund Jephcott and Gunzelin Noeri (Redwood City: Stanford University Press). https://doi.org/10.1515/9780804788090

Huber, Marty. 2013. *Queering Gay Pride: Zwischen Assimilation und Widerstand* (Vienna: Zaglossus)

Lin, Kai. 2016. 'The Medicalization and Demedicalization of Kink: Shifting Contexts of Sexual Politics', *Sexualities*, 20.3: 1–22. https://doi.org/10.1177/1363460716651420

Sedgwick, Eve K. 2003. *Touching Feeling: Affect, Pedagogy, Performativity* (Durham, NC: Duke University Press)

Serlin, David. 2012. 'Touching Histories: Personality, Disability, and Sex in the 1930s', in *Sex and Disability*, ed. by Robert McRuer and Anna Mollow (Durham, NC: Duke University Press), pp. 145–62

Weiss, Margot D. 2001. *Techniques of Pleasure: BDSM and the Circuits of Sexuality* (Durham, NC: Duke University Press)

——— 2006. 'Working at Play: BDSM Sexuality in the San Francisco Bay Area', *Anthropologica*, 48.2: 229–45. https://doi.org/10.2307/25605313

——— 2008. 'Gay Shame and BDSM Pride: Neoliberalism, Privacy, and Sexual Politics', *Radical History Review*, 100: 87–98. https://doi.org/10.1215/01636545-2007-023

Index

Abascal, Santiago 218
Abbey Theatre (Ireland) 1, 5, 10, 14, 71–2, 74–9, 83, 85, 86nn4–6. *See also* Mac Conghail, Fiach; McClaren, Graham; Murray, Neil
   actors' protest 77–9
   Peacock Theatre 72
Abramović, Marina 48
Adams, John 149
Aeschylus 5
Afriyie, Jerry 160
Against Modern Opera Productions (AMOP) 145
Agranovich, Aleksei 59–60, 66n12
Aisling Ghéar 14, 71, 79–82, 85
Aisteoirí Bulfin 81
Akhedzhakova, Lia 62–3
Albania 39, 41
Alföldi, Róbert 97, 99, 101nn9–10
Algeria 6
Almási-Tóth, András 148
Amharclann de hÍde 81
Amnesty International 176
Amón, Rubén 220, 224–5, 225n4
Anđelić, Srđa 39
Andersen, Hans Christian 60, 62
antisemitism 15, 124–30, 132, 134
Apostolopoulos, Giorgos 201, 206
archives 7, 9, 86n12, 107, 115n3, 116n4, 123
Arsenijević, Vladimir 39
Arts Council England 149, 152n13
Arts Council of Ireland 14, 71, 73–4, 77–85
   Gender Counts report 73–4
   Making Great Art Work 83
Arts Council of Northern Ireland (ACNI) 14, 79–82, 86n7
Atelier 212 (Serbia) 42–3, 47
Athenagoras, Ecumenic Patriarch 203
Atkinson, Paul 139
Auslander, Philip 126

Austria 99, 107, 115n1, 121, 142, 151n2, 158
Azas, Anestis 204
Azzopardi, Clare 30–1

Bailey, Brett 4, 6, 192n4
Bakhtin, Mikhail 93
Bakoyannis, Pavlos 204
Balme, Christopher 47, 186, 188, 190, 191
Barbican (England) 6, 188
Bardari, Giuseppe 141
Barrio, Víctor 219
Barry, Kevin 84
Barthes, Roland 8
Bartís, Ricardo 213
Basha, Doruntina 41
Battersea Arts Centre (England) 182
Baudet, Thierry 162–3
Bean, Richard 180–1
BEATS 149, 150
Beasant, John 140
Beckett, Samuel 6, 80
Belarus 5
Belarus Free Theatre (Belarus) 5
Belgium 122, 133, 157
Bell, Lian 72
Belmonte, Juan 212, 214, 224
Bezjak, Primož 121
Bhatti, Gurpreet Kaur 4, 179, 185, 187
Bieito, Calixto 145
Bienvenida, Antonio 220
Bitef Theatre (Serbia) 39, 41, 44
Black Lives Matter 148, 160, 162, 164n5
Black Pete 156–66
blackface 5, 6, 12, 16, 19n2, 138, 143, 144, 146–8, 156–66. *See also* racism
blacklists 3, 37, 41, 107, 199
Boadella, Albert 214

Boccaccio, Giovanni 59
Bocharnikov, Aleksandr 60
Bödőcs, Tibor 93, 100n1
Bodó, Viktor 95
Bogataj, Janez 110–11, 113, 116n12
Bogavac, Milena 39, 41–2
Bogomolov, Konstantin 59
Boland, Eavan 71, 76
Bolshoi Theatre (Russia) 56–7
Bond, Edward 79
Bonnici, Owen 29
Bosnia and Herzegovina 40, 43. *See also* Srebrenica genocide
Boult, Adrian 137
Bourdieu, Pierre 9
Boyd, Madeleine 142
Bradić, Nebojša 45
Brenton, Howard 7
Brešan, Ivo 35, 105
Bridges, J'Nai 148
Brighton, Pam 81
British Broadcasting Corporation (BBC) 182
Britten, Benjamin 137
Bruna, Luis Pelayo 220
Bulc, Mare 109–15, 116n14, 116n16, 117nn17–20
Buljan, Ivica 44
Bunn, Matthew 4, 9, 11, 197–8
Bush, George H.W. 9
Butler, Judith 9, 85, 139, 160, 197, 231

Camus, Albert 203
cancel culture 6, 16–17, 19, 138, 145, 163, 169–72, 176, 212
Cantarella, Robert 6
Carlos, King Juan 223
Carr, Marina 72
Castellucci, Romeo 17, 179, 188–92
censorship
  assassination 13, 26–7, 31, 139, 204
  cancelled productions 3, 17, 37, 119, 150, 169, 174–5, 179, 181, 184, 186, 187, 198
  definitions of 2–7, 37–41
  imprisonment 3, 5, 19, 36, 37, 57, 58, 66n6, 105, 107, 140
  rewritings 46, 111, 112, 137, 141–4, 146, 180

sources of 25–49
  financial 3, 14, 36, 37, 39, 49n6, 56, 61, 80–5
  government 5, 7, 13, 15, 37, 54–6, 61, 63, 64–5, 66n12, 104, 107, 110–11, 115, 140, 147, 205, 217
  local authorities 4, 30, 37–9, 95, 96, 106, 108, 160, 183
  pressure groups 4, 10, 37, 41, 43, 49, 149, 184, 187, 200
  prosecution (or threat of) 5, 7, 9, 57–60, 64, 65, 105, 182, 183. *See also* Abbey Theatre (Ireland)
  self-censorship 9–10, 13, 15, 17, 19, 26, 34–51, 59, 65, 100, 104, 106, 115n2, 116n5, 119–35, 139, 145–7, 149, 150, 172, 175, 179–82, 184, 186, 197, 198, 230
  theatre management 6, 30–1, 35–7, 109–15
Centre E8 (Serbia) 44
China 54, 100n1, 149, 151
Chitirion Theatre (Greece) 201–2
Chraniotis, George 206
Churchill, Caryl 181
Clanchy, Kate 171–2, 176
Coetzee, J.M. 8
comedy 72, 77, 93, 95, 105. *See also* Hungary
communism 7, 11, 15, 35, 36, 43, 54–5, 100, 104–8, 114–15, 138, 199, 218–19
  Bijela knjiga 36
Corcadorca Theatre Company (Ireland) 14, 71, 79, 82–5, 86n12
Correia, Tiago 4
Croatia 35–6, 43, 46–7, 105, 122
culture wars 6, 12, 16, 17, 19, 138–9, 144–5, 169–76
Cunha e Silva, Paulo 4
Czech Republic 105

Dafoe, Willem 126
DAH Theatre (Serbia) 42, 44, 49n3
Dale-Jones, Josie 171
Deevy, Teresa 75, 77, 85
Delia, Manuel 29

Demeter, Szilárd 96
Demirski, Paweł 121
Denmark 2
Dent, Donna 73
Diappi, Carlo 143
Didenko, Maksim 59
Dimitrakopoulou, Pigi 18, 201, 203, 205
Domingo, Placido 147, 213
Dominguín, Luis Miguel 220
Donizetti, Gaetano 141–2
Dörner, György 5, 97
Doss, Mark S. 143
Dowden, Oliver 170
Dragomán, György 96
Dunbar, Andrea 5
Dyas, Grace 74

Eagleton, Terry 215
Ecuador 214
Edgar, David 181, 182, 186–8
Egypt 143
El-Khairy, Omar 17, 169, 173
England 2, 79, 82, 149, 152n4, 152n13, 181, 182
Eötvös, Peter 150
Exorcist, The 143

Facebook 145, 146, 148, 163. *See also* social media
Fandino, Iván 219
far-right politics 96–7, 145, 147–8, 162–3, 184, 202, 216, 218
Farrugia, Anġlu 30
feminism 14, 71–3, 75, 86n2, 93, 218–19, 230
Fenech, Yorgen 31, 32n2, 44–5
festivals 34–5, 72
  Avignon Festival 188
  Belgrade's International Theatre Festival, 39
  'Days of Sarajevo' festival in Belgrade 39
  Dialog Festival in Wrocław 121
  Druid Theatre Festival 83
  Dublin Theatre Festival 83–4
  Dubrovnik Summer Festival 122
  Festival at the Crossroads in Niš 44–5
  Festival of Experimental Scenes in Podgorica 38
  Festival Without Translation 44
  Fortress Theatre Festival 38
  Galway International Arts Festival 84
  Gate Theatre Festival 83
  Glass House 72
  Golden Mask Festival 57
  Kilkenny Arts Festival 84
  Kunstenfestivaldesarts 120, 122
  Malta Festival in Poznan 46
  National Festival Borštnikovo 42
  Wiener Festwochen 120
financial crisis 195–6, 198, 200–1, 207
Fo, Dario 80
Formenti, Mario 183
Foucault, Michel 9, 139, 158, 197, 230
Fraga, Manuel 217
France
  censorship 1–2, 5–8, 191
  colonialism 6
  Golgota Picnic 183
  Opéra-Théâtre d'Avignon (France) 188
  Paris Opera 149
  religious freedom 185
  racism 5–6
  self-censorship 149
freedom of expression 1, 4–5, 7, 12, 17, 18, 25, 35, 45, 64, 79, 100, 108, 138, 169, 170, 172–3, 176, 179, 183, 185, 197, 199, 204–5, 216
French Connection, The 143
Freshwater, Helen 1, 7, 9–10, 81, 139, 185–6
Frey, Rudolf 142
Friedkin, William 143
Friel, Brian 80
fringe theatre 64
Frljić, Oliver 15, 37, 42, 43, 44, 45–9, 49n2, 49n5, 50n6, 119–23, 125–7, 129–34, 135nn1–2

Gądecki, Stanisław 183
Galán, Edu 212
Galizia, Daphne Caruana 13, 26–8, 32n2

Gallagher, Sean 181
García, Rodrigo 183
Gardner, Lyn 175
Gario, Quinsy 160
Gate Theatre (Ireland) 74
Gavrilović, Žarko 40
gender 146
   in East Asia 138
   in Greece 198
   in Ireland 71
   in Irish theatre 73–7
   in the Middle East 138
   North American attitudes 144
   Pour un temps sois peu 6
   stereotypes 75
Germany 7, 15–16, 45, 121, 186, 188
   Polish biases against 123
   restriction of free speech 145
Gershwin Estate 147–8
Gestalta 18, 228–37. *See also* queer
Gibbons, Scott 188
Golden Dawn 200, 202. *See also* Greece
Goldman, Lisa 187
Goncharov, Ivan 59
González, Ana 219
Gothár, Péter 98
Goya, Francisco de 211
Grech, Herman 31
Greece 195–210. *See also* Golden Dawn
   censorship and artistic expression 18, 195, 198–200, 207
   financial crisis 200–1
   freedom of expression 205
   religious censorship 202
Green, Stephen 182
Greene, Eric 150
Gregory, Lady Augusta 72, 75, 77
Gremina, Elena 63
Gross, Jan Tomasz 128
Grotowski, Jerzy 131, 213, 221
Grubić, Marko 39
Grum Award 108–9
Guerrin, Michel 149
Guimarães, Regina 4
Gulyás, Márton 94–5

Habermas, Jürgen 49
Hackney Empire Theatre (England) 150
Hands, Terry 180
Harlow Playhouse (England) 183
Harms, Kirsten 145, 186
Háy, János 96
Henriquez, Mitch 160
Herranz, Faustino 220
Hervé, Frédéric 6
Holten, Kasper 146
homosexuality. *See* LGBTQIA+
Horkheimer, Max 230
Hubač, Željko 42, 44
Hull Truck Theatre (England) 180
Hungary 14, 93–100
   comedy and subversion 93–4
   Porgy and Bess 147–8
   history of theatre censorship 94–8
   Hungarian Theatre and Film Academy 98–100
   state interference in theatre 5, 121
   Two-Tailed Dog Party 93, 94
Hynes, Garry 75

Iakovlev, Anton 60
imprisonment 5, 19, 36–7, 58, 105, 107, 140, 206
Index on Censorship 181, 192n1
Injac, Goran 119–20, 133
Instagram 59. *See also* social media
intimidation 4, 37, 41–2, 46, 95–6, 105–6, 113, 184
Ireland 70–85, 183. *See also* Abbey Theatre (Ireland)
   Aisling Ghéar 14, 80–2
   arts in 75
   Corcadorca 82–5
   #MeToo 74
   Speak Up: A Call for Change (Irish Theatre Institute) 74
   #WakingTheFeminists 72–4
Ireland, David 76
Island Theatre Company (Ireland) 82
Israel 133
Italy 15, 143, 147, 152n5
   whitening of Black performers 147

Jančar, Drago 107
Janion, Maria 124
Janša, Janez 42
Japan 228

Jarocki, Jerzy 122
Jevremović, Zorica 44
Jiménez, David 217
Jones, Marie 80
Jovanović, Dimitrije 43
Józefczak, Zygmunt 125, 127, 129–30
Jung, Carl 190

Kaczyński, Lech 121
Kálmán, László 99
Kantor, Tadeusz 122, 131
Kapkov, Sergei 53, 66n2
Karczmarska, Anna Maria 120
Karsai, György 100
Katona József Theatre (Hungary) 95–6, 98
Kazantzakis, Nikos 203
Kick Out Black Pete (KOZP) 160, 162, 163
Kiernan, Pat 82, 84
Klata, Jan 120–2, 131–3
Kneecap (hip-hop band) 80
Kno'ledge Cesare. *See* Afriyie, Jerry
Koncz, Zsuzsa 96
Koper Theatre (Slovenia) 110
Kopitović, Zoran 38
Korea 6
Kosovo 41
Kott, Jan 125, 133
Kovačević, Siniša 40
Krasiński, Zygmunt 127, 135n1
Krupiński, Wacław 132–3

Latif, Nadia 17, 169, 173–4, 181
Laušević, Žarko 40
Lawrence, D.H. 137
Le Brocq, Marc 150
Lee, Hye-Youn 150
Lee, Stewart 182
legislation 10, 14, 207. *See also* LGBTQIA+: propaganda law
anti-LGBTQ 96–7
on blasphemy 182
in Hungary 5
in Russia 10, 14
Lengyel, Anna 12
Lescaut, Manon 147
Letunić, Ana 44
Lewis, Kristin 143

LGBTQIA+ 45, 56, 63, 96, 147, 199, 228, 231. *See also* queer
anti-LGBTQ legislation 96–7
homophobia 97, 170, 172
propaganda law 53, 56
Liddell, Angélica 211–12, 214
Lijtmaer, Lucía 219
Livathinos, Stathis 201, 204–5
Llosa, Mario Vargas 215
López, Julián 222
Lorca, Federico García 211–12, 214–15
Lowe, Louise 75
Lukashenko, Alexander 5
Lukić, Darko 45
LUNG Theatre (England) 17, 169, 173, 175
Lupa, Krystian 122

Macedonia 40, 49
Mac Conghail, Fiach 76–7
Madigan, Josepha 77
Maestri, Ambrogio 143
Maffei, Andrea 141
Majewski, Sebastian 120–2, 131–3
Malevich, Kazimir 61
Malibran, Maria 141–2
Malobrodskii, Aleksei 58, 66n6
Malta 25–32. *See also* Galizia, Daphne Caruana
abolition of censorship 30
ad hoc street protests 28
arts and social criticism 30–1
Great Siege Monument 28
'Occupy Justice' protest group 28
public space 26–30
Running Commentary blog 26–7
'Repubblika' protest group 28
Manzanares, José María 222
Marín, Serafín 216
market pressure 37, 74, 137–51. *See also* opera
Markowski, Stanisław 132
Marlowe, Christopher 180
Marx, Laurène 6
Máté, Gábor 96
McCabe, Pat 84
McCarthy, Paul 48
McGrath, John 225

McGuinness, Frank 1
McIntyre, Clare 14
McLaren, Graham 77–9, 86n4
McLaughlin, Caitriona 75
McMahon, Phillip 76
McNally, Terrence 18, 201–2
Mears, Oliver 151
Media 15, 98, 113, 128, 134 *See also* Malta; social media
  and *Behzti* 187
  cancel culture and woke culture 170–1
  and Chitirion Theatre 202
  foreign media organizations 30
  in France 183
  government-sponsored 39
  in Hungary 96, 98
  and Labour Party (Malta) 27
  local media establishment 26, 30
  in Poland 133, 183
  pro-government 95–7
  tabloid campaigns 37, 39
Medinskii, Vladimir 13, 54, 56, 60–1, 66n4, 66n8
Medvedev, Dmitrii 52–3, 58
Merczyński, Michał 183–4
Merkel, Angela 145, 186
Merritt, Stephanie 180
Messina, Antonello da 188–90
#MeToo movement 74, 98
Meyerhold, Vsevolod 61
Michaels, Walter Benn 127
Michieletto, Damiano 16, 145–6
Michnik, Adam 128
Mijač, Dejan 43
Milatović, Slobodan 38
Milčin, Vladimir 40, 49n4
Miljanić, Ana 39
Milosavljević, Aleksandar 45
Milošević, Slobodan 40
Miłosz, Czesław 41
Milovanović, Spasoje Ž. 45
Mim theatre (Serbia) 39
Mitsotakis, Kyriakos 204
Mladenović, Kokan 39, 42–5
Mnouchkine, Ariane 6
Monks, Helen 173, 175
Montenegro 38, 40, 43
Mouffe, Chantal 44, 127

Murphy, Brenda 79
Murphy, Cillian 84
Murphy, Elaine 77
Murphy, Isabel 141, 143
Murray, Neil 77–9, 86n4
Music Theatre Wales (MTW) 149–50

Nádas, Péter 96
'National Fiesta' 18, 211–25. *See also* Spain
National Old Theatre (Poland) 15
National Stary Theatre (Poland) 45, 119–20, 127, 130, 132
National Theatre (Bosnia) 40
National Theatre (HNK Zagreb) (Croatia) 44–5
National Theatre (Greece) 201, 203–4
National Theatre (Hungary) 42, 44
National Theatre in Niš (Serbia) 44–5
National Theatre (Slovenia) 42
National Theatre (Montenegro) 43
National Theatre (Scotland) 77
National Youth Theatre (NYT) (UK) 17, 173–4, 181
Navalny, Aleksei 61
Ndiaye, Pap 149
Neef, Alexander 149
Neilson, Anthony 178, 192
Netherlands 156–66. *See also* Nicholas (Saint); KOZP
  Black Lives Matter demonstrations 162
  Black Pete portrayal 156–9, 164
  image repertoire 157–9
  racism awareness 160–2
  tradition and performative protests 162–3
Neuenfels, Hans 16, 145, 186
New Censorship Theory 9, 197–9
Newtownabbey's Theatre at the Mill (Northern Ireland) 183
Neziraj, Jeton 39, 41–2, 44, 48
Nicholas (Saint) 16, 156–64, 164n2
Nicholl, Charles 180
Nicholson, Steve 7, 11, 180
Nikšić Theatre (Montenegro) 38
Nordhaug, Bishop Halvor 19

Northern Ireland 14, 70, 79, 80, 82, 183
Norway 19
nudity 144, 146, 183
Nureyev, Rudolf 56
N.V. Gogol Drama Theatre (Russia) 52, 53, 55, 57–60, 63–6

Ó Cairealláin, Gearóid 80
Ó Cairealláin, Naoise 80
O'Casey, Sean 70, 76, 85
'Occupy Justice' 28
O'Donoghue, Éadaoin 84
Ó Gallchóir, Bríd 80, 82
Ókovács, Szilveszter 147, 148
O'Leary, Catherine 3, 8–9, 11, 19n3, 152n4, 198
Oman, opera in 140–4
  Aida 143–4
  cultural diplomacy 140–4
  cultural norms 144
  Maria Stuarda 16, 140–3
opera 11, 137–51
  Aida 16, 140, 144, 152n8
  Anna Bolena 142
  Buondelmonte 141
  Canadian Opera Company 149
  Carmen 213, 216
  crises 145–6
  Deutsche Oper 145, 179, 185, 186
  Doña Francisquita 223
  equality, diversity, and inclusion (EDI) themes 150
  ethnographic approaches 139
  in European culture wars 144–5
  global circulation of 138
  Golden Dragon, The 150
  Guillaume Tell 16, 145
  historical context 137–8
  Idomeneo 16, 145, 179, 185–8
  Jerry Springer: The Opera 182, 184
  La forza del destino 151n3
  Madama Butterfly 149–50
  Maria Stuarda 16, 140–3
  Metropolitan Opera 149
  Nixon in China 149, 151
  in Oman 140–4
  Opéra-Théâtre d'Avignon (France) 188

Paris Opera 149
Porgy and Bess 147–148, 152n12
power and agency in 140
and race 147–51
Rape of Lucretia, The 137
Roberto Devereux 142
Royal Opera House (Oman) 16, 140, 142
Royal Opera House (UK) 145, 151
Salome 137
Santa Fe Opera 149
Scottish Opera 149, 150
self-censorship 145–7
Turandot 147
Welsh National Opera (WNO) 16, 141, 142, 143
Orbán, Viktor 5, 94–7, 99, 100nn1–2, 101n6, 147
Ortega y Gasset, José 222
Ortombina, Fortunato 147
Oručević, Tanja Miletić 40
O'Toole, Fintan 75, 77
Out of Joint theatre company (England) 5

Paković, Zlatko 39, 42, 44
Panagopoulou, Vasia 201–2
Parker, Lynne 75
Pasqual, Lluis 223
Patlai, Anastasiia 63
Paula, Rafael de 212, 221
Peacock Stage (Ireland) 72, 79. See also Abbey Theatre (Ireland)
Pegan, Katja 110, 114
Perera, Miguel Ángel 217, 222
personal attacks 26–7, 49n3, 58, 61, 96–7, 101n9, 106, 113, 133
Peskov, Dmitrii 56
Pessoa, Fernando 18, 201, 206
Petković, Dejan 45
Petőfi Literary Museum 96
Petrović, Goran 45
Piano, Renzo 29
Picasso, Pablo 211
Pintér, Béla 95, 97–8
Pirozzi, Anna 143, 146
Pizzi, Pier Luigi 147

plays, performances, musicals. *See also* Un-Divine Comedy. Remains
11 septembre 2001/11th September 2001 6
25.671 42
A Common Story 59
A Midsummer Night's Dream 58
All That is Left is for You to Die in the Plaza 212
Aleksandra Zec 45, 47, 49n2, 120
Ako dugo gledaš u ponor 39
Akropolis 131
Arlington 86n6
Authentic Interpretations: '68 39
Bacchae, The 45
Balkan macht frei 47, 121
Battle of Kolubara 43
Battle of Warsaw, The 121
Behzti 4, 7, 185–8
Billy Elliot 147
Censor, The 178, 192
Champion, The 95, 101n4
Coming Out of the Closet 63–4
Complete Word of God (Abridged), The 182, 184
Corpus Christi 18, 195, 201–3
Cowardice 46
Crime and Punishment 49n2
Croatian Theatre 45
Curse, The 46, 121, 134
Damned Be the Traitor of His Homeland 47, 49n5, 120, 121
Danton 122
Decameron, The 59
Disco Pigs 82, 82
Encyclopaedia of the Living 39
Endgame 82
England People Very Nice 181
Exhibit B 4, 6, 192n4
Family Sex Show, The 171
Fine Dead Girls 49n2
First Bread 62, 63–4, 66n9
Ginger Ale Boy 82
Golgota Picnic 183–4, 192n2
Gorki: Alternative für Deutschland 47
Guests of the Nation 84
Hamletmaschine 121

Homegrown 17, 169, 172–6, 181, 184, 192n1
Hour of the Devil, The 18, 195, 201, 205–6
I Hate the Truth 120
In God's Name 19n4
Inspector General, The 95, 100n4
Iphigénie Hôtel 6
Jami District 39
Jesus Christ Superstar 202
Kanata 6
Kathleen Ni Houlihan 72
Le Tartuffe, ou l'imposteur 1
Les Coréens 6
Les Huissiers 6
Little Tragedies 57, 59
Maria Stuart 141
Merchant of Venice, The 124
Misterman 82
Nash Equilibrium, The 18, 195, 201, 203–5
Nečastivi na Filozofskom: fakultetu 105
On the Concept of the Face, Regarding the Son of God 17, 179, 188–92
Our Violence, Your Violence 47
Oxygen 66n11
Patriotic Hypermarket 41
Piel de toro 216
Politika kao sudbina 38
Portia Coughlan 72
Pour un temps sois peu 6
Predator 39
Prince Paul 43
Princess Ksenija from Montenegro 43
Repubblika Immakulata 31
Request Programme 84
Rita, Sue and Bob Too 5
Romans in Britain, The 7
Saint Sava 40, 43
Same, The 84
Shush 77
Slovene National Theatre 42
Smalltalk Place at 'Lucky Shot' 45
Spiro Crne 49n4
Spreading the News 72

Srebrenica: Kad mi ubijeni ustanemo 39
Što je čoek do li biciklista? 38
Suppliants, The 5
Sveto S ili Kako je 'arhivirana' predstava Sveti Sava 40
Tamburlaine the Great 180, 184
Tebut isfar 30
They Blew Her Up 31
To Damascus 131–2
Trilogia Pass-port 39
Troilus and Cressida 43
Trojan Horse 17, 169, 172, 173, 175, 176
Udarna vest 39
Up on Roof 180, 181, 184
Valjevo Hospital 43
Waiting for Godot 6
War is Close 63
Wielopole, Wielopole 131
Zoran Đinđić 43, 120, 121
Plazzi, Gianni 188
Pocket Theatre (Serbia) 44
Poland 15, 45, 119–35, 183, 184. See also Frljić, Oliver; Un-Divine Comedy. Remains
  antisemitic discourse in 125–6, 129–30
  cancellations 119–20, 122, 134, 135n2
  Nazi atrocities 128
  independent theatre 184
  nationalism 131
  political context 125
Poland, Christine 79
policing 17, 65, 104–7, 116n4, 169
political correctness 6, 12, 148, 157, 161, 219
political parties 5, 15, 26–8, 35–8, 54–5, 93–5, 97, 104–7, 162, 182, 183, 200–2, 204, 216, 218
political representatives 9, 27, 29, 38, 43, 45, 64, 93–5, 98, 100, 113, 115, 160, 183, 218
Polony, Anna 133
Polyák, Gábor 98, 100n2
Pomerantsev, Peter 57
Ponce, Enrique 213

populism 10, 13, 16, 34, 36, 38, 54, 94, 162–3, 180, 218
pornography 178, 229. See also sexual content
Portugal 2, 4, 11, 214, 216
Powszechny Theatre (Poland) 134–5
Prešeren Day 109–15
Prešeren, France 109, 110, 111, 114–15, 116nn12–13, 117n19
Prešeren Fund Management Board 109–15
Prevent Strategy 17, 169, 173, 174, 175, 176, 181
  Channel programme 181
protests 4, 16, 28–30, 40, 47, 53, 99, 182–3, 192–3
  religious 202, 206–7
  women's protests 76. See also feminism
Puebla, Morante de la 218–19, 221
Pullman, Philip 171
Pushkin, Alexander 57
Putin, Vladimir 10, 11, 13, 52–5, 57, 61, 63, 65

queer 73, 228–37. See also shibari performance art
  assimilation 229–30
  queerphobia 171
  queer subjectivity 18, 231–2
  persecution 53
  resistance to censorship 228–37

race 2, 16, 19, 82, 139, 145. See also Black Lives Matter
  Black voices in opera 148–51
  protests against racial stereotypes 163, 181
  racial tropes 149
  racialized voices, 17, 171–2
racism 6, 11, 127, 147, 148, 158, 160–2, 164, 170–2, 176, 200. See also blackface; Netherlands
  'Black Pete is Racism' 160, 163
  culture wars 144, 169–76
  woke culture 170–1
Radwan, Anna 129–30
Rajesh, Monisha 171
Rancière, Jacques 28, 48, 162
Reade, Simon 180

Reagan, Ronald 9
realism 55, 60–1, 150
Reduced Shakespeare Company
    (USA) 182
Reedijk, Alex 150
Reflektor Theatre (Serbia) 44
rehearsals 35, 38, 119–20, 125–9,
    131–4, 139–40, 146, 174, 200
Reinelt, Janelle 7, 185–8, 197–8
religion and theatre
  as sensitive issue 145, 180, 186, 192
  in *Behzti* 4, 7, 185–8
  Church 8, 36, 38, 46, 54, 70, 74–5,
    121, 124, 125, 134, 196, 197,
    199–203, 206–7
  Christianity 17, 100, 124, 147, 158,
    171, 179, 182, 183, 184, 187,
    188–92, 201–3, 206
  in *Corpus Christi* 18, 195, 201–3
  in France 183, 185, 190–2
  fundamentalism 179, 184, 191,
    219, 220
  in Germany 185, 186
  in *Golgota Picnic* 183–4, 192n2
  in *Homegrown* 17, 169, 172–6,
    181, 184
  in *Idomeneo* 16, 145, 179, 185–8
  Islam 145, 173, 174, 175, 176, 179,
    181, 184, 187, 216
  in *Maria Stuarda* 16, 140–3
  Greek Orthodox Church 199, 200,
    201, 202, 203, 206, 207
  in *On the Concept of the Face,
    Regarding the Son of God* 17,
    179, 188–92
  in Poland 183–4
  politics and 141, 195–208
  Russian Orthodox Church 54
  pressure from religious organizations
    183, 184, 198, 200
  taboos in the Balkans 41, 48
  in theatrical performance, historical
    roots 179
  in *Trojan Horse* 17, 169, 172, 173,
    175, 176
  in UK 179–83, 184, 185–8
  in Verdi's operas 137
Repubblika 28
Rey, Andrés Roca 224

Ríain, Ailís Ní 84
Ribes, Jean-Michel 183
Ristovski, Ljubica 46
Rivera, Francisco 224
Rivière, Constance 149
Robinson, Morris 149
Romania 11
Romero, Curro 221
Roseby, Paul 174, 181
Roselli, David Kawalko 218
Royal Court Theatre (England) 5, 180
Royal Shakespeare Company (RSC)
    (UK) 180
Rozman, Branko 107
Russia 5, 10, 11, 13–14, 19n1, 52–65,
    65n1, 66n3, 66n10, 67n13, 94,
    98, 100n1, 130, 133
  independent theatres 56, 59
  models of censorship 62–5
  self-censorship 59
  Serebrennikov case 5, 37, 52–64,
    66n7
  westernization of Russian culture 65
Rutte, Mark 161–2
Ryzhakov, Viktor 63, 64, 66nn10–12

Salazar, António de Oliveira 7
satire 27, 38, 93, 180
Scandinavia 1, 11. *See also* Norway
Scannell, Ray 84
Scarlatella, Sergio 188
Schenkman, Jan 157
Scheppelmann, Christina 141–2, 144
Schilling, Árpád 94–5
Schneemann, Carolee 47–8
Scotland 77
Serbia 37–41, 43–7, 49n3, 105, 121,
Serebrennikov, Kirill 5, 37, 52–64,
    66n7
Serlin, David 234
Šešelj, Vojislav 40
sexual content 7, 12, 18, 40, 41, 46,
    53, 62, 74, 132, 134, 138, 141,
    143, 171, 178, 198, 229, 231,
    234–6
Shaw, George Bernard 78
shibari performance art 228–37. *See
    also* queer
Shubert, Adrian 218

Sievers, Lieke 162
Singh, Sunny 171
Sky Arts Award 150
Slavko Grum Award 108
Slovenia 15, 103–15
  independence 108–9
  practice of denunciation 107
  Prešeren Day 109–15
Smock Alley Theatre (Ireland) 80
Snyder, Timothy 97
Socialist Alliance of Working People (SZDL) 104
social media 47, 72, 95, 98, 114, 138–9, 145, 150–1, 171, 202, 219. *See also* Facebook; Instagram; media; Twitter; YouTube
Socìetas Raffaello Sanzio (Italy) 188, 189, 191
Soho Theatre (England) 187
Sovremennik Theatre (Russia) 62
Spain 18, 156, 158, 164n1
  bullfighting 11, 18, 211–22, 224–5
  culture wars 218
  Franco dictatorship 18, 212
  theatre criticism 222
Spiteri, Simone 31
Springer, Jerry 182, 184
Srebrenica genocide 39, 41, 46–7
Stafford-Clark, Max 5
Stone, Maeve 72
Stoppard, Tom 170
Strauss, Richard 137
Strindberg, August 131
Strzępka, Monika 121
Suleyman, Chimene 171
Summers, Sean P. 76, 85
Surkov, Vladislav 52
Šuvar, Stipe 36
Svich, Caridad 8
Swinarski, Konrad 122–34

Targoń, Joanna 122–3
Tashimov, Rinat 62, 66n10
Távora, Salvador 215–16
Tchaikovsky, Pyotr 56
Teatro Massimo (Italy) 146
Teatro Regio di Torino (Italy) 144
Téllez, Ángel 221
Théâtre 13 (France) 6

Théâtre de la Ville (France) 188, 190–1
Theater der Welt (Germany) 188
Théâtre du Rond-Point (France) 183
Thoday, Jon 182
Thomas, Richard 182
Thompson, Mark 182
Tomás, José 211, 215–16
Torbica, Igor Vuk 44–5
tragedy (theatre form) 132, 213, 215, 225n3
Trela, Jerzy 133
Tsakirakis, Stavros 206
Tsinikoris, Prodromos 204
Tsoi, Viktor 56–7
Tumbas, Nikola 46
Twitter 72, 74, 76, 150. *See also* social media

Ukraine 10–11, 14, 54, 56, 60, 63, 65, 133
Un-Divine Comedy. Remains 15, 45, 119–35
  antisemitism 134
  cast of 126
  performance on hold 131–5
  rehearsals 120–2, 127, 129
  and self-censorship 119–35
  uncertainty 126–7
United Kingdom 15–17, 66n1, 137, 149, 169–70, 173, 176, 225n1, 228
universities
  on artistic freedom 5–6
  Hungarian Theatre and Film Academy 98–9
  performances 98
  student demonstrations 5–6, 28, 99, 190
Urbán, András 39, 42
Užice City Theatre (Serbia) 44

Vágó, Gábor 94–5
Valletta Campus Theatre (Malta) 31
van Hove, Ivo 1
Vasiliou, Laertis 201–2
Vázquez, Curro 224
Verdi, Giuseppe 137, 143, 151n2, 151n3,
Vezjak, Boris 114–15

Vidnyánszky, Attila 99–100, 101n11, 101n13
Villán, Javier 222
Vinaver, Michel 6
violence 39, 48, 53, 57, 134, 138, 152n10, 160, 184, 202, 204, 205, 206, 225
   sexual violence 74, 98, 145–6
   violent content 47, 191, 235
   violent threats against artists 26, 37, 46, 119, 184, 186, 198
Vrgoč, Dubravka 44
Vučić, Aleksandar 44
Vyrypaev, Ivan 63, 66n11

Wajda, Andrzej 122
Wales 16, 80
#WakingTheFeminists (#WTF) 14, 71, 72–4
Walsh, Eileen 84
Walsh, Enda 82, 84
Waterloo Vaults (England) 192n4
Webber, Andrew Lloyd 202
Weiss, Margot D. 230, 235, 236
Weiss, Peter 47
Western Balkans 13, 34–49
   blacklisted artists 37, 41
   counterpublic 4, 34, 36, 42, 44, 45, 47, 48
   direct censorship 34, 37–8
   financial censorship 36–9, 42, 48
   historical context 35–7, 43

   indirect censorship 34, 36, 37, 38, 39, 42
   moral and religious coercion 45–8
   self-censorship 37
   street-censorship 37
   verbal offence 36
Westwood, Vivienne 142
Wichowska, Joanna 119, 120
Wilde, Oscar 137
Wilson, Tamara 146
woke culture 170–1, 172, 212
Wolff, Francis 214
Wonderland is For Everyone 96
Woodhead, Matt 173, 175
Wyspiański, Stanisław 46

Xiros, Savvas 203, 205
Xiuzhen, Yin 54

Yeats, W.B. 72
Yugoslavia 12, 15, 35–7, 40, 41, 43–5, 104–8, 114–15, 115nn1–2, 116n6, 120–1
Yugoslav Drama Theatre 40, 43
YouTube 94, 148, 162–3, 225n1. *See also* social media

Zahumlje Theatre (Croatia) 38
Zakharov, Mark 59
Zeffirelli, Franco 145
Žižek, Slavoj 61–2

www.ingramcontent.com/pod-product-compliance
Lightning Source LLC
Chambersburg PA
CBHW020645300426
44112CB00007B/250